The Borderline Patient

ARLENE ROBBINS WOLBERG

Director, Department of Community
Services and Education, Postgraduate
Center for Mental Health, New York, N.Y.

INTERCONTINENTAL MEDICAL BOOK CORPORATION
New York

CONTENTS

To
My Husband
Lewis R. Wolberg

INTRODUCTION

In view of the large number of borderline patients seen in both clinics and in private practice, interest in this problem has been constant from the time that Freud wrote of "borderline and mixed conditions" in his preface to Aichorn's book, "Wayward Youth" (1924), up to the present, when the first definitive research study was reported by Grinker and his colleagues (1968).

It is the purpose of this book to discuss the dynamics of the borderline patient and his family, to delineate the psychoanalytic principles involved in the treatment process, and particularly to explain certain projective therapeutic techniques, thus integrating theory with practice. It is a further purpose to trace the historical development of ideas as these are reflected in psychoanalytic thinking, and to show their relation to modern concepts of the borderline syndrome.

Descriptions of the psychodynamics and psychopathology of the border-line do not fit the categories of either the neuroses or the psychoses; neither do the traditional therapeutic approaches seem entirely applicable. To gain a proper perspective on therapeutic practices which apply to the borderline case it is necessary to trace the historical roots of our concepts in the studies of the hysterias, the schizophrenias, the depressions and the character disorders. Throughout the past fifty years, certain authors have contributed ideas which, if integrated into our present day methods, can go far in helping to appreciate the modifications in therapeutic technique that are crucial to successful outcome with borderline patients.

A basic tenet in our conceptual framework is that emotional problems develop within the womb of family living; a peculiar contagion of psychopathology is passed along from parent to child. There is no intent here to assume that the adult is like the child, even though Freud once said that childhood thinking patterns contaminate adult life.[1] While the child may be "father of the man," the man is not a replica of the child. Neither is the child similar to the ancestors who lived eons past. In agreement with Kurt Goldstein (1959), there is no assumption in this book that what Freud called regression is, in fact, a revivification of a former stage of development, nor that developmental epochs recapitulate the mental states of the race as it existed thousands of years ago. One looks upon the phenomenon that Freud considered to be regressive as a withdrawal mechanism with its accompanying detachment; and a function of this maneuver is a constellation of defensive phantasies which show a delusional content. The delusional phantasy is a version of the *identification phantasy* which every neurotic and psychotic employs in the interest of controlling anxiety; the phantasies have a functional relationship to the past experiences of the patient in the family as well as with his immediate present, his current social milieu.

A basic tenet, then, for understanding the dynamics of borderline patients is that identification phantasies are the mental representations of the child's principal defensive maneuvers in his need to adapt to a traumatic family situation, and that these phantasies indicate *the sado-masochistic role assigned to the child by his parents when he becomes enmeshed as a transferential object in service of the parent's defenses.* The ensuing neurotic and psychotic processes are defenses against a harsh reality with which the individual tries to cope, and the crucial mechanism is identification with the parents. My thesis is that neuroses and psychoses are defenses (A. Wolberg, 1960), a tenet set forth by Freud in his early papers on the "Defense Neuropsychoses" (1896, 1898).

The identification phantasies of the borderline patient resemble to a great extent those of certain types of schizophrenia. The eventuating interpersonal transferential encounters are similar to what Freud described as object relations in the narcissistic neuroses. Projection, an identification defense, is, as Freud has indicated, more pronounced in these problems. The "projective therapeutic techniques" recommended in Chapters IX and X are organized around this premise. As the projection mechanisms become more pathological, the identification phantasy tends towards delusion (A. Wolberg, 1968). However, there are differences in the manner in which schizophrenics and borderlines use delusion.

The most difficult forms of mental organization to treat are those which involve delusion and other types of projection. Because of their early frustrating interpersonal experiences, borderline patients particularly are least prone to trust other persons, including therapists. We may expect that any psychotherapeutic effort, no matter how ardently the patient seeks it, will precipitate aggression and other defensive operations.

The severe transference reactions of the borderline patient have unfortunately led to an attitude of therapeutic nihilism. Confirmation for such hopelessness seemed to be found in the experiences of the early analysts with the narcissistic neuroses, which were considered to be irreversible. It was assumed that the individual, being loosely knit from the inside, interpreted any pressure from the outside as evil, forcing his withdrawal from people and organizing the kind of mental dynamics which could not be changed, namely, delusional and hallucinatory processes. This formulation included ideas taken from Freud's structural theory to the effect that the patient's ego was weak; the "id impulses" had taken over; the ego had lost its boundaries or had never gained them; the ego needed strengthening; the defenses were chaotic; and the superego was primitive. Under the circumstances, nothing could be done except supportive therapy, which was organized around being a "good" mother or a "good parent" who provides a protective experience and a relationship which could go on the remainder of the individual's life.

We do not share this pessimism today. Observation soon revealed that the ego does not disintegrate or disorganize (in borderline patients) even though it does take on forms of organization which are rigid and difficult to change. Several authors, including L. von Bertalanffy, in 1950, have suggested that systems do not disorganize, that change is ever occurring, and that what happens in systems is a unity of forms of mutually interactive parts. Merton (1947) has aptly pointed out that this unity can change so far as the functional relationships are concerned: certain forms can disappear and new forms can appear, but organization does not cease. The sociologist, Simmel (1950), had made similar statements in 1908 and 1917 in relation to social systems. These principles seem to apply to mental dynamic systems as well as to social phenomena. The principle of homeostasis should include the idea that there are alternate choices for the individual in methods of adaptation. Some of these methods make life more miserable than others; this is true of the neuroses and the psychoses. In treatment we must be aware of the social system that supports the individual's neurotic or psychotic adaptation (identifications) and we must understand the intrapsychic processes of the members of the social system. With appropriate techniques the individual can be helped to change his ego organization, and in turn he can influence the social system so that certain shifts make his life less anxiety-laden and more constructive.

Freud's idea of *id, ego* and *superego* was an attempt to apply to mental dynamics the concept of homeostasis and the unity of systems in the midst of emotional conflict. With some modification in the theory and the meaning of these concepts, we might still employ these terms. The mind, the personality, the family and society are obviously interrelated open systems; each has an influence upon and is a reaction to the other systems.

An important clue in working therapeutically with borderline patients is the understanding that they utilize a rapidly shifting defensive process in interpersonal relationships in spite of the fact that they possess a passive-agressive personality organization, acting at one time helpless, and on other occasions aggressive. The patient is attuned to interpersonal cues (as is the paranoid) and he can change his defenses easily, showing in quick succession such behavior as hostility, detachment, masochism, appeasement, and flight into phantasy (Wolberg, A., 1952). Hoch and Pollatin (1949) reported on this shifting mobility of defense in patients whom they called pseudoneurotic schizophrenics. These patients, like the borderlines, were found to have a loosely defined delusional system which was brought out in a dramatic manner under sodium amytal narcosis.

Compounding this defensive fluidity is another difficult resistance in the borderline patient, a fear of success, which inspires undoing mechanisms to enhance self-defeat. This is a manifestation of sado-masochistic behavior. In our therapeutic efforts we must be concerned with both the patient's penchant for failure and his guilt concerning success. In his past history it will be found that there have been areas of success. Even though the individual may have been a school "dropout," he may have gotten "A" in certain subjects in which he was interested. Although he seems completely defeated and a "washout" now, he may at one time have reached heights of accomplishment in the arts, on the stage, or in the sciences. Failure then is only a surface characteristic. The patient has made himself fail because he is locked in a sado-masochistic interpersonal bind with others. He may fail due to fear of success or may fail in order to frustrate the person or persons with whom he is closely related in one way or another; or, he may succeed out of revenge, so as to lord it over others. This sadistic or revenge motif operates in treatment as well as in other relationships; the other side of the coin is the masochism and self-defeat. Since the sado-masochism has evolved in the service of the defenses of the parents, self-defeat has a relation to the patient's neurotic needs. The parent interrupts certain of the child's normal activities when these create too much anxiety in the parents. Interesting data obtained by several investigators relevant to interrupted tasks are of interest to us in this respect and should enhance our study of borderline patients; they point to personality mechanisms operative in individuals who have suffered frustration: Abel (1938); Adler and Kounin (1939); Alper (1948, 1952); Atkinson (1953).

The aim in psychoanalytic treatment of the borderline is to reduce the anxiety and tension created by the conflict over living and the feelings concerning success and failure, and to resolve the basic identification with parents around which all other defenses are organized. The basis of Freud's interpersonal and family theory, and the crux of what he called the oedipal dynamics, was the identification process. He wrote that, in the dream, identification is represented by the group of persons the patient uses to express certain meanings. He also claimed that in the schizophrenias, persons can be symbolized as things, or as symbols of things or as ideas. Thus the disguise helps express the problem or the conflict and deny it at the same time. In this displaced (projected) form the defense helps to relieve anxiety or "give the ego distance." It was when Freud decided to call identification one of the organizing forces in the ego, relating it to his developmental system and "normality," that confusion entered into psychoanalytic theory. In this book, identification will be defined as a neurotic defense, sado-masochistic in nature, a necessary ingredient in the maintenance of the parent's neurotic homeostasis (A. Wolberg, 1960). Reich (1933) suggested, and Fenichel (1941) later reiterated, that in treatment the therapist must show the patient that he is defending, when and how he is defending, and then help him find out what it is that he is defending against. It is just this task of showing the patient that he is involved in a process of defending which is so difficult in working with the borderline patient. The projective therapeutic technique, which will be elaborated in this volume, is an important aid in this task.

NOTE

[1] In "Civilization and Its Discontents," Freud wrote (1930): "The earlier phases of development are in no sense still preserved; they have been absorbed into the later phases for which they have supplied the material. The embryo cannot be discovered in the adult. The thymus gland of childhood is replaced after puberty by connective tissues but is no longer present itself . . . The fact remains that only in the mind is such a preservation of all the earlier stages alongside of the final form possible . . ." This lent credence to his theory that childhood thinking patterns were preserved and reanimated in regression.

CHAPTER I

PSYCHOANALYSIS AND THE
BORDERLINE PATIENT

Psychoanalysis has its friends and its foes; its experts and its neophytes. In the present form it is a theory and to some extent a mystique, due to problems of definition, the esoteric ideas incorporated within its framework, and the fact that its tenets have never been appropriately delineated. Yet it is amazing how much it has contributed to our understanding of mental illness. The borderline patient is a case in point. As a distinctive syndrome, the dynamics were never described. Nevertheless, even in the beginning of the psychoanalytic movement, much was written on the schizophrenias that we now know applies to borderlines. Some of the most important concepts derived from Freud's work with his hysterical patients—cases that most certainly we would describe as borderlines or schizophrenics. In the literature, the borderline case was largely ignored as a definitive entity.

It is only in the last five or six years that more intensive studies of the borderline patient have been attempted; yet scattered throughout the literature of the past fifty years there is much to be learned that is relevant in the recognition of the dynamics of these cases and an astounding amount that can be gleaned on treatment method.

One of the many confusing problems in psychoanalysis which hampered the understanding of borderline cases is the dichotomy that appeared when Freud attempted to separate the neuroses from the character disorders, the latter

6

being considered the less treatable problems. What seemed to emerge was that neurotics were not thought of with pathologies involving a character structure, and characterological problems were not considered amenable to psychoanalytic treatment techniques.

The greatest confusion of all, however, centered around the fact that almost every concept in psychoanalysis came to have several definitions. Thus, repression was of three kinds; identification was of more than four kinds; displacement and projection were differentiated by various labels. Resistance and defense would at one time be regarded as synonymous and at another time be appraised as completely different. Added to this was the factor of Freud's strong and lively personality, his insatiable drive for writing, his sparkling mind, his penchant for changing theories and his personal problems which colored his work and were fused with his concepts. Freud's talent for accurate reporting of clinical material, regardless of his speculative premises, has given us a vast store of data which even today has not been surpassed. The impossible task of self-analysis, which Freud tackled, allowed him to work through a personal phobic problem, but his rejection of some of his findings and ideas in favor of others was apparently the product of some unresolved emotional difficulties. His turning away from the "accidental cause" to the libido concept and the theory of infantile sexuality was based on a fifteen year struggle over the meaning, the origin and the dynamics of perversion. He wrote to Fliess while undergoing self-analysis (1897, Letter 69) that he no longer believed in his neurotica, due to the continual disappointment in his attempts to bring his analysis to a real conclusion, the running away of people who had seemed most in his grasp, and the absence of the complete successes on which he had reckoned. In addition he was surprised at the fact that in every case the father, not excluding his own, "had to be blamed as a pervert." The realization of the unexpected frequency of hysteria, in which the same determinant is invariably established, made him think that such a widespread extent of perversity towards children was not very probable. "Perversion would have to be immeasurably more frequent than hysteria, since the illness can only arise where the events have accumulated and one of the factors that weaken defense is present."

As a result of the shift to the libido theory, psychoanalytic literature became permeated with certain mystical ideas. These, at first uttered as casual pronouncements, soon became dignified in writings; then, through reiteration and restatement, they were converted into dogma. In a field as fluid as psychoanalysis this unfortunate trend retards the development of solidifying scientific thinking.

Among the curious phantasies perpetuated as facts are staunch expressions of what the infant must think and feel. Some of these concepts have a bearing on interpretations of the dynamics of the borderline patient. In particular, the defenses of omnipotence (megalomania) and what Freud called the "oceanic" feeling are still conceived of in terms of his developmental system. For example,

Carmichael (1954) notes that one analyst said: "When a child comes into the world he comes in lonely and he is afraid." This pronouncement was quite sincere, but we do recognize the projection of personal feeling into this early developmental phase of childhood. A second analyst writes (Rado, 1960): ". . . pleasurable infantile experience encourages a delusional sense of magical power"; and another excerpt from this same author gives the opinion that "the experience of pleasure and unpleasure effects the quality of self by expanding or contracting the sense of magical omnipotence." This same analyst states: "Enchanted by its success in sucking, the young organism attributes unlimited power to its willed (intentional) actions and pictures itself as an omnipotent being. . . . From this vantage ground the infant views his parents . . . as deputies who exercise his magic powers for him." The idea that the infant has a "delusional sense of magical power" is undoubtedly a projection of adults, couched in the idea of regression to earlier phases of development. Our understanding of family dynamics and the meaning of early effects of family relationships in the here-and-now has been obscured further by Freud's displacement onto the racial heritage (the totem group) away from the actual family.

Treatment methods, too, underwent drastic changes in the course of the development of psychoanalytic theory, beginning with the topological theory. This at first was involved with the technique of hypnotic suggestion used to "strengthen the defenses" and "hypnotic catharsis" employed in the effort to "undermine the defenses" toward the objective of "making the unconscious, conscious." Then, moving to the dynamic point of view, the goal was to "abolish the resistances" (Fenichel, 1939). But when the developmental theory of the libido was incorporated into the topological theory, the genetic point of view stimulated analysts to ask such questions as, "Does the analyst educate the patient's ego to a tolerance of the instincts, and thus function as the patient's 'superego'? " It was thought that part of the ego develops in treatment through identification of the patient with the analyst. The therapist is introjected like a parasite into the superego and into the ego as well.

Wilhelm Reich, focusing on the delineation of defenses, introduced such ideas as "interpretation of resistance precedes interpretation of content. . . . Analyze always from the surface." A dissolution of the transference was a second goal. Fenichel was critical of Reich's technique although, apparently, he agreed with his therapeutic formula regarding defenses. He accused Reich of being too active and implied that his work was hostile and grandiose; he commented that "shattering of the defensive armor" is masochistically enjoyed by many patients and specific transferences can hide behind such enjoyment and escape discovery. Fenichel alleged that Ella Sharpe's (1937) emphasis on "defense analysis" coincided with his own view.

There is no doubt that Freud's fundamental observations, made early in his career, continue to be a lasting contribution to our knowledge of defensive operations and they have a utility in our modern approach to borderline patients. Indeed, his work has so influenced the therapeutic field that even those who reject him use many of his concepts without knowing that they do; others employ his material deliberately without acknowledging the source. Although Freud indulged in some mystical ideas when he finally developed the libido theory, nevertheless, we can glean from some of his original work concepts and meanings which have stood the test of time and have paved the way for further knowledge. Reich's idea that analysis must focus on the understanding and the delineation of the dynamics of defense is the most important concept in psychoanalytic literature. The idea originated in Freud's initial work.

Freud's early interests were primarily in neurology, biology and histology. In 1886 he entered the practice of neurology, working for a time with Charcot, who had created the greatest neurological laboratory of all times at Salpêtrière. He soon discovered that neurological theory and treatment methods were not adequate to ameliorate certain disorders which seemed to him to be psychological in nature rather than organic. It was in the pursuit of more psychological knowledge which might lead to new discoveries that Freud became interested in the "magnetists" and hypnosis.

In Charcot, Freud had found a dedicated investigator who spent years studying and describing various neurological syndromes. Among Charcot's original works was a differentiation in the study of muscular atrophy of ordinary wasting from amyotrophic lateral sclerosis (1874), and a description, with Pierre Marie, of the progressive neural peroneal type (1886); a classification of the essential lesions of locomotor ataxia; a description of the conditions, gastric crisis and joint affections (Charcot's Disease); and he distinguished multiple sclerosis from paralysis agitans. Charcot had spent many years recording data concerning hysterical attacks and demonstrating their characteristics as opposed to diseases based on neurological conditions. His notable brain studies were recorded in articles on cerebral localizations. He wrote about aphasia and discovered how miliary aneurysms influenced cerebral hemorrhage. In addition, Charcot published articles on gout, kidney and liver diseases, senile disorders, chronic pneumonia and tuberculosis. Even though Charcot was essentially organically oriented, he did not discount the influence of psychological factors.

Freud's interest in psychological treatment was stimulated not only by the work of Charcot, but by that of Bernheim, Breuer and Janet, all eminent neurologists who had spent many years studying the problems of the hysterias and the use of hypnosis as a treatment method. Such studies revealed the many defenses common to neuroses and psychoses in general, and initiated attempts at classification.

Charcot, for example, described four stages that were operative in hysterical attacks. But what was more important, he proved through demonstrations with hypnosis that "hysterical paralyses were the result of specific ideas

holding sway in the brain of the patient at moments of special disposition." [1] *
He considered hysteria a psychosis superinduced by ideation, even though he
believed it was essentially caused by a constitutional defect. In spite of the
constitutional factor, Charcot insisted that the individual could be helped by
paying attention to the psychological aspects of the disease. Toward this end, he
employed a hypnotic method in the face of the prevailing prejudice of the
general medical community, which considered it a form of medieval legerdemain.

Aside from demonstrating the efficacy of hypnosis, Charcot had performed an experiment which had many dynamic implications: he succeeded in
reproducing a hysterical attack in a patient through the use of certain verbal
stimuli. In this way he provided the appropriate cues to set off a particular
neurotic response. In essence, this was an experiment which can and has been
duplicated by others countless times and provides a paradigm of interpersonal
activity that has both constructive and destructive implications for the treatment
process. Charcot's pupil, Janet, used hypnosis to uncover memories[2]; he thought
that the hysterias were due to traumas which were recorded in noxious
memories. Breuer had similar ideas. It was during 1880-82 that he worked with a
case of hysteria (Anna O.) with whom he used hypnosis to uncover the
circumstances under which her symptoms first occurred. Freud quotes Binet and
Delboeuf (1889) as recognizing the principles of "recall with affect" as a means
of relief of neurotic symptoms (1889 and 1892), a principle we still hold to
today. As a student, Freud met Breuer at a clinic directed by the physiologist,
Ernst Brücke. He soon became fascinated with Breuer's accounts of his
psychological treatment methods, and this provided him with the direction that
was to result in the formulation of his psychoanalytic theories.

Receiving a traveling fellowship on the recommendation of Brücke, Freud
spent several months in Paris (1885-86) studying with Charcot, then returned to
Vienna to set up his practice. He was convinced that the hysterias were
psychologically motivated, yet, he too postulated a biological foundation.

In 1886 (second ed., 1887), Bernheim's book, "De la Suggestion et de Ses
Applications à la Thérapeutique," attracted Freud's interest to such an extent
that he translated the volume and wrote a famous preface, in which he praised
Bernheim, but disagreed with aspects of his psychological theory; this preface[3] is
considered to be Freud's first published psychological paper. Freud visited
Bernheim in the summer of 1889 at Nancy. One of the points of Freud's dispute
with Bernheim was that the latter leaned to the idea that "all the phenomena of
hypnotism have the same origin"; they arise ". . . from a suggestion, a conscious
idea which has been introduced into the brain of the hypnotized person by an
external influence and has been accepted by him as though it had arisen
spontaneously." [4] Freud (1888) commented: "On this view, all hypnotic
manifestation would be mental phenomena, effects of suggestion," and if this

---

* Notes for this chapter start page 25.

were true then it would be impossible to find the syndrome picture in any given case since the constellations would fluctuate with the influencing person. Freud, like Charcot, was continuously trying to provide order in the existing chaotic field of psychopathology. He was seeking to describe syndromes even though he felt at times that the task was impossible, due to the overlapping of symptoms in the neuroses and psychoses.

The concept that, through suggestion, ideas are introduced into the brain of a person and then he accepts them *as-if* they were his own, is a chief dynamic in *identification* (A. Wolberg, 1968). Undoubtedly it explains a conditioning factor that is most important in the relationship between parents and those children who become borderline cases, for without a suitable reinforcement from the parent, without an adequate reward, the identification behavior, or the phenomenon of taking over the ideas of others, would never have been organized in the first place. Suggestibility as a learned trait is a central factor in the *role behavior* which is an aspect of the identifications operating in all pathological emotional states.[5]

One could substitute for the words, "as though it had arisen spontaneously," in the above quotation from Freud, the concept of the *as-if* motif, and thus make the connection between parents' behavior and identification behavior in children. In identification the child acts in some ways like the parent and he behaves as-if this were what he wanted.[6]

The borderline patient has many of the qualities that Freud saw in his hysterical patients. But it was not until 1931 in his essay on Female Sexuality that Freud wrote what seemed to indicate his belief that the parent does have an active role in the neurosis and that, at bottom, the problem is one of the parent's hostility and aggression toward and rejection of the child: "We find aggressive oral and sadistic wishes in a form forced on them by early repression, i.e., in the dread of being killed by the mother—a dread which on its side justifies the death wish against her if this enters consciousness. It is impossible to say how often this dread of the mother draws countenance from an unconscious hostility on her part, which the child divines. (The dread of being eaten, I have so far found only in men: it is referred to the father, but is probably the result of the transformation of oral aggressive tendencies directed upon the mother. The person the child wants to devour is the mother who nourished him; in the case of the father there is no such obvious occasion for the wish.)" What is implied here is that the patient is motivated in neurosis by parental rejection, but there is nothing to indicate *the activity of the parent's aggression* in promoting the neurosis. Freud emphasized the role of the mother, excluding the father in the early phases of development. Today we recognize the father's pre-oedipal role.

The fact that an individual will take the ideas of another person and make them his own, despite the problems that this creates, is one of the basic concepts in understanding neurotic behavior; the trait of suggestibility is the medium through which identification behavior is made viable.[7] Freud's idea that suggestibility was one of the personality characteristics operative in the establishment of *transference behavior,* and that this played a decisive role in the working relationship with patients, was based in part on Breuer's observations that if he went out of town for a short period of time his patient's symptoms would often return. But it was Freud (1912) who eventually described the dynamics of transference, relating negative transference to hate, and to Thanatos, the death instinct, and positive transference to love, and Eros, the life instinct. Freud said that a fusion of these instinctual trends resulted in what Bleuler (1910) called *ambivalence,* i.e., opposing feelings of love and hate, which caused contradictory behavior. Bleuler seems to have considered the trait of suggestibility in the more seriously disturbed patients, as evidenced by his paper written in 1912 at the same time that Freud was publishing his essay on transference. Freud's theory of Eros and Thanatos, and their relationship, was an effort to describe a theory of constancy, or equilibrium, a concept of homeostasis.

The joint papers with Breuer spoke of a "sum of excitation." Freud later postulated the "pleasure-principle" (Eros), or the libido, which represented a rise in tension within the nervous system, and the nirvana-principle (Thanatos) as an opposing tendency of the mental apparatus to reduce tension to zero. Conflict was eventually represented in economic terms, i.e., according to the distribution of energy through the three mental systems (id, ego and superego). Transference, related to the superego, is actually what we now feel to be an important conditioned reaction which generalizes and provides cues for anxiety responses in the individual's relations with others; the *neurotic role* is an important characteristic of the transference. Freud considered transference part of the neurotic process and recognized that it operated in all of the patient's interpersonal relationships. One of the most important contributions Freud made, to aid us in understanding the workings of any neurosis or psychosis, was his insistence that transference behavior contaminates the patient's relationships and results in many complications.

Using role theory, we can define transference behavior as conditioned behavior, contingent originally on a projection of transference needs by the parent upon the child, with a response demanded by the parent. The child is provoked to play a role which helps to quiet the parent's anxiety. The idea that *transference behavior is identification behavior,* and that it is inspired or *demanded* by the parent, is illustrated in the following "battered child" report brought to the attention of the New York Women's Bar Association in a speech by Harry Gair, January 27, 1970. Roxanne Felumero, 3 years old, on March 25, 1969 was dragged out of the East River. She had been beaten to death and her body weighted down with rocks. When she was a year old, on the petition of the Society for the Prevention of Cruelty to Children she had been placed with the

New York Foundling Hospital. She was then put into the care of foster parents. When she was three years old and still living happily with her foster parents, her natural mother appeared in the family court and asked that Roxanne be returned to her in her home. The mother was a prostitute who had been convicted of criminal assault, was mentally unstable and had made several attempts at suicide. The mother had married a George Poplis. The mother was allowed to take the child on December 12, 1968. Three weeks later, January 3, 1969, the child was brought back to the family court. Her former foster parents were petitioners before the court. They had seen Roxanne and spoken to her and they asked the court to see the marks of violence to the child's head and body. The mother attributed the injuries to falling, once from a swing, and at another time as a result of an injury sustained when the child struck her face on a bicycle. The foster mother testified that Roxanne had told her that "Georgie," the step-father, had struck her. The child, in response to a question by the Judge, said: "I dropped on the rocking chair and fell on my head and eyes." Left with her mother and the step-father the child was eventually killed. What is of interest is that this three year old child had gotten the idea that she was to lie about her bruises and protect the parents, thus denying reality and substituting phantasy instead. In this case, the child did not live to perpetuate further identification behavior, but the incident illustrates the fact that a child will deny reality even though he understands reality, and that he can organize a sado-masochistic mode of life, identifying with the aggressor, eventually repressing many of the memories of events which led to the identification. Roxanne acted as-if her life was not in danger.

Sarbin (1950) has offered a reasonable explanation of the links between the identification process, as-if behavior, transference phenomenon, suggestibility and hypnosis in bringing forward the idea that suggestibility is a learned trait. He applied the as-if formulation to repression as an ego defense, impunitiveness as a response to frustration, and hypnotizability as a personality trait. He found that in repression the subject behaved as-if an event threatening the maintenance of the self-concept had not occurred; in impunitiveness the person acted as-if the frustrating event was no longer frustrating; and in hypnosis the individual behaved as-if certain qualities and events were different from what they were actually. One can readily see that in such experiences the individual learns to be masochistic and the frustration creates feelings of aggression. The positive and negative feelings experienced by the patient towards the treatment person in transference can be considered aspects of ambivalence, but Freud was loath to say that negative feelings and sadism arise as a consequence of sado-masochistic relations between parents and children. Masochism was related to the "need for punishment," which we now assume to be a conditioned factor, created, as are the sadistic feelings, in the relations with the parents. Freud called the masochistic act a "gratification of the feelings of guilt." We recognize that guilt feelings are connected with both *permitted* and *unpermitted aggressions*.

(Wolberg, A., 1960) as well as with fears of assertion. Freud (1922) was inclined to credit "giving in to the other" or "retiring in favor of someone else," which was a form of giving up of certain assertive strivings (masochism) to a trait in homosexuality. Schreber showed this trait to an inordinate degree and it is found in milder forms in the borderline patient.[8]

Adler (1925) referred to suggestibility as the quality that made the child educable and credited it to the child's feelings of inferiority, his helplessness and his need to learn in order to develop coping mechanisms that would enable him to adjust. The trait is complicated since it also contains repressed feelings of guilt and aggression, as well as feelings of humiliation that the child experienced in the relationship with parents. The feelings of inferiority and acts of masochism have much in common; indeed, most psychologists believe that there is no masochism without inferiority feelings, and no sadism without superiority feelings or feelings of omnipotence. Moreover, we find clinical evidence for the fact that there is no masochism without sadism. Freud felt that sado-masochism is instinctually based (1915), recognizing that the individual will show anger and aggression if frustrated even in infancy and childhood. Freud fused "normal" with "abnormal," insisting that the neurophysiological response to attack is the root of a sado-masochism based on the instinctual life. At the present time there is a tendency to credit sado-masochism not to instinctual processes but to learning experiences.

A *learning model* for the neuroses, the psychoses, and the borderlines, can be based on the assumption that the "ideas holding sway in the mind of the person," or the "clichés in the mind," are in fact identification phantasies, a reaction to traumatic experience with parents. The phantasy is a defensive reaction and is sado-masochistic because the experience that it simultaneously depicts and defends against has been sado-masochistic. We now feel that sado-masochism is also evidence of some kind of seduction. While Freud never denied that seduction could be a factor in neurosis, it was never made clear that this involved perverse sexuality on the part of the parent, which was basically a rejection of the child qua child.

Adler (1925) also wrote of the as-if motif in neurotic behavior, referring to Vaihinger (1924) saying that this has a connection with *fiction* and *phantasy* and is part of the *private logic* of the patient. Freud made sarcastic reference to Adler's *as-if,* but he seems to have used similar concepts at times. In the volume entitled "The Structure and Meaning of Psychoanalysis" (1930), Freud's ideas on fixation are presented as having some *as-if* concepts: When part of the libido is left behind in fixation, the "libidinal current in question then behaves in regard to later psychological structures as though it belonged to the system of the unconscious, as though it were repressed." Adler said that fiction and phantasy were the rationalizations (a word suggested by Jones, 1918) that the patient presented to explain his neurotic behavior, and were the foundations of his *private logic.*

The concepts of *private logic, as-if,* and *rationalization* have much in common. Although Jones seems to put rationalization in the same category as Freud put forgetfulness, i.e., as a dynamic in normal behavior, nevertheless he showed that it had a relation to *conflict, repression* and other defenses. Allport (1954) wrote that rationalization is a mechanism noted by many writers, and it has been reflected in history by statements about what the "state" or the "crown" wishes. In modern times, we hear of the wishes of the "corporation." Allport says that rationalization also excuses the bad or destructive behavior of our loved ones. He refers to Lippman (1922), Machievelli (1946), Hobbes (1904, 1st. Ed., 1651) and Bentham (1789) as touching upon the subject in their various civilizations.

The concept of private logic seems another way of saying what Freud alleged when he spoke of distortion, condensation and displacement as being forms of thought in phantasy formation, and disguises to give the ego distance. He said (Freud, 1954, p. 197): "For phantasies are psychical outworks constructed in order to bar the way to memories"; and "symptoms and phantasies, like dreams, have a similar mental construction." *Hysterical symptoms are not attached to actual memories but to phantasies erected on the basis of memories.* This important concept was reiterated in the early editions of the "Interpretation of Dreams" (1900), but later it was contaminated by the instinct theory. By 1897, Freud was beginning to study the relations to anxiety of symptoms, phantasies and dreams, and his dynamic concepts were beginning to take final shape.

Charcot recognized the suggestibility trait and let it work for him. He took an authoritative role with patients, however, commanding them to give up their symptoms. Bernheim worked in a different way, i.e., more dynamically; he felt, as Janet, that the patient's past unpleasant experiences had a good deal to do with his problem. He engaged himself communicatively with his patient, asking him to remember his past. Janet employed a somewhat similar technique organized around the idea that hysteria was the result of *mental dissociation* produced by mental or physical shock. While the cause of shock was forgotten,[9] the memory remained latent in the subconscious, and disturbed the individual's behavior or activity—particularly his bodily activity; thus, such symptoms occurred as were found in the psychasthenias, i.e., physical symptoms which Freud called *conversions.* There was to be much speculation and many attempts to distinguish between the somatizations in the hysterias and those of the schizophrenias, which Freud finally referred to as the *hypochondrias* (1914), since he saw a developmental difference in the phantasies attached to each type of somatic symptom. He distinguished in the two syndromes the libidinal attachment to objects: in the hypochondrias, the attachment was to part objects (in regression) and in the hysterias to whole objects (the oedipal phase and the oedipal object).

Janet thought that symptoms were the result of a person's constitutional inadequacy which caused *defects in recognition* and *readiness to meet situations,* resulting often in phobias. Janet also posed a constitutional defect as the reason for the individual's inability to handle the contents of his mind under stress and shock. This was apparently a forerunner of what later was developed by others into an *ego defect concept.* Breuer had the idea that hypnoid states (also credited to a defective constitutional state) were the cause of dissociations in the mind. For Freud, dissociation and denial had the same kind of psychological implication as the mechanisms of displacement; these were connected with "motives" which eventually he attributed to the instincts but which originally he conceived of as resulting from experience. In the end, he finally came to a conclusion similar to that of Janet: it was not so much the quality or the character of the traumatic experience that mattered in the development of the neurosis, but *how the individual reacted to it,* and this in turn depended on a constitutional factor, and an ego defect was implied. In spite of his dilemmas, Freud gave us the important papers on the defense neuropsychoses, which are still basic in our understanding of psychodynamics.

The methods of treatment in the late 1800's when Freud began his practice were primarily "electric-therapy," hydrotherapy, rest cures and hypnosis. Janet, Bernheim and Breuer all used hypnosis to encourage their patients to remember incidents that happened the first time their symptoms occurred. "Of great importance too," said Freud, "was Breuer's request that they remember their feelings, the affect which had been dammed up." Patients were encouraged to speak the thoughts that they had repressed and to *express their untoward feelings without fear of reprimand:* the "strangulated affects" were released. This was the *cathartic method*, an improvement on the *command method* of Charcot.

Two schools of thought emerged: the "suggestion theorists" as opposed to those followers of Charcot who looked upon hypnotic effects as "phenomena in their own right," divorced from interpersonal relationships. In this dispute as in many others to come, Freud's penchant for duality made him state that there are two kinds of hypnosis: one dependent upon suggestion, and one which has its roots in "normal" physiological phenomena, particularly in the dynamics of sleep. He also insisted there were two kinds of suggestibility, and three kinds of repression, a word first used in the paper, "On Hysterical Mechanisms," written with Breuer in 1893. In describing two kinds of hysteria, he elaborated concepts concerning several kinds of thought: Ucs, Pcs, Cs (the topological theory). There were, however, two categories of thought: *biological* and *psychological.* Biological thought embraced an evolutionary connotation which Freud was to expand in his phylogenetic concepts. And the concept *wish* eventually was to have phylogenetic implications. It was not simply the experience of the individual in his ontogenetic existence that produced the wish for the love object, resulting in *satisfaction* in possession of the object, and *dissatisfaction* in rejection by the object. It was also the memory of phylogenetic experience that could produce the same reactions of satisfaction and dissatisfaction. We have, then, the concept of *phylogenetic memory,* and with this concept Freud revived the Platonic postulate of *innate ideas,* and finally the hypothesis of a type of phantasy or hallucination which has no connection with ontogenetic experience. This formulation is at odds with the more modern idea that all phantasy is a reflection of actual individual experience, a view Freud initially held.

In describing a borderline patient, there is little to be gained in using phylogenetic concepts; empirically it is more practical to consider phantasy as a representation of actual experience, albeit in disguised form, the individual using displacement, condensation, symbolization, dissociation, repression and denial as defenses, and employing distortion as an aspect of defense. Projective therapeutic techniques which are so successful with the schizophrenias, borderlines and some character disorders are based on the idea that in delusions and hallucinations, as in other forms of phantasy, there is reflected the memory of actual past experience, as well as current, or her-and-now, relationship.

Freud got around the problem of suggestibility as a learned neurotic trait by developing the concept of *autosuggestion,* a phenomenon which he said could be described apart from the hypnotist as an operator. Autosuggestion was different from direct suggestion: it was an independent mechanism, a stimulus from "within" rather than from "without."[10] To illustrate this concept, Freud used one of Charcot's demonstrations as an example (1888). Charcot would say to a hypnotized subject: "Look at that hideous face. Hit out at it." And the subject would strike out, then his arm would drop down as if paralyzed. Freud explained this phenomenon as follows: "An external stimulus has, to begin with, produced a feeling of painful exhaustion in the arm; and this, in turn, spontaneously and independently of any intervention on the part of the physician, has suggested paralysis . . . in other words, it is a question . . . not so much of suggestion, as of stimulation to auto-suggestion . . . and these, as anyone can see contain an objective factor independent of the physician's will, and they reveal a connection between various conditions of innervation or excitation in the nervous system. It is autosuggestions, such as these, that lead to production of spontaneous hysterical paralysis and it is an inclination to such autosuggestions rather than suggestibility which . . . characterized hysteria." Freud's autosuggestion appears to be a forerunner of his later concept of the wish as an innate factor. Autosuggestion was an impulse from within, and Freud seems to have denied that this response was a result of previous conditionings. The wish became the motivator of behavior and was a combination of innate ideas, or biological thought, and the energy from the instinct. Together these constituted an internal stimulus of somatic origin in the form of *libidinal energy* (later connected with the id).

Bernheim, said Freud, worked with indirect suggestion as well as with direct suggestion. His method for bringing about sleep was an example, as Freud

(1888) pointed out: "suggestion pushes open the doors which are in fact, slowly opening of themselves by autosuggestion ... Indirect suggestions in which a series of intermediate links arising from the subject's own activity are inserted between the external stimulus and the result, are none the less mental processes; but they are no longer exposed to the full light of consciousness which falls upon direct suggestions. For we are far more accustomed to bring attention to bear upon external perceptions than upon internal processes. Indirect suggestions or autosuggestions can accordingly be described equally as physiological or as mental phenomena, and the term 'suggestion' has the same meaning as the reciprocal provocation of mental states according to the laws of association." Freud, as we know, was influenced by Wundt's association experiments. He continued: "Shutting the eyes leads to sleep because it is linked to the concept of sleep through being one of its most regular accompaniments: one portion of the manifestations of sleep suggests the other manifestations which go to make up the phenomenon as a whole. This linking up ties in with the nature of the nervous system and not in any arbitrary decision by the physician. It cannot occur unless it is based upon alterations in the excitability of the relevant portions of the brain, in the innervation of the vasomotor centers, etc., and it thus presents alike a psychological and a physiological aspect." Objecting to the ideas of some who called hypnosis "an experimental psychosis" and suggestion a set of "compulsive ideas," Freud said it is realized that "suggestion only releases sets of manifestations which are based upon the functional peculiarities of the subject's nervous system, and that, in hypnosis, characteristics of the nervous system other than suggestibility make themselves felt." Freud affirmed that the human organism had self-propelling propensities, some goals of which the individual was not completely aware (the unconscious as reflective of the instincts). We see here, however, his need to attribute to the innate characteristics of the organism itself much of what is surely conditioned and learned.

Freud tackled this problem of suggestibility again in his paper, "Psychogenic Visual Disturbance According to Psychoanalytic Conceptions" (1910), saying that it is possible to produce hysterical blindness experimentally through the use of hypnosis. Further, it can be demonstrated that the "hysterical blind do see." But in the essay, Freud attempts to connect suggestibility with his concept of autosuggestion and the instincts, attributing the denial and negation of the object in hysterical blindness to a conflict of interest of the instincts rather than to a conflict which has resulted as a matter of learning in traumatic experience with objects; "... every instinct seeks to come to expression by activating those ideas which are in accordance with its aims. These instincts do not always agree with one another, and this frequently results in a conflict of interest." Then Freud mentions the inevitable contradiction between the sexual instincts and the instincts of self-preservation: these are opposites. "The mouth serves for kissing as well as for eating and speaking; the eyes perceive not only those modifications in the external world which are of import for the preservation of life, but also the attributes of objects by means of which these may be exalted as objects of erotic selection. . ." The role of *perception* and the *reactions to experience* thus were identified as important variables as the individual was thrown into conflict as a result of his contacts with objects. But the instinct theory tended to deny that conflict was a result of learned behavior, giving it a mysterious origin; and later the more serious neuroses were said to have an "organic" or constitutional factor, thus supporting the idea of defects, some classed as genetic and others called "ego" defects.

The infusion of objects with libidinal energy became an important concept as Freud abandoned the seduction theory and developed his instinct hypothesis. This idea was highlighted in the essay on narcissism, along with the concept that withdrawal from objects, as in schizophrenia, was accompanied by a diffusion or withdrawal of libidinal energy from the object: withdrawal from objects meant that more libidinal energy was transferred to the self. In the relation with objects the processes of cathexis and decathexis of libidinal energy were stressed, and this was a different concept from that of defense as formulated in the essays on the "Defense Neuropsychoses" (1894), i.e., the ego's struggle against painful or unendurable ideas and affects. Yet even in that essay, in the last paragraph, Freud began his speculations about energy. Breuer parted company with Freud over this concept. Breuer's "excitations" in the nervous system and the concept of displacement were neurophysiologically and biologically different from Freud's. Freud's concept of regression finally emerged from his theory, and differences arose over the sexual concept, which are of relevance in our current ideas on borderline patients. Some authorities say that the borderlines are not as "regressed" as other syndromes, but they are "fixated." Some authorities feel that borderline conditions have more of a "constitutional factor" (page 131) than some of the schizophrenias and the neuroses. It was said that Breuer suggested the idea of regression when it was noticed that dreams had a hallucinatory or picture character, the thought being that the hallucination was the response when motor reaction or associative reaction was inhibited. Thinking and phantasy, said Freud, replace action. One does not see why the idea of regression would follow from the concept of hallucination, but Freud's theory involved the notion that, developmentally speaking, the infant hallucinates the satisfaction of a wish when he cannot have the object to satisfy his urge. One aspect of perception is to see things as pictures. Hallucination should be defined in a specific way as having a relation to delusion; this is different from the memory of an object, although delusion and hallucination are undoubtedly based on what Freud and Breuer called noxious memories, but they are defenses against the memories.

Freud's notion of displacement was much more important than his developmental concept for our present-day formulations about the borderline patient, and this embraces the concept of the acting out of roles (a motor response) which are associated with phantasy and the other defenses of the borderline.

The idea of the innate impulse as a factor in the development of neuroses and psychoses should be replaced by the idea of a conditioned role. Such a view would contend that the borderline patient's neurotic impulses stem not from instinctual origins but from anxiety and other responses to parental behavior. A prior experience of traumatic consequence in striking at a face (or some other aggressive series of acts on the part of the parent) could have conditioned the reaction of paralysis in Charcot's patient, who is protecting the object from his aggression out of guilt. Patients who show extreme forms of guilt have been made to feel guilty about their reactive aggression in response to the aggression of parents. The problem is compounded by the fact that the parent accepts some aggression due to his own masochism, but then rejects other instances of aggression; thus there are "permitted" and "unpermitted" forms of aggression (Wolberg, A., 1960). When Charcot gave his patient the cue to action, resulting inhibition of function came about as a learned response. This was a conditioned defensive reaction. Early analysis connected the inhibitory reaction to a protection of the object (Freud refers to this as Stekel's idea) against the individual's own aggression, and this motif was thought to be a factor in depression in obsessive-compulsive defenses, in schizophrenia and in other emotional conditions. Spotnitz (1969) considers this the main dynamic in schizophrenia. As a matter of fact, both ideas tend to be true: the individual through inhibition protects both himself and the other person—himself from the aggression of the other, and the other from his own counter-aggression, stirred up by the initial aggressive attack of the other. An experience in the present can set off the response which was inhibited in the past. This behavior can be thought of as a form of acting out.

Freud's study of the hysterias gave rise to several complicated ideas: (1) the beginnings of a concept of defense; (2) the organism as its own conditioner of behavior after trauma; (3) the idea that a set of thoughts which are associated with conditioned behavior can become the stimulus for the repetition of that behavior (a "learning" and an "associative" concept); (4) thought as a reaction to an experience; (5) symptoms as a reaction to experience; (6) experience as an inhibitory factor in behavior (frustration); and (7) suggestibility as a learned response related to overevaluation of the object and a willingness to identify with the object out of the need to have wishes satisfied, out of the need to be cared for, or out of fear and the hope of protection.

After he gave up the seduction premise, Freud turned more and more to the idea of inner stimuli as opposed to the accidental factor. Inner stimuli were biologically founded and created pressures over which the individual seemed to have no control and against which he constantly had to fight and defend himself. Thus, there was considerable difference in the idea that neurosis is stimulated in the child as he rejects or finds experience intolerable and unacceptable, as opposed to the theory that his innate impulses and his sexuality are unacceptable and, therefore, he must build defenses against the anxiety resulting from his conflict with repudiated sexual impulses and the innate ideas associated with them. Freud was of the opinion that not only was a constitutional factor present in the form of an innately unacceptable sexuality, but that, in addition, civilization or society made the individual feel guilty about his normal sexual feelings. He expressed the opinion that constitution and environment were thus interactive and in the long run had an effect upon each other. Both society and the instinct threw the child into defense. This circular reasoning caused Adler (as faithfully reported by Freud) to quip: "If you ask where repression comes from, you are told 'From civilization'; and if you ask where civilization comes from, you are told 'From repression.' You can see, therefore, it is nothing but playing with words." (Freud, 1914)[11]

The works of Bianchi (1920), Pavlov (1928), Sherrington (1936), Papez (1937), Penfield (1952), Penfield and Roberts (1959), Vogts (1951), and Magouen (1954) have given us neurophysiological information about such matters as the neural mechanisms and functions of the frontal lobes; the intricacies of conditioning; the levels of nervous integration; the organization of the limbic system; the delineation of brain centers (through electrical stimulation); the precise physiological mapping of the cerebral cortex; and the mechanisms of the reticular activating system. The psychoanalyst is only peripherally interested in these neurophysiological phenomena. He is more concerned with those elements of the interpersonal and intrapsychic systems that communicate to the individual, from the parents, the role he is to play in the parents' defensive system. Ultimately science may, as Freud once speculated (1914, 1931), provide a physiological explanation (perhaps even a chemical explanation) for all of our psychological functions. As matters stand, we do not yet have the information that permits us to do this. While *thinking*, as L. Wolberg has reminded us (1966), may be conceived of neuro-psychologically as "the product of electrical impulses coursing through the multiple synaptic connections of cortical neurons with their ramified dendritic networks, circumscribed by the selective discrimination of multiform subcortical influences, as well as of intracortical associative excitations," we as analysts deal with other variables related to thinking and are concerned with the *mental systems* which are reflected in dreams, phantasies, symptoms, and the demonstrable behavior which includes acting out. We are also concerned with memories of traumatic experiences, and with the patient's aspirations and efforts towards eliminating inappropriate defenses. Wolberg notes (1966) that memories, once stored, "and their associated emotions and action tendencies, are not extinguished easily . . ." but "the reason may be that such memories are being reinforced daily, satisfying random inner needs not apparent on the surface." Freud (1900) was of the opinion that "nothing that we have once mentally possessed can be entirely lost." This thesis is certainly tenable and appropriate to our current knowledge. Penfield elicited in his patients both vivid memories and the emotions associated with them. The conflicts investing past experiences are reflected in the here-and-now symptoms, dreams, and phantasies. Sheffield and Tenner in 1950 reported some work in a paper entitled "Relative Resistance to Extinction of Escape Training and Avoidance Training" which applies to defense.

Freud understood that the brain and the nervous system were storage systems as well as active dynamic systems. He mentioned that the imagoes were reflections of past experiences with significant figures in the family, i.e., mother, father, brother, sister. He spoke of the imago as delineating a *pattern.* While he never succinctly defined this concept of *pattern,* he undoubtedly was referring to experiences with parents which reflected the conflicts, fears, inhibitions and conditionings which emerge from life in the family *and result in neurotic or psychotic role behavior.* Freud enjoined the psychoanalyst, through the process of free association and the patient's dreams, to discover the associations between the past and the present as these were reflected in the patient's current conflicts. In this way, we are able without electrical stimulation of the cortex, such as Penfield had employed, to activate the past in the present.

In their papers on the hysterias, Freud and Breuer emphasized a number of interesting points: (1) there is a "constancy," a "sum of excitation" [1] [2] in the nervous system (later becoming associated with the economic theory); (2) symptoms are displacement activities, they are attempts at reaction; (3) on the mental side, they represent memories of traumas—the symptom is the recurrence of a psychical state experienced earlier, i.e., a memory of thoughts, feelings and words, but the memory has been suppressed so that it is wholly absent from the patient's consciousness or recollection at the time the symptom is in operation, and the symptom is its substitute; (4) the memory itself has entered into the "second state of consciousness," and (5) the traumatic, or the "exciting" experience, more precisely, *the complex arising as the consequence of traumatic experience,* continues to be effective even years after the event. Freud at first thought that the past was associated with the neuroses not "indirectly" by means of a chain of causes linking up with one another; but as the "actual exciting cause." The memory of the psychical trauma, he said, acts as a kind of *foreign body* constituting an effective agent in the present. In this reference, Freud and Breuer said that "patients suffer from reminiscences" (1893). The paper stated that the reminiscence persisted because proper reaction had not taken place. "An insult which is returned, if only in words, is remembered differently from one that had to be endured in silence." The eventuating revenge motif was a way in which experience stimulated aggression. The patient forgets because he wants to forget; he represses and "does not know" because he does not want to know. Freud began to realize this aspect of the neurosis in the treatment of Elizabeth von R., who refused to remember. Freud began to understand that *defenses* were at work in the process of the treatment when the patient was resistant.

What was omitted in these early theories was the idea that the relations with parents are what caused the humiliation, the degradation and the revenge feelings. No syndrome makes this more clear than that of the borderline patient. The "reminiscences," it is obvious to us now, are not pure memories, nor are they "noxae" or festerings (Freud later gave up this idea in favor of the concept of fixation of the libido in developmental phases); rather they are aspects of the patient's mental defenses, his sado-masochistic phantasies, which are the *mental representations of the identifications with parents displaced and symbolized to give the patient's ego relief from the anxiety created in interpersonal relationships.* Seduction was considered a problem, but the dynamics of perverse behavior on the part of the parent in relation to seduction were denied. Freud noted much later in his essay on Female Sexuality (1931) that where seduction intervenes there is trouble, but the interlocking aspect of the neurosis with that of the parent was merely hinted at and was never considered essential for the development of perverse behavior on the part of the child.

The fact that later in life the individual finds another with whom he can interact as he did with his parents seems to signify that he must replace the parent with a substitute, one who is in some ways like the parent, in order to maintain his own neurotic balance. Displacement mechanisms are used not only in interpersonal relationships per se, but also in defensive phantasies, dreams, phobias and other symptoms. Since the neurosis is, in a sense, a life-saving mechanism in the relationship with parents, the emotional need to hang on to neurotic symptoms is an aspect of the patient's fear of testing out new situations out of terror of hurt or destruction. Animals, or even pieces of furniture and other inanimate objects may be used as projective objects (i.e., objects of displacement) in phantasies or behavior. The *meaning systems* are what we must uncover. The delusion, which is a particular form of phantasy often employed by the borderlines, embraces many objects or things as projective instruments.

It was the problem of the perversions, which seemed associated with family dynamics and perverse attitudes in parents and that Freud found in his hysterical patients, that led him to the instinct theory (in defense). The patients that Freud called hysterics were primarily schizophrenics and borderlines, as well as character disorders and obsessionals, so that much that related to his discoveries of dynamic mental systems referred to these syndromes. Since we are using the term identification to connote defense, we must note that the early analysts defined identification in several ways: (1) an interpretation having the meaning of both defense and conflict stemming from problems with early authorities and thus having a relation to transference and imagoes (this latter seems to have embraced both mental patterns and acting out patterns, i.e., transference behavior); (2) a means through which an object gives satisfaction of an instinct through incorporation (the taking in or assimilation of the object), the "cathexis" of the object (investment of the object with libidinal energy and the assumption that one could "decathect" the object when no longer useful); (3) a wanting to be like the object; and (4) wanting to have or possess the object. The fourth connotation had a relation to Freud's thesis of fixation. We find a use for this idea in the borderline case in the sense that the rejected child clings to the object as a defense, and moulds himself according to what he feels the object wants him to be in order to appease the object. Then he remakes the object in his mind into a more acceptable person. A fifth interpretation of the term identification was a conglomerate of various psychological, sociological and mystical conceptions and had to do with the phenomenon of peers banding together for a social purpose. This idea Freud used in his book, "Group Psychology and the Analysis of the Ego," but he now applied the oedipal theory in his formulations. He specified that the social behavior of individuals who join in a common cause derives from the homosexual impulse originated in the archetype of the sons dominated by the harsh and cruel father who refused them their birthright of independence. To break their bondage, the sons were forced to band together to kill the father. Sociologists and anthropologists depreciate this idea as highly speculative. It is probably significant that in the concept of peers, Freud classified males and females as one sex, that of males. In certain passages Freud referred to *identification as a substitute for object relations*. The several meanings given to identification were often fused in the use of the libido theory. At different stages of development identification was presumed to take on different forms.

In Freud's essay on the Uncanny (1919) he touched upon an important subject for understanding the dynamics of borderline patients, dealing with what Melanie Klein later called "projective identification." In the essay he referred to identification with the "double," i.e., with persons who are considered identical by reason of some similarity. "There is a transference of mental processes from one person to another." Freud alluded to Rank's statement that the "double" was originally an insurance against destruction of the ego, and an "energetic denial of the power of death." This was another way of talking about the familiar defense of identification, and the fear of separation from the parent or the fixation on the parent. We can see that the fear of death comes from the fear that the parents will abandon the person or, in their destructiveness, kill rather than protect. To prevent this they have to be appeased. This idea is found in the "language of dreams." To save himself the child identifies with the parent. When in transference the individual finds someone who acts like the parents, he in turn acts toward them in some ways as he did toward his parents. His projective defense involves his transferential object, but in the transferential object he sees, hates and denies that aspect of himself with which he is identified.

In summary, we may say that the early studies of the hysterias, and particularly the original hypnotic experiments provided information concerning the dynamics of identification and the various roles the individual assumed in his adaptive defenses. The roles we now observe played by the borderline patient are similar to what Freud originally described as *hysterical* (1908) and which he later said were transferences based on *identification.* The early studies clearly depicted identification as based on hysterical mechanisms, and although Freud's libido theory confused this fact, we must keep clearly in mind the concept of hysterical maneuvers if we wish to understand the dynamics of acting out in our borderline cases.

NOTES

[1] Freud (1856-1939), Charcot (1825-1893), Breuer (1842-1924), Janet (1859-1947), and Bernheim (1840-1919) can be called pioneers in the exploration of depth psychology. They discovered most of what we know today about psychodynamics. Freud (1893) wrote of Charcot: "While he was occupied with the study of hysterical paralyses appearing after traumas, the idea occurred to him to reproduce ... such paralysis as he had previously carefully differentiated from organic disturbances; for this purpose he took hysterical patients and placed them in a state of somnambulism by hypnotism. He succeeded in producing a faultless demonstration and proved thereby that these paralyses were the result of specific ideas holding sway in the brain of the patient at moments of special disposition. With this, the mechanism of an hysterical phenomenon was for the first time disclosed, and on this incomparably fine piece of clinical research his own pupil Janet, and also Breuer and others, based their theories of the neurosis."

The concept that symptoms and other forms of neurotic or psychotic behavior are connected with "ideas holding sway in the brain of the patient at moments of special disposition" is an important formulation in understanding any kind of neurotic behavior; indeed, these "ideas in the brain" are *specially organized* and are interesting to us in the consideration of the borderline patient because they have to do with the familiar processes of *identification, transference, acting out, withdrawal, phantasy,* and *anxiety,* and the relation of these to the sado-masochistic use the parent has made of the child in the interpersonal transactions in the family.

[2] Janet wrote a book (1889), "L'Automatisme Psychologique," in which there is a description of a cure attained in an hysterical girl by the employment of a method similar to that reported later by Breuer. Freud (1893) explained, however, that Breuer's work was done first in 1880-82, even though it was reported in subsequent years.

These early studies stressed the concept of repression, a major defense in neuroses and psychoses, and the role of memory and the relation of traumatic events to memory as central concepts in understanding emotional difficulties. *Memory, learning,* and, we shall presently see, *the need to identify with parents who are neurotic or psychotic,* due to the trauma recurring in the interpersonal encounters with them, are variables considered important in the development of borderline problems and probably of all neuroses and psychoses. The concept of the "binding of excitations" in memory became an idea which led Freud to the theory of libidinal energy.

[3] Freud's translator gave this paper the title "Hypnotism and Suggestion" in the

Collected Papers; it was originally published in parts in 1888-1889.

4 This important point is the basis for the idea that *suggestibility is a learned response* and that it is a factor in symptom formation, and the organization of phantasy. We now say that the parent is the active agent in promoting *social roles* which are pathological in nature, the motivation being that these roles appease the parents' neurotic needs, and temporarily reduce the parents' anxiety each time the role goes into operation. The experience is traumatic for the child, and when it occurs is always of a sado-masochistic nature, creating such anxiety in the child that he must organize defenses, *phantasy being one of the defensive reactions.* These "ideas in the mind" were later called "clichés in the mind" by Freud in his paper the "Dynamics of the Transference" (1912) and they were related to the "infantile imagoes." The "infantile imagoes" were unconscious conflicts, the outcome of relations with "archaic objects" (Bychowski's phrase, 1967). This experience with objects at an early age led later to the idea of the superego. Thus, we see in Charcot's formulation the forerunner of the concept of *phantasy*, i.e., *the mental representations of the neurotic problem, as it evolved in the early object relations.* It was the work in hypnosis and the factor of suggestibility that enabled Freud to come to certain conclusions about the role of identification in neurotic problems. He established the connection between object relations, experience with parental figures in the early years of life, identification and the "imagoes" of transference, which were in essence phantasies representing patterns, conflicts, or "complexes" (Jung's word) created in the early relations with parents. Freud noted that Gabriele Reuter in 1895 was aware of the dynamics of transference.

5 It is essential to understand the *active role* of the parent in the conditioning process which calls forth *as-if* behavior, an important element in the organization of identification and thus of neurotic and psychotic behavior. "In defending their own neuroses, parents project onto the child certain 'roles' which gratify neurotic needs, generally unconscious within themselves. Through the mechanism of controlling tendencies the parent regulates the child's behavior so that it will fit the role that will most relieve the parent's pressing anxiety. The projected role is that aspect of the parental neurosis that the parent wishes most to deny—projection and denial are twin defenses. The interlocking neurosis between the parents and the child is set up on the basis of identification, for the child has no other choice but to conform; this kind of identification is predicated upon a sado-masochistic relationship. Eventually, the child has secondary gains of reward from the parents for his neurotic behavior; but these rewards are complicated for the parents have guilt feelings, and this guilt has to be assuaged. The fear is that the child will expose their forbidden aims, and so punishment is sometimes the reinforcement which the child receives for the encouraged or the 'permitted' behavior. The punishment is fused with rewards for the same behavior. Thus the superego has aspects which are not associated with 'good values,' instead, they are motivations for 'bad' or destructive behavior. It was probably this perplexing state of affairs that caused Freud (1924) to comment, '. . . a complication is introduced by the existence of the superego which, in some connection not yet clear to us, combines in itself influences from the id as well as from the outer world.' " (A. Wolberg, 1960)

6 In the paper "Patterns of Interaction in Families of Borderline Patients" (A. Wolberg, 1968), there are illustrated the *roles* that parents encourage in their children and the as-if motif present in the child when he carries out these roles. As-if behavior is identification behavior, in essence, defensive behavior, but it must be accompanied by several kinds of other defenses, not the least of which are repression and denial. Fairbairn (1952) has discussed such roles.

7 Freud incorporated the characteristic of suggestibility into his concepts of transference; and Ferenczi (1909) connected the "character of suggestibility" with the

"parent complex." When Freud spoke of the parent complex it would seem that this was another way of talking about the infantile imagoes of his essay on transference, those mental organizations (now unconscious) acquired as a result of conflict in childhood. Freud made a connection between fixation, masochism, and suggestibility in the following way after he gave up the seduction hypothesis and adopted the instinct theory. In "Three Contributions to the Theory of Sex" (1905) he wrote: "The psychic estimation in which the sexual object shares as a goal of the sexual instinct is only in the rarest cases limited to the genitals; generally, it embraces the whole body and tends to include all sensations emanating from the sexual object. The same over-estimation extends to the psychic sphere and manifests itself as a logical blinding (diminished judgment) concerning the psychic attainments and the perfections of the sexual object, and in a credulous yielding to the judgments emanating from the latter. The absolute faith inspired by love thus becomes an important if not the primordial source of authority . . . I must mention here that the blind obedience evidenced by the hypnotized subject to the hypnotist causes me to think that the nature of hypnosis is to be found in the unconscious fixation of the libido on the person of the hypnotizer (by means of the masochistic component of the sexual instinct)." There is credence in believing that suggestibility is a masochistic trait learned in the interpersonal relationship with parents. The "over-estimation" of the "libidinalized object" in Freud's concept of the "ego-ideal," elaborated in the essay on narcissism, later an aspect of the superego, is an example of the employment of this dynamic.

Cantril (1941, 1957) did some interesting work on interpersonal relations in which he showed that *confusion increases suggestibility.* Nightmares, phobias, obsessive-compulsive and psychotic symptoms appear more frequently, he said, when the individual is in situations where many opposing cues are present. Cantril has related this phenomenon to what he calls perception. It is probably nearer the truth to say that the trait of suggestibility was already present in Cantril's subjects, due to training in childhood with parents who demanded identification behavior because of their own anxieties. Thus we could say that *suggestibility increases confusion in the presence of conflicting cues.* This would be the basis for the *double bind* problem postulated by Bateson, Weakland et al., and it would account for the reactions observed by Stanton and Schwartz (1954) when disagreements among the staff created psychotic behavior in certain patients. There are several other kinds of data which may possibly be explained on the basis of the suggestibility factor. For example, Searles in writing the essay, "The Effort to Drive the Other Person Crazy" (1959), undoubtedly has pinpointed obsessive-compulsive and paranoid trends in parents who "drive their children crazy" in the sense that they do not let them have an opinion—they always question a decision, or cut off the behavior which might result from a clear-cut decision; they offer so many alternatives that they prevent decision; and finally they show dissatisfaction with any decision. This creates a problem which eventually prevents the child from operating on his own, making him dependent on the vascillating opinion of the "other," i.e., the parental figure. Obsessive bugging leads to obsessive doubting in the child and dependence on the opinions of others. The suggestibility factor is present due to the identification required by the bugging punitive parent. The underlying hostility and aggression in such parental maneuvers is obvious. In this same vein Freud noted that disagreements between parents are among the most anxiety provoking situations for children.

There are two other kinds of phenomena which perhaps may be accounted for by the suggestibility factor. One is what has been called the "pre-logical thinking" or the "regressive thought" of the more severely disturbed patients. The theory was that this type of symptom is a regression to early patterns of thinking in the stage before the id/ego differentiation. Some writers refer to this as a disturbance in abstract thinking and they talk of the "language of schizophrenia." One sees that in this kind of communication a disguise is developed, so that what the person is thinking or feeling is not immediately evident since *he is not supposed to think on his own.* He has been trained by his parents to believe he should not think on his own. The fact is that there is much symbolic and abstract thinking in what has been called pre-logical thought. A word, for example, can symbolize a whole constellation of ideas, as Freud pointed out in some of his early papers. The disguise may be in part due to the guilt the individual feels in being able to perceive. Another kind of data comes from the reports of investigators like Charles Fischer (1969) and his colleagues (1964), who compare nightmares to temporary psychotic attacks. Freud said that dreams were temporary psychotic attacks in view of the fact that there was no motor discharge. In his dream studies, Fisher found that when he woke people from nightmares they were often delusional, paranoid and hallucinating, i.e., they use projective defenses. The borderline patient has brief, evanescent psychotic episodes which may easily be set off when the patient is in a situation where conflicting cues are present and he feels he is expected to respond. Freud suggested that the mind "works over" stimuli that are anxiety provoking and we may assume that this is what happens in the dream. The nightmare is an aspect of the defense, a projection of the anxiety response to a traumatic situation, and a "working over" of the situation to master the anxiety. The suggestibility of the borderline is a factor in the conflict situation when two opposing cues are given; the defense is to use delusion. The "positive transference" which Freud considered essential in analysis is predicated upon suggestibility.

L. Wolberg employs psychoanalysis with hypnosis, and uses the "positive transference" to help induce motivation in the patient and to align himself with the "observing" or the "rational ego," at the same time that he explores the projective defenses.

8 The ambivalent attitude may be observed in all patients, but in the more disturbed patients it is pathologically pronounced. Because the ego is more rigid and the so-called superego more punitive, guilt is more severe and masochistic traits more pervasive. The denials of reality are greater in the more seriously disturbed patients, and one finds a "split" attitude: at one time the patient denies something that he does not deny on other occasions. Freud noticed this phenomenon in his hysterical patients and in those with fetishes, this latter having, of course, many hysterical defenses. Freud noted also that in the obsessional neuroses the patient has two kinds of knowledge: "he knows" and "he does not know" (1909). Ambivalence was defined as love and hate for the same object, but it is probably more related to indecision and obsessive-compulsive attitudes on the part of the parent who infuses the child with uncertainties than it has to do with love; there is a relation to hate and revenge, certainly a displacement from the parents' parents to their child, and it is this kind of problem that interferes with the child's self-assertiveness. Mowrer (1950) suggested a guilt theory of neurosis rather than an instinct theory, since guilt is a primary factor in every neurosis and in every psychosis. It would seem obvious that the parent initially instills the guilt feelings in the child when the latter's normal behavior gives the parent anxiety; then, later, the child feels guilty for his own aggression and fearful lest he lose the parent who is already mostly lost. One will remember that Schreber used to shout threats and abuses at the sun (God the father) and he got so that he could rage at it without any difficulty; however, on other occasions he felt a great deal of guilt and fear that God would sever his connection.

The borderline patient is especially ambivalent and shows negative attitudes in the transference. Negative and hostile behavior often evokes untoward reactions in the therapist. In essence, ambivalence in an excessive amount, is found in the passive-aggressive characterological manifestations typical of the schizophrenias, the borderlines and the character disorders.

9 An important basic formulation in these early days of pre-analytic thinking was the dynamic concept introduced by Janet that *forgetting* in the face of trauma and its twin

phenomenon *dissociation* were connected. Freud (1898) wrote a paper on forgetfulness which placed it within the "normal" range, but nevertheless described it as a dynamic related to conflict and repression. These concepts were to be the basis of later disagreements between Freud, Breuer and Janet and they undoubtedly moulded some of Freud's later ideas about repression. The concepts of defense and repression led to the topological theory: the Conscious (Cs), Preconscious (Pcs), and Unconscious (Ucs). What was repressed was what was unacceptable to the ego, i.e., to the individual sense of decency. But fear is also a primary motif for repression. In the case of Roxanne (page 12), denial and a made-up story was her defense at the same time that she gave an accounting of the reality situation to her foster parents. Did she repress? She certainly had to repress her feelings about the way her parents used her. She must have had fears of being destroyed. She tried to save herself by appealing to her foster parents.

[10] In Freud's illustrations, one can readily see that as first described it was a conditioning factor that set off the suggestive response emanating from within. Our theory will contain the idea that some of the experiences of borderlines in the family tend to condition displacement behavior (see page 172) in the form of "permitted aggressions."

[11] The difference between what Freud finally considered to be inner impulses, particularly in relation to neurotic and psychotic syndromes (his preoccupation with the innate) and what we now consider to be the source of these impulses in ontogeny is of great theoretical importance. Neurotic impulses are, in our present formulations, learned responses, while physical growth and development which occur in all individuals, whether they are neurotic, psychotic, or "normal," are based on genetic factors, or what Freud at one point called the "innate schedule." We are concerned in psychoanalysis with the effects of identification, rather than with developmental considerations.

[12] At that time the concept of libido as instinctual energy was not clearly defined. It was later that the economic theory was elaborated, although even in the "Project" there was an energy concept, as Holt has mentioned (1962, 1963, 1965, 1967).

CHAPTER II

THE "WOLF MAN": A BORDERLINE CASE STUDY

Freud came nearest to describing a borderline patient in his paper "The Infantile Neurosis" (1919), although one can see from the material that he was dealing with a patient who had more complex trends than are usual in borderlines. It is interesting to examine aspects of the case, however, for some of the dynamics meet the criteria we might set up for the diagnosis of borderline conditions—particularly those cases that have an obsessive overlay. The patient might, for example, fit into Grinker's Group One Type, which will be referred to later. The family dynamics are of special interest.

The case study ("The Wolf Man") concerned a young man, age eighteen, who, after an attack of gonorrhea became incapacitated and completely dependent upon other people. Ten years of his boyhood seemed "normal," yet his earlier years were actually characterized by a neurotic disturbance which was evident shortly before his fourth birthday and which took the form of anxiety-hysteria (animal-phobia); later, this changed to obsessional neurosis, with a religious content, that lasted with its reverberations into his tenth year. At that time, the symptoms subsided, and he seems to have had some years free from neurotic problems until his eighteenth year, when his sexual experience with its venereal outcome brought on his long-term illness.

The patient's father had spent many years in sanitaria and was diagnosed "manic-depressive insanity." The father's life (although he was active and had

30

many interests) was marked by several attacks of severe depression. The patient's illness, said Freud, was a condition following upon an obsessional neurosis which had come to an end spontaneously but which left a defect behind it after recovery. The case report deals with the infantile neurosis which existed in the patient's earliest years. The essay was an attempt to explain the meaning and dynamics of the childhood neurosis which was the forerunner of the adult condition. The original problems revealed to Freud the significance of the individual's later illness.

As with most borderline cases, Freud noted the difficulty of establishing a relationship: "The analyst must behave as timelessly as the unconscious itself if he wishes to learn anything, or achieve anything. And, in the end, he will succeed in doing so if he has the strength to renounce any short-sighted therapeutical ambition." One cannot expect that "patience, adaptability, insight and confidence will be forthcoming from this kind of patient" (nor, we may add, would we expect that his relatives would have these qualities).

"The patient had an attitude of apathy. He listened, understood and remained unapproachable" (detached). "His intellect was cut off from the instinctual forces that governed his behavior in the object-relations that remained to him" (detachment, isolation). "It required long education to induce him to take an independent share in the analytic work. When he finally did, he began to feel relief and immediately knocked off work in order to avoid any further changes."

> (Obviously the patient wished to remain in the "transference cure" or a "flight into health," and relished the secondary gain of a new dependency. . . . Through passive compliance he frustrated the therapist by putting an end to his own therapeutic goals. Freud was dealing with a *passive-aggressive* and *sado-masochistic* character pattern. The patient was suspicious of human relations, and he had reason in his past to feel so, for his relations with adults had been painful. "Love" was not given, but had to be extracted and his interpersonal encounters in the family were tinged with sadism. Such a patient develops "distrust," as Erikson would put it, though he needs to trust in order to survive.)

The patient's family lived in two country estates and they used to move from one to the other during each summer. The estates were not far from a large town. Near relations used to pay long visits—brothers of his father, sisters of his mother, and their children, and his grandparents on his mother's side. Usually, during the summertime, his parents went away for a few weeks leaving the children with nurses, governesses and relatives. Freud was able to establish time sequences to pinpoint historical data by reference to the periods when the family was at one or the other of the estates, and to discover where the parents were at these given intervals. Freud described "the child's world" in some detail. The parents had married young. They led what Freud called a "happy life" until ill-health set in after a few years; the mother began to suffer abdominal disorders; the father began to have attacks of depression for which he was hospitalized; thus, he was out of the home for long periods at a time. The patient was aware of his mother's ill-health from the first but became conscious of his father's illness only years later. As a consequence of her problems, the mother had very little to do with the children.

(One may properly assume that the burdens of family life were too much for these parents. They were wealthy and could afford the servants they needed, but the demand in marriage to maintain an uninterrupted, interpersonal relationship seems to have been an inordinate emotional strain, and the parents were saving themselves and each other, by their separations and illnesses, from the aggression each felt towards the other. Each parent took refuge in symptoms, a sado-masochistic mode of adjustment.)

One day, while walking beside his mother and holding her hand as she accompanied the doctor to the station, the patient overheard her bewailing her condition. These feelings of the mother made a deep impression on the child and later he "applied them to himself" (identification). The mother complained of her somatic symptoms in a hopeless and resigned "why me" attitude.

(This, one will recognize, is a kind of paranoid feeling—"I am being tortured by these illnesses," the *why-me* mechanism being a masochistic defense with sadistic overtones: "You must feel sorry for me, and guilty, doctor, that you can do nothing to relieve me of these symptoms." The veiled hostility is evident here, as is the obvious transference, being couched in the *projective identification* form of defense. This is illustrative of the mechanism Thompson described in 1957, i.e., the paranoid quality, the masochism, and the controlling mechanisms, in her paper: "The Interpersonal Approach to the Clinical Problems of Masochism." The mother is acting towards the doctor as someone acted towards her in her childhood; this is the mode of projective identification—the mother, in her interpersonal relations acts the role of the aggressor with whom she is identified. She acts out her aggression in a passive, martyred way, making everyone feel guilty. She represents not herself, per se, but the individual with whom she is identified. Horney's paper (1948), "The Compulsive Drive towards Revenge," explains some of these dynamics too.)

As a child, the patient had a sister about two years older than himself—lively, gifted and precociously "naughty," who played an important part in his early life.

(We now know from the work of several authors, Woolf and Fries, for example (1953), who delineated the development of an obsessive-compulsive problem in a child, and from the studies of Mittelmann (1954), that some children are more active than others by nature, some more passive. This activity or passive mode can be fostered or inhibited, or it can be directed into constructive or destructive aims by the parents or the parental substitutes. In the family of Freud's patient, neither the parents nor the nursemaids protected one child from the other, and the sister, being older, soon took advantage of her younger brother, manifesting hostility, rage and death wishes against him.)[1]*

As far back as this particular patient could remember, he was taken care of by a nurse, an uneducated, old woman of peasant birth, with an "untiring affection" for him. He served as a substitute for her own son who had died young.

(Thus, this patient had two, if not three, female objects with whom to identify: his mother, his sister, and his nurse. It is interesting that most children who have been cared for by nurses remember being the "pride and joy" of the nurse, even though at the same time they remember the nurse as stupid, vapid, or cruel and neglectful. This is apparently the same kind of defense the child raises against feelings of rejection by parents—the *idealization* that Freud spoke of in connection with "introjected objects." It is typical of borderline cases that even though the father and mother are present in the home, they are, nevertheless, rejecting and preoccupied with themselves. They reject and resent the parental role, as Grinker has pointed out, and they reject their sexual roles as well. The child in his own defense denies this and idealizes the parent at the same time that he blames himself for not being liked, and hates the parent for using him in this way, often projecting the hate to a sibling. This may have been the problem of this patient's sister who, later in life, committed suicide. The nurse, too, although she professed love for him, was using him to appease her own neurotic needs. He had a role to perform with her that had nothing to do with his own needs, being rather a projection of her need for a son.)

Freud noted that on one occasion the patient produced a screen memory, in which he saw himself with his nurse standing and looking at a horse-drawn carriage which drove off with his father, mother and sister, after which he went peaceably back to the house with the nurse. He was two-and-a-half at the time. (Even though the patient by this maneuver "possesses" the nurse for himself, this is a second-best choice, an aspect of a passive defense, covering his aggression, depression and fear of abandonment.[2])

During the summer that followed the period when the patient remembered having stood passively with his nurse as his parents drove away, he and his sister were at home with, in addition to the peasant woman, an English governess who had been engaged to be responsible for the supervision of the children. The parents were away.

When the patient was questioned, Freud discovered that his personality change began during the summer when the English governess was with them. She turned out to be an eccentric and quarrelsome person, an alcoholic. The mother

* Notes for this chapter start page 40.

blamed the governess alone for the change in the child, but the grandmother, who had spent the summer with the children, felt the boy's irritability had been provoked by the dissension between the English woman (the governess) and the nurse, his "Nanya," the uneducated, peasant woman who had the immediate care of the patient.

> (It was undoubtedly true that the conflict between the governess and the nurse had something to do with the child's conflict. Incidentally, Schwartz and Stanton reported in 1950 that disagreements between staff members affected the patients' moods and behavior [incontinence]. Our interpretation of this behavior is that it is reminiscent of fights and disagreements between parents. What is basic is the conflict between the father and mother, expressed in their attitudes, resentments, withdrawals and illnesses, which the child understands but cannot face directly. It was easier and safer for this child to react to the quarrel between the nurse and the governess and project his feelings onto these persons; the conditioned response in the patient is the anxiety and the defensive behavior, the projection or displacement from the family members to others which is the essence of the transference, a basic ingredient of all neuroses. In transference, all situations of disagreement are felt as family situations. Freud wrote that fights between parents created intense anxiety in children which they had to handle through defense. We are reminded of Laing's poem (p. 55), for there is a game being played in this situation with denial and threat implied if the child expresses openly what he sees, so he must defend by "not seeing"; but his problem is reflected in his projective identification defense and in the phantasy which depicts the family situation.)

The new governess had repeatedly called the nurse a witch and had ordered her to leave the room on several occasions when arguments occurred. (We can infer the kind of transferential relationship which existed between these two.) The little boy took the side of his "Nanya" and let the governess see his hatred. The governess was eventually sent away but there was no change in the child's behavior. The patient "preserved the memory" of this "naughty period."

> (As we now see it, he was able to use the nurse as a "projective object" in his defense against his feelings of rejection by his parents and his nurse, and to handle his fears by becoming both passive and explosive. He idealized the inadequacy of the "Nanya" and thus the inadequacies of his parents. We are reminded that the temper tantrum is a forerunner in the history of the passive-aggressive personality and we see that this patient's behavior also is reminiscent of Arieti's "stormy personality." The patient clung to the memory of the disagreement as a defense. In addition, by preserving this memory the patient used it as the basis of his *identification phantasies*, i.e., as his defense against the rejecting reality in which he lived. "Patients suffer from reminiscences," said Freud and Breuer. The patient is defending against recognition of his own destructive impulses, created in his early relations with objects, by focusing on these memories and using them as the impetus for his present behavior. To get well, the

patient, according to Melanie Klein, would have to recognize that he is using these other objects to hide from himself his desire to kill his parents. Freud's patient's sister killed herself rather than the parents and avoided facing her problem with the parents. The patient seems to have turned his sadistic feelings onto himself and others while his sister used him as an object in childhood to vent out her sadism and later, herself as the prime object.)

Freud said that what brought about the patient's change in character at this early age was inextricably connected in his memory[3] with many pathological phenomena which, in retrospect, he lumped together as having happened in one particular period of his life, although it could not possibly have been that way. Before the age of five, he remembered he had many fears which his sister exploited for the purpose of tormenting him. Freud noted the patient had amnesia for his early years. When he was older he was told many stories about his childhood. He said that he knew a great deal himself, but when he recalled what he knew, he disconnected times, events and subject matter.

(This is the typical constellation in repression with its attendant defenses. These *disconnections* are certainly brought about by the use of hysterical mechanisms: displacement, denial, dissociations and repressions. We see in this case that transference, i.e., the patient's relation to Freud, the identification, the patient's phantasies as expressed in the screen memories, the acting out, the idealization, the withdrawal, are all related to the sado-masochism, accompanied by undoing, going against the self, isolation, and apathy which masked depression.)

The patient was told that, at first, he was a very good, tractable, even quiet child, so that they used to say of him that *he should have been a girl, and his sister, a boy.*

(It is obvious that when this theme is repeated over and over again in a family, it usually means that the parents do not accept their own identities as male and female, and that they resent having to acknowledge the masculine and feminine aspects of their children. They resent their duties as parents and their roles as husband and wife (Grinker, 1968). Such rejections of sex roles are typical in parents of borderline patients—indeed, in parents of all patients who become seriously, emotionally disturbed, such as the character disorders, borderline cases, and the schizophrenias. This attitude is often typical of servants who are unattached to members of the opposite sex. This patient's parents were able to maintain "distance" from each other, while living together, as they fostered the perpetuation of their illnesses, and the denial of their sexual roles.[4] It is this state of affairs that creates the situation Erikson has described as "lack of role identity" in adolescence, a characteristic that Freud assigned to the unresolved oedipal problem. These parents took the differences in children's personalities and their constitutional differences as a focus for projecting their own phantasies which contained the roles they wished the children to play. The hostilities towards the same sex, and the opposite sex, become evident in the attitudes of the parents. This problem also has a relation to the perversions that Freud found so difficult to explain in terms of accidental causes. In denying their proper sex roles, parents express instead perverse sexual feelings and attitudes, for in perversion there is an overt expression of sado-masochism with an acting out of a revenge motif).

When his parents came back from the summer's holiday, they found this child "transformed." He had become discontented, irritable, violent, took offense on every possible occasion and often flew into rages, "screaming like a lunatic" (the stormy personality). His parents expressed doubts as to whether they would be able to send him to school later on.

(This is an example of the Von Domarus principle (Chap. IV, p. 64)—one thing has nothing to do with another; i.e., the fact that the child screams at home does not mean that he will scream at school. Screaming is the common factor in the parents' premise, but the situations are not equivalent. The conclusion has little to do with the basic premise. But the parents are *suggesting* that he perpetuate this behavior and it is presented not in the form of a wish but a fear. Sabath (1965) has written a paper noting that this form of suggestion is a negative reinforcement of behavior. He emphasizes the nagging or "bugging" quality of this kind of parental behavior, and there is a connection between this and the "compulsive drive toward revenge," using the child as a projective instrument. I have found that the parents need to maintain such behavior in the child in order to perpetuate their own neurotic homeostasis. The sado-masochistic pattern seems to have been played out with the patient's sister as well as with the adults.)

The sister used to frighten him (tease him) with the picture of a wolf. There was a particular picture-book which had a wolf walking upright, and whenever he saw this, he imagined the wolf was coming towards him to eat him up, and he would scream "like a lunatic." His sister always made certain to show him this picture. As an adult, he used this memory as a basis for his identification phantasy. In childhood he was already "identified" at an early age with his mother, who was passive, complaining, withdrawn and unavailable, but hostile and controlling at the same time, through illness. So he had, in this behavior, the same masochistic role with his sister that the mother experienced in her illness.[5] He was identified with the masochistic position in these phantasies, using the fairytale book as the projective identification stimulus. He was denying his sadistic impulses; *these were repudiated and projected*, but he showed his sadism in the temper tantrums and in his hostility towards the governess.

In his analysis, the patient did remember some sadistic behavior and feelings as a child. He recalled running after a butterfly with striped yellow wings which ended in points. All of a sudden he was seized with fear and he stopped running; he felt a loathing for beetles and caterpillars. He remembered that he used to torment beetles, and cut caterpillars to pieces. Horses gave him an uneasy feeling. If a horse was being beaten he began to scream, and once he had to leave the circus for that reason. On other occasions, he said, he himself enjoyed beating horses. (The fears and phobias were connected with sado-masochistic phantasies and behavior which were identifications with the behavior of the parents and of the parental substitutes.[6] All the patient's phantasies were sado-masochistic in essence; and they were "oral" and "anal" as well as "oedipal." The mother continued to complain that no matter what was done, nothing could really relieve her pain.[7])

The patient talked about a time when he experienced many obsessional ideas, and Freud felt that the "naughty period" was replaced by the obsessional period—one was a substitute for the other.

(The guilt over his sado-masochistic behavior made him resort to his masochistic role with his sister; his inability to be assertive and to stand up to her, seems to have been a precursor to the formation of the obsessional symptoms and his passivity, and his latent homosexual trend. At the same time, he developed the habit of venting his hostility on bugs. It is well to remember that patients show sadistic traits, even those whose presenting façade is more masochistic. His passivity and his "screen memory phantasies," the sado-masochistic phantasies based on actual occurrences, i.e., his relations with his nurse, his sister and his parents, were defenses against his recognition of his own sadism and the reality situation which stimulated his sadistic behavior.)

Freud's patient, as a child, went through the following types of obsessional attacks. Before he went to sleep, he had to pray for a long time and make "an endless series of signs of the cross": every evening he used to make the round of all the holy pictures in the room, taking a chair with him so he could touch them; at the same time he had blasphemous thoughts which kept intruding upon his consciousness. Such phrases as "God-swine" and "God-shit" entered his head. (We are reminded here of Schreber and also of Dr. Daird's hostile outpourings and their concomitant fears of aggression.) Once, when the patient was riding to get a health examination he had a compulsion to think of the Holy Trinity whenever he saw three heaps of horse-dung or other excrement lying in the road. He felt sorry for beggars, cripples and very old men. He had to breathe noisily *so as not to become like them*, and, under other circumstances, he had to draw in his breath.

(We see here his guilt over his hostile feelings, his impulses to express aggression, and his defenses so as not to recognize his true feelings about his parents and their role in his difficulties. We see also his denial of his identification with his parents, and here particularly, with his father. His defenses gave his ego distance from thoughts of his parents, that is, from his repudiated thoughts concerning his parents, and also helped him deny his identification with his parents whom he loathed. He had no respect for himself when he was identified with his parents. His need to talk in a "dirty" manner is a small way of venting some hostility, but the phenomenon is one that seems to come from "within," said Freud, and he insisted this was partly instinctual. In this maneuver the patient denies that he has anything to do with the matter or that he can control the impulses, or that they have specific meaning. In the Schreber case, the patient threw invectives at God, and when he described God as cold and unfeeling, having no consideration for others, he was describing both his father and himself, their characteristics of withdrawal, hostility, detachment and contempt for others. Many individuals who are never hospitalized or who never seek treatment on an out-patient basis speak in a filthy way, albeit in a so-called humorous way. The shock value and the aggression in this kind of talk is obvious. It is a kind of counter-phobic mechanism. But in the more disturbed patient, the aggression is either directed towards a third party or a series of third persons or "objects" with whom the patient acts out or has the phantasy of acting out. The verbalizations, which are in effect aspects of the phantasy, serve as a substitute for action. Schreber shouted obscenities at the sun; but, on the other side of the coin, Flechsig, his physician, he said, called him dirty names. The hallucination and the delusion are forms of "going against the self" and striking out at others but in the third person, or at things,[8] a displacement from the parents and a denial of his identification with them.)

The borderline patient does not develop such obsessional rituals as cleaning or hand-washing, but he has other obsessional patterns which are acted out on the interpersonal level. Neither does he develop full-fledged phobias, although he has many hysterical phobic-like characteristics. Avoidance mechanisms and undoing in the form of failure, in certain areas, seem to be characteristic of borderlines. The defenses against aggression are great.

One of the clues Freud gave us which has a bearing on borderline patients, as well as paranoids and other types of schizophrenics, was his thought that *in paranoia the identifications which resulted from object relations are dissociated rather than integrated, and thus there is a kind of "splitting" into a number of objects, both good and bad.* One can perhaps make these "split objects" more specific by thinking of them not only as male and female but as displacements for identifications with father and mother.

I suspect that this dynamic is the origin of the "multiple personality," that this is *a defense against recognition of the characteristics of father and mother and the patient's identification with them.* My patient, Dr. Daird, for example, needed several objects upon whom he could project certain characteristics. There was his girlfriend, a girl in the office, his colleagues in staff meetings, a senior professor, his roommate, Jerry. This constellation of "objects," was a necessary part of his defensive system and it helped him to maintain his neurotic equilibrium. As his analysis proceeded, he was able to give up these objects and recognize their relation to his early family objects. Freud apparently speculated that this "splitting," was a main defense in paranoia and a "regression": accompanying the regression was the "break-up of the identifications" (the ego and the superego or the "object cathexes") into their original parts. The ego, one will remember, according to Freud was a composite of abandoned object cathexes. It is important, I believe, to remember that "splitting" as a defense is associated not only with paranoid feelings and ideas, not only with a systematized delusion around which the patient organizes his life, but it can also be connected with a loosely defined delusion as well, which can come into play during periods of intense anxiety. This is the type of delusion operative in the borderline. Since Freud's premise was that paranoia was a step above schizophrenia (this latter would be regression to the auto-erotic stage or the "part object" stage), the break-up of identifications in paraonia would mean regression to some later stage. Fleiss (1950), for example, places "some forms of schizophrenia" in the sucking stage, depression in the biting stage, and paranoia in the early anal phase, i.e., the phase of partial incorporation and explusion.

Apparently Freud finished the treatment of this particular man by setting a date for ending, and then keeping to the date although the therapy was not complete. Some years later, Mack Brunswick(1928) worked with the patient, going further towards a resolution of his problem. Freud's tactic with the patient, at the close, seems to have been an attempt to deal with his passive-aggressive mechanism, which is a difficult task in any case. The passive-aggressive personality is revengeful and exploitive, and is loathe to give up his obsessional hate, for to do so brings him face to face with his murderous feelings which he fears he will act out. If this problem is not dealt with appropriately, the patient often saves himself by resorting to homosexual behavior, which is a substitute for the murderous impulses, and which perpetuates his masochistic pattern of *giving in to the other* (appeasement). The homosexual phantasy is a most complicated affair, referring not only to a member of the same sex but including members of the opposite sex. There is an overtone of depression associated with the homosexual trend, for it is a manifestation of the results of rejection and devaluation. For example, one of my patients has a homosexual phantasy which he has acted out on occasion when he feels exasperated at work by competitive feelings, particularly a desire to win out over the other. The idea of winning rather than losing sets up an anxiety and a kind of contrition and depression for wanting to win. He will then feel remorse, but to counteract the feeling he will go out looking for someone to pick up so that he can "lord it over" the other by making him do fellatio, then refusing to give the other satisfaction. This phantasy gives him excitement and counteracts his feeling of depression. On one or two occasions he has put himself in extreme jeopardy. On the other hand, he has the phantasy of bringing home a homosexual partner and throwing him at his mother's feet in a kind of flaunting manner, saying "Here he is—this is what you wanted." This phantasy he has never acted out, for he has not made a homosexual adaptation. When he feels competitive to win, he thinks of his father, who belittled him, and he becomes depressed. When he thinks of becoming a homosexual he thinks of his mother, who always implied that she made the wrong choice in marriage and whom he always remembers as talking of strong he-men. While looking at television, for example, she would say: "Just look at that physique, those muscles; look at that chest." The patient himself was considered by the mother to be "weak," "puny," "unathletic," "unable to hold his own with others." Both father and mother demeaned his abilities and capacities, although he was a brilliant boy mentally. This oedipal theme is employed in the interests of a homosexual aim, and thus his phantasies include members of the opposite sex as well as members of the same sex. One of his early phantasies in analysis was the fear (or desire) to kill his girlfriend. He would become so angry at her that he would feel like choking her to death. This frightened him and enabled him to detach from her, necessitating his having to seek for another. Another way in which he was able to leave was to be perfectionistic and find flaws in the girl's character. It is this type of transference that we deal with in the borderline patient. The transference operation begins as soon as the relationship with the patient commences. This form of transference is extremely complicated, however, and involves the kind of dynamics Melanie Klein called *projective identification*. We shall see later just what the operations of projective identification mean in the case of the borderline patient.

An interesting book entitled "The Wolf-man," published in 1971, substantiates that some of the analysts who saw the patient after Mack Brunswick considered the diagnosis of borderline. The sexual acting out which is so obvious in the new book was not clear in Freud's report of the case, since Freud's paper focused primarily on the childhood neurosis.

NOTES

[1] Freud called aggressive behavior *instinctual*, but today we call it *reactive*. Man's inhumanity to man is so pervasive in this world that Freud came to the conclusion that the impulse to destroy was instinctual. He cited the hostile wishes of children when a new child is born into the family: the wish that the new baby die. We know that parents can help foster a fear of abandonment and intensify the aggressive reaction by pitting one child against the other, or simply by doing nothing and watching the aggression between the children build, the younger often becoming the masochistic one, while the parent enjoys the sado-masochism secretly or perversely. On the other hand, an older child can become the masochist while the younger one is sadistic if the parent makes the older child feel guilty about his feelings towards the younger child. A new child is usually a threat to the child already in the family, for he must share the parents and the attention of others.

[2] See page 107, the case of Kenneth, in which both the Rorschach protocol and the other projective tests revealed the passive-aggressive personality. Kenneth often recalled the memory of his nurse, which was always anxiety-provoking to him and which he conjured up whenever the problem of self-assertion arose. In such circumstances, he remembered his nurse's pattern of giving him a bath: instead of attending to him, she left him in the bathtub and went into the kitchen to have coffee with the nurse of the patient's sister; he would sit in the bathtub and scream for her to come and get the soap which was in the soap dish,

refusing to help himself. In the park, he also remembered standing around and not participating with the other children in play. He says he was made to feel "above the others"; they were not good enough for him as playmates. He felt "like an outsider." This elaboration of omnipotence and grandiosity, and aloofness, is obviously a compensatory feeling for passivity and the withdrawal from others. Freud spoke of this mechanism in his essay, "Family Romances," attributing it to a paranoid defense, later saying it was a function of the oedipal problem. The feelings of inadequacy which such a patient experiences come from his actual inadequacy in view of the inhibitions of function he develops as a fear of assertion and his need to remain dependent or in a masochistic position. The passivity is associated with anger and aggression and the need to control the other person, and the parents' interference in the child's attempts at peer relationships. This child was able to feel superior by virtue of the prominent position his family held in the community, while at the same time feeling inferior due to his own fears and lack of social techniques. It is interesting that when Kenneth spoke of his nurse, he would idealize the situation between them, thus denying the reality and perpetuating the defenses he had in childhood. He would say that his nurse loved him, that she was a kindly woman, that he used to visit her and her husband when he was older and spend the night with them. She would put him in her bed. He was the "apple of her eye." On the other hand, he would call her stupid, vapid, ignorant, and unfeeling.

Freud and Adler, as we have seen, argued about the dynamics of such mechanisms, Freud at first refusing to call this a defense mechanism but rather a regression to the stage of auto-erotism, omnipotence, being, according to his developmental scheme, the phase-appropriate mental organization for this early period. Adler insisted that the feeling of inferiority is the basic problem for the neurotic defense. Adler said that the struggle for superiority (the masculine protest) is the motif for omnipotence of thought. Freud, as we have seen, considered omnipotence primordial in the child, part of the "inherited" or "instinctual," or "totemistic mode of thinking," an aspect of the "primal stock of ideas." On the biological side, omnipotence was related to the pleasure-principle, which was, in Freud's terms, innate in living matter (the organism moves towards the source of pleasure and away from the source of pain—a principle which Freud conceptualized in philosophical terms as hedonistic). Freud eventually solved this problem by calling regression a defense, insisting on his concept of "primitive thought." Freud was constantly disparaging Adler, and he wrote of him on one occasion that he was "formerly" an analyst (1909).

3 Freud stressed the significance of traumatic memories in the neuroses and psychoses; and even when he organized the libido theory, he did not discard the importance of memory. Memory and perception were linked. The ability to perceive and "take in" the meaning of a situation is apparently one of the factors creating conflict. Memory is being studied at the present time by many types of investigators. The recognition that memory is a long-term proposition is fascinating to the learning theorist as well as to the biochemist. A DNA ticketing theory of memory was presented by Griffith and Mahler (1969). The original work was reported by James V. McConnell at the Mental Health Research Institute at the University of Michigan in 1962, and recently investigators at Baylor University (Unger et al. on "Memory Transfer by a Protein") are reporting new work, the meaning of which we can scarcely understand at present. Indications tend to make one wonder whether humans have the same propensity as the planaria for behavior patterns to be repeated in a new generation without training. There is speculation that some such phenomenon accounts for the changes in the biological development of man as time goes on, and may be an aspect of what is called "instinct."

4 Some of the studies done by Robert J. Stoller (1968) at the University of California suggest that "one's conviction regarding the feeling that he is a member of his assigned sex is directly the result of his parents' unquestioning belief that he is a member of that sex ... that the assigned sex was the proper one." One may say with certainty, too,

that in those cases where the parents do not accept the sex of the child and, more especially, do not accept their own sexual roles, there will be a problem regarding sexual identity—and this, with its attendant meaning, seems, in essence, the crux of the unresolved oedipal conflict which Freud insisted was "pre-individual."

[5] One will remember that Freud described this kind of attitude, albeit in a more severe form, in the Schreber case. Schreber took a masochistic role in the relationship in his phantasy (delusion). He was tortured, thus denying his sadistic trend and projecting it outward, using the characteristics of his father and mother and his identification with them in the projection (the upper God and the lower God). Schreber held it against his wife that she prevented him from having children, expressing his hostility in this way. And he expressed hostility towards God in a way that seemed "justified" in view of all that God was putting him through.

[6] Boyer and Giovacchini (1967) mentioned this case, with special reference to the patient's offering himself to Freud so that the latter could use him in an anal sexual attack, thus revealing the homosexual side of the masochistic phantasy. It is not unusual for the borderline patient to have sexual phantasies concerning the therapist, but usually they take the form of seductions between the sexes. The patient does have homosexual phantasies at times, and towards the middle of the analysis he deals with his latent homosexual trends. There is often the feeling on the part of the patient in the initial stages of treatment that the therapist would be shocked and would think of the patient as a "no good bum" if it were to be discovered in the course of the analysis that he had perverse trends. The patient has massive guilt feelings concerning his perverse trends, for they would reveal his sadistic pleasure in torture and frustration even if he must torture himself to make another feel guilty.

[7] David Levy (1932) once wrote a paper called "Body Interest in Children and Hypochondriasis," suggesting that a parent who has this interest may overemphasize it and that this is what may preface a hypochondriacal trait in a child. This patient's mother apparently had an obsessional interest in her own body, which would account for the patient's hypochondriacal traits (identification with mother), a preoccupation with her health, and a need to deny her feminine sexual role in favor of one with homosexual implications. This was connected with her feeling that her children should be the opposite sexes of what they really were.

It seems to me that excessive "body interest" often betrays a secretive sexual interest. "Gazing" has a scanning quality and can be an obsessive defense against acting out some kind of perverse behavior. The "looking" can express either "pleasure" or "displeasure" and it may focus on one or more body parts. A "bugging" demeanor is operative in this nonverbal maneuver, the same as if the parent were obsessively talking and reiterating a theme. The response on the part of the child is often of a paranoid nature, displacing the problem to the outside world as a defense against what is happening in the family. Some one "out there" is doing the persecuting, a projection of the sadistic identification with the parent; but the delusion also includes the child's feelings about his own body, and his anxieties are expressed in fears concerning disease, disfigurement (body-image) or some dire outcome of living in a certain way—thus the masochistic side of the defense comes into play.

[8] The use of a projective therapeutic technique in psychotherapy in such cases was suggested by Clark (1919, 1926), who recognized the denial in identification. He talked with the patient as if the hallucination and the delusion were a third person. Therapists can learn the technique of discussing psychodynamics, motivation and defenses in the light of the "third person" so that the patient's detachment and defense will be respected and, at the same time, his guilt and fear can be reduced and thus the problem can eventually be tackled "straight on." This technique in its various forms is explicated in Chapters IX and X.

CHAPTER III

EARLY PSYCHOANALYTIC SPECULATIONS

When Freud used the term *borderline* in his preface to Aichorn's book (1925) he was apparently alluding to a delinquent, acting out child. He said that such a child was not neurotic, meaning that his relations with objects (i.e., with people and things) were not the same as those of a neurotic, but he did not attempt in the short essay to make the distinctions between the neuroses and the delinquencies.[1]*

Freud thought that more would be learned about the delinquencies as the study of children became more important and as *psychoanalysis* came ever more into use. The understanding of "borderline and mixed cases," he said, would stem from the work of those who were interested in the rehabilitation of delinquents, mainly educators, especially those who had psychoanalytic indoctrination and who worked closely with psychoanalysts, particularly educators who had experienced psychoanalysis themselves. However, even though psychoanalysis had been called a re-educational process, it was not to be confused with education. Delinquents would need both education and a modified psychoanalytic treatment. Those who administered this combination would need special psychoanalytic training. With these acting-out youths, the problem of forming a relationship was great, and Freud thought that Aichorn was intuitively able to do this. It would require a great deal of additional study to enable the average educator to work with such problems successfully. Much more would have to be known about techniques which could achieve desired effects.

* Notes for this chapter start page 55.

From the earliest days, Freud had doubts about the treatability of borderline problems, psychoses, and character disorders, feeling that therapeutic success would come only through modification of his psychoanalytic method. He seems not to have used the term "acting out" explicitly in relation to these problems, but he outlined the dynamics of such behavior through references to acting out behavior in other syndromes. Mention has been made of his paper, "Hysterical Phantasies and Their Relation to Bisexuality" (1908), in which Freud said that some individuals "realize their phantasies in action" and some "bring about sexual attacks." His descriptions indicated the *sado-masochistic motif in acting out behavior and the relation of this behavior to phantasy.*

An understanding of the dynamics of acting out is important if one is to help borderline patients, for this is an aspect of behavior that must be considered early in the treatment. Acting out takes many forms and is associated with sado-masochism. Freud, in the paper, "Fragment of an Analysis of a Case of Hysteria" (1905), referred to Dora's acting out of childhood phantasies when she broke off treatment; and in the "Psychopathology of Everyday Life" (1904), he described what may be called acting out in the illustrations of "faulty actions" and other forms of symptomatic behavior. Note should be made also of Freud's essay, "A Case of Successful Treatment by Hypnotism" (1898), where he discussed an acting-out phenomenon which he calls "counterwill." The patient does in some form what he fears he should not do. If the inhibition were to be carried out to its full extent, Freud said, the patient might have a phobia, but in these instances he does, in some form (either through a somatic symptom or some other kind of behavior, or both) what he dreads doing. This is a description of what is now commonly referred to as counter-phobic manifestation, which is in essence an acting out phenomenon. In some of the other descriptions of acting out, Freud gives the example of "well brought up" boys who, when they suffer from hysterical attacks, "give free play to every kind of rowdiness, and every kind of wild escapade and bad conduct"; and he mentions the nuns in the Middle Ages whose "hysterical deliria" took the form of "violent blasphemies and unbridled erotic language."

In the essay, "Further Recommendations in the Technique of Psychoanalysis: Recollection, Repetition, and Working Through" (1914), Freud wrote of acting out as being connected with transference and resistance. It is this concept of transference behavior that deepens our insight into the dynamics of acting out. Transference is *action instead of remembering*. In the essay, "Recollection, Repetition and Working Through" (1914), Freud remarked that the patient *does not remember* how "critical and defiant he was with his parents," but he "reproduces" or "expresses it in action," he "behaves that way towards the analyst." These were manifestations of *negative transference*, as opposed to *positive transference*. Transference was one of the main resistances in the treatment, and Freud related it to the *early identifications*. He mentions that

Adler felt that the "not remembering" and the "by-play" in transference behavior is the essential element in the whole neurotic process. This "by-play" we now refer to as acting out; and the "not remembering" we still think of as an hysterical response associated with the defenses of repression and denial, and particularly with *displacement*. *Projection*, which is a defense characteristic of the borderline and associated with identification, is a form of displacement. Identification in Freud's earliest papers was considered to be hysterical behavior. Repression has a relation to identification and the concept of splitting the mind into Cs and Ucs. These early speculations we still employ in describing the dynamics of borderlines.

There is no doubt that Freud was touching upon the dynamics of acting out in several other essays, particularly: "A Special Type of Object-Choice (1910); "The Taboo of Virginity" (1918); "Some Character Types Met with in Psychoanalytic Work" (1915); "The Uncanny" (1919); "The Psychogenesis of a Case of Homosexuality in a Woman" (1920); "Certain Neurotic Mechanisms in Jealousy, Paranoia and Homosexuality" (1922); and "Fetishism" (1927).

In recent years, Helene Deutsch in "Neuroses and Character Types" (1965) described the patient who repeatedly creates a situation in which he will suffer disappointment—"the fate neurosis" she calls this, describing it as "a form of suffering imposed on the ego apparently by the outer world with a recurrent regularity." The motivating factor in this fate lies "in a constant insoluble inner conflict." The patient is thus bound to be disappointed. Deutsch also refers to this phenomenon as the "hysterical fate neurosis." It is apparent in reading her description that the patient projects onto others certain feelings he had towards his parents. He acts within a pattern of transference behavior learned in his relations with his parents so that he is rejected or frustrated (or both). Freud called this process the "destiny neurosis" in "Some Character Types Met with in Psychoanalytic Work" (1915). In this paper he emphasized the *patient's sense of guilt*, in relation to a kind of masochistic acting out behavior. These patients could not stand success. Freud also wrote that a person's need to perform criminal acts (to act out) was often a reaction *in the face of guilt which derived from the oedipus complex*. He did not, as we do now, stress the active role of the parents in promoting these acting out patterns, nor did he emphasize in the above paper the "introjected object." He did believe that there was a "defective superego", and *an identification with an anti-social father in such cases*. Others have said that the *hostile introject* will not let the patient enjoy success, and that it insists upon frustration and disappointment.

Freud characterized hysterics as people who could not let themselves be happy. As individuals who had doubting mechanisms which prevented their carrying through certain normal intentions, they did the opposite of what they thought they should do, "as if a demon were in control of them." The paranoid projection in these cases was not particularly accented in the early descriptions of the dynamics, even though both the masochism and the paranoid projection were evident. Someone or something else (or their instincts) had taken over. It was *as-if* they had no responsibility for their behavior.

Adler (1925) underlined some patients' needs to project and to become involved in a neurotic way with another so that they could feel "justified" in the expression of aggression; thus he outlined the destructiveness in ordinary forms of acting out. The aggression could at first be countered by passivity, or masochism (receiving aggression), but finally the individual reacted with retaliatory anger, rage and punitive behavior. The patient's guilt was relieved by his defense of rationalization. He felt justified in his own aggression by singling out certain unworthy aspects of the other person's behavior. This was his "private logic."

In the essay, "The Psychogenesis of a Case of Homosexuality in a Woman" (1920), Freud focused on the sadism in acting out. The particular homosexual girl he described "wanted her father to know occasionally of her intercourse with the lady, otherwise she would be deprived of satisfaction of her keenest desire—namely, revenge . . . ." The unusual lack of caution "displayed by this otherwise ingenious and clever girl" was an indication of the revenge goal towards her father. In the same essay the family dynamics were described in some detail. The mother obviously had secret desires to drive her daughter toward homosexuality. What is missing in Freud's description is the fact that the father, too, undoubtedly had secret desires for her to act out, and that on some unconscious level the girl "knew" all of this. Her revenge was geared not only towards her father, but toward her mother as well, and it came about through her exposure of herself as a homosexual. The "humiliation" was for her a triumph. However, what is important in such humiliation, in my opinion, is that her act of exposing herself reveals to them, or confronts them with, their own hidden aims—the very aims for which their defenses are operative. The mélange of acting out, father's, mother's, the girl's and her homosexual partner's, is carried on in the context of denial, i.e., as-if all of their needs did not exist. Yet their verbal and non-verbal communication systems expose such needs. The pleasure of the revenge adds to the essence of the sexual excitement. There is implied in Freud's writings that the negative transference is manifest in acting out; the revenge has a relation to a homosexual trend, to sado-masochism, and to identification; and that there is a connection between identification and projection within a kind of paranoid frame of reference. In exploring the dynamics of borderline patients we often find confirmation for these ideas.

Aichorn (1945) influenced by Freud's structural hypothesis and the libido theory, adapted them to the behavior of the delinquent. The delinquent, he contended, was controlled by the pleasure-principle and the primary process (*the id*), as against the *reality principle* and *secondary process*. Thus acting out was a form of id-behavior. But he also noted that poor training was a factor in delinquency. In this he again followed Freud, whose partial explanation of emotional difficulties involved the concept that, when an individual does not have an adequate *identification figure*, he tends to become upset. Freud and Aichorn agreed that the delinquent child does not develop an appropriate *ego-ideal* or *superego* from his identifications, particularly his identification with his father; the delinquent has identified himself with a "criminalistic parent," and it is this that drives him into anti-social behavior.

Early practitioners of psychoanalysis undoubtedly observed what Hoedemaker (1955) later stressed in an essay, namely, that the schizophrenic patient usually attempts to devalue the therapist and that this should not be allowed. The patient, out of revenge, seeks out weaknesses or characteristics he feels he can use to "put the therapist down." The maneuver has been referred to as "identification with the degraded object." In the paper, "The Most Prevalent Form of Degradation in Erotic Life" (1912), Freud described the acting out of a sado-masochistic phantasy. A similar theme was elucidated in "A Special Type of Choice of Objects Made by Men" (1910) and in the paper, "A Child is Being Beaten—a Contribution to the Study of the Origin of Sexual Perversions" (1919). Freud connected the problem with the oedipus complex and with the child's phantasies about the meaning of the parents' behavior towards him and others in the family.[2] We now say that the paranoid mechanism in the defense is organized to protect the patient from the painful recognition that he has been degraded and rejected by his parents. The identification helps him deny and ward off his anxiety and the fear of desertion. The negative transference is associated, too, with a depression and a tendency toward delusion. Moreover, it is a defense against what has been called "separation anxiety." In a sense the anxiety is avoided by a perpetuation of the sado-masochistic relationship. It enables the patient to deny he is now like the parents.

Klein's concept of a projective-identification with some theoretical modification is more and more accepted as a basic dynamic in borderlines, schizophrenics and certain kinds of character problems. (It would seem that acting out is inherent in the concept of projective-identification.) While Klein's explanations, from the developmental point of view, may be unacceptable to some, and her interpretations tend to focus on "content" (fixations, according to Freud's developmental concepts), rather than on defenses, nevertheless, she has touched on important aspects of the defensive system of the borderline and other schizoid types. Money-Kryle (1966) lists Klein's contributions to theory under the following: (1) elaboration of the early stages of the oedipus complex and superego formation; (2) understanding of the early operations of introjective and projective mechanisms in the building up of a child's inner world of phantasy, and a clarification of the difference between the two types of identification, i.e., *introjective* and *projective*; (3) delineation of concepts of paranoid-schizoid and depression positions; and (4) emphasis on the importance of a very early form of "envy." Punishment begins early in the lives of most children, and, thus, one can support Klein's tenet that *guilt*, as well as *envy*, emerge in the earliest stages of development.[3]

Klein assumed with Freud that *introjection* (the form of identification some early analysts said was operative in the beginning stages of development) was a normal developmental motif, and a consequence of relations with objects and the ambivalence which occurs is not necessarily a reaction to the parents' aggression, hostility, punitiveness and rejection, but is a consequence of the normal living experience itself. Since the human condition does not allow us to have everything we want, frustration results, along with the arousal of feelings of hate toward objects which do not meet every need and demand. Conflict develops between loving and hateful feelings toward the object. Freud similarly alluded to the fusion of the instincts of love and hate toward an object, which he said was a necessary dynamic in the organization of the ego. Ambivalence had a phylogenetic origin as well. The basis of ego structure, in libido theory terms, was that it is a precipitate of abandoned object-cathexis formed out of early identifications. Such ideas have been central in psychoanalytic thinking ever since Freud turned to the libido concept and developed his interpersonal theory around the idea that instincts seek objects. Identification could thus be "normal" or "neurotic." While it was never clearly stated that neurotic identification was a function of acting out, all writing seemed to lead in that direction.

Why Freud stressed certain developmental aspects to the exclusion of others and why he focused so much on bodily cavities in speculating on complex interpersonal relations is difficult to say. It is possible that his areas of selection and his focus in development, were connected with the many perplexing dilemmas posed by his discovery of the problem of *perversion* as it relates to sado-masochistic impulses in the various neurotic syndromes. There is much more that goes on, for example in the early phase of infancy, than sucking, and in the later phase of infancy than biting, but Freud chose to concentrate on these to the relative neglect of other developmental activities, probably because these were found in the perverse sado-masochistic phantasies. In his conception of the developmental scheme, Freud insisted that the ego and the body were fused with the biological functions of biting, swallowing, spitting-out, and with anal functions, and he referred these primarily to sexual development (infantile sexuality). Once the theory of infantile sexuality was introduced, and the idea that interpersonal relations were activated by libidinal (sexual) energy, the sado-masochism in perverse traits was equated with the instincts and the normal functions of sucking, biting and expelling. Schizophrenia and the borderline and mixed conditions were due to fixations in the earliest phases of infantile sexual development.

In the beginning, Freud alleged, the ego was auto-erotic and, therefore, had no need of the outside world. But self-preservation (ego instincts) forced a recognition of the value of objects. The infant resented the fact that he needed the objects. His equilibrium was disturbed by the outside world. Although external objects helped him survive, he developed ambivalence (love and hate) towards the objects of his need, for they could not give him all he wanted when he wanted it. Later, Freud (1915) added that objects, insofar as they are sources of pleasure, were "introjected," but the unacceptable parts of the objects were rejected and "projected." First, all objects, both "good" and "bad," were introjected and then the bad parts were *projected* and *idealized*.

Ferenczi accepted Freud's formulations and described introjection as the first stage in the adaptation to reality. In this stage, the ego had itself as object: the ego and the id were still undifferentiated. Introjection was considered the first stage in the differentiation of the ego, the process by which objects are psychically assimilated. He used terms like "ingestion" and "oral incorporation" to describe behavior typical of the oral phase. Jones defined introjection as an unconscious tendency to incorporate the environment into one's own personality. As we have seen, the idea of "incorporation" stemmed from Freud's developmental concepts, which attributed to this stage the "drive" or "need" or "impulse" to assimilate by eating or swallowing—the "oral incorporation phase."

A thesis of some of the early analysts was that *those patients who showed criminal or delinquent tendencies had been most deprived of love and satisfaction in early childhood.* This thesis we still use today. Many modern Freudians, however, while accepting this idea in formulating a diagnosis, still attempt to fuse symptoms and syndromes with particular phases of sexual development[4] in accordance with Freud's developmental scheme. The problem is that borderlines were considered to be narcissistic neuroses rather than oedipal problems, narcissistic problems being preoedipal; and Freud felt that transference was lacking in these problems so that treatment was not possible.

Freud's psychological theory purported that at the narcissistic stage of development the infant's typical mental mode was characterized by omnipotence. He said that in the schizophrenias, and in the narcissistic neuroses, one finds this trait and that it indicates a regression back to the oral stage. There was never any clear distinction between acting out in preoedipal problems and acting out in oedipal perplexities.

Those early analysts who believed that in order for the child to survive in the family with neurotic parents, he must identify with them (the aggressors) and that this identification was a defense against the child's feeling that the parents' aggressions would destroy him, posed the idea that idealization was also one of the conditions of identification. It helped to relieve the anxiety aroused by the fears of destruction. Freud wrote of idealization and the ego ideal (both associated with the superego) as a gradation in the ego based on identification. It seems to me that Rickman (1927) was on the right track when he called the superego *a technique for maintaining object relations.* I would call that technique *a defense.*

It occurs to me that ominpotence is a step beyond idealization and is an aspect of turning around upon the self; i.e., the self becomes powerful in phantasy as a means of reducing the anxiety created by the fear of destruction. But now the patient fears his own counter-aggression as well, his own murderous and revenge feelings, so he looks for a powerful figure to help keep himself under control. At times, through identification, he takes over many of the qualities and characteristics of the aggressor. When the behavior of the parent is repugnant, and is interpreted as threatening to the child's life, he responds with overwhelming fear. His humiliation by the parent, and his rage against the parent, provide the basis for his self-contempt and contempt of others. At the same time he fears his own destructiveness which is like the parents'. We find this commonly in borderline patients. In projective identification, denial mechanisms come into play to control anxiety. Through idealization the aggressor becomes "good," and the "bad" part of the object is projected onto someone else. Or the aggression may be turned back on the self in a masochistic denial of the true source of the aggression. *The parent has trained the child in masochism.* The "split objects" are represented in the phantasies. Usually they are four in number: two for mother and two for father. One could think of this as the superego being split four ways ("good" and "bad" male and female phantasies). But "good" refers to idealization, and "bad" refers to aggression. Freud called sado-masochistic phantasies manifestations of "active" and "passive" instincts, i.e., either sadistic-active or masochistic-passive, and he connected passive with female behavior and active with male behavior. Freud tended to judge these male and female characteristics of phantasy as aspects of the bisexual biological nature of the individual, rather than as solely representative in phantasy of the relations with parents. The defense of identification thus included not only a phantasy, but an accompanying form of sado-masochistic acting out behavior, which Freud said was based in part on instinct and in part on unresolved conflicts of childhood. (These split objects are aspects of the defensive system.)

In contrast with the instinctual emphasis, we are more and more recognizing that sado-masochistic responses are consequences of particular kinds of conditioning in the family. Szurek and Johnson (1954) and Stoller (1968) have demonstrated that sexual attitudes in children have a definite relation to similar attitudes in their parents. Perversions, which were the ground over which Freud shifted from the seduction hypothesis to the instinct theory, we now feel are evoked by cues from the parents. Freud discovered this but apparently he repudiated the idea. He evolved the oedipal concept as a special phase in *normal* development as a substitute for what in the "Studies of the Hysterias" he had called the *accidental cause.*

In our work with borderline patients, we are persuaded that the degree of emotional disorder from less severe to more severe is proportionate to the greater or lesser degree of hostility to which the child is subjected in the family. The concept of ego defect, considered the source of emotional difficulties, is giving way to the concept of *defense*. In the borderline patient a basic defense is to shield the individual from perceiving the true nature of this reality situation, erecting barriers to reason.[5] The ego, according to libido theory formulations, may not be able to contain the id and this accounts for acting out which is based on an id-impulse and as an identification with an id-ridden parent.

As a substitute for the instinct theory, attempts have been made to reinterpret many of Freud's clinical observations from the standpoint of conditioning. Accepting the fact that transference is a repetitive pattern originally evoked in the parent-child relationship, we must inquire into the child-rearing studies which clearly indicate that it is a form of conditioned behavior, the paradigm of which is the *role expectation* set up by the parent on the basis of forcing the child into identification. Identification behavior is stimulated by precise kinds of communication from parent to child, reinforced through reward and punishment. Freud noted that acting out had a *pantomimic quality,* thus emphasizing the nonverbal aspects of such behavior. Identification is an interlocking defensive maneuver used by both parent and child to relieve anxiety and to maintain themselves in a stressful situation. Repression, displacement, dissociation and denial are major dynamisms buttressing identification. We could, if we so desired, apply to this phenomenon some aspects of Freud's topological theory, elaborated prior to his dedication to a phylogenetic stance. The mechanisms of denial, displacement and repression shield the individual from awareness of his conflict, i.e., the conflict that was resolved by identification, relegating it to the unconscious. We cannot use the structural hypothesis in any attempt to explain the complexities of identification. The id, ego and superego concepts related to a developmental theory of the libido confuse the issues. It is constricting to apply the libido model to neurotic behavior since it is tied to biological, developmental and neurophysiological variables, which we do not find useful in understanding neuroses in the light of modern knowledge.[6]

Our explanations for the observations that Freud recorded concerning love and hate and identification are somewhat different from his. We find more and more that seduction is a factor in love and hate or, to be more precise, in sado-masochism. Although it does not have to be the kind of seduction Freud thought of in the first instance, i.e., actual manipulation of the child's genitals by the adult, nevertheless seduction is an element in the kind of frustration he wrote about when he said that the formation of ideas with a sexual content produce "excitation processes in the genital organs similar to sexual experience itself." He speculated that this *somatic excitement* "transposes itself into the physical sphere." But, if the sexual experience occurs during sexual immaturity and the memory is aroused during or after maturity, then the "exciting effect of the recollection" will be much stronger than that of the experience itself because, in the meantime, "puberty had increased to an incomparable degree the capacity of the sexual apparatus for response." Freud commented that an inverted relation of this kind between real experience and memory appears to be the psychological condition of repression. What Freud seems to be writing about here is a *sexual phantasy*, using memory as stimulus. As Freud realized the implications of his discoveries, he began to doubt that parents could influence their children in totality. He then assumed that sexual experience could be both *endogenous* and *exogenous*: the stimulus for the experience could come *from within the organism as well as from an object*. The "endogenous concept" was the biological forerunner of the libido theory of the instincts and their derivatives and was spelled out more clearly in the three essays on the theory of sexuality (1905), originally called "The Problem of Sexual Excitation." In the Project, Freud said that one of the functions of the ego was the "binding of excitation" in the memory. This was a precursor of the idea of *anxiety*.

In "Studies of the Hysterias," Freud called the conversion symptom a displacement mechanism, a way of handling anxieties created by certain sexual events. As the libido theory developed, *anxiety* was thought of as converted libido or *sexual energy*. Conversion was the sign of a pathological condition, associated with a damming up of libido. Freud said that Breuer's cathartic method had achieved its results by deliberately affecting a retransmutation of excitation from the somatic into the mental field, in order to enforce a resolution of the opposed elements by a process of thought and a motor discharge of the excitation in speech. In the paper, "On the Grounds for Detaching a Particular Syndrome from Neurasthenia under the Description 'Anxiety Neurosis' " (1894), Freud said that neurotic anxiety was transmuted sexual libido. Psychoanalytic (psychological) treatment helped the patient complete the reaction (a sexual response) in a normal way. It enabled him to discharge energy on the "motor end" of the neurophysiologic apparatus in an appropriate way *through verbalization of his sexual ideas and feelings*. The neurophysiologic tenet upon which Freud based many of his ideas included the thought that "the psyche develops the affect of anxiety when it feels itself incapable of dealing (by an adequate reaction) with a task (danger) approaching it externally." On the other hand the psyche "develops the neurosis of anxiety when it feels itself unequal to the task of mastering (sexual) excitation arising endogenously .... it acts *as-if* it had projected this excitation into the outer world." An exogenous factor acts like a single shock, while an endogenous one is like a constant pressure. Later this idea became incorporated into ego psychology, and the thought was that a failure by the ego to handle the problem might be due to a constitutional defect. Initially he said that a trauma "might be defined as an increase in excitation in the nervous system" with which the individual is unable to deal adequately by motor reaction. In Letters 32, 39 and 52 to Fliess, Freud had suggested that, when for some reason adequate motor discharge after stimulation was impossible, the organism would react in some way even by using the sensory end as a reaction through phantasy, dream or hallucination. Phantasy, Freud stressed, plays an important part in understanding the nature of neuroses and psychoses. We hold to this tenet today, but reject the idea of the endogenous concept and fixations of the libido, except as the idea of fixation might be reinterpreted. The phantasy is an aspect of the sado-masochistic defense based on identifications with the parents.

On August 16, 1895, Freud wrote to Fliess (Letter 27) that psychology was really an "incubus." He said: "All I was trying to do was to explain defense, but I found myself explaining something from the very heart of nature. I found myself wrestling with the problems of quality, sleep, memory. In short, the whole of psychology." The endogenous concept took away the onus from the parent as the stimulus for perverse behavior, but modern researchers such as Szurek and Johnson, Don Jackson and Stoller place the "blame" back with the parent.[7]

In considering the dynamics of identification and acting out, it is important to emphasize the work of Ferenczi, particularly his ideas concerning the "introjected object," a concept that we still use to explain identification and neurotic roles in acting out. Ferenczi gave us important insights toward understanding the transference process, and introjection, and his observations of the introjected object were recorded even before Freud wrote the essay on transference, in a paper called "Introjection and Transference" (1909) (translated from the German by Ernest Jones in 1916). But Freud often referred to another paper of Ferenczi: "Stages in the Development of a Sense of Reality" (1913). This paper seems to have been a forerunner of what we might now call *the ego function school of psychoanalysis*, since it attempted to describe stages of ego organization in relation to Freud's developmental theory and the individual's ability to perceive reality at these various stages. This idea was an elaboration of what Freud had initiated in his early writings (see page 175 in "Origins of Psychoanalysis") and which formed what later was called the *genetic* aspect of Freud's theory, i.e., his attempt to give a historical account of the development of the individual "ego functions" within the context of general development of the mental apparatus. While we may not see eye to eye with Ferenczi in his ego concepts, we may well regard him as blazing the way to some of our modern notions about delinquent and acting out behavior. Thus he has contributed to our understanding of borderline conditions. Ferenczi wrote that intolerance of other people's wrong-doing is a sign of an uneasy conscience and of the strain on the individual in repressing his own desires to act out some criminal or delinquent act which is based on his own forbidden, unconscious impulses. The researches of Szurek and Johnson have attested to the validity of the concept. Ferenczi felt that the retribution principle in law is based on intolerance and the unconscious urge for vengeance. We are unconsciously indignant that the criminal dared to do something which we all unconsciously have the greatest inclination to do. While Ferenczi felt that these impulses were stimulated by the id rather than the parents, he wrote that the punishment of criminals allows the non-criminal (who has these aggressive revenge and sadistic impulses repressed) to find expression for his impulses in the act of punishment. The individual who wishes to punish the wrong-doer, we can see, acts *as-if* he were justified in his sadistic behavior, being able to torture or hurt others with less guilt, since he is only injuring a person whom society has chosen for punishment. In this notion, Ferenczi was accenting an idea of Freud, who said that when members of society get relief in punishment of the criminal, they feel so because their unconsciously repressed *revenge feelings* have been appeased. Freud also pointed out the need for the criminal and delinquent to requite his own guilt. He found this dynamic to be present in cases of theft, fraud and arson. After the deed was done, the oppressive sense of guilt was relieved. The punishment freed the individual from the deep anxiety that stemmed from guilt. Freud said that the origin of the guilt *was to be found in the poor resolution of the oedipal problem.* The dynamics of projective identification emerged from these ideas.

While the borderline patients do not commit crimes as a rule, nor do they murder or commit suicide, they do have murderous and suicidal feelings, and chronic feelings of depression and guilt feelings are ever present.

The work of the early psychoanalysts has helped greatly to understand the interactive defensive mechanism between the criminal and his punitive authority, society. We find this to be similar to the model in the family, where the children are used as "scapegoats" or as transferential, projective objects; this introduces a destructive dimension. For years, most people have had feelings of shame about psychotic individuals and some of the more severe neurotics. The shame and guilt of family members caused them to want to hide the victim's illnesses or emotional discomfort, often "putting them away" in a hospital or sending them to another area to live and financing their extended sojourns. This attitude, particularly the denial by the family of their role in initiating and fostering the illness, is largely responsible for the fact that treatment techniques have lagged far behind knowledge. Society has not felt it important to treat the criminal nor the seriously immobilized patient. Punishment and custodial care have been the order of the day. This attitude is slowly changing but the change is fraught with the desire to find short cuts in the use of drugs and certain superficial group techniques which do not touch the basic problems. One of the reasons for the change is our better knowledge of the dynamics of schizophrenia and our realization that some of the dynamics are similar to those found in borderlines and character disorders. A review of pertinent material on schizophrenia is therefore in order, and may encourage therapists to take a more optimistic view of treatment in the borderline patient.

NOTES

1 By 1924, Freud had evolved the structural theory, having earlier incorporated the topological concept (Cs, Pcs, Ucs), the libido theory and a developmental scheme. In 1924 several papers were published which showed Freud's preoccupation with problems related to borderline and schizophrenic patients, for example: "Neurosis and Psychosis; The Economic Problem in Masochism;" "Loss of Reality in Neurosis and Psychosis." He was concerned with negativism, sado-masochism, perversion, denial, withdrawal—all problems which have meaning in considering the dynamics of the borderline. In the essay, "Neurosis and Psychosis" (1924), he made his well known statement that a transference neurosis represented a conflict between the ego and the id; a narcissistic neurosis (this included the borderline) between the ego and the superego; and a psychosis between the ego and the outer world.

2 It is interesting that recently in some cases of drug abuse the patients have made comments to the effect that when they are "straight" they cannot bear to think of their parents, for when they do, *they think of what terrible creatures they are or want to be.* There seems to be awareness on the part of the patient of his extreme contempt for the parents and their behavior. It seems to me, however, that what the patient is denying in these instances is that he is like the parents. Patients see qualities in themselves that they hate in the parents, and they fear and deny these characteristics.

3 We are inclined today to credit the child's disturbed emotional reactions to distortions in his relations with parents, and to regard the results as the oedipal problem. When Freud discussed *oedipal dynamics he stressed the child's relation with the parent of the opposite sex.* But we must, it seems to me, include the child's relationship with *both parents* in our concept of the oedipal problem, in particular the child's position in the *interlocking defensive system between the parents who use the child as an object of projection.* This is the principal dynamic in the stimulation of neuroses and psychoses and the basis of the identification problem which is at the root of acting out. Guilt is a factor in the oedipal problem not only with respect to sexuality but also in relation to any kind of behavior that upsets a neurotic parent. Punishment, for example, often takes the form of making the child feel guilty for normal behavior, particularly as the behavior tends to unmask the parents' neurotic aims (A. Wolberg, 1960). Laing in his book, "Knots," has recently given us succinct expressions of this "bind" and the ways in which the individual must handle this conflict through identification and hysterical mechanisms on the mental level: Poem one, stanza one, on page one, poignantly illustrates how children become enmeshed in the defenses of the parent:

> "They are playing a game. They are playing at not
> playing a game. If I show them I see they are, I
> shall break the rules and they will punish me.
> I must play their game, of not seeing I see the game."

Identification is based on this dilemma. It is the child's way of solving the problem while the adults maintain their interlocking defenses. (The poem is quoted by permission of the publisher, Pantheon Books, a division of Random House, Inc., New York: R. D. Laing, "Knots," copyright 1970.)

4 Stealing, for example, can be traced back to the castration complex, according to the libido theorists: if "object transference" in stealing is found, i.e., stealing from superiors, this is symbolic of penis-envy and active castration wishes. Compulsive stealing, on the other hand, is based on the longing for the first source of pleasure, the mother; it shows that the first refusal of the mother's love had not been overcome. Pyromania is considered a urethral-erotic character trait. Some analysts retain Freud's idea that there is an unconscious

urge to confession based on guilt rooted in the unresolved oedipus complex. Confession rests upon these pre-existent feelings of guilt.

Some analysts still endorse Freud's confusing explanation of kleptomania. Kleptomania, he said, found almost exclusively in women, was derived from "no object-choice"; therefore, the aim was not revenge but could be traced to "penis envy." By their thefts, women are trying to make good the "cosmic injustice of their bodily configuration"—their thefts have more of a "narcissistic" tone. Current theories support the fact that revenge does seem to be a motif in kleptomania—the object is degraded and humiliated; but in the acting out, projective identification is evident in that the kleptomaniac is masochistic and humiliates herself as well as the members of her family. She acts out roles arranging to be caught and punished. Aggression and degradation are fused in one symbolic move. We do find many male kleptomaniacs, so that it is not an exclusive female trait as was originally assumed.

5 The concept of *ego defect* comes from two sources: one, the hypothesis of a constitutional factor; and two, the proposition that trauma at early ages creates conditions under which the ego cannot develop properly. Freud (1937) wrote: "The etiology of all neuroses is indeed a mixed one; either the patient's instincts are excessively strong and refuse to submit to the taming influence of his ego or else he is suffering from the effects of premature traumas which his immature ego was unable to surmount. The borderline patient would certainly fit this latter description. Freud insisted that symbolism, as well as some of the defenses, were determined by heredity, an idea that many analysts cannot accept, but it may be that displacement as a defense has roots in neurophysiological reactions. Tinbergen (1952) has suggested this. We do know that aggression can be aroused as an aspect of defense (fight-flight is said to have biological roots) if enough aggravation and frustration is present. The concept of a death wish does not seem tenable. In analysis we need the cooperation of the ego and we focus on the study of "ego modification" as we determine the defensive patterns in all their forms. As aspects of their own defense (Wolberg, A, 1960) parents help mould the child's displacement behavior.

6 Breuer had introduced the subject of excitations (energy) entering the nervous system in greater or lesser degrees. In the Project, Freud mentioned his idea of "quantity" as related to energy. There was a "sum of excitation in the nervous system." Part One of the Project dealt with various topics affiliated with Freud's reasoning about the concept of energy. "Energy" became finally and specifically "sexual energy" and later "destructive energy": these two were opposites—opposed energies which feature in the elaboration of the instinct theory. Freud remarked in his essay, "Analysis Terminable and Interminable" (1937), that Empedocles of Acragas (Girenti), born about 495 B.C., considered Love and Destructiveness as elements—principles in life. Apparently this idea has a long history in the philosophical thought of the human race.

7 Lashley (1957) criticized early analytic thinking in this way: "Neural activity has been sufficiently well explored to rule out such broad assumptions as of the energy of the libido or the id. Summation, potentiation, irradiation, and inhibition are fairly well, though not completely, understood. The energy of the nervous system is that of transmitted excitations, with its implied limitations and specificities. Energy disassociated from this as postulated in field theories is ruled out by definite experimental evidence . . . the derivation of psychic energy from one or a few 'instincts' finds no support in the nature of the neural activity."

Holt says that the Project reveals that Freud had a feeling about feedback in his postulations of *pleasure* and *unpleasure*; and that the mechanisms of *defense* can be related to a theory of self-regulating systems which control themselves by the use of informational feedback. This is possible through the awarding and aversive centers in the mid-brain. While there is not a specific quantity of excitation, not a constancy of quantity, or a definite sum of excitation, there are nevertheless, steady states, a dynamic of inputs and outputs.

Freud changed his ideas about libido several times. In 1894 he said that libido is a sexual psychical energy and when libido is frustrated symptoms occur. He used the term libido here to mean *conscious sexual feeling*. He wrote that *anxiety arises from a transformation of the accumulated tension from excessive excitations (sexual) which stem from the instinct*. But in situations where symptoms occur such as in phobias and obsessions and forms of inhibition such as impotency and frigidity, the reason for the accumulation of undischarged excitation is a psychological one: *repression*. Energy is used to reject unpalatable thoughts and feelings (sexual) and to keep them in the Ucs. Defense was a conscious attempt to hold back unacceptable sexual ideas. As he began to move, after 1895, towards a libido theory (an instinctual theory rather than holding to the seduction hypothesis) he wrote in 1897 to Fliess (Letter 75): "I have decided to regard as separate factors what causes libido and what causes anxiety." But this idea found no place in his theory until years later (1926, "Anxiety, Inhibitions and Symptoms"). By the time Freud wrote the first edition of the "Interpretation of Dreams" in 1900 he used the topological concept, saying that *anxiety is a libidinal impulse which has its origin in the unconscious (Ucs) and is inhibited by the preconscious (Pcs), the censor.* He was of the opinion that the anxiety in anxiety dreams, like neurotic anxiety in general, "arises out of libido." In the paper on narcissism (1914) Freud defined libido as *sexual psychic energy*; and later he said that *libido is a "force" of variable quantity by which the processes and transformation in the sphere of sexual excitement can be measured.*" (This was the economic concept.)

In the 1920 edition of "Three Essays," in a footnote, Freud said: "One of the most important results of psychoanalytic research is the discovery that neurotic anxiety arises out of libido; that it is a transformation of it; and that it is thus related to it in the same kind of way as 'vinegar to wine.'" In 1926, in "Anxiety Inhibition and Symptoms," Freud went back to his early formulation relative to the ego and anxiety; and, in Letter XXXVI of his "New Introductory Lectures" (1933), Freud wrote: "We shall no longer maintain that it is the libido itself that is turned into anxiety." He made the full circle, going back to the idea he had expressed in the "Defense Neuropsychoses," that it is the ego that experiences anxiety; the "danger" could come from the outside, or "from a persistent impulse arising endogenously."

Finally, the *concept libido* began to include *all feelings which motivate a person to desire pleasureable contact with others or even with himself.* Some libido was transformed by the process of *sublimation*; i.e., a certain amount of libido which is originally devoted to a sexual focus is directed into ostensibly non-sexual channels from which either esthetic or utilitarian pleasure is derived. *Sublimation* is the unconsicous gratification of sexual desire by a substitute activity which conforms to a personal and social definition of acceptibility. Out of sublimation grew the whole superstructure of human civilization and the resolution of the oedipal problem.

Breuer did not accept the libido theory. He had mentioned three kinds of energy, "a potential energy which lies quiescent in the chemical substance of the cell; a kinetic energy which is discharged when the fibers are in a state of excitation; and yet, another quiescent state of nervous excitation, tonic excitation or nervous tension."

CHAPTER IV

RELATIONSHIP OF STUDIES ON SCHIZOPHRENIA TO THE CONCEPT OF THE BORDERLINE SYNDROME

In the studies of the schizophrenias from the time of Morel (1860) and the work of Kahlbaum (1863, 1874), to the present day, one finds references which apply to borderline conditions. It is interesting to trace the historical roots of our present ideas, for in the descriptions of the schizophrenias we find allusions that are helpful in our understanding of the psychopathology and psychodynamics of borderlines. Indeed, the diagnostic manual of the American Psychiatric Association (1968) has designated certain forms of schizophrenia that have common ground with the borderline patient. Chronic *undifferentiated schizophrenia* is a type described as covering *mixed* syndromes without any clearly defined symptomatology. It is said that while these patients present definite schizophrenic personalities, they cannot be classified as a specific type of schizophrenic reaction. Many psychiatrists include here what Bleuler called the "latent," the "incipient," or the "pre-psychotic" schizophrenic reactions which are referred to by others as borderlines. *Schizoid personality* is another A.P.A. classification, describing a patterned disturbance, the characteristic traits of which are: (1) a basic sado-masochistic phantasy thinking organization; (2) an inability to express hostility or even ordinary aggressive feelings in a direct manner; and (3) avoidance of close relationships with others. Common traits described here are coldness, aloofness, emotional detachment, fearfulness, avoidance of competition, and daydreams concerned with the need for omnipotence. These patients are said to be extremely sensitive and shy, having few or no friends, suffering acutely crippling feelings of inferiority, and demonstrating little self-assertion. It is obvious that the schizoid personality described in this A. P. A. category has many of the features of the paranoid, without a self-defined and projected delusional system. The prevailing passive-aggressive personality organization of such patients is evident and can be found in other seriously disturbed individuals, i.e., those suffering from manic-depressive disorders. The borderline stays in an interpersonal relationship, however, and thus is not as isolated or lonely as some of the paranoids or the schizoid personalities as described in this category. But the borderline has the passive-aggressive personality and the sado-masochistic orientation.

Arieti (1955) thinks of schizophrenia primarily as a functional disease. He has suggested that we use as a basic definition, the one found in Blakiston's "New Gould Medical Dictionary" (2nd Ed., 1956), which refers to schizophrenia as a "reaction" characterized by a tendency to withdraw from reality, inappropriate moods, and unpredictable disturbances in stream of thought, regressive tendencies, to the point of deterioration, and often hallucinations and delusions. The borderline patient has many of the symptoms mentioned by Arieti. He has periods of withdrawal from reality, but does not remain withdrawn. He has a loosely defined delusional system, but is not always motivated by the delusion. In periods of great stress, he can become quite unreasonable. We can think of the borderline personality as a reaction, but more precisely as a defensive reaction (as Freud originally suggested of the neuroses in his paper "The Defense Neuropsychoses" (1894)). But the early investigators were inclined to regard schizophrenia as an organic condition and ascribed its symptomatology to a "splitting" mechanism constitutionally based and physiologically inspired.

The concept of *splitting* so frequently found in the literature on borderline patients has derivations in Kraepelin's (1896) idea that schizophrenia was due to an injury resulting in a splitting of the psychic functions. This produced loss of the integrating unity of the personality. Kraepelin believed that treatment was difficult because of a deteriorating element in the schizophrenic process, probably the result of a degenerating disease of the brain or of a metabolic disturbance causing auto-intoxication.

As has been indicated in previous chapters, Breuer felt that in the hysterias the mental functions were disturbed by a dissociative process which prevented the patient from integrating the contents of his mind. This process, which caused *hypnoid states*, was, according to Breuer, undoubtedly due to a constitutional factor. Breuer also emphasized the *excessive excitations* in the nervous system resulting from trauma, and he felt that these physiological effects were related to the development of the hypnoid states. What Freud later described as anxiety seems to be what Breuer meant by "excitations"; however, Breuer was thinking, in neurophysiological terms, of an overflow or excess of ennervations at a given time, which the patient could not handle, while Freud was speaking of libidinal energy which he conceived of as being present in the human system in a given quantity. Freud used the concept of defense in the sense of rejection of reality, and repression as a splitting of the mind, to explain what Breuer called hypnoid states.

Many of our current ideas about the hopelessness of treating borderline conditions stem from the contention that certain syndromes, like schizophrenia, had an inherent deteriorating element (Kraepelin, 1896) and that they resisted treatment because of what Morel (1860) described as a pervasive "stupidity." Some ego-psychology analysts adapt Morel's notion of constitutional "stupidity" to their psychodynamic model by insisting that the traits of "poor judgment" and "poor perceptual capacities," that make up a patient's "stupidity" are the product of "ego deficit," which they say is due to a developmental problem.

We now know that schizophrenics do not necessarily deteriorate. If they withdraw and neglect themselves and encourage others to neglect them, the result is due to their sado-masochism rather than to an intrinsic propensity. The stupidity described by Morel is related, as we think of it at present, not only to underlying mechanisms and sado-masochism but also to certain hysterical defenses which schizophrenic and borderline patients put into operation to prevent the expression of their aggression and assertiveness, which they sense unconsciously would be against their parent's wishes. The guilt over the aggression and the fear of retaliatory punishment are factors in the defensive operation. The aggression in these instances is felt as a desire to injure or defame the parent while gaining success. The child was made to feel guilty for wanting success, the parent being competitive, envious or hostile, and developing anxiety if the child's behavior became threatening to his own neurotic adjustment. Such a parent is fearful of action and experimentation, having been inhibited by his own parents. If the child expresses freedom of thought and feelings, he becomes a potential threat to the homeostasis of the parent. The child's reactive withdrawal is associated with the defense of identification with the parent.

But the child is not indelibly crippled as a consequence of his early upbringing. In his interpersonal encounters with parents, *complete submission* or *complete inhibition* is rarely required. There are usually one or two areas of functioning that are not a threat to the parent—thus what has come to be known as the "anxiety-free areas of the ego." Hartmann (1939) has written of these free areas and of the "autonomous ego functions," an idea introduced by Breuer in his concept of anxiety-free states, or "bound" and "free" energy (Freud, 1915). In most instances when the individual is exposed to other important personages than the parents, he utilizes his ego functions and his creative intelligence to distinguish between his parents' ways and the ideas and actions of others. Unfortunately his ability to perceive this difference causes him to feel guilt, since he is tempted to act assertively or aggressively.

The stupidity-mechanism, as manifested in borderline conditions (and even more pronounced in some of the schizophrenias), has a relation to what Freud wrote about in his paper, "Some Character Types Met with in Psychoanalytic Work" (1915), when he described the kind of person who falls ill with success: the destiny neurosis. Helene Deutsch's *hysterical fate neurosis* (1965) is a similar concept, the probelm undoubtedly being based on a fear of success and a masochistic maneuver which serves both as an undoing function and as a defense against the aggression stimulated by parental envy and fear. Freud (1913, 1916, 1919) on several occasions attributed what some investigators have called "aggression in the interests of self-assertion," or "aggression (or regression) in the service of the ego" to sadism and obsessive-compulsive mechanisms. He discovered, too, that some individuals do not inhibit or undo their achievement but they force themselves to succeed and they then become apathetic and disinterested after performance. The idea Freud had was that the individual was interested in outdoing someone else rather than in the accomplishment of a task out of genuine creative desire. The "desire for knowledge" or for activity was attached to an impulse for revenge. In itself it constituted an act of aggression (Freud, 1913), even though the individual might do outstanding work. Freud's clinical descriptions have accurately depicted what we observe now in some borderline patients, i.e., accomplishment gives only momentary satisfaction, and boredom sets in when the aggressive thought or feeling has been satisfied. If the therapist helps the patient reduce his guilt over the impulse to create and express his ideas and feelings, the aggressive impulses can be analyzed. The need for revenge and the satisfaction of sadistic feelings is a conditioned response which must be dealt with in the therapeutic process. We see this problem today in the masochistic form in school children who "drop out" from their studies, a good number of whom turn out to be borderline reactions. Levinson's study (1965) reported that a certain number of children cannot permit themselves to lean on another's experience. (This seems like a reaction to defend against sadism. The obsessive mechanisms that go with the drop-out pattern attempt to undo the desire for revenge or to kill the other. The pattern is a masochistic way of eliminating oneself so that the individual will not have to face the problem.) Such children, for example, when they have to do a brief presentation on a particular topic, "rather than reading one or two concise references on the subject, will take 15 huge . . . books from the library and . . . try to read through every one of them. . . . They are in some ways so hostile and insubordinate to any kind of authoritative learning experience that they must learn everything all over again, from the beginning, by themselves." Rich (1972) has found that school failure is a function of aggression.

Bleuler (1911) made an attempt to explain some of the thinking processes typical of schizophrenia: psychic complexes, he insisted, do not combine in a purposeful conglomeration of strivings, ideas and feelings; rather, they invade consciousness, usually in fragments, but sometimes in totality, and they foster scattered thinking, incoherence, then blocking. There is a loosening of conceptualizations, and an impairment of the capacity for the association of ideas (Breuer's concept), with resultant confusion. In his idea of function, Bleuler (as have the more modern ego psychologists) borrowed liberally from Freud's material in describing the ego and its operations. Particularly he was intrigued with Freud's idea that the confusion of the schizophrenic patient was due to a flooding of the ego with "id" material.[1]* Bleuler believed that if the "total complex" invaded, then a complete phantasy erupted, and a change of personality took place. A total projection resulted in delusion.[2] Bleuler suggested that *fragmented ideation* be thought of as a "stuttering" kind of thinking process, causing a scattering of associations. The fragments, he insisted, represented the unconscious which promoted autistic behavior (this was disordered thinking in the form of phantasy, or dereistic thinking created by a dissociation of ideas).[3] Bleuler's concepts are interesting for, as we know, there is a distinct projective reference in the mental organization of borderline patients as well as in the schizophrenias, but we are probably more accurate if we think of this presumably chaotic mental organization as having a specific structure in the form of purposeful delusion (a defense) rather than conceiving it as a disintegrating operation, or as a primitive early form of thinking (primary process).

The neurotic, said Bleuler, could come back to reality by getting over his thinking block, but the psychotic did not recover because the block was always there. The neurotic was aware of blockings; the psychotic, on the other hand, was "disloyal to reality." The borderline was partially disloyal to reality. We must remember that Bleuler, like Kraepelin and Freud, felt that schizophrenia was due basically to a physical or constitutional disorder, with psychological precipitating factors. He speculated on the theory of a toxin. The borderline patient's symptomatology was included in what Bleuler termed "simple and complex functions." [4]

In contrast to Bleuler, Adolph Meyer (1910, 1912) thought that schizophrenia was a habit disorganization due to faulty reactions acquired during the life experience of the individual. He discounted the toxin idea, basing his theory on an *adaptation concept* to the effect that faulty conditioning interfered with development and adjustment. A great many authorities agree with this formulation. Meyer's concepts, however, did not take into consideration what Freud called the symbolic meaning of behavior. While Meyer put emphasis on conditioning in the family and the social environment, regarding the individual and the environment, to use Moreno's phrase, "as a fish is to the water," a unity, he

* Notes for this chapter start page 90.

laid more stress on the idea of habit formation rather than on intrapsychic processes of phantasy or autism, which related to and disguised the meaning of neurotic behavior, or the habit patterns, and defenses.

Certain adaptationalists, who support some aspects of psychoanalytic theory, disagree with Meyer's concepts, clinging to Freud's biological bias. For instance, Rado believed (1962) that schizophrenia is due to a defective gene, a "schizotype genotype." Heath (1958) has been searching for a chemical reaction which will account for schizophrenia, and he reports having isolated a specific protein factor, taraxein, believed to be related to ceruloplasmin, the alpha globulin transporter of copper in blood plasma. Other investigators have been unable to duplicate Heath's experiments. There are many authorities who believe that anxiety does, indeed, produce varying types of physiological and chemical reactions that may account not only for symptoms which have bodily effects but also for certain kinds of symbolic behavior which can be looked upon as displacement behavior. (See Psychiatric Annals, July, Vol. 2, No. 7, and August, Vol. 2, No. 8, 1972.)

In contrast to this biochemical direction, a number of attempts have been made to study schizophrenia through a careful dissection of the personality structure in operation. Arieti (1955), for example, speaks of the "stormy personality" of the schizophrenic, emphasizing the aggression and the distancing (withdrawal) mechanisms. The schizophrenic tries to reach people, but each attempt leads to hurt. The concept seems similar to that of Zilboorg (1931) who felt that the psychotic attack has the function of letting the individual act in an assertive, albeit aggressive, manner. It allows the individual to break out of his passivity (we might appropriately refer to this as his masochistic position) and his dependency, and to act with aggression (what we might more truly term his sadistic response). This comes at a point when, after a series of incidents during which the individual feels he should have asserted himself but did not, a cumulative or summative affect accrues and then he breaks out in action. Arieti has emphasized the futility of this episodic attack: it drives the other person away. It seems likely that such behavior is actually a rage reaction, a temper tantrum meant to punish the other person in the relationship. In its extreme form, murder may be the outcome of such emanatory responses.

Several authors have thought of this kind of activity as self-assertion and have used descriptions such as: regression in the service of the ego, or aggression in the interest of self-assertion. As a matter of fact, this sadistic position does not appear to be associated with self-assertion; it is not in the interests of normal creative or free behavior. It is merely the reverse of the masochism: a shift in the patient's position from masochism to sadism. Such behavior is not a step in the resolution of the problem, but rather a perpetuation of it. Levy (1953) associated this kind of behavior with what he called the *oppositional syndrome*. The *fate neurosis* and the *stupidity syndrome* noted by Morel seem to be the opposite of the stormy personality, the other side of the coin, so to speak, for in this, the individual maintains the masochistic position, his passivity, while in the stormy episode he expresses his sadism. It is quite possible that these actions are similar to what has been described as a patient's phobic and counter-phobic activities just as depression and manic behavior may be. Underneath the stormy personality or the over-active one is a feeling of depression. The oppositional syndrome as described by Levy, begins in what Levy calls the I-do-it-myself period, at about eighteen months of age. This is, according to the Freudian model, the anal period of development. While Freud stressed the associated anger, rage and opposition, Levy reminds us that at this stage the child is normally being assertive. When the child is frustrated, of course, a rage reaction will occur. Levy suggests that the oppositional trait is connected with important ego defenses, and that is one reason why it is so difficult to give it up in treatment. One wonders whether in the stormy personality, activity is meant to counteract the feeling of depression, such depression being a function of the masochism. There is reason to believe that in these moods the delusion is being used as a defense and that when these attacks occur, masochistic maneuvers are hiding a deep fear of assertiveness or a fear of success. The undoing mechanism includes the kind of phantasy Freud (1920) described as "retiring in favor of someone else"; but the abiding motif is revenge. It is as if the patient is saying to the object: "I will keep myself from doing these things, so that I can continue to punish you," or the opposite, "I will do these things to punish you, by exposing you."

There has been ascribed to the schizophrenic, and to the borderline a "paleologic" form of thinking based on the principle promulgated by E. Von Domarus (1944): whereas the normal person infers identity on the basis of a similar subject, a typically schizophrenic way of thinking infers identity on the basis of identical predicates. As an example, the patient might say: "I am a virgin; I am the Virgin Mary." The explanation follows that being a virgin is the common predicate. The patient can, in this way, deny her feelings of unworthiness and inadequacy and identify with an "idealized" image of female perfection. One is reminded that such thinking is often the basis of particular kinds of humor which we find in patients, the "shaggy dog" type of humor, through which the patients make fun of themselves and others, a sado-mashochistic trait. The *idealization concept* was introduced by Freud in his ego psychology as one of the important dynamisms in defense, and by implication it had a relation to his concept of splitting and the formation of the superego.[5]

As Freud developed the libido theory, "schizophrenic thought" gradually began to contain the idea of *biological and inherited thought*. The child, said Freud, filled in the gaps of his knowledge with phylogenetic thought, *and this kind of ideation was related to pre-history and the early phases of the experience of the race.* Inasmuch as schizophrenic thought was unconscious thought or "id-thought" breaking through into consciousness, it was archaic thought in two senses: in the context of early ontogenetic experience and within the conjecture of how such early ontogenetic thought was associated with phylogenetic thought (ontogeny recapitulates phylogeny).[6]

Arieti calls the Von Domarus concept of *paleologic thinking* a regressive phenomenon and he believes it to be associated with a motivational mechanism; but he does not make clear whether the motivational mechanism is due to conditioning and defense or to a biological or instinctual substratum which may be associated with a defective gene, the resulting phylogenetic thought causing defective ego functions. Arieti seems to believe, with Sullivan, that psychosis is due to innumerable conditionings, and if this be true, then his concept of motivation in the neuroses and the psychoses might have a relation to conditioned responses. One gets the impression that "paleologic thought" can be thought of as part of the patient's phantasy constructions, and thus as an aspect of the *identification phantasy*. This latter, I would suggest, is in turn related to Freud's concepts of infantile imagoes, idealization, defense, transference and delusion.

If we eliminate the phylogenetic aspect of the theory, we find an explanation in ego terms which agrees in essence with the fundamentals of the topological theory, and this theory, it seems to me, can best be thought of as an ego theory. The conflict is presented in ego terms which are understandable if we say that the patient who is revolted by reality experience becomes frightened by it and flies into defense. He reacts, not only to the "other" with disgust, but also to himself, and he becomes enmeshed by the other in the identification. In order to disguise this whole problem, he remakes reality by forming a delusion, which is a projective way of handling the identification, at least on the mental level. The fact that this kind of solution brings him into conflict with people other than the original objects is simply another way of making a statement concerning the transference: others are not the original others, the ones who were such a threat to him and against whom he had to defend. His projection onto others of the traits and characteristics of the original others is what keeps him in a state of anxiety and yet helps him maintain a kind of equilibrium. The new others challenge the transference, not deliberately but simply by virtue of their differences from the original others. The wish to avoid the challenging of these differences helps the patient to maintain the defense. The patient wants to hold onto feelings, not only because he wishes to avoid having his defenses challenged, but also because he does not wish to face the fact that he was in fact rejected and demeaned by his parents, and it will now be necessary to extricate himself from them and from others like them. He suffers what has been called *separation anxiety*. If he gets well, he must reorganize his ego and he must give up his aggression. He must eliminate part of his ego, the defensive part. He must forgive and forget, and either he will become friendly with his parents, or he will have to separate from them completely. Should they die in the interim, he will have to face the realities of their lives in relation to him. He must relieve his guilt toward them so that he is not compelled to consider that they were his friends, if indeed they were unfriendly and hostile. He will have to work through his guilt at making these kinds of decisions and he will have to work through his aggression and his identifications and in fact eliminate them. This task I have found to be fundamental in the treatment of borderline patients.

In a related way, LaForgue (1926) outlined a particular kind of obsessive defensive system which he said was operative in patients with a schizophrenic overlay. The borderline patient has some of these mechanisms. While obsessive symptoms are prominent in some borderline patients, hysterical maneuvers seem predominant in others. LaForgue apparently described the former kind of case. According to this author, when the mother is rejecting during the first years (in infancy or the early stages of psychological weaning, he intimated that rejection is a factor in all such cases) the child reacts by creating a "narcissistic substitute" for her. He does this by "introjecting" two images of her: he "scomatizes" the real mother from whom he withdraws and whose care he denies he needs, and he then substitutes for the existing hostile, punitive, and obsessive mother an idealized good mother. The obsessive "narcissistic substitute" enables the child to avoid the suffering of the rejection in the forced process of "psychological weaning." The child neutralizes the feelings of inferiority which are inevitable and as a consequence remains fixated at the anal-sadistic phase, developing a particular kind of "personality split." Such a child has a specific kind of personality organization: easily traumatized by frustrations, he tries to live up to the demands of the introjected mother—the ideal—which he cannot do, and so he feels guilty and worthless. The child then identifies one aspect of the introjected object with excrement. In order to kill the parents, he withdraws; and in order to castrate them, he castrates himself. He depersonalizes people, makes them into feces, and he then chooses feces as his libidinal objects. (Dr. Daird, the borderline patient described in Chapter VIII, had an intense feeling of pleasure in looking at a well-formed and especially long stool. He had phantasies while doing this that he apparently repressed, for when he began to talk about them, they "disappeared." The phantasies of feces and his practice of scrutinizing the stools, in his free associations had homosexual connotations, and were associated with a phantasy of giving in to another).

LaForgue goes on to say that these schizoid patients become receptive to destructive impulses and they "scomatize" that which is constructive. They choose their own egos as love-objects, but they dissect every thought. The obsessional (paranoid) persecutor is "introjected" and then "projected" outside the patient. A sado-masochism element is evident in this description, and one may deduce that Freud's concept of the ego-ideal is actually a description of a defense against a nagging, compulsive-obsessive hostile parent who has paranoid trends. The description of the father was usually missing in Freud's and others' delineations of preoedipal dynamics, but today we understand that the father, too, is an important factor in the early stages of development. The father can be the "persecutor" as well as the mother, for his interlocking defensive relationship with the mother supports their mutual obsessive-paranoid trends.[7]

About the time that LaForgue was accenting the role of the "sadistic archaic superego," Freud had completed such works as "Civilization and Its Discontents" (1920), "The Ego and the Id" (1924), and "The Economic Problem in Masochism" (1925). He was at this period evolving the structural theory. The problem of sado-masochism was still urgent and perplexing and stimulated such workers as Abraham (1927), who elaborated on Freud's preoedipal, anal-sadistic stage, breaking the period into sub-stages. LaForgue seems to have dealt with clinical material along more topical descriptive lines. Thus he spoke of the compulsive mother who "bugs" or "bedevils" her child with constant criticizing and harping, and with perfectionistic demands, a kind of "driving the child crazy." (Note the paper by Searles referred to on pages 27 and 70, which deals with this same subject.)

In 1927, in his paper on "Fetishism," Freud insisted that LaForgue's ideas were not developed through the application of psychoanalytic conceptions of the psychosis, and could not be applied to the process of development and the formation of neurosis. Freud avowed that the individual who was "ruled by a fetish" had an oedipal problem. The fetish was a substitute for the mother's phallus, which the little boy believed once existed. The fetish represented a belief the child did not wish to forego; he simply refused to accept the fact that a woman had no penis. If a woman could be castrated, then his own penis was in danger.

Freud's concepts of castration and penis envy, notable as they were historically, have not explicated in a useful way the tremendously complex relationships that develop within the family structure. They do not help much in understanding the dynamics of borderline problems,[8] but they do reflect some of the phantasy found in some patients, due to the rejecting attitudes (castrating attitudes) of parents.

In elaborating on ideas concerning the ego we must pay acknowledgement to Bellak's writings (1969) on schizophrenia. When we consider the psychoanalytic treatment of schizophrenia, says Bellak, we must recognize that Freud's topological model was predicated upon the fact that behavioral phenomena can be seen as part of a continuum, some of the links of which were, or had become, unconscious. But interpretation in the early days of psychoanalysis depended upon "content analysis," i.e., analysis of the fixations of the libido according to Freud's developmental scheme. Bellak wisely avoids the problem of defining the unconscious, but he implies that the words *conscious* and *unconscious* have something to do with the "splitting of the ego." Bellak, following along the lines of Knight (1953), who emphasized the ego functions of the borderline, undertook research to develop an *ego function scale*. In applying his *ego function test,* he shows that the *ego function scores* of schizophrenics are lower than those of neurotics and that the scores of neurotics are lower than the scores of "normals." This phenomenon can be interpreted in various ways, since the meaning of such a finding is open to many theories. Ego functions are defined by Bellak as: reality testing; judgment; sense of reality; regulation and control of drives; object relations; thought processes; adaptive regression in the service of the ego; defensive functions; stimulus barrier; autonomous functioning; synthetic function; and mastery-competence.[9] The items which make up the ego function process scores, Bellak admits, cannot be precisely delineated with respect to the various syndromes, since no clear pictures are evident. In some of his other writings, there is an indication that Bellak believes we should think of symptoms, particularly acting out, in terms of hysterical phenomena (1965). In this sense, he implies the ego may have a special form of organization in one emotional problem as compared to another. This idea is central and important, it would seem, in any theory of neurosis.[10]

There are many psychoanalysts today who speak of *defective perception* in the context of a *defective ego,* implying that there is a defective developmental factor in schizophrenia. This idea was applied to the borderline patient described in a paper at the 1970 meeting of the American Psychiatric Association, entitled: "Management of Specific Ego Defects in the Treatment of Borderline Patients" (Frosch, 1970). The author used the example of a patient, a highly skilled and successful commercial artist, who, while walking on the street, inched near a policeman smoking a marijuana cigarette. It was his contention that this man's ego was operating in a defective manner due to developmental causes and that this accounted for his neurotic behavior. He was emphatic in saying that it is erroneous to think of this man's behavior as defensive. The patient, he said, does not perceive his danger; he is not capable of perceiving his danger nor the foolishness of his behavior. Such an explanation is puzzling, since we know that a successful artist would have to exercise acute perceptive capacities to draw, to paint, and otherwise to operate successfully in a commercial milieu. It is only in *selective areas,* as Sullivan would say, that the man's denial, repression and masochistic behavior operate. Frosch's patient seems to be *acting out a sado-masochistic role,* placing himself in a position to be punished, just as Freud noted that some of his hysterical patients acted out in roles that were aimed at retaliatory assault. These patients, said Freud, were "realizing their phantasies in action" (1909), and he inferred that there was a repressed homosexual trend operating in this type of behavior. Yet Freud recognized that an individual's ego, no matter how "sick" he was, was never completely "defective." In his essay concerning the two laws of mental functioning, the idea is put forward; and in the "Outline of Psychoanalysis," Freud (1938) wrote: "The problem of psychoses would be simple and intelligible if the withdrawal of the ego from reality could be carried through completely. But that seems rarely, if ever, to happen.

Even in conditions so far removed from the reality of the external world as hallucinatory confusional states, one learns from patients, after their recovery, that at the time in some corner of their minds, as they express it, there was a normal person hidden who watched the hubbub of the illness go past, like a disinterested spectator. I do not know if we may assume that this is so in general, but I can report the same of other psychoses with a less tempestuous course. I recollect a case of jealousy, in which a dream conveyed to the analyst a correct picture of the cause, free from any trace of delusion." In this passage one senses that Freud considered denial and distortion as defenses in psychosis, at the same time that the psychotic "understands" and "sees" reality. Observations such as Freud expresses here would seem to contradict the idea that the schizophrenic cannot perceive reality or that he has a defective ego so far as ego functions are concerned. Rather it would seem to coordinate with concepts of hysterical-like defenses of "seeing" and "not seeing," and the Sullivanian formulation of selective inattention.

Sullivan wrote extensively on schizophrenia in the context of "faulty interpersonal transactions." His concepts are of value in working with borderlines. Schizophrenia, like all other neuroses and psychoses, he said, is an outcome of unhealthy interpersonal relations between the child and his parents. These "faulty relations" perpetuate anxiety which then interfere with the development of the self-system (Sullivan's term for the dynamism that is the motivating factor in behavior, interpreted by Clara Thompson (1958) to be Sullivan's idea of the "ego"). The self-system formulation bears a resemblance to Freud's descriptions of the ego and the superego, in that it is a constellation of "precipitates" of early and later identifications. According to Sullivan, as a consequence of faulty interpersonal situations, which he called *parataxic distortions* (Sullivan's phrase for transference), the self-system develops out of the search for security. Later the individual, distorting his interpersonal relations with others loses, in his communication with them, "consensual validation," i.e., recognition by others that his statements contain any validity.[11]

Another "ego psychology" pioneer who worked with schizophrenia was Paul Federn (1934, 1952). He considered the borderline patient a type of "latent schizophrenia," and he cautioned that the most important defense against schizophrenia is an accompanying neurosis which is usually of the hysterical or obsessional type. No attempt, he insisted, should be made to cure the latent schizophrenic of his neurosis. He definitely should not be treated by the standard form of psychoanalysis. Federn felt that the schizophrenic reaction could be modified, but that the defenses against the psychotic reaction should be reinforced. While the individual could be helped to reduce some of his guilt and anxiety, the basic ego structure would remain the same.

The contributions of Frieda Fromm-Reichman (1939, 1948, 1950, 1952, 1954) are notable particularly for her sensitivity to the needs of schizophrenic and borderline patients. She described the picture as follows: "The schizo-phrenic is painfully distrustful and resentful of other people. This is due to the severe early rebuff and rejection he encountered in important people in his infancy and childhood, as a rule mainly in the schizophrenic mother. During this early fight for emotional survival, he begins to develop the great interpersonal sensitivity which remains his for the rest of his life. His initial pathological experiences are actually, or by virtue of his interpretation, the pattern for a never-ending succession of subsequent similar experience. Because of his sensi-tivity and his never satisfied lonely need for benevolent contact, his threshold is all too easily reached. The schizophrenic's emotional regression and his with-drawal from the outside world into an autistic private world with its specific thought processes and modes of feeling and expression, is motivated by his fear of the repetitional rejection, by his distrust of others and equally by his retalia-tive hostility which he abhors, as well as by the deep anxiety promoted by his hatred."

Searles has written many important works on the treatment of schizo-phrenia (1959, 1962, 1963). Essentially a Sullivanian, he has noted particularly the exploitive attitude as an expression of aggression and the masochistic defensive system, with the paranoid undertone also stressed by Clara Thompson (1959) and Reich (1949). The mechanism of vindictiveness (Searles does not necessarily call this an expression of sadism) and the controlling aspects of passivity (masochism) are characteristics typical of the more disturbed patients. Actually these are elements of the passive-aggressive character. "Frustrated dependency needs are the source of hostility," says Searles, thus giving credence to the frustration-aggression hypothesis of Miller (1948). He notes that in inter-personal behavior, the patient acts *as-if* the other person, "the object of the dependency striving," is a rejecting and hostile person. The schizophrenic in turn also projects his own hostility upon others. He is afraid his hostility will be destroyed by his good or kindly libidinal feelings, so he must defend against them as they are a threat to his ego. His potential self-assertiveness is bound up with aggression. Searles considers "the-effort-to-drive-the-other-person crazy" an element in the etiology of schizophrenia. Searles mentions other authors who have touched upon this idea: Arieti (1955) for example, and the group of researchers headed by Johnson, Beckett et al. (1956) at the Mayo Foundation. In superego formation the child identifies in defense with the parent (the aggres-sor) and becomes his own persecutor (this seems an apt description of an "intro-ject"). The child has no other choice than to defend himself in this manner, the parent giving him no other alternative. There is a connection here between "obsessive bugging" and Freud's concept of "delusional belittling" explicated in the essay on Melancholias (1917). One finds obsessive and paranoid trends in the borderline patient, but the "bugging" motif is not quite so severe as in the paranoid. The paranoid is the kind of individual who secretly has sworn to revenge himself, to "pay back," and he does so deliberately on every occasion where he can manage to make himself feel "justified." Many years ago Adler (1925) stressed the fact that the paranoid mechanism helped the individual to rationalize his aggressive feelings and his rage. This secret vow to "pay back"[1 2] is repressed and held below the level of awareness, but it can reach consciousness if the situation is such that it calls forth the feelings. The secret vow to pay back can become such a pervasive symptom that it stimulates the individual to acts of violence, even murder. This motif is present in practically all of the incorrigibles and the individuals who perpetuate crimes of violence. They have no trust in others and their vengefulness is all-consuming; they have paranoid feelings and they plot consciously to injure others. These in the extreme are the paranoids and the psychopaths, the unreachable individuals who, when they were children, reached out and were always disappointed and rebuffed. Included are those who had nobody who really cared; those who were the most lonely of children.[1 3]

Searles has brought forward the idea that in interpersonal relations, the other person's dependency needs stir up great anxiety in the schizophrenic patient; he feels so starved and empty himself that he cannot bear to "give" to others. For this, he feels guilt. The schizophrenic also projects on to the other person his own "undependability," his feeling that he is unable to give, and will always "let the other person down." Usually, the patient's undependability is a defense against closeness and one can see that it is also a sadistic maneuver, as well. Dr. Crane, one of my patients, has the phantasy that if he "gets well" through analysis his wife will leave him and he fears this outcome. The projection is clear and his own fear and need of closeness is also evident. His relationships in this need-fear dilemma are sado-masochistic, and it is this kind of relationship he fears leaving. Searles has in fact described the defense of *projective identification*, for not only does the patient project his own undependability, but also that of the parents with whom he is identified. When good feelings emerge and there is danger of closeness, the patient does something to gain distance or to discourage the relationship, at least temporarily. This mechanism can be found in borderline patients, but the borderline, unlike the paranoid, maintains the relationship with the object and is able, at times, to let his good feelings come through. His parents, in his experience, have fended off good feelings too.

The schizophrenic's "vulnerability," says Searles, can be interpreted as an aspect of the patient's hostility and his need to control people through masochism, making the other person feel guilty. This maneuver is observable in the treatment of borderline cases. *The patient attempts to conceal his sadism through presenting a masochistic façade, and, in this way, projects his guilt on to the other person. The vulnerable attitude in analysis is a masochistic defense meant to throw the analyst out of his analytic position and is an effort to force him to play the role of a guilty parent.* In moments of anxiety in the session, the patient resorts to this defense. The sado-masochistic child plays on the sado-masochistic parent's guilt, and vice versa. This transferential maneuver must be dealt with early in treatment. While the characteristic of vulnerability is an aspect of the patient's sensitivity to rejection, it is also part of his controlling mechanism which has been incorporated into his sado-masochism. If he is vulnerable, he makes the other person feel guilty when the latter says anything or does anything that would impinge on his defenses. He is highly attuned to cues from the environment or ideas in his own head which might challenge his own defenses. This is apparently how his controlling parent acted toward him. Denial is all important. Such a motif is found in all of the more disturbed patients, and in borderlines and certain characterological disorders.

The vulnerability is associated with an obsessive-paranoid kind of hostility stimulated by the transference phantasy (the *identification phantasy*). The phantasy takes many forms. In the paranoid it may be the kind of phantasy that Freud described in the case of Schreber, who had an idea running through his head (a phantasy) to the effect that it could be stimulating to be a woman who was being raped by a man. Many borderlines have this obsessive kind of phantasy with paranoid trends, but it is not so highly developed and projected as in Schreber's case, since the delusion is not so well organized. These phantasies, while obsessive and repetitive, are similar to what Freud noted in his essay, "Hysterical Phantasies and Their Relation to Bisexuality." Both male and female figures are represented in the phantasies and the masochistic motif is variously depicted. In telling of the phantasies, it is usual for the patient to emphasize the masochistic rather than the sadistic motif, although, in homosexuality and in certain kinds of psychosis, this is not always the rule. The borderline patient tends to deny or overlook the sadism at first as he talks of his phantasies. Occasionally, a patient will verbalize his fear of his own aggression, but the thought is usually couched at first in terms of hostility rather than sadism. We have mentioned that Freud at one time (1919) suggested such phantasies were manifestations of the bisexual disposition: activity representing maleness, and passivity representing femaleness, characteristics of the related instincts of sadism and masochism.[14] (See page 50.)

Some interesting material has recently been distributed by the Sandoz Pharmaceutical Company of Hanover, New Jersey, in a report (Vol. VI., No. I) of a conference on schizophrenia which took place at the Menninger Foundation on April 3-5, 1969. It was evident that specialists at this conference held the opinion that schizophrenia is a complex, multi-faceted problem. Most felt that diagnosis was difficult but necessary, and there were several suggestions as to how to go about making the diagnosis. The concept "borderline" was included in the category of schizophrenia.

As might be expected, many investigators supported the belief that there was a constitutional factor in schizophrenia; they put forward the idea that there may be more of a genetic element in borderline cases, in catatonias and in the hebephrenias than in the paranoids. There was the general feeling that there may be as many as ten or fifteen types of schizophrenia, that Kraepelin was near the truth when he made the division between endogenous and exogenous, and that Bleuler was on the right track when he suggested the terms endogenous or organic, and reactive exogenous or psychogenic.

Several participants in the conference, however, tended to disagree with the geneticists, following along the road of Adolph Meyer with some Freudian, Sullivanian and sociological concepts added. Adaptational concepts were advocated particularly in the patient-environment-system theory, which includes the sociological dimension as well as the psychobiological. (One would presume that modifications of Freud's object relations theory, especially as this has been constructed by Fairbairn, might be called a patient-environment-system theory.)

On the biological side, it was pointed out that the physical phenomenon of tension is important. It was said that biochemical reactions can be the result of both intrapsychic stress or environmental pressure, or both, in the sense that an equilibrium (or homeostasis) exists which is upset by intense stress, the unbalance initiating and sustaining various kinds of biochemical reactions.

Some authorities felt that one should look at diseases, both physical and mental, as "equilibriums" of a sort, noting that functional operations persist even with disease. From this point of reference there is no purely physio-chemical, physiologic, psychologic or sociologic illness. It would follow, then, that treatment in schizophrenia should take this fact into consideration.

Most authorities at the conference agreed that even if there were biological or genetic reasons for the development of schizophrenia, nevertheless, in early childhood, the individual who became schizophrenic found himself in a family that did not offer him the kind of security in which he could develop his potentials without intense anxiety. Out of his environment he had to emerge with a plethora of ego defenses of the most severe and inhibiting kind. As a consequence, the schizophrenic does not develop the interpersonal skills and habits of performance that will allow him to feel confidence in his ability to get along with people, even though he knows he needs to accommodate himself to others in order to adjust to the demands of society. Nor can he work in a way that will bring him both success and satisfaction, avoiding the patterns which will result in pain. The problem here, as we have stated previously, is that the schizophrenic's intense anxiety in interpersonal relationships creates the need for detachment and distancing mechanisms. His rage is too great for him to feel comfortable in interpersonal encounters. His guilt over wanting or approaching success is too intense.

Most authorities at the Menninger Conference felt that the schizophrenic's "life style" is organized around feelings of hostility and fear, along with the underlying need for love. Such individuals feel unwanted, inferior, inadequate and unloved; they do not find satisfaction in accomplishment.[15]

It was agreed that the schizophrenic's relationships were contaminated by fears and that he used detachment as a means of avoidance; thus, in treatment, it was important to maintain some kind of relationship, any kind, so that he could feel less threatened. Some individuals avoid relationships by being attacking or hostile, thus driving others away. (The person who wishes to help the schizophrenic, or the borderline, must attempt to break through these defenses, but this has to be done very gradually, respecting the patient's fear of closeness. The projective therapeutic techniques described in Chapter X are helpful in accomplishing these aims.)

The conference report indicated that the schizophrenic was hypersensitive to subtle "cues" from the environment, and this could be demonstrated even in the hospital. Where the patient requires hospitalization, the hospital, like the family, should be thought of as a *social system*. The work of Stanton and Schwartz (1950) was cited as evidence that covert disagreements of staff lead to excitement in patients. While the patient has not been told directly of staff disagreements, he picks up this piece of reality from verbal and non-verbal cues which are given by the staff. Schwartz observed that fecal smearing by four chronic schizophrenic patients was uniformly stimulated by a "break-off" of relationships by the staff. This, one would say, is a sado-masochistic response to what the patient experiences as a threat, a desertion which is also considered a rejection. Perhaps, as LaForgue has said, these patients "scomatized" the parents as well as the substitute parents (as constituted by the staff) and then they identify these authority figures with feces. In this kind of acting out the patient can represent the staff as the despised or the devalued and degraded objects (he is disappointed in them and he feels hopeless if he finds they have hostilities and competitive feelings), and at the same time he smears himself as an equally degraded object. Thus the patient by his behavior invites rejection,[16] and demonstrates his identification with the degraded object.

The schizophrenic patient is not only highly attuned to cues of rejection but also to situations which arouse in him fears he had as a child—the kind of prohibitions and suggestions that were implied in the patient's childhood conditionings related to the inhibitions he had to set up in his childhood so that his behavior would not arouse undue anxiety in his parents. An interesting "finding" was reported at the Menninger Conference by the "perception theorists" who stated that the schizophrenic patient's communications become more intelligible when he feels less threatened, such as when the person or persons he is working with do not act fearful and do not signal to him that he is hopeless or that he cannot be helped. In such a situation, the patient does not have to employ so many symbolic kinds of communication nor so many restitutive mechanisms; he does not have to deny reality quite so much nor to defend against it, nor interpret it so often in a transferential way. This is in line with another "finding" of the behavior therapists, which is that positive action should be reinforced in treatment. These are complicated problems in the treatment of the borderline patient, and techniques will be explored in Chapters IX and X as to how reinforcement can be done effectively without arousing the patient's defenses and guilt feelings.

The perception theorists confirm Freud's observation that the schizophrenic restructures reality, replacing the intolerable "inner" and "outer" reality with a version (the delusion) that is more tolerable. He does this out of anxiety. Now it seems that what Freud referred to as dynamisms or defenses, i.e., displacement, delusion, projection, denial, repression, splitting, idealizing, and certain hysterical and/or sado-masochistic mechanisms, the perception theorists speak of as: "reality restructuring by replacement," "misperceiving people as bad," "denying by reduplication of time, place, or word-play," or "reexperiencing" painful events. And what Freud called "working through the repetition compulsion" the perception theorists refer to by such statements as "working through to more satisfying conclusions than when the events originally occurred."

Freud observed that when patients verbalize, even those who are delusional, there is always a grain of truth which is concealed or symbolized. We must remember that direct action, either verbal or non-verbal, has not been tolerated in the patient's family. He has had to find some secretive way to make statements about his own and his parent's neurotic behavior and to communicate this to others. In this respect, one is reminded of Freud's essay, "The Unconscious" (1915), in which he said that the Ucs of one person can communicate with the Ucs of another person without their consciousness being involved at all. Non-verbal communication is one of the means that the neurotic parent uses to let the child know the role he is to play in the family drama, and denial of that communication is an important dynamic; thus on the occasions when Ucs speaks to Ucs we see the hysterical maneuver of not seeing and not hearing. In this reference, patients will say that the analyst knows what the patient is thinking—as their parents did, they feel. I often think it was the subtlety of this kind of communication that was one of the factors in Freud's belief in the occult.

The "Von Domarus principle" might be considered a way of communicating in the context of delusion. The woman who says, "I am a virgin; I am the Virgin Mary," would, if she could say it more directly, make some comment to the effect that she is suffering from a sexual problem. She may or may not be asking for help, but it is certain that she is using the statement as a phantasy to stimulate herself sexually while denying sexual feelings. At the same time that she is suffering, she seeks a kind of masturbatory relief. This type of delusional defense mechanism is usually the result of relationships with parents who have secretly and non-verbally communicated their personal neurotic sexual or other repudiated needs, stimulating the child to act in some neurotic way to appease the parents' wishes and then denying the entire operation. To expose the sexual problem in a direct way would be to expose the parents' sexual perversion. To respond to such a patient with a statement such as: "I wonder how the Virgin Mary really felt!" or "I wonder what most virgins really feel," might be a way of communicating to let the patient know the therapist is aware of a conflict.

Perception theorists have come to the following conclusions concerning schizophrenics:

(1) There is a "high state of basal psychophysiological arousal" which must affect the perceptive responses to stimuli and their subsequent integration. (The "dynamic" psychologist might interpret this phenomenon to mean that the schizophrenic is in a high state of chronic anxiety, and is attuned to cues from the environment in such a way that he must constantly be prepared to defend against and restructure reality by distortion if his defenses are threatened.)

(2) There is an under-reaction to certain stimuli, such as pain or threat-connecting stimuli. (Here we might say that the defenses of "not-seeing," "not-hearing" or of "selective inattention" with the accompanying defenses of denial, detachment, isolation and masochism are used in such instances, but this does not necessarily mean that there is an under-reaction in the physiological sense. The reactions are there, but the defenses are such that the patient acts "as if" both the stimuli and his reactions were not present. This phenomenon was described by L. Wolberg in one of his lectures at the Postgraduate Center for Mental Health in New York City, citing the case of a business man who, in the session, verbalized in tortured language and facial expression his experiences with his girl friend, but who, when he talked of his business, seemed calm. However, he did not show significant electrical changes in the skin as measured by the G.S.R. apparatus when talking about his girl friend, but as he spoke calmly of the business, the indicator scored the upper limits of response even though he did not betray his emotional turmoil through his behavior or speech.)

(3) "Performance deficits" improve when tasks are simple, when backgrounds are under-arousing, and stimuli are unambiguous. (In life, many schizophrenics perform in highly complicated ways: they write plays; they do highly skilled tasks in acting and remembering long parts; they obtain Ph.D.'s in universities and they do all of the complicated problems in mathematics and physics that non-schizophrenics do. It is true, however, that they must isolate themselves, and they find functioning difficult. Furthermore, by denial and withdrawal and hysterical mechanisms, they minimize the stimuli around them.)

(4) There is a slower response-time to visual and auditory stimuli, regardless of the complexity of the response called for, although a normal response-time to tactually presented stimuli is found. (This interesting finding might easily fit the concept that the schizophrenic has been trained by parents from early childhood to scan visual and auditory stimuli and to respond through selective inattention, *denial, undoing, negation, splitting, dissociating,* and other

hysterical and obsessive-complusive defenses. It is probable that non-verbal and non-visual stimuli and cues are less anxiety or guilt provoking, that is, *are less revealing* than the visual and auditory. It is probable here that parents have used these methods in communication to conceal their aims. It is evident that the individual decides which stimuli will receive attention and which have to be defended against. There is always a response to stimuli, but some responses apparently are handled by *displacements* of one kind or another, which are, in essence, defenses. Since the patients are able to sort out cues and determine which shall receive overt response and which shall not, one realizes that the *ego functions of patients are intact* and operative. Sullivan's concept of "selective inattention" would fit this finding and, of course, hysterical maneuvers and defenses of denial and repression are needed to sustain these responses. Freud's observation that delusional patients understand reality and that a delusion can be corrected in a dream (page 147) is a kind of proof that the individual's reality testing is always present.)

(5) There is an altered sensitivity of the vestibular mechanism, an important organ in integrating various sensory inputs and proprioceptive responses. (This finding might also follow from the fact that the schizophrenic has been trained to act selectively to stimuli, and that certain of his responses must be concealed or inhibited. The process of concealment necessitates the use of substitutive behavior such as displacement, and the use of opposite trains of thought to counteract the impulses being avoided as well as other disguises. The act of perception, it is said, can be defined as the "transferring of physical stimulation into psychological information." The mechanism can be broken down into the component phases of *reception, registration, processing* and *feedback*. Holt (1967) suggests that these processes are operative in defense. There is no doubt but that the schizophrenic patient, along with all others, has no problem so far as the processes of perception are concerned. The method in which information is handled depends upon previous conditionings.)

Freud's paper on "Formulations Regarding the Two Principles in Mental Functioning" (1911) reminds us that psychotics, like neurotics and "normals," have perceptions of reality. They have *accurate memories of events,* and their *attending* or *alerting mechanisms* are operative. Also present is *the act of coding or judging what a given piece of reality means.* Freud spoke of the place of thought and the role of past experience before the selection of a type of action or behavior takes place. But in symptom behavior, or in acting out, the reaction was said to be impulsive or automatic. This he called instinctive behavior, but we now believe that symptoms and acting out are learned products of long periods of conditioning in the family; they are forms of *displacement behavior.* The fact that the patient elaborates defenses means that he is able to understand reality and to know what to defend against. Reality concepts are necessary in the ordinary acts of life, such as eating, walking, reading, writing, adding, subtracting, making plans, and so forth. Without some reality testing capacity, our patients would not be able to participate in the process of psychotherapy, to report dreams or to tell of experiences. With Fairbairn we change the meaning of the id so that it is a denied or repressed part of the ego.

Reminiscent of some of the observations of Kraepelin and Bleuler are data from the "Special Report on Schizophrenia" issued by the U. S. Department of Health, Education and Welfare, April 1970. In this, it is said that the schizophrenic shows: (1) an inability to use language logically and effectively; (2) disturbed patterns of learning and performance; (3) decreased motivation or apathy in many situations; (4) a distorted sensory acuity and perception; (5) disturbed conceptual processes; (6) alterations in body chemistry and brain wave patterns; (7) extraordinary reactions to ordinary situations, which put him under almost continuous emotional stress; (8) a deficiency in the ability to perceive the passage of time; (9) indulgence in faulty thinking; (10) a defect in the ability to "get ready" to respond; (11) an inability to vary response as the task demands; (12) *more arousal* than normal by stimulation, but *less responsiveness*. Many investigators in this report said that most, if not all, of these symptoms are related to the idea that *certain situations have special meaning for the schizophrenic and that, therefore, the above twelve kinds of reactions are not universal for all situations.* In this one can agree and refer again to Sullivan's selective inattention concept and Breuer's and Freud's discussions of the mechanisms of the hysterias.

Unlike Bleuler and earlier observers, this report emphasizes that the *meaning* of certain situations is responsible for a prolonged stimulation (both physical and mental) at certain times, which prevents the individual from attending to tasks in the ordinary way. Thus, autonomic and attentional phenomena seem to be related to the presence of the disturbing symptoms rather than due to some genetic or primary defect. The H.E.W. report emphasizes that many of the phenomena reported above can be cleared up by use of certain tranquilizing drugs.

The fact that schizophrenics can accomplish certain tasks at certain times and not at others becomes evident when working with patients. One of my patients, Gertrude Belen, said in a session that try as she would, she could not follow a pattern in making a dress. Her friend had finally given up explaining to her that the measurements must be exact and that a tape measure had to be used. She said that the problem was basically her inability to do arithmetic. She could not compute the addition. I told her that sometimes I feel as though I cannot add and that I have met many people who made mistakes in addition. I referred to an incident in a store where I had recently purchased a particular kind of pocket book and had made a mistake in the price. I thought that the ticket indicated $5.00 when, in fact, it was $25.00. She laughed and responded that $20.00 didn't mean anything to me because "you are rich and don't worry about money." Then she said: "I could have saved you $11.75 for I know where to get that kind of pocket-book on Delancy Street for $13.25. You know I'm a better shopper than you are." I said then, realizing that she had computed sums in her head, that the other day I had bought seven items, six of which were $10.50 each, and the other $1.25, and I had given the man $70.00 but he gave me back $6.75. She flashed back that I could give her the extra dollar of change if I wanted to since she needed the money much more than I. These lightning calculations were made by a person who insisted that she could not add!

Most authorities now agree that it is the *meaning* to the individual of the particular stimulus, at the particular time, that makes the difference in performance. In Gertrude Belen's case, it is evident that the meaning of the situation had a connection with a transference problem and that what was involved was the patient's use of a phantasy—the identification phantasy—to cope with anxiety. The obvious *role* required in the phantasy, and in the situation, was one of *inadequacy* (a kind of masochistic maneuver), while secretly she sought to "best" the other person (her sadistic side). She is "competitive in her mind" and she is also "orally-oriented." She likes to receive and does not hesitate to ask for things. She has great difficulty in performing, so that she herself gets little for herself. She operates on an economy of scarcity, both materially and emotionally, but she resents being in this position. Adler stressed that the goal of behavior or its *aim* was all important. The aim or the motive depended upon the meaning of the situation to the patient and, in essence, this related to the transference which we now consider is a phenomenon based on training and learning, the identification phenomenon. Gertrude persists in hanging on to her hostility, for it is associated with her feeling of being alive, a feeling of power.

Some of the findings reported by sleep investigators are of interest in the survey of literature on the schizophrenias. For example, certain investigators report that in acute psychosis, both REM and non-REM sleep are decreased; during the recovery phase, there is incomplete "rebound" or "makeup" of REM sleep. Chlorpromazine results in the reversion to a normal sleep pattern. Depressives apparently go to sleep more quickly than schizophrenics and have more intense REM activity, and a more variable total percentage of such activity. Chronic schizophrenics tend to have a "normal" pattern of sleep. Anxiety is reflected in the sleep pattern and in the pictorialization of the defenses organized and recorded in dreams to defend against anxiety. In sleep, dreaming reflects the kind of thinking that continues even in mere relaxation. Freud noted that in the construction of a dream or phantasy, perception and memory, both remote and immediate, are represented in pictorial form.[17]

Often the borderline patient responds to the dream as if it were a play, and this represents a more projected form of ego defense. One can, in fact, use the construction of the dream to gauge the degree of anxiety, and the nature of the defenses. Thus one may discover *the area of least anxiety* which should always be the initial point of interpretation in the analysis of borderlines. Of equal importance is a determination from dream content of what has been "split off," the areas of denial of reality that have been relegated to the unconscious. As has been mentioned before, the "splitting mechanism" is, we believe, a dissociative phenomenon and it accounts for the kind of material Freud assigned to the unconscious. Freud realized that the child may have an awareness of reality at the same time that he represses his knowledge of it, when he said (1931): "We find aggressive oral and sadistic wishes in a form forced on them by early repression, i.e., in the dread of being killed by the mother—*a dread which on its side justifies the death wish against her, if this enters consciousness. It is impossible to say how often this dread of the mother draws countenance from an unconscious hostility on her part which the child divines.*" (My italics.)

It is interesting to note that in this passage Freud comes close to saying that the aggression of the parents towards the child is the stimulus for a counter-aggression on the part of the child, and, we must add, constitutes the necessity for his defensive reactions. We would not exclude the father in this process, however, even at the early phases of development.

A paper by Epstein and Coleman published in Psychosomatic Medicine, the Journal of the American Psychosomatic Society (March-April, 1970), entitled "Drive Theories of Schizophrenia," provides commentary on some of the modern neurophysiological, "drive" or "arousal" theories of schizophrenia. All assume that the basic defect in schizophrenia consists of a low threshold for organization under increasing stimulus input. *Drive* as used in this paper refers to the "energetic aspects of behavior independent of directional tendencies." This is not a directed or motivated behavior, such as in the psychoanalytic conception where the term refers to "instinctive impulses." These modern theorists agree that "organisms must deal with the quantitative aspects of the total amount of effective stimulation to which they are exposed," and that the mechanisms for doing so have widespread implications for complex functioning. The paper reports the behavior theorists' attempts to explain the same kind of data that psychoanalysts interpret on a "structural psychological level." The dynamics of perception, memory and thought, the effects of various types of sensory stimulation, and the defenses (the inhibitions) that the organism uses are topics of exploration. Much of this work is predicated on original experiments done by Pavlov, and the report refers to Pavlov's contention that there are two fundamental processes which account for all behavior: *excitation* and *inhibition*. Epstein and Coleman believe that Pavlov's ideas about the three basic forms of inhibition (*internal, external,* and *transmarginal*), and the concept of *paradoxical phases,* explain some of the ways in which symptoms occur. "Pavlov noted that while, on some occasions, excessive arousal produces paradoxical responses and disorganization, on others, it accomplishes the opposite, and produces fixation—given a highly focused source of excitation and a strong, momentary response tendency, fixation should be favored because of negative induction." These authors comment that Pavlov had the view "that given a source of strong focalized excitation, negative induction encapsulates the excitation, thereby protecting the cortex from widespread over-excitation."

One may speculate as to whether such neurophysiological manifestations are not similar to what we call hysterical or dissociative mechanisms. As a defensive reaction, part of the cortical impressions become isolated from the rest, and associations and response tendencies governed by this reaction are removed from the influence of that part of the cortex. Whether this interpretation is valid or not, it is certain the resulting inhibitions are important in borderline and schizophrenic reactions, and that dissociating mechanisms are common.[18] Perhaps the explanations of Pavlov tell what happens on the neurophysiological level when hysterical (dissociative and displacement behavior) phenomena take place. "Excessive stimulation" would mean some kind of trauma—some repetitive event causing over-stimulation and anxiety, as Breuer originally pointed out.

Evidence is usually cited by behaviorists that part of the reason schizophrenias are difficult to treat is that they have unstable associating responses and do poorly on tasks with words that have more than one meaning; they have trouble with proverbs that encourage competing responses. We have seen that such reactions have a relation to feelings about authority as displaced from the parents to others. Some patients will refuse to respond if the answer is needed immediately and there is conflict. This is an aspect of the negativism or the passive-aggressive personality. On the other hand, we know that schizophrenics, who are otherwise resistive, can be highly suggestible and often make good hypnotic subjects. They often cannot wait to please certain authorities, particularly if the latter are openly hostile aggressive authorities who relish attack and with whom the patient is identified in a positive way.

It has been said that the schizophrenics who have an overlay of obsessive mechanisms are more prone to be "dropouts," or more likely to refuse to respond due to oppositional and other tendencies, than those who have more pronounced paranoid mechanisms. The paranoids become the better responders if their ideas are not too firmly fixed in delusion and if they can use knowledge as the organizing vehicle for their revenge. In this reference, we have referred to the work of Levinson with college dropouts (page 61). Perhaps, as Freud and Stekel once remarked, the obsessive has more guilt concerning his revenge feelings than does the paranoid. The guilt in the paranoid is probably more egosyntonic, if one can use such a term. The *competition* which schizophrenics are able to endure is stimulating so long as it is connected with the acting out of the sado-masochistic phantasy (knowledge is used as a way of demeaning or of controlling others). But when the guilt over rage and revenge is too intense, the result is undoing and the "dropout" syndrome. The behaviorists say that the way in which *attention* is handled by the schizophrenic is of a *selective nature*, an observation which, we have pointed out before, was made a long time ago by Sullivan and implied by Freud in his early concept of "motives," and phobic and counter-phobic manifestations. The schizophrenic screens out certain responses or inhibits them. We know that both neurotic and psychotic individuals respond to some stimuli in the same way as do "normals." But neurotics and psychotics inhibit many responses or conceal and distort them. Actually *displacement* is probably the proper word to describe what happens in these situations, for there is in fact a response on some level to all stimuli.

Sechehaye (1947) and Axima and Witthauer (1956) take the position that a symbolic mother-child relationship must be lived through with the therapist, the therapist deliberately taking the role of the mother. A similar technique has been tried and suggested by many others. Sechehaye recommended "explaining," "reassuring," "bodily contact," "taking the side of the ego against unconscious self-punishment," and "giving in symbolic form," things the mother had denied the patient as a child, such as apples (breast). Axima and Witthauer gave the patients materials which were symbolic of frustrated basic needs at oral and anal levels—"milk," "brown clay," "baby bottles," "mud." The idea of acting towards adults as if they were frustrated infants is a questionable practice although the concept of working with clay, paints, poetry, drama and so forth, is a useful part of a rehabilitation program for the more disturbed patient, enabling him to express his feelings and his creativity. Fleischl and Waxenberg (1964) write of such a program.

Burnham (1969) has recently co-authored a book with Gladstone and Gibson called "Schizophrenia and the Need-Fear Dilemma." What I called sadomasochism in my early paper (1952) these authors refer to as the *need-fear dilemma*. Obviously they are talking of conflict. They note that the schizophrenic has an inordinate need for what they call a "supporting structure," that is, a source outside of himself to provide him with the regulation and organization that he is unable to provide for himself. Another way of thinking of this maneuver is to call it a paranoid defense or a *projective identification*. It is a passive and masochistic mode of behavior with sadism as its goal. One of the patients said that it was as if he were a ship at sea without navigational equipment and he needed direction by radio. In my 1952 paper, I noted a similar statement from one of my patients who said: "When I am with you, I am you; and when I am away from you, I must take part of you with me, otherwise I am nothing." At that time, I looked at this phenomenon as an aspect of defective development, as a consequence of a weak ego, as the need to cling and be dependent. But as I began to study such mechanisms I realized that the patient's ego is strong, not weak, that it is hostile and driving, that passivity is in fact a form of sadism, not weakness. We have always looked at this kind of phenomenon as indicating that the patient is incapable of acting for himself due to developmental defect and a weak ego. A better and more accurate view is in terms of sado-masochism and the insistence on a sado-masochistic position. In libido theory terms this has been called oral aggression, or an inordinate demand for the attention of the other person, or the need for "narcissistic supplies" or a passive-aggressive personality. Hostility and controlling mechanisms are operative.

Burnham, Gladstone and Gibson say that they found three types of reaction to the need-fear dilemma: object-clinging, object avoidance, and object redefinition. These reactions never appear in pure form. These types have been described by psychoanalysts as the familiar *oral aggressive,* the *isolated* or the *phobic,* and the *paranoid,* this latter as the type that redefines the situation or remakes reality, as Freud put it, in delusion. All of these display a sado-masochistic way of life. Burnham, Gladstone and Gibson speak of "personality deficits" or "ego function deficits." Using the terminology of Jacobson, Kernberg, Erikson, and Bellak, they say that disordered object relations in infancy and childhood interfered with the normal developmental processes of differentiation and integration to the extent that the patients were predisposed to schizophrenic disorganization. They stress that the patients have no autonomy. There is another way of thinking of this mechanism and that is that patients *deny* their autonomy and, out of rage, force the other to do for them what they should do for themselves. The original rage was towards the parents; the perpetuation of it is in revenge. What looks like the inability to function without guidance from the other is actually based on a revenge motif, or sadism. Symbiosis, meaning a dependency such as the infant has on the parents, is quite a different matter from sadism. The adult acts in a "symbiotic" way and seduces the other to think that he is weak and "undifferentiated" because he wishes to punish and revenge himself on others for what he was deprived of in his childhood; he will force others to maintain him. In addition he has great fear in acting in an autonomous way due to his guilt feelings.

The acts of denial, idealization and restructuring embrace the acts of "seeing" and "not seeing," evident in all patients, and of "remaking reality." In spite of Freud's attempts to give other metapsychological explanations of these phenomena in the schizophrenias as opposed to the hysterical and the obsessive syndromes, we must admit that all patients solve this conflict dilemma by the use of phantasy and the acting out of the phantasy, and in this act they play roles and use mechanisms such as identification, dissociation, displacement, projection, and other hysterical defenses. When my patient says "I am you" and "when I go away I must take part of you with me," she is verbalizing the identification process in projective form in transference. The statement means a variety of things: she is passive-dependent; she is masochistic; she is sadistic, for she will hold me responsible, not herself and her parents, for what happens to her; she will flatter me, seduce me, control me, throw me out of my analytic role and she will incorporate me in her sado-masochistic phantasy. She will give me burden of controlling her acting out. She will imitate me; and she will ridicule me and hate me, and appease me. She is also telling me that she has been a rejected child and that her parents are exceedingly hostile to her. I suspect she is verbalizing in this statement the whole concept of "loss of object" that Freud and Abraham pointed out to be an aspect of the dynamics of depression.

There is a great deal of speculation today as to the applicability of work with animals to the human condition. The implications in terms of psychopathology cannot be properly evaluated at this time. Harlow, for example, has done major studies with monkeys, showing the effects of social deprivation. Inhibition of functioning appears to be the result of certain attitudes of parents or certain conditions in the environment; the attitude of parents affects both the social and the psychological life, including the sexual responses of the individual. He has shown, to quote Gadpaille (1972), "that inadequate mothering and lack of peer-group social contact and sex play during childhood produced subsequent adults who lacked totally the capacity for adult sex behavior, successful copulation and conceptive function. What surprised behavioral scientists most was the clear evidence that peer-group social and sexual play was more important than mothering; and that lack of mothering could be overcome by peer experience but lack of peer experience left ineradicable incapacities." This finding with monkeys may help us to understand why it is so difficult for the schizophrenic person to break out of his isolation, an isolation generally fostered by parents who have prevented adequate peer-group contact. The paranoid parent makes the child suspicious and mistrustful of all people, and he prevents the child from having a meaningful contact with others; hostility is his main affect in relationships (A. Wolberg, 1952). Very often the mental pathology of the parent is concealed from persons outside of the family by a casual social façade. An interviewer taking a case history from a parent of a schizophrenic or borderline child may report little or no abnormality in the mental states and behavior of the parent. It is essential to realize that the role the parent plays with a child is different from that with an interviewer. Hostility and perverse tendencies may come out solely within the emotional matrix of family life.

The American Medical Association pamphlet "Dynamics of Violence" (1971) contains several papers which make connections between the sadistic behavior of the parents and the sado-masochistic problems of the child. Three papers in particular are relevant to this theme: "Homicide in Adolescents: Fantasy and Deed" by Kalogerakis; "Individual Violence, Prevention in the Violence Threatening Patient" by Menninger and Modlin; and "The Assassin and the Assassinated as 'Non-patient Subjects of Psychiatric Investigation'" by Rothstein.

Five factors are present according to Menninger and Modlin in the background in these cases—all of which, it seems to me, can be tied to the clinical finding of Szurek and Johnson who found that the acting out patterns of delinquents are related to the phantasies of the parents. It follows from this thesis that the phantasies of the children are similar to the phantasies of the parents, and that interlocking sado-masochistic phantasies represent interlocking defensive interpersonal patterns in the family where the child is the instrument for acting-out the parent's sadistic impulses. This does not mean, of course, that the parents are not themselves sadistic—quite the contrary—they definitely are; but their mode of defense, which is projective, is the stimulus for both maso-chistic and sadistic behavior in the child. It is evident that the sado-masochism is acted out in a variety of ways at home, and that cues are sent out by the patient to people outside of the home in the community who can be provoked to engage in sado-masochistic behavior so that the family pattern can be perpetuated. The dynamic is often operative in suicides, murders, delinquencies, in behavior prior to car accidents, and of course in acting out patterns in neuroses and psychoses.

The five factors as delineated by Menninger and Modlin in the background of "violence threatening patients" are: (1) severe emotional deprivation or overt rejection in childhood; (2) parental seduction; (3) exposure to brutality and ex-treme violence; (4) child fire-setting; (5) cruelty to animals or other children. In all of these patients, they also found that there were (1) fears or concern about losing control; (2) evidence that the person has been looking for help; (3) reports of suggestive actions, i.e., sadistic actions, or actions that might be conceived of as intending to carry out destructive actions; (4) episodes of "altered states of consciousness" (these, the authors say, have to be investigated to determine whether they are due to hysterical states, epileptiform states, neurological condi-tions or, perhaps to drug states, such as drunkeness from alcohol or from nar-cotics or other drugs); (5) previous suicidal or homicidal attempts or acts.

One finds a persistent theme in these papers, emphasized also in previous studies to the effect that the seducer and the seductee have mutual aims; that the victim of accidents is often accident prone and invites the assaults on his body.

Borderline patients do not commit extreme forms of violence, but, it is clear that they sometimes encourage their children to do so. They do have fears of being violent and they often have suicidal thoughts. They frequently have fears of doing harm to their own children or to the children of others.

At the 17th Annual Meeting of the Academy of Psychoanalysis in Dallas, Texas, April 28-30th, 1972, the theme of the conference was "Psychoanalysis of Psychoses: Schizophrenic and Affective." Of particular interest were papers by H. Kelman (1972) and D. Shainberg (1972). Kelman's paper, "Chronic Analysts and Chronic Patients: The Therapist's Person as Instrument," stressed the fact that the psychoanalyst would not have such intense counter-transference reac-tions towards the schizophrenic patient if he accepted the patient as a person rather than a "non-person," i.e., a fragmented, half-developed, lower order of human being. The analyst bent on establishing a relationship with his patient, should understand the struggle the patient goes through in psychodynamic terms rather than in developmental terms, which consider the adult a composite of infantile mechanisms. This can be misleading and confusing. Shainberg's paper, "The Dilemma and the Challenge of being Schizophrenic," discussed the patient's struggle to "become someone." Shainberg contended that the family milieu is responsible for the schizophrenic reaction and that the patient has been made to feel that he is "not a real person," a "nothing" so to speak. His struggle is to "become somebody" or to accept himself as an entity. The patient fights against being obliterated as a person. My own theoretical postulation is that the "non-person" described by Shainberg is, in fact, the surviving feeling the patient had as a child when he was used as "projective object in the interests of the parent's defense." The patient was not accepted for himself by the parent, but was used as a projection of the hated and denied identification of the parent with his own parent. Not enough emphasis is put on the guilt the patient feels in wanting to be "his own man" and to express his own individuality, nor is cognisance given stress as Freud gave it, to the fact that the patient's defenses are a way of resolving the problem. In the case of the schizophrenic the defense is the identification: "I am nothing; I am a non-human thing," or the reaction formation: "I am the greatest person in the world"; or "I am one of the most important persons in the world"; or, "the world will hear from me." The delusion, although based on certain factual premises, is never-the-less a phantasy defense; it is an obsessional way of expressing aggression rather than resolving the aggression. Wolfson (1972) has written a case study called "The Struggle for Autonomy in Hank, a Borderline Patient" which graphically describes the kind of conflict the patient who is motivated for treatment goes through when he strives for self-expression, i.e., when he struggles to "become" and to accept himself as a person.

Boyer and Giovacchini, in their book, "Psychoanalytic Treatment of Schizophrenic and Characterological Disorders" (1967), have summarized certain ideas relating to treatment that have accrued over the years, culled from various writings. While these authors apparently see no need to modify orthodox psychoanalytic technique in the treatment of these disorders (a principle one can hardly support), they do a great service in outlining some statements that have relevance in the treatment of borderline conditions, as well as schizophrenia. They point out that:

(1) schizophrenia is a meaningful system of defense;
(2) the schizophrenic projects hostility onto the therapist;
(3) the schizophrenic stimulates hostility in the therapist;
(4) the schizophrenic feels that he or his physician, or both, are in danger of magical destruction[19];
(5) one should establish a working relationship with the schizophrenic by any practical means, that is, by unorthodox methods, if necessary—simply talking casually, just "getting acquainted," discussing topics of the day;

(6) the schizophrenic reenacts events of his childhood even in the session—these are aspects of his "acting out" patterns and demonstrate his "split transferences";

(7) like the rejected child he conforms to parents chiefly through fear of estrangement from them—he senses his need for them in order to survive;

(8) all psychotic behavior can be called transference behavior;

(9) often the therapist disparages the activities of the patient unwittingly rather than investigating the dynamics and genetics of the problem—this happens because the patient so often goes against the moral grain of the therapist;

(10) treatment with schizophrenics can be sustained even if the "positive transference" is not operative—the therapist can learn to work temporarily with a negative transference;

(11) why (?) questions arouse guilt in the schizophrenic and are felt as accusatory;

(12) Klein's term *projective identification* can be used to describe the *introjective* and *projective* processes that occur as a consequence of the patient's relations with his parents and his identification with them;

(13) free association is not advisable in the beginning of treatment with schizophrenics while a meaningful relationship is being established;

(14) it is mandatory to give positive recognition to the patient's forward moves[20];

(15) one should work first with the "peripheral field," the relationships with relatively innocuous persons;

(16) reassurance makes the patient feel that the therapist considers the patient helpless—this appeals to the "rejected" side of the patient and promotes regression, or, in other words, fosters the neurotic patterns;

(17) one must respect the integrity of the patient and this attitude should be conveyed in verbal terms to him;

(18) the therapist should address himself to the patient's adult side, that is, to the healthy side of the ego;

(19) one should try not to fear the patient's aggression, for the patient will sense this and the result will be a reinforcement of the patient's feelings that there is a magical quality about his aggression; when the therapist does, in fact, fear the aggression, this may be openly stated, but it should be explained that the therapist's fear is not so great that analytic work has to be discontinued;

(20) treatment involves modifying, or better, replacing cold, unloving, and archaic ego and superego "introjects" with new, warm, loving and reasonable introjects;

(21) the garbled, symbolic, transferential communication of the patient must be given up for more rational, normal, clear communication;

(22) the aims of treatment are to restore a reasonable ego and superego; "ego introjects cannot be altered efficiently, unless simultaneous changes take place in the superego introjects, in the direction of reducing the archaic, sadistic nature of the psychical structure;

(23) in the beginning one should make interpretations about *defense* rather than *content*, i.e., avoid the "fixation" type of interpretations;

(24) one should interpret first depressive material rather than paranoid material (this is in line with Eisler's parameters and with Kleinian methodology);

(25) steady but "gentle confrontations with distortions, contradictions and other abandonments of reality," should be tried relating these to defenses;

(26) direct superego support should not be given;

(27) silences must be interrupted—the therapist should talk if the patient hesitates, using nods, grunts, encouragement for the patient to talk more, or about anything in particular to break the silence;

(28) interpretations of content that emphasize forbidden or frightening "wishes" should not be given in the beginning (i.e., while the patient is psychotic), although to make such interpretations once in a while may be expeditious (in general, however, these interpretations arouse guilt, whereas interpretations concerning defenses give the patient the sense that the therapist, whom he perceives to a large degree as a superego figure, appreciates how much he struggles against his impulses);

(29) firm, consistent and realistic limit-setting must at times be used in the treatment of schizophrenia;

(30) the destructiveness of the schizophrenic patient must be successfully encountered in treatment;

(31) the patient's developing identification with the analyst increases his fears of his hostile impulses and this must be recognized and handled;

(32) the schizophrenic's ego has been prevented from acting in its own best interest in many ways so that if the therapist does not strive for his own success in the treatment, he will not help the patient; however, the patient's destructiveness works against the therapist's success so this problem has to be faced. Where the patient "acts out" against the therapist and others, as well as against himself outside the therapeutic hours, thus, perpetuating his problem, the therapist must make it plain that he cannot go on working efficiently if the misbehavior, that is, the destructive "acting out," continues indefinitely—sooner or later, the therapist will have to withdraw from the work if the "acting out" persists. The patient, confronted with this fact, can then make a choice: he possesses the power over his fate. This confrontation will have to be done intuitively and delicately and early in the treatment. The "hostile introjects" which thus threaten treatment have been challenged; later, these can be analyzed. This position is not a threat of abandonment by a substitute parental figure whom the patient is trying to learn to trust, but a realistic statement that treatment cannot proceed under the circumstances; a "partnership" with the "healthy aspect of the patient's ego" must exist; the therapist can help the patient become well only insofar as the patient has a wish to become well and can cooperate with the therapist—(this latter was one of Freud's main treatment tenets for all patients);

(33) the patient behaves towards the analyst as the "parental introject," i.e., the non-listening, inattentive, demeaning, disregarding person (The therapist has to fight for his existence in this situation; sometimes he gets angry at the patient's need to throw him out of his therapeutic role. If he expresses anger, he should do so without guilt. The patient on his part should not have to feel guilty about his anger towards the parent who was cold and non-listening);

(34) insofar as the ego gains structure from an interpretation, this process constitutes a positive feedback, and the ego's capacity to form an analytic introject is increased. (The introject leads to further integration which enables the ego to introject more effectively and expansively and respond to further interpretations. The analyst's main interest is to foster the patient's autonomy, and it is this aspect of the analyst that the patient really incorporates);

(35) the patient's need to see everyone, including the therapist, as a rejecting figure, is a defense against underlying painful feelings becoming

conscious if, in his hostile world, he discovers the therapist as being truly unhostile. (The realization of the contrast between the therapist and the patient's parents threatens the patient with consciousness of overwhelming poignancy and rage regarding his past; the schizophrenic defends against this painful awareness);

(36) Eissler's parameters in treatment, as agreed upon by Jones, are relevant in the treatment of schizophrenia: (a) reduction of traumatic reactions to past and present situations which produce or have produced excessive excitations can best be done by *giving preference to the depressive aspect of the case at first*—this means *paying attention to "pathogenic introjects;"* (b) *then turning attention to projective manifestations,* which will have been rendered more accessible by the preliminary work on pathogenic introjections, *one can reduce the introjective and projective systems;* when this is accomplished, the regressive products will diminish without direct analysis.

Boyer and Giovacchini espouse the "orthodox" classical model and theory, to wit, that the patient learns an adequate way of life through identification with the analyst, i.e., through "analytic introjects," and that this identification must be fostered if the patient is to gain an understanding of reality. Freud originally had this idea, but he also said that identification must be worked through and eliminated if the patient is to get well. But in this seeming paradox he made the statement, as was his wont with many other kinds of concepts, that there were two or more kinds of identification—normal and abnormal. The normal kind was, of course, with the analyst, who represented the all-wise, all-good, all-reality-oriented person.

Boyer and Giovacchini (1968) appear to believe that regular psychoanalysis, without great modification, is successful with schizophrenics. They refer to Garma (1931), who also held this view.

The sins of the parents are unfortunately too often reinforced by stimuli from the environment. The conditionings which are brought about in the culture by the sanctioned patterns of fear, rage, and aggression cannot be overestimated. On the radio and television, and in the movies, children and adults are subject to rage, violence, war, murder, and criminality, almost constantly. These "permitted" reactions are encouraged, but only under certain circumstances. The inconsistencies of the culture bear untold havoc on family, social and even international relations: for example, at times murder is not only permitted but demanded; at other times it is punished. The distinctions are understood but not rational, as the murderer Manson so aptly pointed out in his defense. The defensive system of the schizophrenic and perhaps some borderline cases may tend toward violence in the face of existing contradictions sustained by the culture.

In summary, we may well bear in mind, in our attempt to understand borderlines, the lessons taught us in our work with schizophrenics. But this can become a two-edged sword. Because borderline patients so frequently in their symptomatology resemble schizophrenics, many analysts still have a hopeless attitude toward treatment. Such professionals consider the schizophrenias incurable and they justify their pessimism by tagging the patient with such labels as "weak ego," "genetic defect," "ego unable to resist flooding with id material," etc. Their attitude, together with the fact that borderline patients tend to be hostile, makes treatment difficult. If the therapist evinces such denigrating convictions, and the patient possesses them as well, then treatment becomes doubly difficult. If, on the other hand, one were to think of borderline conditions, and even of schizophrenia, as systems of massive defensive maneuvers, recognizing that projection and delusion are major aspects of the most severe kind of defense, then therapeutically one will not be handicapped by the schizophrenic affiliation. Recognizing that in moments of intense stress the defensive balance may be tilted in the direction of perversion or psychosis, one may deal more appropriately with the underlying dynamics. The therapist will then not be handicapped by such notions as "infantile and uncorrectable ego." A different attitude will emerge toward the patient, encouraging the greatest potentialities of therapeutic benefit. To feel that one can deal with the "introject" or the "identification" (pathological defense) in either a projected or a direct transferential way and to have the technical know-how to determine when the transference in the interpersonal situation or in the projected form should be delineated is the essence of good therapeutic practice and adequate skill. In addition one must learn how to use dream interpretation and the material in the session as a means of outlining phantasies, so that the relation between character defense and intrapsychic mechanisms can be made. If one thinks of ego functions as being intact but the ego as burdened by the defensive introject and the anxiety of this burdensome sado-masochistic defense, then one has a different feeling for the patient than if one feels he is symbiotic and defective.

NOTES

[1] Freud's work can be divided into four epochs. The first was when he used the *seduction hypothesis,* studying the ego or the personality and *the dynamics of defense,* i.e., the dynamisms and energy systems which were meant to handle the ravages of traumas, resulting in the hysterias, the obsessional neuroses, the anxiety neuroses, and the paranoidal conditions with their attendant perversions. He came to the idea that accidental causes, and particularly the child's relations with parents, were of great importance. Some of his most important concepts were touched upon at this early time. His second period was ushered in by the introduction of the topological and libido theories with an attendant developmental system which purported that the instincts (libido and perverse impulses) sought objects. A lasting contribution was the concept of transference. After a long struggle, Freud gave up the seduction hypothesis and adopted the idea that resolution of the oedipus complex was the apex of the developmental system. The *accidental cause* receded in importance and the *constitutional factor* took precedence: the greater the constitutional factor, the more disturbed or the nearer to psychosis was the patient. Along with these ideas eventually came the introduction of *phylogenetic concepts* associated with repressed memory, regression, the backward flow of libido, fixation and defense against instincts which were perverse, un-

organized, fickle and polymorphous. The energy concept was a contribution at this point. In his third period, Freud put forth the *structural hypothesis* (an elaboration of the instinct theory), dividing the mind into psychic energy systems—the ego, the id, and the superego—associating these with the concept of two opposing instincts, Eros and Thanatos (life and death). Freud was attempting at this time to construct a model depicting conflict and in the *structural theory* he incorporated the *topological* (Cs, Pcs, Ucs), the *genetic* (origins of the ego including the phylogenetic), the *economic* (a stated quantity of libidinal energy that could cathect objects and decathect them), and the *dynamic* (the defensive systems against reality and against the instincts). In his fourth and last period, Freud returned to ego concepts and the dynamics of defense. An expansion of his ideas about ego psychology were expounded with special reference to anxiety and the subsequent defenses against both "exogenous" and "endogeneous" threats.

2 In 1896, in the essay, "Further Remarks on the Defense Neuropsychoses," the word *projection* was used by Freud and applied to a case of paranoia.

3 In his studies of the hysterias, Freud had been concerned with the dissociation of ideas and one of the purposes of his and Breuer's early treatment method was to bring ideas back into their appropriate associative focus. The dissociation was connected with the defense of repression, which Freud said was a form of flight from reality and a condemnation of some part of reality (Freud, 1915). We know that in the borderline, as in the schizophrenias, there are areas of repression that reach the depth of denial. But denial is present in the neuroses and the character disorders as well. The differentiative characteristic between neurosis and psychosis seemed to Freud to be the delusion, or the remaking of reality which was associated with an extensive personality change.

4 The splitting process and the disturbances in associations were emphasized by Freud, particularly in his concepts of dissociation, displacement, repression, denial and negation. In 1938, in the unfinished essay published posthumously, "The Splitting of the Ego in the Defensive Process," Freud apparently was still trying to explain the phenomenon, this time in terms of the structural hypothesis, i.e., the energy balance as applied to the id, the ego and the superego.

5 Idealization could occur in the sphere of "object libido" or "ego libido," terms elaborated in Freud's essay on Narcissism (1914). These concepts, as is well known, were connected with the idea of withdrawal from objects and attachment to objects. There was a stated quantity of libidinal energy, and the individaul could withdraw his libido from objects or attach his libido to objects. When he withdrew, the libido went back into the self from whence it originally came; the libidinal cathexis shifted from an external object to the self. In this maneuver, sadism was turned into masochism; thus withdrawal was associated with anger, rage and revenge, and fear of assertiveness, which was "turned around upon the self." In object love, said Freud, idealization was manifest in "sexual overestimation of the object"; this was the origin of the feeling of "being in love." By this standard, love would always be a defensive maneuver. For instance, Freud, in writing of the resolution of the oedipal complex, said that the anxiety was relieved as a consequence of hate being turned into love in a reaction formation. Idealization, as it concerned ego-libido, involved the process of setting up the ego-ideal, and later the superego. Idealization was a way that the individual dealt with "infantile imagoes," i.e., representations in the mind of parental figures. A number of puzzling questions present themselves: Is it that the individual's perception is actually inaccurate, or is this a defense? Is idealization based on an ego defect or is it a defense? Is the superego as it relates to idealization merely a form of ego defense? Is idealization an aspect of identification?

6 Freud was of the opinion that the *id* contained phylogenetic thought and that this was an aspect of phantasy. Distortion came to have two meanings: one, connected with

phantasy in the sense of denial of reality and the making over of reality; and, two, distortion of reality associated with the idea that when the individual could not understand or perceive reality, this was due either to a developmental defect or a constitutional factor. An extraordinary amount of phylogenetic thought was capable of breaking through the defenses to "fill in the gap." The usual concept of paleologic thinking had the connotation of antiquity and phylogenetic meaning. It was this idea upon which Freud and Jung based their concept of the archetypes. The id was a constellation of archetypes. *Id* conceived of in Freud's terms, however, usually referred to sexual ideas.

It is interesting that in the midst of his more fanciful writings, "Totem and Tabu," for example, Freud provided an excellent basis for a theory of schizophrenic thought in the essay on the "Unconscious" (1915). Having introduced some phylogenetic concepts in this essay, he postulated the economic concept of *anti-cathexis, cathexis,* and *hypercathexis* of ideas in his discussion of repression (censorship and rejection of certain thoughts and feelings). He now spoke of the *hypercathexis of words and ideas* which he said had to do with the *secondary process* (related to the ego) a higher form of ideation than thought associated with the id and the pleasure principle. Linking up thoughts and ideas with verbal and active behavior is one of the functions of the process of hypercathexis, he said, and this is a means through which ideas have the potentiality for becoming both conscious and unconscious. Words, of course, were learned symbolizations of objects and would be associated with the ego. According to Freud's ideas, however, all thought originates in the unconscious (one of his more nebulous concepts). Freud asks us to consider the idea that in schizophrenia words can become subject to the same process as that which makes dream images out of dream thoughts; i.e., they undergo condensation, displacement, transfering their cathexis to one other—"thing presentation" Freud calls this. And a bodily sensation can be converted into "organ speech," which in turn may be a manifestation of the *hypochondria* which is usually connected in the narcissistic neurosis with a delusion. According to Freud's theory of development a different kind of reaction was involved here than in the conversion dynamism prevalent in hysteria. Freud cites cases and then says that one finds many other indications of this type of reaction in the works of Bleuler and Jung. (The examples show us that the delusion is none other than the *identification phantasy* presented in a variety of disguised ways. Thus delusion is not only a defense, but is a specific kind of defense, and as in the dream, often contains the essence of the sado-masochistic relationship that existed between parent and child.) In psychological terms, Freud explains that a *substitute idea* which is connected (remotely) by association with a rejected idea is cathected, but it escapes repression due to its distance from the original idea. The substitute or displacement is thus a "return of the repressed" or a symptom.

[7] LaForgue was using many of Freud's concepts, particularly that the schizophrenic takes his own ego as object in the process of introversion and regression and withdrawal from objects. This concept was a factor in Klein's idea of projective-identification. In 1912, Freud spoke of the feelings of *degradation in erotic life,* attributing the dynamics of impotency in men and the desire to degrade women (women are of no value) to an unresolved oedipal problem, and to incest wishes. The guilt and worthlessness felt by the patient and stressed by LaForgue was in a sense similar to Freud's idea of degradation.

In 1922, when Freud wrote the paper entitled, "Certain Neurotic Mechanisms in Jealousy: Paranoia and Homosexuality," he referred to three kinds of jealousy: one, normal or competitive; two, projected, and three, delusional. He began to elaborate on a more dynamic picture of the interactions between neurotically related people, and there was a hint that at least one person in the relationship had an investment in the patient's illness. A number of observers have concluded that it is just this investment or motivation that urges the parent on to use the child as a projective object or as a "scapegoat" (Eissler, 1949; Ackerman, 1958). Employing the child as a projective instrument or an object of displacement is a safety-valve for the expression of the parents' aggression. He uses the child to release his aggression accumulated during the course of his everyday interpersonal relations. The child not only becomes a substitute for the parent's parents, but is also a replacement for the "boss" or any other current authority. In the 1922 paper, Freud discussed the interlocking neurotic relationship of a husband and wife. The husband became jealous when he saw his wife flirting with another man at a social gathering and was unduly disturbed when she inadvertently appeared to brush against the man's shoulder. This kind of verbal as well as non-verbal behavior is a good example of the type of interlocking neurotic interactions that so commonly occur among borderline cases. Each uses the other as a projective object and each identifies with the neurotic roles that the other plays. Thus each person is denying his own role. There are paranoid elements in this maneuver which we may classify as *projective-identification*. It is this meaning that is used conceptually in this book and that underlines the rationale of the suggested projective therapeutic techniques. We must not forget that the wife does have phantasies of another man and in some instances does act out.

8 Throughout Freud's writings, as has already been indicated, we find references to phenomena characteristic of borderline symptomatology. With an extraordinary perceptiveness, Freud attempted valiantly to distinguish the dynamics of schizophrenics as differentiated from neuroses, and to discriminate among the neurotic syndromes. He was handicapped in this task by the models he erected to explain the involved psychopathological complexities. For example, at one point when he was using the seduction theory, he said that obsessional neurosis was the result of guilt over enjoying seduction, while hysteria came about as a reaction of disgust. He explained perverse tendencies, employing the libido hypothesis, as polymorphous perverse instinctual manifestations. In his voluminous works it is apparent that Freud was conscious of the role of parents in schizophrenic and borderline disorders, but he tended to deemphasize this. He elaborated on the oedipal problem, for example, but then resorted to phylogenetic reasoning to explain it.

There is a tendency at present to reinterpret some of Freud's concepts in terms of ego psychology and this may lead to a more hopeful attitude toward treatment. For instance, Freud commented on guilt and the primitiveness of the superego. Its chief function, he said, is criticism (perhaps punishment would be a better word), which creates in the ego an unconscious sense of guilt. The implication was, however, that the child was innately bad, so that it was against the innate id impulses that the values of the parents were pitted. At the same time he admitted that the parents could be poor "superego models." A more modern look makes us say that some of the values of the parents are "bad," and that they wish to maintain these values and have the child identify with them, punishing the child when he challenges these. Freud said that it is through an internalization of the values (introjection and identification) of the parents and later of the other agencies in society (such as the school in the person of the teacher, the church in the person of the priest, the society in relation to norms, laws and other regulatory measures) that cultural attainments are made and a working through or sublimation of the bad instincts is made for the good of all.

Freud believed that the superego is operationally independent of the conscious ego, and largely inaccessible to it even though initially it is an outgrowth or a modification of the ego itself. It rules the ego as a deposit left by earliest object-cathexes of the id. Thus, it represents an energetic reaction formation against early object choices of the id. The superego acts as a "categorical imperative," assuming a "compulsive character." In an attempt to explain the relations of "bad" values in the superego, Freud engaged in the practice of anthropomorphizing the id, ego and superego. He said that the superego was in touch with the id, and, since it is so close to it, it helped defend the individual against the id. Free communication was possible between the superego and the unconscious instinctual trends; the superego had many points of contact with the phylogenetic endowment of each individual, his archaic inheritance. It is possible that the reason Freud believed that the superego made contact with the id was that he sensed the "bad" or aggressive values of the parents and that, in order to defend parents, he assumed that they always stood for the "good." We realize that parents have both bad and good qualities, but in our own country, at least, they support a flawed social system and then complain of it, not accepting their own responsibility for it. Yet Freud, too, condemned society, saying that it supported neurosis and psychosis. We have the kind of society we want and we rationalize our motives. This point is made by Ramsey Clark (1970) in his book, "Crime in America." Crime reflects more than the plight of the few who commit it: "We are cruelly afflicted with crime because we have failed to care for ourselves and our character." One can paraphrase this sentence, using instead of the word *crime* the word *neurosis,* or *poverty,* or *neglect,* or *hunger,* or *war,* or *poor schools,* or any of the other words that signify our failings in society. In the same way we may substitute the word *aggression.* Frustration leads to aggression and is usually the instigation to aggression. Aggression is most often expressed within the family, and this extends even to the most violent forms of aggression.

9 As the ego functions are named and defined in Bellak's study, some appear to overlap in meaning. Bellak says that his ego function list is based, in part, on items suggested by Beres and Hartmann. One gleans these latter have based their ideas on Freud's statements concerning the characteristics of the *secondary process* and the ego. Bellak reports that lists of ego functions have been provided by Hartmann, Bellak, Rappaport, Beres, Arlow, Brenner, Rangell, Kanzer and others.

10 It is my contention that to speak of "ego weakness," or "ego dysfunction," or "ego defect" is to be confusing; we should instead talk of various forms of *ego organization.* Ego functions, however these may be defined, seem to be intact in all individuals. All persons perceive the reality situation; they employ defensive maneuvers; they employ thinking, feeling and behaving functions in a more or less integrated way. In my opinion, the most reasonable approach to the problem of understanding the psychiatric syndromes is to be found in the concepts of *conflict* and *defense.* What has been called "distortion" or "misperception" is not, in fact, based on an inability to perceive but on a defense which disguises what has been perceived. One must use all the ego functions in the process of defense. The ego (if the concept is used at all) should be thought of as a *mental organization, a system.* To think of it in terms of disorganization or dysfunction is to misunderstand the concept of organization and mental systems. Several authors have veered in the direction of the concept of organization in their use of such terms as "ego patterns," "ego structure," and "ego organization." Another type of concept, and one that is perhaps not so useful is "ego deviation," suggesting a norm; this latter idea seems inherent in the concept of ego function scores.

If one wishes to discard words and concepts like ego, superego and id, then one must find another way of conceptualizing the mental and behavioral aspects of defense. Erikson (1946, 1959) has made such an attempt, but his concepts, some therapists insist, deny the existence of instinctual patterns at the same time that he speaks in other words of what Freud meant by "id." Erikson's work, as Freud's, has led to speculation as to what the normal stages of development are. Erikson uses the terms *introjection, identification* and *identity* to describe three phases of ego development.

11 One will recognize that when Freud described the hysterias, the "not knowing," the "not seeing," he was, in fact, describing denial tendencies. Sullivan added to this the important idea of *selective inattention.* In the family, the child is taught to deny that he sees what his parents are doing and saying to promote the neurotic role. They themselves deny and they force the child to deny. Sullivan felt that, in schizophrenia, the parents' needs for security did not allow them to feel the child as a separate entity. "Separation" was a threat

to the parent, for it meant accepting one's identity apart from a controling parental figure. This attitude was carried over to the child. One can see that this situation could account for what has been called "symbiosis." But I contend that the phenomenon is based on psychological anxiety rather than on the sustaining of a biological function. This observation of Sullivan is in line with our present day thinking of the child as an *object of displacement* (a transferential object), a means through which parents maintain a neurotic or psychotic homeostasis. Sullivan thought that the child is felt as necessary for the parent's survival. The child, in turn, will accept this situation because of his own dependency needs. He will mould himself according to the wishes of the parent for the sake of security. Thus identification is similar to the "lesser of two evils" defense described by Wilhelm Reich. Sullivan said that all relationships between such parents and their children were transferential. The mother transfers to the child as if the child were her own parent; and the father does this too. Sullivan did not specifically call this an ego defense, but it is obvious that these "transferential relationships" are what we now call the "projective identifications," or the "use of the transferential object" (Wolberg, A., 1968). In the borderlines, character disorders and schizophrenias, this "object projection" or "transferential interpersonal relationship" is based on what has been called the "projective" and "introjective" dynamics of identification.

12 The revenge motif, as an aspect of the patient's sado-masochism, has been noted by several authors. All of these, with some modification, refer to the "frustration-aggression" aspect of the problem and to "separation anxiety." Some references here are Stärke (1921), Abraham (1927), Fenichel (1945), Horney (1948), Thompson (1959), Bychowski (1952), Searles (1965).

13 As I write this, the trial of Charles Manson and his family of assassins is in progress. He and his "family" seem to be the living examples of this type of destructive vengefulness.

14 A paper by Gadpaille entitled, "Research into the Physiology of Maleness and Femaleness: Its Contribution to the Etiology and Psychodynamics of Homosexuality," reports some of the work being done today which gives us insight into the importance of external stimuli in the outcome of maleness or femaleness, not only on the psychological level but on the physiological level as well. The work suggests that there are psychological differences as well as physiological differences in males and females but that external stimuli provide the basis of the psychological sexual image.

15 We have mentioned that this feeling of no-satisfaction-in-accomplishment was explained by Freud in his essay, "Predisposition to Obsessional Neurosis," as relating to the fact that the patient's activity in these instances was associated with his sadistic impulses; he accomplishes things in order to outdo others, to humiliate them or to kill them symbolically. When the acquisition of knowledge is used in this way, the patient feels no satisfaction in knowledge or achievements. If the focus is not on outdoing or defeating, the person becomes bored. It is only in the pleasure of the symbolic kill that he can find satisfaction. So long as the sadistic impluse is being gratified, the individual feels alive and his depressed emotions are lifted. On the other side of the coin, he can "downgrade" his accomplishment and masochistically humiliate or devalue himself. This constitutes a "turning around on the self" of the sadistic impulse, with feelings of depression and a mild paranoid defense, and with the need to make the object feel guilty.

16 In treatment, the patient constantly invites abuse as well as gives it. The therapist must, in some way, *let the patient know that his fear and anger are understood,* and that the self-attack is recognized. When the interpretation includes hostility from the patient towards the treating person, it may be pointed out that this must be how the patient was used at home. The patient is either prodding the other person on to attack or he is attempting to humiliate or degrade the other, or he is trying to make the other feel guilty for an attack. In

the use of his paranoid defense there is concealed a suicidal and homicidal tendency. The patient tends to interpret the interpersonal encounter in the session as a way of feeling attacked and abused. The therapist is a monster and the patient a victim; more precisely, the patient is a victim and the therapist is a murderer (in phantasy). When such a patient functions at work he experiences his day as an ordeal, an abomination and an abuse. At the end of the day he often feels he must act out in order to gain relief. The acting out helps him express his aggression in a disguised way, but in doing this he often puts himself in jeopardy. The acting out takes the form of some aspect of the role that has been promoted by the parent. There are an infinite number of ways this acting out takes place. Meerloo (1968) suggests that even suicide can be such a role. The near death escapades of several suicidal attempts are seen as masochistic maneuvers—the only way the person feels *alive* is to experience *pain*; other manifestations of this defense are over-eating; over-working; sexual acting out; suicidal acts; alcoholism (a semi-suicidal or suicidal act—more than 50 percent of car accidents are caused by drivers who are drunk—51 percent of the drivers killed in New York City in 1965 were intoxicated at the time); undoing chances by creating a problem or a condition where the other must reject, and deny an opportunity. On the other hand, the person may neglect an illness, fail to be examined when he feels sick; refuse to take the precautions the doctor suggests once the illness is known. Sexual acting out takes a great variety of forms, depending upon the early conditioning: homosexuality, whoredom; being hurt or humiliated during the sex act and so on. There is a connection between the acting out patterns and the parents' phantasies, as we have stated, and thus between the acting out and the parents' motives. Horney has touched upon these motives in her paper, "The Compulsive Drive Toward Revenge" (1948); these are the obsessional paranoid forms of hostility that we see in the sadistic side of the problem: in these obsessional traits there is *pleasure* in the torture.

Such patients always employ therapeutic interpretations masochistically in the beginning phase of treatment. The therapist often responds to this reaction countertransferentially by feeling guilty, or angry, or both. *He should respond by pointing out the masochistic maneuver.* We find that, not only rejection, but success as well, will often set off a barrage of anxiety in the patient. For example, a woman, a writer, came to her session one day acting as if she should be hospitalized, saying that she felt positively suicidal. Upon exploration of the reality situation, it was revealed that she had written a story that had been accepted for publication. The suicidal feeling was intense and repetitive.

The borderline patient would not go so far as to smear feces on himself as might the disturbed schizophrenic, but he will indulge in some milder kind of self-destructive or self-demeaning behavior.

Schreber's attacks seemed to have had something to do with his inability to tolerate success and honor due to his identification with the degraded object, since both attacks occurred when he was being promoted. This mechanism, as we know, has something to do with what Freud called the *"homosexual tendency,"* and in this trait one sees the pattern of giving in to the other, or as Freud put it: "retiring in favor of someone else." Let us understand that the patient can reverse roles and make the other play the masochistic role.

One can see a connection between homosexual phantasies and fears of success, for these are related to the patient's fear of punishment by parental figures, and his need to degrade himself or someone else—usually both. My patient, Dr. Daird, for example (see page 183), had symptoms when he was invited by a prominent university to spend an exchange year with one of their professors. The invitation stimulated his competitive feelings and his grandiosity. He felt he wanted to accept merely to "down" his current associates and he condemned himself for such feelings; on the other hand he had phantasies of giving a lecture before distinguished colleagues and having them attack him unmercifully. He thought of running to his former professor and now colleague whom he hoped would comfort him but who in reality would probably ridicule him. He thought of homosexuality with this colleague and of the unfaithfulness of the colleague's sister in her marriage. He felt "weak, crazy, incompetent," and said: "If they knew what I am really like, they never would have invited me." But unlike Schreber, he did not resort to a psychotic episode; he went to the university and controlled his anxiety. He felt that, without treatment, he never would have been able to do so. Before, he had operated under the aegis of a surrogate figure, a senior professor, who often belittled him and degraded him but who nevertheless associated with him and to some extent helped him.

17 Freud attributed phantasy to a turning away from reality, an introversion, and his examples showed that the mechanism was associated with a "turning on the self." He said that hallucination and phantasy are the effects of shutting out external stimuli, thus allowing reactions only from the sensory end of the apparatus, and, we must assume, only from memory. This is an interesting idea and one which finds credence in some sensory deprivation experiences. We know, however, that even in sleep the individual is responding to external stimuli and that these are often what set off the dream. In the use of certain drugs, young people have reported that their current sensations are highly exaggerated and so are their memories, which are disguised in the form of phantasy; these reach frightening proportions, often delusional, and create intense fears in the individual in the form of dread that something terrible will happen. Freud's suggestion that the form of the hallicination phantasy or delusion was determined phylogenetically is regarded by many as less comprehensible than if he simply were to have said that they were part of the defensive maneuvers of a person in the face of deprivation, and that the phantasy is constructed of disguised and symbolized memories, representing the identifications with hostile parental figures.

18 L. Wolberg in his book, "Psychotherapy and the Behavioral Sciences," writes of the Pavlovians who consider the role of *protective inhibition* of the "utmost importance in the integrative activity of the central nervous system. But *where* in the conditioned reflex the inhibitory process takes place is disputed. In the nerve cells of the conditioned brain foci? In the internuncial neurones? In special inhibitory structures which are apart from excitatory structure in the cortex? Irrespective of locus, cortical inhibition is a fundamental tenet in Pavlovian theory. Important in understanding how some neurotic patterns originate and continue to perpetuate themselves are certain experiments described by Kupalov in which delayed conditioned reflexes result in consistent abnormal irradiations of inhibition that spread extensively over various functions unrelated to the original conditioning. Such inhibitions initiated by the cerebral cortex spread expansively over the cortex and subcortex, and many persist for years. . . . Probably all pathology of higher nervous activity involves the formation of pathological conditioned connections which nurture pathological functional reactions. Eventually, these become stabilized and are set into motion by conditioned stimuli in the environment. What accounts for the involvement of the selected areas of the brain is also of interest in understanding conditioned reflex connections. It is probable that all stimuli at first excite the brain as a whole. However, certain regions are more sensitive than others, being in a functional state of subliminal excitement. These regions will be most susceptible to low increments of stimulation and will most readily offer themselves for the establishment of conditioning connections . . . In Pavlovian descriptions of personality typology, the relationship of two signal systems operative in man played an important part. The 'first signal system' was the primary or concrete system which was supplemented by the 'second signal system' in which words and abstractions took the place of direct stimuli. The systems could be balanced ('intermediate personality type'), weighted in the direction of the primary system ('artistic type') or in the direction of the secondary system ('thinking type'). . . . Psychoses such as the schizophrenias, according to Pavlovian theorists, are based on pathological excitations of connections of the *second signal system,* with a derangement of their interrelations and their dominance over the first signal system. A

measurement of bioelectric potentials of the cerebral cortex indicates that as a result of consistent inert excitation, exhaustion and protective inhibition develop in the cells of the cerebral cortex and then spread to individual signal systems or analyzers. A developing chain results in an increasing signification of the pathogenic lines. As one observes the bioelectric mozaic in the chlorpromazine therapy of schizophrenic patients, cortical activity is gradually increased. Disturbances in the bioelectric mozaic are found in divergent areas of the brain in different forms of schizophrenia and the depressions. Clinical changes brought about by psychotropic drugs are accompanied by rectification of these disturbances toward normal bioelectric activity."

[19] M. Klein's hypothesis, taken from Freud, was that the phantasy was of destruction by oral means—eating or being eaten, while Stärcke, in 1921, was of the opinion that the situation of being suckled played a part in the origin of projection and that the neurotic need to devour had a relation to controlling tendencies; he also spoke of the patient's need to "suck" the therapist into his world, or, as we say today, the patient's need to throw the therapist out of his role of analyst into a parental position, but, a specific kind of parental position. Schizophrenic patients, said Starche, worry that their aggressive tendencies will destroy the object, or be projected onto the object and this will result in their own destruction.

[20] This point has been documented by studies which show that reinforcement in terms of noticing and speaking of forward moves and constructive behavior helps the patient to greater success and he makes better progress than those patients who are not treated in this way; such notice should be made by appropriate verbalization about the efforts (not "supportive" or complicated statements but straightforward statements).

CHAPTER V

THE ROLE OF DEPRESSION

One of the persistent symptoms in the borderline patient is a mild, but chronic depression. That depression was a ubiquitous manifestation was understood many years ago by Freud, who indicated its universality in all neuroses and psychoses. Depression, he said, was essentially due to the real or imagined *loss of a love object*. In "Mourning and Melancholia" (1919), he tackled this problem in light of the libido theory. Depression in the borderline patient often goes unrecognized. Detachment as a way of controlling depression can be another masked symptom, since the façade of sociability may deceive the therapist. It is a fairly well documented thesis that depression can be a function of rejection, and where one searches intensively for the phantasies accompanying depression, one usually finds that these are sado-masochistic in nature.

Freud noted that depression was not "pure," but was associated with moods of elation. He emphasized the connection of feelings such as rage, anger, revenge, disappointment and real injury with the loss-of-object, and his illustrations indicated the same mechanism that we have described as a sado-masochistic defense. What Freud meant by "real injury" was only sporadically spelled out and dispersed through his writings, except during the initial period when he was convinced that *seduction* had a great deal to do with the derivation of emotional problems. Seduction was never associated in Freud's scheme with *rejection* but it was considered to be a great *trauma*.

99

In my paper, "Patterns of Interaction in Families of Borderline Patients" (1968), I presented a formula which was an attempt to connect the oedipal problem with rejection and loss of object. It is my feeling that "imagined injury" represents a phantasy which is a transferential consequence of real injury, suffered through parental rejection and the aggression that is involved in forcing the child to play a neurotic role for the parent. Depression, under these circumstances, is a reaction to the rejection, and a further reaction is aggression, which creates guilt and fear of retaliation.

Freud said that the feelings of depression were similar to mourning. The love object could, in reality, have been taken from the family through death or separation, but this was not absolutely necessary. As we shall see, there are several studies indicating that the real loss of a parent may be a factor in schizophrenia.[1]*

Freud agreed that a love object could be alive yet *lost*. We have explained that according to the libido theory, all objects related to infancy are "lost" in the ordinary course of developmental events. The child learns that he cannot have the parent and he experiences a depression; then he recovers and goes on to other objects. But how can one understand the depression that persists? Or the depression which is more closely associated with the psychoses than with the neuroses?

As we look over the historical material on depression and compare Freud's descriptions with our concepts of schizophrenia, we are hard put to see differences, psychodynamically speaking. Certainly there are similarities in the dynamics of depression and the borderlines. I am inclined to think that depression is a defense against rejection and active abuse (either mental or physical or a combination of both). In actual fact, there are no isolated defenses, only defenses operating in combination. Depression is probably associated with all of the known defenses. Depression is a function of masochism and is associated with delusions, especially paranoidal ideas. These delusions are reflected in dreams, as one may see in the dreams of the borderline patient. Theoretically, we may confirm from our borderline cases dream activities that seem to support Freud's hypothesis that the dream is a kind of psychosis. Fisher (1969) explored this thesis but did not connect it with depression. However, he differentiates "anxious REM dreams" from "stage 4 nightmares," and says that nightmares are not ordinary dreams but violent, often paranoid disturbances, brought about by the ego's inability to stave off the breakthrough of anxiety. Anxious REM dreams seem to be accompanied by a motor paralysis, while in the nightmare the person calls out for help, he wakens and often seems catapulted out of bed, followed by a period of dissociation, confusion and hallucinatory experience during which the person is unresponsive to the environment. We have already noted that some sleep investigators have said that both the chronic

* Notes for this chapter start page 123.

schizophrenics and the depressives seem to have "normal sleep patterns." What this all means is not clear at this point, and several theories have been brought forward. At any rate, it seems to document the idea that in the more disturbed cases there is a connection between depression, fear of aggression and/or fear of attack and paranoid feelings and ideas, common phenomena in the borderline patient. I do wonder whether there is a person alive who has not had a nightmare at one time or another. The dreams of the borderlines seem more like "anxious REM dreams"; the reactions, "motor paralysis."

Confusion about the psychodynamics of the borderline case is not difficult to understand since there is rampant disagreement about the psychodynamics of even the more clearly defined syndromes. One discovers that in all of the literature on the neuroses and the psychoses, six themes are constantly being repeated in an infinite variety of ways by many different authors, and that myriad interpretations are made for the same phenomena. These intertwining themes seem to be: fears of annihilation; rage, revenge and aggression; sado-masochism; perversion; defensive operations of varied types associated with inhibitions; acting out. All of these seem to be related to depression and all appear in one form or another in the borderline patient, and perhaps in all patients.

There have been innumerable ways of looking at the meaning of depression both as a syndrome in itself and as a symptom in schizophrenia, as well as in the neuroses; for example Melanie Klein's differentiation of the *schizoid* and the *depressive* positions and Fairbairn's idea that *depression is a feeling rather than a defense*, a feeling which must be defended against. If one utilizes the libido theory as a model it is difficult to pinpoint these distinctions, since all of the psychotic and severe neurotic syndromes are subsumed under the rubric of *narcissistic disorders*. These imply some delusional factors in sado-masochism.

It may be helpful in the effort to differentiate the borderline patient from the schizophrenias and the manic-depressives if one considers the *manner* in which the delusion takes hold of the personality organization, particularly the kinds of roles that are evident in the acting out behavior, as these are connected with the identifications as contained in the delusion. Those cases where the delusion is only fleetingly operative and the individual maintains object relations, yet obviously has a paranoidal or other slightly delusional attitude, we might call "borderline," although certain authors have called these character disorders. But in instances where the delusion occupies much of the patient's waking hours, and his life style is organized primarily around it, we would be more inclined to regard these as "psychotic."

What is the function of depression for the borderline patient? Does it serve any purpose in his *adaptational* scheme? One of the values is as an outlet for hostility that rages within the individual and is focused on the "love object" who has hurt and humiliated the individual; but he divides the aggression, directing part towards himself (masochism), and part towards others (sadism). This is the splitting defense.

In his treatise on melancholia, Freud did implicate the parent in what he later called the "punitive superego" but which he spoke of in this particular essay as the "criticizing faculty of the ego" and "the ego as altered by identification." "If one listens patiently to the many and various self-accusations of the melancholic," Freud wrote, "one cannot in the end avoid the impression that often the most violent of them are hardly at all applicable to the patient himself, but they do seem to fit persons with whom the patient has been in a relationship, i.e., some person whom the patient loves, has loved or ought to love." The reproaches against a loved object have been shifted onto the patient's own ego. He then made an observation which, if he had followed it through, *would have shown that the melancholic uses a defense of projective identification*—a motif similar to that in borderline conditions and in schizophrenias. Some of the derogatory statements the patient makes about himself are really true, Freud said. The patient *is* lacking in interest, he *is* incapable of love and of certain achievements. He may well *be* petty, jealous, somewhat dishonest and lacking in independence. We may ask: "Why must he become ill rather than face the way he is?" Why must the "identification with the abandoned object persist?" Freud answered the question by noting that when "object cathexis" in "object love" is replaced by identification, the ego is *remodeled*, implying that the patient resorts to delusion as a defense; there is a change in the ego's character. Such people, said Freud, make a great deal of trouble for everybody, perpetually taking offense and "behaving as if they had been treated with great injustice." He did not really answer the question, "Why?" We recognize that Freud was describing the projection of the individual's sado-masochistic relations with his "love objects" and the way in which the individual accepted blame as a consequence of having been jockeyed into the masochistic position. The important point was that in depression there is a paranoid defense. Such individuals are, in fact, treated with injustice in their families, and thus, revenge feelings are great; it is also true that *the feeling of injustice* has been incorporated into the mechanism Freud called "delusional belittling," making it a kind of paranoid projection. The individual protects himself from the knowledge of his intense aggression and his desire to kill his parents for their rejection, at the same time that he denies the role of the parent and his identification, and projects it outward. Schreber used this mechanism. In the therapeutic situation the "delusional belittling" is projected onto the analyst and the patient acts *as-if* the analyst was demeaning him. And then the reverse can take place: the analyst can be demeaned by the patient, *as-if* he were the patient's parent who had previously demeaned the patient. This kind of hostility fused with masochism and paranoid feelings is the essence of the negative transference in projective-identification. The patient projects his own guilt onto the analyst, and in his acting out with the analyst attempts in a variety of ways to make the analyst feel guilty. The patient says, for example, that he is not being helped, he is not understood, he cannot communicate or "get through" to the analyst. Often, we find that this kind of patient is so provocative that the therapist does, in fact, become angry and inaccessible; then the patient is able to make the therapist feel doubly guilty, but these circumstances do not alter the fact that the patient's mechanisms are sado-masochistic in nature and that he is using the mechanism of projective-identification with the analyst. What the therapist often misses is the fact that these mechanisms are always accompanied by depression. Paranoid feelings are an indication of depression, i.e., they are one of the defenses against depression, and depression, it seems, is a defense against aggression and feelings of rejection. But paranoid feelings are also an expression of aggression in an attenuated and projected form! No wonder Freud said that psychology is an incubus!

The paranoid feeling has roots in the reality of rejecting hostile parents who have treated the child in a way that he had to project in order to save himself. His fear of destruction in the face of parental hostility is great and rocks his self-preservative feelings and needs.

The second function of depression is to counteract the fear of annihilation, which causes the "split in the ego," i.e., the defenses of repression, denial, delusion and detachment. Thus the individual may try to save himself by making himself helpless and in a remorseful and forlorn state entreat the people around him to come to his aid. With this is an intense feeling of anxiety. Freud stressed this fact when he said that patients suffering from "narcissistic disorders" seem to be wedded to anxiety. Without severe anxiety, the patient feels an "inordinate fear" that he cannot function at all; he has a dread of being completely immobilized, dead. Perhaps this was the meaning of the "end of the world phantasy" that Freud attributed to paranoia: without the anxiety and the image of the object (projected in delusional form) the patient fears he will disintegrate. This mechanism has to do not only with defenses against aggression, but also against the impulses for certain kinds of self-assertion as well. "Separation anxiety" and the "end of the world phantasy" and "regressive symbiosis" of the paranoid appear to be outcomes of the extreme sado-masochistic positions organized in the early stages of development. The fear of the object, the realization that the object can kill and yet is needed for survival, is what we have called "oral dependency" or "symbiosis." But this is not simple dependency based on a childish need; rather it is a complicated sado-masochistic defense associated with identification. The patient fears that if he gives up the identification he will die or be destroyed. The identification is an aspect of the adaptations he made to save himself as a child; it is also a saving of the parent. We have noted that Freud insisted that aggression is an aspect of normal development; and that hate "is derived from the primal repudiation by the narcissistic ego of the external world whence flows the stream of stimuli." The idea was based on Stekel's premise that hate is, developmentally speaking, older than love. In narcissistic identification, said Freud, the ego takes flight and regresses into itself, and thus love escapes annihilation; the neurotic does not take the self as an object, he does not revert to primary narcissism.

Laing in his book "The Divided Self" speaks of three forms of anxiety, his concepts being helpful in understanding the depression in borderline cases: the anxiety over fear of annihilation; anxiety over the impingement of reality; and anxiety that makes the person depersonalize, "play possum," "feign death," "turn himself into stone," "turn himself and others into things"—in other words, anxiety that makes the person immobilize himself and detach (not see, not hear, not do). Laing says it is as if the person were saying: I am arguing (does he mean defending?) to preserve my existence; you are arguing to have the pleasure of triumphing over me (this is the familiar sadistic motif). The anxiety which creates depersonalization is due to the patient's fear of killing and of being killed—the expression of aggression in some formidable form. (Freud's discussion of his own feelings on the Acropolis are relevant here.) The identification with the aggressor, the ego-ideal, the punitive superego are all defenses so that the child can tolerate the relationship with his parents (an idea Freud was defending against). As we know, the impulses to self-assertion, the true feeling of pleasure over success, and the ability to perceive reality can be felt as an abominable aggression and can cause intense guilt feelings, in view of the fact that the parents have made it necessary for the individual to inhibit many of his normal self-assertive drives, or to feel guilty about them. This latter idea seems related to Freud's comment that the mechanism in depressives is that "Their reactions proceed from an attitude of revolt." The revolt that Freud speaks of should perhaps be understood as revolt associated with revulsion, fear and rage, and the sadism felt towards the object, plus the knowledge that one can be adequate, "normal," realistic.

As James, one little ten year old boy verbalized in his relationship with his alcoholic mother who neglected him shamelessly: "In spite of everything, I have to stay here. I need you." His mother was receiving relief from the public welfare department. "If I don't live here, I can't eat." This little boy saw his situation with clarity. He was disgusted with both his father who had deserted, and his mother who stayed with him, albeit giving him little real care. He tended to feel that he was not good enough, and, that if he acted differently, he would be more loved. His father had gone, driven from the house by the mother. When the father was around, on rare occasions, he was punitively critical of every move the little boy made, undermining him and demeaning him. The boy had a deep underlying rage at the parents, and he was angry at being in such a position. On the other hand, in order to exist in this position, he had to deny the cold, hard fact of the parental rejection and, at the same time, repress his rage and anger. He was able to project these to an aunt who was helping the family, telling the aunt that she was hostile. He often spoke of the aunt's "false values" and of her "supercilious attitude," her intense hatred. Freud put it this way, without emphasizing the rejection theme: he said that the feeling of revolt produced "a mental constellation which by a certain process has been transformed into melancholic contrition (the mental faculty commonly called conscience is here in operation)." In the intensive masochistic defense, one readily sees the paranoid feelings, the hostility *and the guilt*. It is as if the patient were taunting: "Look what you are doing to me—you are torturing me. I am bleeding; I am wounded; I am being destroyed. Don't you feel guilty?" The mother of Freud's patient described in Chapter II, seems to have been this type; we are suggesting that the patient's delusional projections do in fact describe some of the parent's characteristics—and some of the patient's—particularly those by which the patient is identified with the parent. The parent is saying to the child who represents, not himself, but the parent's parent: "I will make you feel guilty even if I have to kill myself."[2] Borderlines, character disorders, and schizophrenic patients usually establish this kind of relationship with a therapist, and if, in the beginning, the therapist attempts to interpret this maneuver in a direct way, the patient either uses the interpretation masochistically to punish himself or he increases his paranoid defense.

A third role of depression is to lessen the severity of the anxiety associated with the defense of identification.

Over and over Freud stated that identification of the ego with the abandoned object causes a split in the ego and the organization of an ego-ideal which is associated with the formation of the superego and idealization of the parent. The "criticizing faculty" of the object is turned around upon the self as part of the defense of identification in order to maintain relations with the parents or the parental substitutes. The child denies and acts *as-if* he does not understand the role of the parent. The mechanism of *isolation* is used to deny the feelings—it is too painful for the child to accept the reality.

The depression is associated with the mechanism of *turning against the self*. Freud reiterated that, in depression, not only was there reproach of others but the self as well. The self-reproaches, however, actually applied to the object, i.e., to the object "that has been lost and which has become valueless through its own fault." This mechanism was obvious in the case of Schreber. The individual who was melancholic, through a process of turning against the self, or to put it another way, through the process of "narcissistic identification," had set up the object in his own ego, the object having been "projected onto the ego." In the "Introductory Lectures on Psychoanalysis," Freud wrote: "The subject's own ego is then treated like the object and is subject to all the aggressions and revengefulness which have been aimed at the object." This masochism, or hostility turned onto the self, is an important element in *projective identification*. The suicidal trend in depression would be due to aggression turned onto the self (masochism).

The various functions of depression that I have outlined above are illustrated in one of my borderline patients, Mabel Claire. Before she was married she anticipated what her relationship with her children would be, and her thoughts were depressing. She did this by phantasizing about her sister and brother-in-law. She thought of how they were slowly bestializing their only child, a son. The father was openly punitive and derogatory toward the boy, now eight years old, and the mother was constantly undermining him. They punished him for the least infraction of their wishes. He was unable to play with other children; his parents would not let him associate with the children in the neighborhood; and the parents of the neighborhood children did not want him around their homes because he was so aggressive and cruel and unable to play cooperatively. The patient said that her own mother and father had a similar relationship with children. Her father was a hostile, screaming type, "a big brute," he could "kill you with one blow," a "powerful man." He paid little attention to his wife and then only to have her attend to his physical needs. He was violent and physically cruel to his sons. This kind of phantasy is a forbidding one in terms of prognosis, for it emphasizes the sadism of the individual, the sadistic trends that have become entrenched in the patient's characterological structure. She felt isolated and detached from her family but attached to her mother.

Before her marriage, Mabel had gotten angry at her boy friend because he refused to go to a movie with her, and she jumped from his moving car in which they were riding, flinging herself onto the road and into a ditch. On another occasion, when she became angry at home, she put her fist through a window. She was prone to hysterical tantrums. When the patient finally married, against advice, she did indeed establish the kind of relationship she had anticipated with her children. Her husband she embued with the characteristics of both her father and her mother. On the one hand, she was hysterical, screaming and tyrannical. She always fought against having sex and when her husband "forced her to do so," as she secretly wished him to do, she would bite and scratch him. He on his part seemed to tolerate this behavior. When her first child was born she had a phantasy in the labor room that she was the mother of God. She could not bear to touch her child until the child was about three months old; her husband took care of the child in the morning before he went to work and during the day her mother came to care for the infant. The patient could not stand "mess," such as feces, or food when the baby "spit up" formula, or wet or soiled her diapers. Mabel would not touch her. Finally, she forced herself to begin taking care of the child. She was meticulous about the house, spending hours cleaning; when she fed the child, she would always have a wet washcloth in one hand ready to wipe away any food that might drop from the child's mouth. The patient remembers that her mother did the same with her. Occasionally, her tension would mount to such a degree that she would begin screaming at the child, and would hit her (even when the child was still an infant, six months old), and then she would run to the telephone and call the visiting nurse service, telling whoever answered the telephone that she was afraid she would kill her child and could someone please come to help her because she could not feed her infant; it was too upsetting to her.

On one occasion, this patient was walking on the street pushing her child in a perambulator. She decided to drop in at a friend's house unannounced. The friend was not there and the house was locked. The patient was so angry that she began to scream and she saw her own face mirrored in the window, distorted with rage. Her child, then eleven months of age, was so frightened by her looks and her behavior that she began to scream. The patient was so upset by this confrontation (that is, by the child's recognition of her inordinate rage) that she began hitting the child.

Mabel's husband gradually withdrew from the family in a flight into work. He stayed away until twelve at night. The couple had two more children. He acted, however, as if all was well, leaving the children each morning in the care of his wife, ignoring the fact that the children had little security. The husband tried many jobs, acting, painting, working as a salesman; then he went into the furniture business and failed. He acquired a partner who set him up in the automobile business and he failed in this as well. Finally, he became a salesman for a furniture firm and was able to keep this position for a number of years. Mrs. Clair, after several years of treatment, gradually became intensely interested in community affairs. She was antagonistic to the "establishment." She fought against the schools, against local political candidates, against local businesses. She was aggressive and vociferous in her antagonism. While she was accurate in her estimation of the school system, and of certain neighborhood problems, her aim was as much to express aggression as to remedy situations.

Kenneth Walcott is another example of a borderline patient who experienced feelings of isolation from his family and open anxiety even at the age of two years. He used to say he had never been free from anxiety in his entire life. Often he would feel depressed. Kenneth was raised in luxury, but with reservations. His father was energetic and an engineer who worked long hours, "played hard" and was extremely competitive with his children. Kenneth, the first son, was a shy child who was brought up, along with his sister, by Scotch nursemaids, women of the "old school," who incidentally hated children, were lazy and hostile. Kenneth's Nana was in competition with the Nana of his sister. With Kenneth, his maid was neglectful. She would, for example, put him in the bathtub and go off to talk with her colleague and have tea, leaving the two year old boy by himself. He would scream for her but she would ignore his screams and stay away, sometimes for three-quarters of an hour. Kenneth recalls that even when he was five years old, and perfectly capable of washing himself and of getting in and out of the bathtub, he would not do so but would wait for the maid, screaming for her help. He would not even take the soap in his hand to wash himself but would yell and wait for the maid to wash him. The parents were seldom home but they did see the children at least once a day when they were in town. In the summer, the children were all sent to the grandparents' estate at the seashore. The parents would visit two or three times during the summer but, for the most part, they stayed in town or traveled. In the summer time, there were many different kinds of people caring for the children—the nursemaids, the grandparents, and usually university students, young men who were hired for the summer to go with the children into the woods, to teach them to swim, and to go hiking with them.

The father was a brilliant man and fancied himself an intellectual; he was an authority on all subjects. He had been in therapy with an "orthodox" psychoanalyst for several years (at least ten), going to treatment five times a week. He was "psychologically oriented" and constantly made interpretations of his, and the members of his family, and his friends' behaviors. When he was at the seashore estates he often urged his friends to join him in nudity: nude walking, nude bathing and nude social gatherings under the trees. The father was an excellent swimmer, a good golfer, a great mountaineer, a woodsman, a fisherman, a sailor, and he gave his children the impression that he was an expert in all of these, and that they could never quite equal him. The patient remembers winning a swimming contest at the seashore town and having his father say that next time he would do better. The individuals he was in competition with, said his father, were not that good. Next time he might join a more important competition. He had not done the breast stroke well but perhaps next time he'd perform more expertly. The father had this attitude about school work, swimming, running, in fact about anything that Kenneth did as a child. The father spent time with Kenneth when he was not busy and at work or socially. Kenneth remembers that when the father came to the nursery things got lively—active play began. Father would take Kenneth onto his shoulders and prance through the rooms of the nursery with him. Almost always Kenneth's head would hit the top part of the frame of the door as they went from room to room. Once he was "knocked out" in this play. Kenneth remembers his father teaching him to swim by throwing him into the water when he was five years old; he went under but finally came to the surface—terrified. He remembers, too, that same summer going with his father into the woods. His father gave him a small axe and told him to use it on the trees. Kenneth hit his foot, breaking into the shoe and hacking through the skin on his foot. He was afraid to mention this to his father and walked around with the wound for two days before anyone noticed it, by which time an infection had set in. However, in spite of these experiences he became an excellent swimmer and a good woodsman. But he was shy socially; he could not talk to people, always felt inferior, and never was able to earn a living. Fortunately, he did not have to, for both he and his wife lived on inherited money. This did not help his self-esteem but it kept him alive.

In his early childhood Kenneth was considered by his father to be awkward and inept. When he went to school, he could not seem to learn to read, although his I. Q. was about 158. His mother, who was a social butterfly, was never at home until suddenly when he was about five she became ill with a serious disease. It was about this time that Kenneth started school. His mother had to give up all social activities and remained at home, mostly in bed. She lingered for three years and finally died when Kenneth was eight. Kenneth felt a terrible loss and was visibly depressed for several months after his mother died. During the time when she was ill she became Kenneth's tutor, helping him to learn to read. But he never did learn and, finally, while his mother was still alive, he was sent to a woman, Mrs. Broderick, who was a specialist in reading disabilities.

Kenneth liked Mrs. Broderick and he felt that she liked him. He had never had such feelings before, not even with his father and mother, or with his nurse, whom he now said adored him. He was the apple of his nursemaid's eye. This hostile Scotch woman he now thought of as a warm, sweet woman, "even though she had her faults"; one fault was that she was on the "stupid side." Even as a small child, Kenneth could tell that the nurse did not have good judgment about things; that worried him often, for his welfare depended a good deal on her. Mrs. Broderick was different: she was pleasant, unhostile, helpful and he responded to her; he was beginning to feel a little less lonely. He remembered always feeling lonely as a child and "outside of things." Even when he was two and three, and the nurses took him and his sister to the private park, where everyone needed a key to get in, he felt alone and shy and unable to play with the other children. One reason was that he had gotten the idea that his family was different from the others—they were of a higher status, had more money. He never remembers ever being taken to anyone else's house, only to the homes of relatives. He never had friends. Mrs. Broderick felt this condition should be remedied and she suggested a certain private school and his sister was sent there too. But he still never really visited the homes of other children and they never came to his home. Even when the whole school went on outings or trips, there was always something happening to him to spoil it all.

When he was twelve his father remarried, a woman who was extremely adequate and talented. She worked for charities and other community causes. She had two children from a former marriage. Basically, she rejected Kenneth and his sister while fostering the efforts of her own children. She had a demeaning attitude towards Kenneth and always, when he would propose something he wanted to do or to have, the stepmother would say: "Are you sure now that you want this or is it just another of your schemes that will come to nothing?" He longed for his own mother, whom he now idealized.

Two school events were outstanding: The first occurred when he was about eleven years old. He had told his father that he was to go to Vermont on a trip with his class. His father said that he had to go to that particular town on business so Kenneth should go with him rather than ride in the bus with the class. Kenneth agreed and waited desolately at the school while the others were leaving in the bus. The father was three hours late and Kenneth missed the party altogether, although his father did drive him to the town. The second trip involved a trip to the Amish Country with his class. He and his two sisters went with their various classes. However, these wealthy children had five dollars each for the trip, while all the other children had fifteen each. Kenneth and his sisters were constantly embarrassed for lack of money. They could not go on all the side trips and when the most important side trip occurred, the teachers had to supplement their funds. They remember the trip only with embarrassment.

When Kenneth was sixteen, his father died while on a mission in a foreign country for a certain organization in the United States. He was killed in an automobile accident. The stepmother took control of the family and "ruled with an iron hand." He became fearful of her but always tried to appease her by being "good" and "helping." She continued with her belittling attitude.

The following testing report gives a picture of Kenneth as he was in his thirty-fifth year. At the time of the report he was working as a salesman but yearning to be independent. He had difficulty in learning the sales pitches and would attach himself to a senior and "bug" him all the time with questions to which he should have known the answers. He did know the answers, but he would not translate the answers into action without checking with a senior salesman. He made a great nuisance of himself around the place because of these habits. He had wanted the test battery so that he could get an evaluation to give him a hint as to what kind of work he would be best suited.

Kenneth wanted to go through the test battery in one day, although it was the custom to take the tests in two different sections on two different days. The first test, the WAIS, took him over two hours to complete. He had a nonchalant manner, was full of jokes, but listened to instructions carefully. Kenneth suggested to the examiner that he should use his help to set up the testing battery so that he would get what he wanted. "I know my needs very well, and without my help you might be testing me in a wrong direction."

When it came to the Rorschach, Kenneth stated that he had taken the test twice before. The first time, it was a serious Rorschach, "but no discussion of the results was given." The second time, the Rorschach was given "off the cuff." Some cards were shown to him, and the psychologist shrugged his shoulders and said, "You still have problems."

Kenneth volunteered that he is now in the seventh year of psychoanalysis and that if he did not have psychoanalysis, he would be "in a nervous breakdown."

During the preliminary discussion, Kenneth sat in the chair, balanced on the two back legs. And twice he almost fell out of the chair. Though he was speaking about a sickness that he considered serious, he would burst into laughter at very inappropriate times. He took the attitude that all of his problems were somewhat funny and never showed overtly that he was worried about them.

This joking kind of an attitude persisted throughout the test. He would make side comments that he was "oversexed" and has "sexy feelings," "sad feelings," "crazy feelings," and then he would laugh. When the test was finished, he said, stamping his feet in a clownish way, "Am I sick, sick, sick?" When the examiner pointed out that he had definite difficulties, but that he was not as sick as he thought he was, he became very serious for the first time. He said, "I hope you send all of this report to my psychiatrist."

Kenneth answered by long rambling responses, some mumbled, others delivered in a high pitch of voice. He had to be stopped at each card, for his responses would go on and on. An extrapolation of the findings follows:

Card I

1) Two little boys, two men with wings, each hanging to the side of the mountain. Boy, men, I don't know. They are not secure, not secure at all.

W:F:M:H
Instability and danger; fear; anxiety. some confabulation.

2) Also I see a pelvis, skeleton of a pelvis like Kennedy's pelvis, as shown in the Herald-Tribune.

WLF:Anat. Confabulation

3) Spooky feeling. I don't know, the whole thing looks spooky.

Feeling of extreme anxiety.

4) Sex picture. Woman and her vagina.

DI F—sex

5) (Reverses the card) evil temple—spooky thing, I am referring to the spooky feeling I had before (3)

W F—Vista

6) Somber, it might be a mandible. Just a feeling, I don't see the mandible.

Anxiety
No response
Lost in the anxiety.

7) Two men at work. I only see a foot don't see anything else, but the foot shows that they are working.

D F—M F

Card II

1) Two contortionists, two ladies sitting at a soda counter having a good confab. Heads are definitely goose-like or chicken-like. Some women look more like geese or chickens than women.

W F plus M H

2) There is a rocket ship blasting off.

W FM Techn. Aggression

3) And there is an oversexed male penis   D F Sex
   (laughs).

4) Two people fighting (cuts off lower   W FC M H
   red and then restores it)—probably
   blood is flowing.

5) Ballet sort of dance, lots of fast action. No score, elaboration on the
   I am referring to the ladies who could   first idea.
   have left the soda fountain and now are   Disorderliness of thinking:
   dancing.   Mr. K. cannot stick to one problem
                                                and get finished with it.

Card III

1) Two butlers lifting a punch bowl or a tug   W F M H
   of war. The base of the object is very   Aggression
   terrifying. Looks like a pair of jaws.   Confabulation
   An aggressive animal, he don't fit.   Fear; anxiety.

2) Bow tie.   D FC Object

3) Spots of blood.   D C Anat.

4) Sex mixed up with a vicious sort of   W F—Sex
   animal. I don't know. Sexual feelings,
   but also an animal. I don't know where,
   but the feeling is there.

5) Bird-like quality. Red parrots, not just   D FC Animals
   spots of blood. (Refers to response (3).)

6) Something feminine about the feet.   Homosexuality response.
   Stylized stance. Might be a dance.
   Something female about those individuals.
   Stylized by precise motion. (laughs).
   He refers to response (1).

Card IV   8"

1) This represents a skin tacked on the wall. W CF Pelt

2) Might be a bat with a funny face.   W FM Animal-Human?

3) Mottled. Everything is mottled. Reminds   Further elaboration response (1)
   me of a snake's skin, not really a skin.   Slight confabulation
   (Makes reference that he tried to make a
   purse out of the snake's skin.)

4) Sliding or swimming through the water, a   W FM A
   flat animal. Big, heavy head. I don't know Schizophrenic type of response
   if I'm scared of this animal. Also, it is
   swimming in two directions.

5) A man standing up. Looking at him from   W F plus M H
   the ground up. Great big feet. No head,
   almost no head. I don't know what dangles
   here, probably a giant. (Goes over the   Father image: child is small.
   details very carefully in describing the   Father huge: the child on the floor.
   giant. Looking at him from the floor as   Fear; anxiety
   he is standing up.

6) Sex in that too. Could be a vagina,   No response (no shape is discerned—
   could be a penis. Sex all over the   more a symbol than an actual
   place.   response).

Card V

1) Bat or butterfly. Two feelers. Two
   proboscuses. Bat's ears. These tails
   are like butterflies. Wings are furry.
   Probuscuses—there is no such word.
   Not probuscuses, but feelers. He is
   speaking of proboscises.

   W FM: Fc Animal

2) Flower opening up

   W F & M Plant
   Original

3) Two rams coming together in a head
   to head charge.

   W FM Animals
   Aggression

4) This must be a beak of a bird.
   See nothing in the rest of it.

   D FM Animal part

5) This area, woody mountainous, looking
   down from airplane.

   D cF Map

6) This is a rabbit, not a bat. First mistook
   him for a bat. Rabbit mound, they
   live in mounds, see no mound, but they
   live in mounds.

   W FM Animal
   Confabulation

Card VI

1) This is a skin. This is a mammal skin
   Woodchuck. It is furry.

   W Fc Pelt

2) Male sex organ. I am very sexy today.

   D F Sex

3) This could be a fan

   W F Object
   Femininity

4) Very much disguised cross. Some people
   don't want to admit religion.

   W F Symbolism

5) Seven stars in a star (laughs).
   (cannot discover what he means.)

   Symbolism

6) Also could be a jacket with a zipper in
   front. Not whole jacket, just the front.
   They tore off the front. Tore it off,
   badly mutilated.

   W F Destruction
   Schizophrenia type response.
   (Sado-masochistic response,
   anger at what parents have
   done to him)
   Depression.

Card IX

1) See an awful lot of opposition, arguing or
   even dueling with small indicators of small
   sticks. They look as if they are sitting
   down. Very funny (laughs).

   DF plus M Human
   Aggression
   (Sado-masochistic response,
   pleasure in aggression)

2) Something very sexual. Big rod going into
   pink clouds. This is active intercourse.
   This is the only thing that it looks like.

   W F FC M Sex
   fear of sexual impotence
   (represents revengeful feeling)

3) Green looks like nothing.

   Color naming

4) Red flower stuck into a vase.

   W CF Plant

5) Face between green and orange. Not a
   nice face, looks worried. Small eyes,
   monkey's face, moron's face. Watching,
   spying.

   D F M Head
   Paranoid type of response.
   Anxiety
   Depression

6) Two men. One biting the other on the chin.
   They do not like each other.

   D F M Aggression; (sado-masochism)
   Head, odd and bizarre.
   Almost confabulated response.

Card X

1) Looks like flowers in the garden (names all
   the colors). Shapes are irregular, colorful
   but unfriendly. Garden overgrown with bugs,
   Don't see any bugs, but I feel it. Tweezer-
   like. The whole thing could be a flower,
   an anatomical representation of a flower.

W CF—Plants
Destruction
Schizophrenic response.

2) Two people, like two seahorses, facing each
   other. They look like people that look like
   seahorses.

D F M Animal-Human
Confabulation

3) Blobs of blue. Crabs or spidery effect.
   Not quite sure what I see, but they are
   indefinite in shape.

D F-M Animal

4) Green fairy tales—beasties, dragging
   each of the other. They are mouse-like
   or rat-like, these beasties.

D FM Animal

5) On the heads of pink seahorses—they're
   like children. They are feeding, they
   are sucking. On the heads there are
   goblins snarling at each other. I am
   back to Grimm's fairy tales.

D F M Human
Symbolism
Confabulation
Aggression
Destruction—rage—revenge
Food
Dependence-infantility

6) Don't know what the yellows and reds
   mean.

Color naming

Card VII

1) Two women. I don't know what they are
   resting on. Talking over the back fence.
   Now they look more argumentative.
   They are quarreling.

W:F plus Human
Aggression

2) You could see feminine sex in all of them.
   Woman lying on her back. Legs spread.
   Is she offering?

W F M Human
Homosexual type of response.

3) Shrimps. One on each side. Fried to
   perfection.

W Fc Food
Dependency

4) Veal cutlets. Fried in bread. Can't
   think what style it is.

W Fc Food
Dependency

5) Also could be polliwogs, four of them.
   swimming in one direction. Toward the
   upper part of the card, thinking of the
   woman's sex organs, that I described
   before. Taking the whole thing as a
   woman's sex organs, they are sperm,
   I guess.

Elaboration on
response (2)

Sexual confusion

6) These are legs, and this is an arch.
   A part of furniture, probably. An art
   object.

W F Crafts

7) Person tiptoeing, gently tiptoeing.
   Delicate, nice tiptoe. I only can see
   the feet. The rest is lost.

W F-M Human Detail
Femininity

Card VIII

1) Pink—they're animals, carefully stepping from one rock to another.	W F M Animals Vista
2) Red color is hot. Blue color is cold. Held over the fire. Cover to keep the heat in. It is the preparation of food.	W C Fm Food Dependency; aggression, fear
3) Rose or some other red flower. Dead stuff underneath. Leaves are falling off.	D FC Plant, Destruction. Feeling of death and destruction; depression
4) Shadow or something. That's it. It is the shadow. I can't see it now.	No response, or possibly F-response
5) Falling petals (reference to response 3).	Elaborates on destruction in a rambling obsessive way and was finally stopped by the examiner.
7) Green inch worms eating my maple.	D FC FM Animal Destruction

"Thank God you stopped me, I'm pooped."

The psychological summary contained the following ideas:

K. feels that life is dangerous. He wishes he could have wings, fly off, and be safe. He feels weak; he has no backbone or strong pelvis on which to build strength. He tries to fight this feeling. He consoles himself that even though the pelvis is sick, one can still become important (a president). He has grandiose feelings—he wants to be important. Although he tries to reassure himself, the anxiety mounts. He cannot quite put his finger on where the danger comes from.

Filled with fear, K. thinks that if he could be a woman and submit, he probably would not be treated so harshly. (This reminds us of Schreber.) He feels that the source of his problem is outside himself—a feeling of doom from supernatural sources. In this way he reduces his guilt feelings about not being a man and taking proper care of his family. The guilt persists, however, and he expects to be punished. Punishment may come from a strong feminine figure; a masochistic fantasy helps him contain his anxiety at times, while at other times the anxiety is free-floating.

K., even though vague, shows some desire to resolve his problems on a more mature and realistic manner—through work. But what is he to do? He has hope of change but still, basically, he feels himself a child and wants a woman's sympathy, nourishment, and attention to his physical needs. But he cannot depend on women. They are "contortionists," tricky and devious. Also probably stupid, and gossipy. They have never lived up to what he desires from them. Annoyed at the women, who do not give him what he wants, he indulges in fantasy that they will be "blasted off." Having destroyed the women, having rejected his own tendency to femininity, he asserts that he is a male and a strong male—so strong that he is "oversexed." Being a male, however, exposes one to danger. Other males will challenge you. There is some doubt about how serious the conflict might be (rejection then inclusion of blood). Most likely it will become serious. K. fears open conflict and competition. He cannot tolerate the idea of being an aggressive male. Rather it would be safer to be with women. They might prove to be gracious and disciplined.

He has several schizoid responses. He becomes unsure of his identity, and what role he is to play in life. Bewilderment and anxiety exhaust him and he feels he needs rest so as to adjust his thinking. Sustained work is debilitating and dangerous. K. cannot be serene for long. Anxieties keep pressing in on him. It seems to be almost a compulsion to continue to investigate his identity. Unfortunately he comes to no conclusion. He seems to use sexual thoughts, feelings and talk as a means of bolstering up his weak feelings of masculinity and as a way of denying his basic fears of annihilation. Intellectually, K. knows how the relations with authoritative male images should be handled, but emotionally he still cannot deal with them. Although he states that nothing should be feared from superiors, he cannot help but worry. He attempts to make light of his fears.

K. implies that not only has he not solved his problem with authority but he has the desire to kill any "leader." He tries to escape guilt by saying that his aggression against the father image was almost like faith, a kind of religious feeling. He did not want to have this aggressive feeling but it happened anyway. No matter how he rationalizes his relations with the father image, he still feels the fear verging on dread. He feels helpless and defeated. Father's penis "dangling" between his legs is a fearsome object. K. does not know whether his father wants him to be a boy or a girl.

Having exhausted himself with his emotional struggle, K. is unable to work in a productive way. He is able to control his impulses as long as new blows and stresses are not forthcoming. During those periods when he feels serene, K. functions well. He shows some intellectual ambition. He is free from anxiety. These occasions are, however, rare, and occur only at periods after he has gone through a great struggle (resembling the oedipal struggle) with some "superior," and has lost the battle. A contest against peers upsets K. less than coping with his hostility toward father figures. The idea of strife of any kind, however, is upsetting. He wants to take himself out of all contests. He has no energy to strive for leadership; he attains leadership only in his grandiose phantasies. He covers his fears with bravado, humor and making himself into a clown. Often when anxiety mounts, he tries to get relief in reverse, which he considers to be a form of religious meditation and philosophy. He uses this as a means of controlling his own aggression and his fears of the aggression of others. What interrupts his defense is the image of the father; he fears that the father figures will attack and molest him (sexual fears). He feels depressed.

Fearing the masculine strong images, K. is almost as afraid of the strong mother images. The difference is that the male is direct and brutal while the female is devious, tricky and undependable. Having considered both male and female strong images, K. seems to lean towards a feminine role. In this way, he can compete with women and seduce the men. The hope is that by seducing men, he will get physical comforts. Is he looking for a "feeding father?" To get what he wants, he is at times almost ready to become a woman completely, to replace a woman in all respects and functions. He warns himself, however, not to be too brazen, to do it gently and delicately, but he repudiates this defense in himself, denies it and projects the problem onto the outer world.

Most of the time, K. is under rather intense emotional strain. With people he sometimes becomes inappropriate in his behavior, almost bizarre. This happens only under intense stress, however. At other times, he resorts to introspection which is obsessive in nature and leads him into his old dilemma: he wants to be nurtured and protected; he wants to resolve the problem; he gets tired and wants to escape. The introspection, his fatigue and the realization that he fails more often than not gives him a feeling of doom and destruction. He resorts to somber musing. He cannot define the source of his feelings, but first he feels pessimistic and then he becomes depressed. Although depressed, it is not a debilitating kind of mood, but rather a nostalgic one. He idealizes the past and longs for it. He feels lonely and left out of life. On the occasions when K. wants to assert his masculinity, he does not quite believe in it and tries to cover up his doubts with humor. This inadequacy as a male is strongly felt. It makes him feel powerless and futile. He is ready to give up his efforts. But the feeling that he might be spied upon revives his energy. He is ready to defend himself, like a rat driven into a corner. Fused with feelings of futility and loss of security in an unordered world, he fights for his life. He reassures himself by engaging in "busy work." He has no real emotional feelings. He is detached and this helps him keep cool in the fray. He tries to be childish on occasions, and seductive so that people will give to him rather than expect something from him. The feeling of helplessness and the desire to have someone to depend on is a childish longing that has never been requited.

On the Wechsler Adult Intelligence Scale, K. tests at a very superior intelligence level (IQ 136, Verbal IQ 138, Performance IQ 130). He ranks in the upper 1 per cent of the general population and in the upper 15 per cent of business executives. His ability in the abstract verbal area is excellent. A very talkative individual, it is difficult for K. to keep to the point. He has an agile mind but this problem of "keeping on the track" undoubtedly cuts down his intellectual effectiveness. He has excellent ability when it comes to picking up new ideas, but his awareness of the world around him—his breadth of information, culturally, politically and economically—is quite limited.

His vocational preference tests show that his interests are highest in areas which are people-oriented and scientific, such as psychiatrist, engineer and chemist. They are definitely not towards work that involves attention to detail, such as office worker or accountant. His interest in people-oriented positions may reflect his therapeutic relationships, his transference feelings (positive ?), but at the same time, they are quite firm. His value system is quite high in the theoretical and political area and very low in the religious.

He has a strong desire to come and go as he pleases, to experience new and different things, and to accept blame when things do not go right. At the same time, he has little need to be loyal to friends or to assist others who are less fortunate than himself. There is a sense of incompleteness within his makeup, a feeling that he has failed, work-wise. There also is an element of sadness and of mood swings. He is somewhat touchy, even to the point of having a chip on his shoulder. The question of parental rejection, or at least his considering that he was rejected, comes to the fore. This aspect of his personality is clearly reflected in his Thematic Apperception Test productions—neglect of himself by both his father and mother, the unhappiness of family life and the refusal of parents to help.

Some of his Sentence Completion material indicates his typical moods:

When I was refused—I got mad.
When they tried to help me—I wouldn't let them.
When my work is criticized—I react angrily.
People in authority—make me feel unappreciated.
When confronted by a successful person—I feel ill at ease.
Working with others—makes me depressed.
Feeling unable to do the job—makes me depressed.

The responses reflect an attitude of underlying anger handled by depression.

K. is often obstinate and negativistic in his attitude. At work, for example, he often simply refuses to function. He will let his work pile up day after day, but his external attitude is one of pleasantness and compliance. He will not get the work done; in addition he pesters people—he goes to them, his immediate boss, for example, and tries to get him to tell him what to do, as though he were a nincompoop who had no brains and had to be told over and over again how to work at simple tasks. At home he resents his role as father. He is married and has three children but he stays away many evenings; presumably he is on business talking to potential clients. These business relationships seldom materialize in the sense that the individual he interviews becomes a customer. Kenneth's psychological report shows the intricate ways in which depression is fused with other defenses and with the rejection theme.

There are great similarities in the way that Mabel Claire felt towards her children and how we assume that Kenneth was used by his parents. How she rejected her child is shown in this interview:

PT.: I hate her (speaking of her two year old child).
TH.: Do you have any idea why?
PT.: I am very annoyed with the problem of her playing with other children. She's little and the other children take advantage of her; then she cries

and I have to go out into the yard. But when I have her in the house, it's just as bad. She either wants me to pay attention to her all the time or she wants to go out to play with other children.

TH.: Either way it's trouble for you. What do you think happens with the parents of other two year olds?

PT.: Oh, I know all the answers. I've read all the books. I've attended all the lectures and I've taken the Mental Hygiene lectures; I've listened to all the lectures at Cooper Union.

TH.: Well, you know as much about it as anyone, then.

PT.: But I just keep on acting the same way although I know how to act. (She says that the other women in the development must think that she is crazy. They go about doing their housework. They have afternoon parties; they look well when their husbands come home at night; they have a well-cooked meal and their children look fine. She is the only one who looks dishevelled. She can't organize herself, or develop a routine. She is the only one who goes around in shabby looking clothes and she is probably the only person who "lets her husband have it the minute he enters the house.")

Lately, Martha (her four year old daughter) has begun to say, when people come to the door, "Hello, come in. Excuse me." She has learned this from me. I scream at salesmen when they come to the door, and then I have to apologize because sometimes the person turns out not to be a salesman but the repairman whom I have called to fix the washing machine or the man from the diaper service. Also, I get mad at Martha and hit her and then tell her I'm sorry. She thinks that saying hello is like hitting someone, and then telling them you're sorry.

The interview continues:

TH.: Is there anything else that the child does that annoys you?

PT.: Yes, she's nosey and she notices things. She wants to know what is going on.

TH.: What do you mean?

PT.: She says: "Mommy mad, mommy mad," or "mommy cry," or "mommy stop crying." She says, "Don't fight!"

TH.: Well, she's an intelligent child like her parents and she notices these things. You couldn't expect that she would not notice, could you?

PT.: No, but if she wouldn't be so observant, I'd like it; it bothers me. She's fresh. If I want her to do something she doesn't want to, she answers me back.

TH.: What does she say when she answers you back?

Upon questioning, the therapist discovered that the child did not exactly "answer her back" but rather made known her wishes to do things. For example, she said, "Me do it" (referring to tying her shoes). She said, "Me go out" when she saw some of her friends in the yard.

When the child showed an ability to think or to reason things out, or to do things spontaneously, Mabel had a reaction as if the child were defying her. The child might say, "Me go out," when Mabel does not want to be bothered getting her ready to go out.

Mabel had a degree of insight when she said: "Maybe I like the infant because she can't talk, walk; she's inactive; she can't notice things. Maybe when she starts to be active, I'll hate her too." The infant was six months old. Mabel was trying not to squelch her children but she found this very difficult and at times impossible.

Melanie Klein theorized that each infant must cope with "death anxiety" and "sexual anxiety" in the first few months of life, just as Rank and Freud felt that each infant suffered birth anxiety. It seems more reasonable to suppose that what Klein referred to as "death anxiety" can be understood not in terms of instinctual or universal fear, but rather refers to the child's sensing the neglect, the aggression and the hostile transference (displacement) reactions of the parent towards him. The threat of death is real. The degree of destructiveness and the rejection of the parent creates the fear of destruction and the defense against this knowledge requires a depressive position, as a defense.

The notion of Melanie Klein that the origins of the *schizoid position* and the *depressive position* begin at early stages (the part object stage at the age of 1-3 months, and the beginning of the object stage 3-6 months) derives from the concept that *separation-anxiety* and *grief* are intermingled; the child cannot be himself if he is deprived of the object *of which he is part in infancy* so he must resort to himself as object. But then he must "reconstitute the parent" *as a defense* in order to survive the rejection. Here the concept of introjection is clearly a defense. Yet, as we have said, Klein was of the opinion that the parent did not have to be rejecting, in actual fact, for the child to feel rejected. Some investigators who are studying the borderline patient today are attempting to utilize a combination of Freudian and Kleinian theory.

Freud had many changes of ideas as to the origin, in time, of the particular neuroses, but he probably came nearest to the truth when he surmised that problems began when the child found it necessary to *repress* certain ideas, thoughts and feelings and to defend against these; he made no connection between *repression* and *rejection*, but there is no doubt that one is a function of the other.

Another way of integrating Freud's theory with biological concepts and development is suggested by Margaret Mahler, who uses the concept of *symbiosis* to describe the second phase of development. In neurosis or psychosis, she says, the child's normal dependency in infancy has been tampered with. The clinging to the object as part of the neurosis is an extended form of symbiosis, or what Freud called the primary stage of narcissism. Abraham felt that in severe forms of depression, the fact that the patient refused to eat had a relation to the early "cannibalistic stage," i.e., the oral incorporation stage of development—a kind of reaction formation to this aggressive developmental phase in repression. This was in line with Freud's theory that in the normal course of events the ego wishes to incorporate its early objects into itself, and in the early oral or cannibalistic stage does so by devouring the object. Identification through introjection or incorporation was a normal motif in infancy.

Depression was considered to be one of the narcissistic affections and Freud felt that the depression in "narcissistic identification" was a lasting one, being experienced by the individual at all times and throughout his life. At various periods, the depression could become greater, associated with a form of grief, *as-if* the individual had lost someone dear to him. In this gloomy picture of profound depression, Freud listed some of the symptoms: painful dejection, abrogation of interest in the outside world, loss of the capacity to love, inhibition of activity, a lowering of the feelings of self-regard, self-reproaches, self-revilings, and a "delusional expectation of punishment." The conflict could become so intense that, in turning away from reality, the individual could cling to the object through the medium of an "hallucinatory wish-psychosis." This kind of person abased himself before people. "He is worthless, incapable of any effort, normally despicable." Freud called this "delusional belittling." Although the borderline patient has feelings of this nature, he does not reach major depths of depression.

In his preface to the volume on "Depressions: Theories and Therapies" in the series Science and Psychoanalysis (Vol. XVII), Masserman writes of his doubts (1970) about using Freud's developmental theory as the basis for understanding the neurosis and the psychoses, particularly in gaining data concerning the symptoms of depression. He noted that Abraham (1911), finding it difficult to fit the newer concepts of "intrapsychic mechanisms" into Kraepelinean nosology, accepted the cyclical nature of manic-depression psychosis, the dynamics of which he differentiated from the "more rapid oscillations of ambivalence in the obsessive-compulsive neuroses." Abraham felt that the depressed patient feels universally hated because he himself feels incapable of loving anyone, and in this self-abasement the patient obtains not only "masochistic gratifications" but also an indirect "sadistic revenge." In contrast, the manic is happy because ego inhibitions are suspended. Masserman questions the validity of this latter observation, noting that patients who are in the manic state do not seem so happy, and suggesting that this state, too, is one of defense. *Abraham made the dividing line between the neuroses and the psychoses the anal phase.* This phase was divided into two parts. The depressive (psychotic) breaks off external object relations and "regresses" to the "expulsion phase of anality," while the obsessive-compulsive "retains his external object cathexes in the relenting libidinal phase," this latter, as Masserman paraphrases Abraham, "maintaining a position safely above the dividing line between the two stages of 'anality.'" Masserman discussed the inconsistency in such "developmental" reasoning, and is of the opinion that we should think in terms of defenses at various levels of organization. L. Wolberg (1954) has suggested a chart which describes several layers of defense. If we were to place the depressives within Wolberg's chart, the mildly depressive would be in the third level (intrapsychic) of defense, while the more severe depressives (endogenous) would be included in his fourth level, i.e., the more physiological of reactions. Freud explained this fourth level in terms of regression. When the libido returned to the ego (leaving its objects), regression took place and on the intrapsychic level the mental contents became fused with megalomania and omnipotence, which was typical of the "objectless state" or when the infant was related to his own body in the "part-object" state. That part of the libido that was syphoned off into the bodily sensations was not a *conversion*, therefore, related to the genitals, but a regression to the auto-erotic, areas and hypochondria was distinguished from conversion in this way—the whole body seemed affected with delusional ideas.

In accounting for depression, Freud's concept of regression has been widely criticized, in particular by Kurt Goldstein. Freud felt that the individual could indeed regress from adulthood to earlier stages of development. The form of thinking which was characteristic, for example, of the age of eight, or seven, or five, or three, or two or six months, could "take over" in the mind of the adult. Goldstein denies that this can happen, saying that what Freud has described as regression is withdrawal into phantasy and isolation.

Freud insisted that when the libido returned to the ego, the individual became "megalomanic" on the mental level, and that the part of the libido that was syphoned off was directed into bodily sensations; but in depression, as in schizophrenia, this was not a conversion, but an indication of the regression to the objectless state. This meant that the physical manifestations of anxiety in the character disorders, the mixed neuroses, the borderline states, the depressions and the schizophrenias were associated not with external objects, but, in regression, with the erotogenic areas, harking back to the time when the child was in the auto-erotic stage of development. Hypochondria embraced thoughts about bodily problems which could become delusional. The individual could imagine, for example, that his body had peculiar sensations for which there was no rational explanation; or, he might persist in a feeling that he had a physical illness in spite of various examinations which showed nothing. These manifestations were often found in the melancholias, as in the schizophrenias.

One can readily find in the depressed patient a feeling of isolation together with a feeling of being "left out." Freud noted this feeling as early as 1897, saying that is was associated with an image of being outside the family. He first thought this to be a definite sign of paranoia, but later decided that the feeling was connected with the "normal oedipal struggle"—the child felt "outside" when he realized he could not have his father and his mother as perpetual love objects, when he realized that he was not the sole interest of his parents, and he would have to "give up these objects." More likely Freud was correct in his first surmise: this feeling of being outside or left out is an aspect of the paranoid projection (the schizoid position) and the child's realization (unconscious) that he is rejected and unprotected, and his need to deny this in order to quiet some of his anxiety. But the feeling of dread is ever present. His feeling of being left out is connected with his feeling of isolation and depression and the reaction formation of superiority, which in turn, reflects his defense against rejection and his hatred of others.

NOTES

[1] The following reports suggest that there is a functional relationship between "lost objects," depression, schizophrenia and rejection.

Wahl (1954) working at the Elgin State Hospital, found that in 42 percent of the cases of schizophrenia, patients had lost either one or both parents by the time they were fifteen years old. He reported that 31 percent were rejected by one or both parents, and 17 percent were over-protected. (Over-protection, it would seem, should be thought of as a reaction formation against rejection; over-protective behavior is essentially rejecting behavior, a denial of the integrity of the person, a demeaning of him as an adequate person. Thus, the study would indicate that 48 percent were rejected.) Wahl combined the percentages of rejection and over-protection and found that 81 percent of the hebephrenics were subjected to these parental attitudes, as compared with 39 percent of the paranoids. In a study based on data from a United States Naval Psychiatric Hospital, Wahl (1956) found that approximately four times as many of the schizophrenic group had been orphaned by the death of either or both parents prior to their fifteenth year than was true for the general population. Furthermore, 34 percent were severely rejected by one or both parents, while 9 percent had been over-protected (a total of 43 percent).

L. Kanner (1949), in a paper entitled "Problems of Nosology and Psychodynamics of Early Infantile Autism," came to the conclusion that "early infantile autism" is "psychologically determined." He found that, in the majority of cases, the parents are humorless, perfectionistic, undemonstrative, and uncomfortable in the presence of other people. They feel repugnance toward physical contact with their children who, therefore, fail to receive any show of responsive warmth. On the other hand, in some families it was found that physical contact was present but in a negative and destructive form. Apparently phantasy and detatchment, like depression, are functions of rejection.

Sauna (1961) reported in a pilot study involving Jewish and Protestant patients that mothers of Jewish patients seemed to be more disturbed than the fathers. Approximately 50 percent of these mothers were categorized as having had a psychotic breakdown, and as being extremely irritable and excessively dull; 20 percent were found to be over-protective; and 15 percent were rejecting. In the Protestant families, the record revealed that fathers had a greater degree of psychopathology than the mothers. One-third were alcoholic and 25 percent were extremely irritable. Physical punishment was found to be quite common. Sauna concluded that if the "schizophrenogenic" label is to be applied to these families, it would be more appropriately applicable to the father in the Protestant family, and to the mother in a Jewish family.

[2] This is revenge turned on the self. It is evident at early ages that a child (even at the age of one year) will hit himself if he is frustrated by a parent or parent substitute and is prevented from expressing his anger. For example, if a one-and-a-half year old child is trying to do something which he finds difficult, like trying to fit a smaller box into a larger box, or if he attempts some other task that requires dexterity, like pouring water from a pitcher into a glass, and he cannot perform these behaviors with skill, then, in his frustration, he might

strike out at an adult. But if the adult remonstrates, he will often hit himself. This is undoubtedly displacement behavior, a mechanism basic in the formation of projections and a reaction that biologists feel is based on a neurophysiological response. The parent, by his behavior, can encourage the child's experimental attitudes or he can foster the child's guilt by criticizing him for his frustration and anger, thus putting an onus on the kind of "normal" behavior that occurs when a young child is frustrated in performance. With enough criticism on the part of the parent, a masochistic attitude will result eventually.

CHAPTER VI

LATER CONTRIBUTIONS TO THE LITERATURE
ON BORDERLINE PATIENTS

Little was written on the borderline case, apart from the writings on schizophrenia, until Zilboorg defined it as an entity in the early 1930's. He described the diagnostic aspects, in part, but made little mention of the treatment process. Prior to this time the borderline case was called the *neurotic character* by some early analysts (Alexander, 1930; Reich, 1933), and there was a great deal of dispute as to whether this category was to be placed between the normal and the neurotic or between the neurotic and the psychotic on Freud's developmental chart. The latter point of view seems to have prevailed. The neurotic character was described as using the defenses of *denial, isolation, repression, reaction formation* and *projection*. Some authors saw similarities existing between the neurotic character and the manic depressive syndrome, particularly in relation to mood swings and the defenses of isolation and denial. The schizoid and depressive traits were especially noted, traits which Melanie Klein described in detail. Certainly, this patient had much of what Kernberg (1966) calls the *borderline personality organization*. Reich (1931) believed that the neurotic character was a more severe type of problem than the neurosis. Ferenczi (1924) considered the neurotic character a "private psychosis" tolerated by the "narcissistic ego." Glover (1955) distinguished between the neurotic character and neurosis in terms of "autoplastic" (in the neurosis) versus "alloplastic" (in the neurotic character) means of discharging tension, thus stressing the projective element and the necessity to express tension in symptom formation.

Reich said that the behavior of the passive-feminine character (a form of "neurotic character" with a patently masochistic trend) is based on anal excitations, but this represents a substitute contact which has replaced the natural contact made impossible by frustration. The young man, in growing up, should, for example, fight against the domination and authority of his father, should become independent and should develop his own capacities. However, he does not have at his disposal the aggression which is necessary for this because it is repressed. In order to maintain the repression he develops his passive-feminine modes of behavior. Moreover, instead of mastering the world with sublimated aggression, he tries to secure his existence by neurotic adaptation, although this involves the greatest personal sacrifice. Reich implied that it was the relation with parents that stimulated these traits in children, but he did not go so far as to say, for example, that if the behavior of the passive-feminine character is based on "anal excitations," then the parents must have had a perverse trend, actively creating these excitations by using the child as a transferential object of perversion, either secretively or openly. Rather, he used Freud's instinct theory as a partial explanation.

Reich spoke of the sadistic attitude, referring to the woman who possessed a compulsive anger toward the man. This has not only the function of warding off her feminine genitality, but also that of compensating for the resulting libidinal *contactlessness* and of maintaining the tie with the original love object, although in a different form. The artificial, exaggerated affectionless attitudes between mates represents a *substitute contact* because of the lack of a genuine sexual relationship. The neurotically aggressive behavior of querulous people is a defense against passive-feminine tendencies and of natural genital tendencies, but, in addition, this is an attempt to remain in contact with the world despite the lack of immediate "vegetative contact" (Reich's phrase for *energy* as a replacement of the libido concept). The masochistic side of the behavior is not only the expression of a defense against sadistic aggression, but also a substitute for direct expression of love, of which the masochistic character is incapable.

"Once one has grasped the difference between the manifestations of free-flowing, immediate vegetative contact and those of secondary, artifical contact relationships, the latter are easy to see in everyday life." Reich proposed the following as examples of *ungenuine behavior* in the neurotic character: loud, obtrusive laughter; forced, rigid hand-clasp; never changing, lukewarm friendliness; narcissistic display of superficial knowledge; stereotyped, meaningless portrayal of surprise or delight; rigid sticking to certain views, plans or goals; obtrusive modesty in behavior; grandiose gestures when talking; childlike wooing of people's favor; sexual boasting; prancing with sexual charms; indiscriminate coquetry; unhealthy promiscuous sexuality; exaggeratedly refined behavior; affected, pathetic or exaggeratedly refined talk; dictatorial or patronizing behavior; exaggerated hail-fellow-well-met behavior; rigid conversational way of talking; wordy or lascivious behavior; sexual giggling and smutty talk; Don Juan behavior; embarrassment. Similarly, certain physical movements often express, in addition to narcissistic tendencies, a substitute contact: shaking one's hair into place in a striking manner, stroking one's forehead frequently in a typical manner, looking suggestively into the other person's eyes in talking, forced swaying of the hips, forced athletic gait, etc. These characteristics we would now call acting out.

Schmideberg (1933) emphasized the detachment and the "no-feeling" of the borderline patient (the inability to experience genuine emotion) and the need that the patient feels to express such emotion. She notes that some patients "work themselves up into hysteric like scenes and over-emotional reactions," or they take drugs, commit offenses, or act out sexually to escape their lack of feeling or to relieve their painful feelings. Schmideberg (1959) also stresses the depersonalization phenomenon which occurs in borderlines.[1]*

Most of the papers immediately following Zilboorg's contribution on the borderline patient have been descriptive rather than dynamic. Eisenstein (1952) felt that borderlines were distinct from the schizophrenias. He said that the former patients appear to function at a neurotic level, but they show abortive paranoid features. They have transient feelings of reference and depersonalization. Eisenstein referred to Hoch and Polatin (1949), saying that they "presented illustrative cases of the variety under discussion in a contribution aptly entitled 'Pseudo-neurotic Forms of Schizophrenia.' " Hoch and Polatin included in their designation such conditions as homosexuality and certain other forms of behavior which we now feel should be excluded from the borderline category since borderlines usually maintain relations with the opposite sex. The homosexual's projective pattern is quite different from the borderline's, and the homosexual's use of himself as a projective object (the masochism) is of a different order from that of the borderline; his hostility and paranoid mechanisms are deeper and more destructive than those of the borderline and more projectively defended. Freud was insistent in pointing to the homosexual trend in schizophrenia, but many of his examples were what have been called "latent," since the "homosexuality" was not always acted out.

According to Eisenstein (1952), improper evaluation of borderline patients at the start all too frequently has led to misdirected therapy. In private consultations, he found 30 per cent of cases to be borderline reaction types. Eisenstein quotes Woltman (1952), who pointed out that, in a random sampling of fifty psychodiagnostic referrals of private adult patients, 32 per cent fell into the

* Notes for this chapter start page 143.

borderline category. Eisenstein remarked that it was paradoxical, in view of the major contribution of psychoanalysis to the understanding of borderline neurosis, that these cases were often therapeutic failures. He avowed that "... the paradox lies in the fact that techniques of therapy, in general application, have not kept pace with the theoretic understanding of these disorders. To treat borderline states as transference neuroses is an error fraught with disappointment and the danger of precipitating psychotic episodes."

In line with the idea that treatment techniques had not been appropriately delineated, Eisenstein referred to a study by Piotrowski and Lewis, who reported that almost 50 per cent of patients (20 out of 41) who had been discharged from the New York Psychiatric Institute at a particular time, with a diagnosis of psychoneurosis, developed definite signs of schizophrenia in the interval between discharge and the follow-up some years later. Rorschach test criteria also suggested a high incidence. We now realize that, in actual fact, treatment techniques always lag behind theory, for it is much easier to develop a theory than to treat a case. The use of one's self in the treatment process requires that the therapist be free of certain prejudicial misconceptions as well as having analyzed his own aggression. This is particularly necessary if one is to treat the more emotionally disturbed patients whose aggression is so intense that it frustrates the treating person.[2]

Zilboorg does not seem to have had a pessimistic attitude about outcome in these cases. His writings encouraged the study of treatment techniques, but he decried brief methods and shortcuts (1952). Today we recognize that often the more disturbed patients fear treatment and hesitate to seek it. They will, however, attempt some short-term measures and these should be given, for in the course of such procedures motivation for further treatment often emerges. In the cases where this is not true, considerable benefit can often be obtained, if nothing more than to start a self-help process which in itself is worthwhile. One of the defenses in some of these patients is their inability to allow another person to help them. In such instances the patient struggles on his own after a brief therapeutic encounter; but others do the opposite—they attempt to settle into a permanent and lifetime dependency with the treatment person; this is the other side of the coin. In these latter cases, termination dates must be set and kept. Such patients may go to someone else after several years of working with one analyst who has now separated himself from the patient. The practice of cutting off at a particular date to interrupt the dependency is a good one, for it shows the patient that he can survive without the surrogate person.

Mahler, Ross and DeFries (1949) described a group of cases of childhood disorders that are undoubtedly borderline cases, referring to them as more benign cases of childhood psychosis. Characterized by low tolerance to frustration, unevenness of development, uncontrollable impulsivity, poor inter-personal relationship, mood swings, poor judgment and many neurotic traits, such as phobias, compulsions, and hysterical and hypochondriacal traits and symptoms, these children were in contact with reality and were said not to be delusional, but at the slightest frustration they could withdraw into their phantasy world. They are prone to tantrums.[3] Geleerd's (1945, 1946, 1958) work emphasized the pathological significance of a type of temper tantrum which she felt was a later edition of the infant's "affectomotor panic." These tantrums tended to indicate that such children do have delusional defenses, for there was a kind of phantasy of external threat along with the tantrum. The broadest lines of treatment with such children, she says, aim at *body-image integrity*, which should enhance a better sense of identity and entity, the development of object relationships and restoration of missing or distorted maturational and developmental ego functions.

Bychowski (1953) spoke of "latent schizophrenia" (Bleuler's term), meaning what many call borderline, and he emphasized five points which he said characterize the disease: (1) neurotic difficulties which, on an appropriate stimulus from the environment, may precipitate into a psychosis; (2) great intensity of neurotic symptomatology, including obsessions and compulsions, hysterical symptoms, schizoid and psychotic features; (3) deviant behavior, such as delinquency, perversion and addiction; (4) an arrested psychosis in the clinical sense, the psychopathology likely to reveal its true nature some day; and (5) psychosis apt to be precipitated by therapeutic or didactic psychoanalysis. Many other symptoms of "latent psychosis" are delineated by Bychowski, including such thinking disorders as scattering, displacement, magical thinking, condensations and symbolism. He mentions, too, symptoms, deriving from a so-called "depressive disposition," which includes various defense mechanisms and disorders of affect.

Otto Kernberg (1966, 1967, 1968) has written some interesting papers which elaborate a theoretical position on the borderline patient. He stresses the splitting phenomenon, which he considers a characteristic mechanism in borderline cases. He connects splitting with what he calls a "comparmentalization of contradictory ego states." He says that at one time an individual may be impulse-ridden and manifest outlandish sexual or hostile impulses, while at another time, he may swing to an opposite stance, conveying highly moralistic, virtuous and compassionate sentiments, acting as if he never had engaged in the impulsive behavior at all. In the latter mood he may project his own impulse-laden motives onto the therapist in transference, and onto other substitutive objects. A vague memory may exist of his own opposing feelings, but this has little effect on his existing antithetic behavior. Kernberg refers to Freud's paper, "The Splitting of the Ego in the Defensive Process," as containing a similar idea. According to Kernberg, Freud used the example of a child who preserved his equilibrium by shifting from one set of reaction patterns which accepted reality to another which denied it. The splitting, while retaining opposing conflicts, had little influence on the expressing of the tendencies, and Freud considered this a psychopathological phenomenon present in the development of a psychosis.

Kernberg cites the case of a man in his late 30's, a borderline patient with a paranoid character structure who, in the third interview, violently accused Kernberg of rejecting him by passing him by on the street without greeting him. It was evident that behind the attack was a feeling that he was being held in contempt by his therapist, but even more importantly, it was a reaction to a beginning need for a dependency in the relationship with the analyst. After a few sessions of expressed verbal attacks, his attitude changed as he voiced expressions of gratefulness and intense positive feelings toward Kernberg. In a few weeks, the shift was back to angry outbursts, and his sadistic, derogatory attitude seemed to make him completely unaware of any good feeling he had previously harbored and expressed. During the period that he manifested sentiments of closeness and longing he had been oblivious to the fact that he had evidenced anger, in spite of remembering that he had possessed feelings of such opposite nature. The memory had no emotional reality for him. "It was as if there were two selves, equally strong, completely separated from each other in their emotions although not in his memory, alternating in his conscious experience." In his daily work and activities, however, there was no such evidence of lack of impulse control, his behavior being socially appropriate. "In other words, he did not present simply lack of impulse control as an expression of ego weakness, but specific, well-structured alternation between opposite, completely irreconcilable affect states." Whenever Kernberg attempted to question either state of unrealistic emotion in its presence, the patient would elicit anxiety. This, he felt, pointed to the fact that the "splitting of the ego" was "not only a defect in the ego but also an active, very powerful defensive operation." In explaining the dynamics of this phenomenon, Kernberg postulates that certain mechanisms of defense operate differently in the borderline than in other patients, particularly the mechanisms of isolation and denial.

Isolation is ordinarily defined as a process by which the memories of unpleasant experiences or impressions are deprived of their affective cathexis, so that what remains in consciousness is nothing but some aspect of the ideational content, which is then judged to be unimportant. Isolation, according to the regular definition, loosens the contents of consciousness from their connections, separating the individual elements and thus concealing their meaning. (While standard definitions of isolation do not include the concepts of displacement and dissociation, we must say that they are factors in such a process.) According to Kernberg, the isolation mechanism of the borderline patient operates imperfectly, so that there is a complete, simultaneous awareness of an impulse and its ideational representation involving *affect, ideational content, and behavior modes*. (This appears to be another way of saying that there are few repressions, and the "id" is evident.)

When we think of *denial*, says Kernberg, we understand this to mean that there is a tendency to eliminate from consciousness a piece of external or subjective reality, and this appears in contradicton to what the synthesizing function of the ego dictates as ego-syntonic. By contrast in the borderline patient, "there exists what we might call mutual denial of independent sectors of psychic life," or "alternating ego states," i.e., "repetitive temporary ego-syntonic compartimentalized psychic manifestations." These are typical defenses of the borderline and "each state seems to represent a specific transference disposition." (Is this Kernberg's way of speaking of what others have called regression back to the part object stage?)

Kernberg explains these phenomena by saying that the borderline patient has a constitutional defect which prevents the normal mode of integration of perceptions. He accounts for this in the following way: object relationships involve drive derivatives, affects, emotions, wishes, fears, images and phantasies. Introjections are the "earliest point of convergency of object relationships and instinctual drive representatives" and "may be visualized as an essential 'switch,' bringing the ego into operational readiness." "Splitting is the normal defensive operation in the early stage of development. There is an undifferentiated phase of development (Hartmann, 1939, 1950), a common matrix to the ego and the id (Freud's concept); and there is a specific stage in which the ego may be considered for the first time as an integrated structure, i.e., the three-month period (Spitz, 1951).

In the borderline there is, according to Kernberg, "a constitutionally determined lack of anxiety tolerance" which interferes with "the phase of synthesis of introjections of opposite balance," i.e., the phase from birth up to eight or ten months, and in addition, there is a "quantitative predominance of negative introjections stemming from both a constitutionally determined intensity of aggressive drive derivatives and from severe early frustrations." Kernberg is of the opinion that in the borderline patient the constitutional defect interferes with the normal mode of integration of perceptions and perpetuates the "splitting" that normally occurs in every child, due simply to the inability of the child in the first few months of life (before the id/ego differentiation takes place) to integrate the contents of his mind. As a consequence, the child never does give up the splitting and it in turn creates a problem in the development of the autonomous ego functions. Kernberg attributes the destructive mental images in splitting to derivatives of the instinct that have not been handled due to the constitutional defect. This is similar to Freud's concept of phantasy life in the narcissistic neuroses and the schizophrenias. Kernberg calls these images non-metabolized ego states or introjects. Freud thought of these phantasies as id-representatives. This idea is reminiscent of Breuer, too, who spoke of "hypnoid states" and felt these to be due to a constitutional inability of the individual to hold together the contents of his mind. But Freud disagreed with Breuer and saw "motives" at work, and developed his ideas of the hysterias, the displacement mechanisms and other defenses. It would appear that hysterical defenses account for much of what Kernberg describes here.

Kernberg says that the constitutional defects and the early frustrations create painful types of object relations and, as a consequence, all-out negative valence increases anxiety and produces the need to project aggression in the form of negative introjections, which then become bad internal objects. Under these circumstances, splitting is reinforced as a fundamental protection of the ego, against diffusion of anxiety. The need to preserve good internal and outer objects leads not only to excessive splitting but also to a dangerous "pre-depressive idealization" (seeing the external objects as totally good, in order to make sure that they cannot be contaminated, spoiled, or destroyed by the projected, bad external objects). When idealization occurs, it creates unrealistic all-good and powerful object images, and, later on, a corresponding hypercathected, blown-up omnipotent ego-ideal, which is quite typical of borderline patients.

The question of the origin of the splitting tendency, the predisposition of the ego toward it, and how other such defensive mechanisms as repression, introjection, and identification are related to it, encouraged Kernberg to formulate a tentative model which fused theoretical concepts from classical psychoanalysis, Kleinian psychoanalysis and the schools of ego psychology: Hartmann, (1939, 1950); Jacobson, (1954); Erikson (1950, 1956); Klein (1946); Fairbairn (1952); Segal (1950, 1954, 1956). The *identification systems* stemming from internalization of object relationships in the psychic apparatus are related, according to Kernberg, to three basic components: (a) "object-images or object-representations," (b) "self-images or self-representations," and (c) "drive derivatives or dispositions to specific affective states." The organization of identification systems begins at the early level of ego functioning "in which splitting is the crucial mechanism for the defensive organization of the ego." Later, a more advanced defensive organization of the ego develops, namely, repression, which replaces splitting, and the degree of ego development and superego integration depends on how thoroughly repression and allied mechanisms replace the splitting phenomena. Kernberg uses Erikson's developmental formulation of the three stages of self: introjection, identification, identity.

The pathology which fixates splitting and prevents its replacement by more mature defenses is residual in severely disturbed, early object relationships. This fosters the "persistence of non-metabolized early introjections which later come to the surface, not as 'free floating' internal objects but as specific ego structures into which they have crystallized." Inhibited in development are specific ego structures and identification systems, that in turn foster ego identity which should ideally take over at the highest level of the synthetic functions of the ego.

Referring to clinical approaches with the borderline, Kernberg considers interpretation a futile way of stopping the contradictions of the patient's behavior. He says that since splitting is not dependent on repression, efforts to deal with the pathology it imposes by delving into repressed, unconscious material yield barren results. To avoid anxiety, the individual will try to maintain the barrier between contradictory states. For this reason, an active attack on the mechanism of splitting as a defensive operation must be maintained. This will stir up anxiety and help mobilize new defensive operations. In this way, intrapsychic change may be brought about. Repeated interpretations of the defensive dissociation which exists between contradictory states, or between lack of impulse control in a specific area and the patient's usual behavior, may mobilize the conflict in transference. This seems to indicate that Kernberg thinks that pointing to defensive behavior is a first step in treatment, and we can agree with this principle. When psychoanalysis is attempted, says Kernberg, reality testing becomes defective and a transference psychosis (loss of reality testing and appearance of delusional material within the transference rather than transference neurosis) eventuates. This indicates that there is a tendency to act out "instinctual conflicts" within the transference as a way of gratifying pathological needs. Yet efforts to treat borderline patients by supportive approaches merely serve to reinforce defenses and leave the patient where he was before. In spite of the effort to avoid transference emergence, negative transference is prone to erupt in an insidious way: it is split up by acting out outside of treatment and with emotional shallowness within the therapeutic situation.

Kernberg (1968) says that modified psychoanalysis is necessary, i.e., a psychoanalytically oriented treatment, and he outlines seven procedures in this modified approach: (1) systematic elaboration of the manifest and latent transference (without relating it extensively to early genetic origins) inside the therapeutic situation while elaborating the negative transference as it occurs in the patient's relationships with others; (2) confronting and interpreting pathological defensive tactics that foster the negative transference; (3) structuring the therapeutic situation (such as the setting of limits to non-verbal aggression) to block the acting out of negative transference; (4) utilization of environmental resources, such as a hospital or day hospital for those patients whose acting out outside of therapy is too disturbing or so gratifying as to prevent progress; (5) focusing on defensive operations which weaken the ego (splitting, projective identification, denial, primitive idealization, omnipotence) and pointing to reduced reality testing; (6) fostering those positive transference manifestations which help the therapeutic alliance with only careful and partial confrontation of the patient with them, and (7) encouraging a more appropriate and mature expression of sexuality where necessary, to free it from its entanglement with pregenital aggression. These techniques, he feels, fall under the rubric of psychoanalytically oriented psychotherapy, rather than formal psychoanalysis.

Kernberg writes that a powerful force interfering with therapy is the patient's attempt to neutralize the emerging negative transference reactions by defensive operations, such as splitting and projective identification (Klein, 1946; Heinemann, 1955; Money-Kyrle, 1956; Rosenfeld, 1954; Segal, 1954). The latter is especially prominent in transference, and is characterized by fear and distrust of the therapist and a need to control him. For example, the therapist may be regarded as a sadistic mother-image, while the patient experiences himself as the frightened, attacked child; then, even moments later, the roles may be reversed. There is danger that the unreasonable behavior of the patient will inspire counter-transference reactions in the therapist which can provide a reality base for the patient's distortions.

Kernberg points to an observation from the psychotherapy research project at the Menninger Foundation to the effect that when therapists attempted to build a therapeutic relationship with their borderline patients, and tried to avoid the latent negative transference, an emotionally shallow therapeutic experience eventuated, along with acting out and interruption of treatment. What was deemed essential was a broadening of the observing ego by a frank dealing with the manifest and latent negative transference. Only in this way could one avoid "the vicious circle of projection and reintrojection of sadistic self and object-images in the transference."

One must always, says Kernberg, in the therapy of borderline patients anticipate the outbreak of a transference psychosis. This is usually in the form of violent verbal attacks, accompanied by delusional content—usually distorted projections onto the therapist—within the therapeutic situation. Outside of therapy the patient appears reality oriented. However, occasions may occur in some patients where the psychosis extends itself to the world in general. In rare instances, hospitalization may be necessary. The most important transference resistance which makes interpretation of transference acting out difficult or impossible is the instinctual gratification that the patient derives from his acting out.

Kernberg points out that counter-transference is very often evident in working with borderline personality problems when, in response to a need to keep in contact with their patients, therapists must tolerate regression within themselves. This is usually in the form of aggressive impulses, which may be difficult to control in the face of the patient's consistent attacks. Other regressive drives, such as masochism, may emerge. "Under these circumstances, pathological, previously abandoned defensive operations, and especially neurotic character traits of the analyst, may become reactivated and interlocked with the patient in a stable, insoluble transference—counter-transference bind." Interpretation of defensive operations may "serve to resolve the transference psychosis and to increase ego strength."

To interpret the acting out in transference as a meaningful reproduction of the patient's past relationships with parents may not be always accurate, says Kernberg. At any rate, it should not be considered as a means toward the working through of conflict. Rather, it is usually a way that the patient gratifies pathological aggressive needs. Yet, the transference regression is an essential part of the treatment process, without which therapy will be ineffective. To sustain emotional involvement entails the risk of transference-countertransference binds. A learning model would contradict Kernberg's idea that acting out in transference is not a representation of early patterns that can be used in working through. Similar techniques are used as in exploring any relationship. The acting out in transference is the essence of the negative transference as operational in the defense of projective identification; thus we use projective techniques. Kernberg believes the working through of negative transference is done by a confrontation of the patients with their distrust and hatred and how these destroy their capacity to depend on what the therapist can in reality provide. Kernberg says his experience shows that when the therapist intervenes as a particular individual, opening his own life, values, interests and emotions to the patient, this is of very little, if any, help. Never yield to dependency.

Kernberg describes his modified psychoanalytic therapy of borderline patients as one which differs from classical psychoanalysis in that a complete transference neurosis is not permitted to develop, nor is transference resolved through interpretation alone. "The focus is on the negative transference and on the pathological defenses. Transference acting out is controlled by a structuring of the therapeutic situation." Some aspects of supportive therapy are implicit in this approach, involving some direct suggestions and advice-giving. While the therapist should try to remain neutral, this does not mean he should not be active. A face to face position helps maintain reality, but the couch may also be used. Kernberg calls this an expressive, psychoanalytically-oriented approach, which should not be used with some forms of narcissistic personality organization in whom non-modified psychoanalysis from the beginning is the treatment of choice. The latter patients are less severely regressed and have much better impulse control. Thus, they can tolerate a classical technique more easily. Kernberg has made a classification of borderline types and he distinguishes these from other narcissistic types.

Nelson has written several papers on the borderline patient, stressing what she calls *paradigmatic psychotherapy techniques*, "the systematic setting forth of examples by the analyst to enable the patient to understand the significant intra-psychic processes or interpersonal situations of his life, past and present." This does not mean "acting as a model for the patient to imitate," although such a tactic might be used, but it is an active form of *mirroring*. Aimed at the analysis of resistances and defenses which cannot be handled in the classical method, they are "designed to educate the irrational ego." Nelson supposes that borderline states are matters of "fixation and retardation," rather than "regression," and the treatment process is geared to promote "remedial emotional growth and mental synthesis." Nelson speaks of "self-dosing," i.e., the patient is asked to advise procedures for the therapist to follow. Nelson believes that the borderline patient has not developed an integrated concept of self and that the "ego is composed chiefly of partial introjects and multiple identifications"; thus the paradigmatic psychotherapist trains the patient as a group, "an aggregate of selves" as well as an individual. She refers to Bychowski's paper, "Struggle against the Introjects" (1958), and Searle's essays, "Integration and Differentiation in Schizophrenia" (1959) and "Positive Feelings in the Relationship between the Schizophrenic and His Mother" (1958). In using the paradigmatic technique the therapist "may elect to impersonate in his communications with the patient any one of the partial introjects (or selves) in order for the patient to ventilate fantasies, experiences and feelings associated with the particular imago." As the patient responds to this technique, the analyst may decide (1) to remain silent, (2) to make a classical interpretation, or (3) to make an observation characteristic of the imago, or to say something that "accords with some relevant self-image of the patient," or "to verbalize the patient's current prevailing or temporary transference image of the analyst." This technique draws from Moreno's psychodramatic method, except that the drama is enacted in the one-to-one situation, rather than in the use of two or more therapists as the "alter-egos." The psychodramatic technique involves switching roles with the patient—he becomes his protagonist (i.e., mother, father, peer, friend, relative, boss, etc.) and the therapist acts as the patient. Searles has developed a similar kind of technique where he verbalizes what he feels the patient would say if he would reveal his phantasies. The "alter-ego" does this in psychodrama.

Nelson (1967) has taken note of certain facts that I find of import in considering the treatment of the borderline patient, but she puts these facts into a theoretical framework that follows libido theory lines.

She says that "the necessity for evolving techniques that circumvent the resistances that certain patients mobilize when confronted by the logic of classical interpretation has been recognized by numerous writers," i.e., Eissler (1958), Greenson (1958) and Lowenstein (1958), for example. She might have added Freud, Ferenczi, Reich, Klein, L. Wolberg and others. She speaks of the "utility of non-interpretive maneuvers" which have the effect of interpretations, and she seems to mean certain kinds of acting out which the therapist performs in order to show the patient what he is doing ("mirroring," i.e., talking with a masochistic tone, etc.—a form of imitation as a means of communication). She mentions that these non-interpretive maneuvers are closely related to a perceptual mechanism that has been discussed by Poetzl (1917), Fisher (1954),

Shevrin and Luborsky (1958), and Klein (1958). Poetzl wrote a paper entitled "Experimentally Provoked Dream Images in their Relation to Indirect Vision." She feels this has a relation to what Fisher notes as the external stimuli that are incorporated in dreams. Shevrin and Luborsky published "The Measurement of Preconscious Perception in Dreams and Images: An investigation of the Poetzl phenomenon"; and Klein and others presented the paper (1958) "Cognition Without Awareness: Subliminal influences upon conscious thought." (We should be reminded that Freud prepared an extensive bibliography and commented on some of these subjects in his "Interpretation of Dreams," 1900. He showed how the individual weaves the affairs of the day into dreams, and how stimuli presented when the individual was asleep were incorporated into the dream.) Nelson notes Holzman's paper, "A Note on Breuer's Hypnoidal Theory of Neurosis" (1959), and considers the similarity between certain conclusions of Poetzl, Fisher, Shevrin and Luborsky, Klein and others, and Breuer's hypnoidal hypothesis. Holzman and Klein apparently tried to explain dream phenomena with a concept of "subliminal perception" in the context of Freud's energy theory and the primary process. Nelson then observes that (1967, p. 83): "If these observations are related to the analytic situation, it may be hypothesized that the non-verbalized interpretations implicit in the paradigmatic maneuvers function similarly, as peripheral stimuli; that—like the blurred tachistoscopic image—the virtual interpretation registers at a more primary level than the overt interchange between analyst and patient. Because the non-verbalized interpretation in the paradigm demands no special, focused attention and because it emerges as an undifferentiated element of the ongoing, conscious encounter, it does not activate resistance as does logical confrontation. When, additionally the treatment of the borderline is regarded as a corrective emotional experience, it may further be deduced that the non-specific, non-intellectual aspect of the paradigmatic encounter more closely approximates the hypnoidal learning situations of early childhood than do the more didactic aspects of formal interpretation." While it is difficult to follow or accept Nelson's and Klein's interpretation of the phenomena, I do believe that one must take these "hypnoidal" factors into consideration. Freud's concept of displacement, denial, symbolization, dissociation, repression, *projection*, and the acting out of hysterical mechanisms based on identification and idealization, as defenses, explain these phenomena much more succinctly than a theory of "hypnoidal learning" (peripheral or latent learning) in early childhood. What is being called hypnoidal learning is an aspect of the defensive operations of the child when placed in a traumatic situation with parents (he "plays dead," as Laing says, he denies; he practises "selective inattention," as Sullivan would say, but above all, the identifications that are based on suggestibility are learned responses). I have posited (1968) that Sarbin and Asch have discovered the mechanisms that are part of the dynamics in what happens in the learning process where identification takes place. The *active behavior of the parent in promoting a specific neurotic role* makes it impossible for the child to engage in incidental learning of the neurotic role. Punishment and reward have played a part in the conditioning process. *The denial of all of this while actively pursuing neurotic goals is what makes the whole thing look like incidental learning.*

The Dutch psychologist, Dr. G. J. M. Van Den Aarweg, apparently uses some of Fairbairn's concepts with respect to role and he does things that resemble Nelson's paradigmatic approach. In a paper presented at the Postgraduate Center for Mental Health, in New York, October 1969, he suggested a treatment technique for male homosexuals that he thought might apply to borderlines and some schizophrenics. The method involved role concepts as the central theme: the "little boy" is held up against the picture of the "idealized male" or father figure and, at the same time, a "laughing technique" is used (which seems similar to some of Nelson's humor and ridicule in the paradigmatic approach), to undermine and delineate the absurdity and the "maladaptiveness" of the way in which the patient carries on relationships with others. One must point out that such a technique with borderlines can be used only when the analyst has an excellent relationship with the patient, for it may increase anxiety and prolong the paranoid defense; while the patient seems to accept the interpretation, he may use it in the service of his masochism. Van Den Aarweg feels that it is not necessary to make the connection between the role the child plays and the relationship with the mother. As the relationship with the father is revealed through holding up the "little complaining boy role" and as this is played out with the therapist, the patient as well as the therapist must learn to play the "father role" in a psychodramatic way in the treatment session.[4]

All of these techniques, i.e., the "paradigmatic," the "laughing technique," the "imitations," the mirroring (acting as the patient does or might), may have a use with certain borderlines at one time or another, but the reasons for using them and the timing are important. They do not constitute a treatment procedure per se. They are obviously used to bring acting out behavior to the attention of the patient so that he will consider the behavior "ego-alien" rather than "ego-syntonic." They are employed to overcome resistances, but they do not in themselves eliminate the resistance. *They hopefully point up the method of defense.* The therapist must still analyze the resistance, delineate the phantasy that is connected with the resistance and analyze that, making the connections between present and past.

Kernberg suggests that the "affect states" of "impotent rage" and "guilt" in transference always relate to conflicts created by early pathology in object relations, and one can readily agree with such a statement. Kernberg, like Freud, however, attributes this pathology, in part, to a constitutional factor which creates specific, defective autonomous ego functions. Apparently Nelson and Searles do not share this view.

Greenson (1968) in his book, "The Technique and Practice of Psychoanalysis," has reviewed some of the opinions of psychoanalysts as to the treatability of borderlines. The majority think that such cases are not suitable for an "orthodox psychoanalytic method" (i.e., four or five times a week treatment sessions with the promotion of what the orthodox analyst calls regression, and the development of a transference neurosis). Greenson defines transference as the "experiencing of feelings, drives, attitudes, fantasies and defenses toward a person in the present which do not befit that person but are a repetition of reactions originating in regard to significant persons of early childhood, unconsciously displaced onto figures in the present." Greenson makes several points of interest, relevant to the problem of treatment of borderlines. He stresses an important dynamic, that of masochism. "Masochists who need their neurotic suffering may enter analysis and later become attracted to the pain of treatment" (1968, p. 54). There is no doubt that this is an important factor that must be dealt with early in the treatment of the borderline and must be discussed almost ad nauseum throughout the treatment relationship. Several authors have commented on analyzability of patients: Ekstein and Wallerstein (1954), Frank (1956), Waldhorn (1960), Knapp et al. (1960). In the field of social psychology many papers have been written on resistance to change: for example, Kelly and Volkart (1952). The borderline patient is resistant to change.

In 1952 I wrote that in treating the borderline patient, "special attention must be given to the patient's masochism, the negative ego, and the projective framework within which the patient operates." Later I stressed the sado-masochistic mode of adaptation, and suggested several projective techniques that should be used, due to "the peculiar composition of the ego which tends to be organized around oppositional tendencies and negativism, the projective framework, the psychotic-like transference" (1960).

Rosenfeld (1952) in contrast to the opinions of other analysts, states that he gets good results from the classical psychoanalytic technique with very sick patients, such as schizophrenics and borderlines, and he reported the successful therapy of a catatonic.

Gadpaille (1967) has drawn attention to a form of acting out in the analytic session (some refer to this as "acting in") which he has called a "screen action," and which is typical of borderline patients and of some other syndromes, such as character disorders and schizophrenics. "Screen-action" is a "substitute phantasy" associated with an action which preoccupies the patient and which he wishes he could carry through. Related to this idea is Boyer's paper on the dream screen (1957). Gadpaille says that the substitute phantasy carries with it all of the emotional intensity of the unconscious phantasy which it represents but which the patient wishes to keep concealed in the unconscious state. In his defense, he substitutes the "attenuated and displaced phantasy" that is an "innocuous representation of the phantasy which is repressed." Gadpaille says that the patient might want to touch the analyst, for example, or leave the room; or, he might feel he wants to undress. Gadpaille suggests that the analyst become active in helping the patient to act out in some way this substitute phantasy, for then material will be forthcoming that will enable the patient to get to the deeper phantasy which is at the root of the problem. The kind of patients in whom he has observed this phenomenon are schizoid, or borderline patients as tested on the Rorschach and the Thematic Apperception Test. But they are not overtly psychotic in their everyday lives; they generally have been functioning acceptably, often very effectively, in family and business or professional affairs, but have been on a "protracted down-hill course." Their emotional impairment often includes seemingly neurotic symptoms, "such as frigidity or conversion reactions," but the problem is most typically manifested "in vague and non-specific depression, anxiety, dissatisfaction, a sense of inadequacy in their total functioning in spite of evidence of some life success, and feelings of never having achieved a valid and satisfying identity." Gadpaille thinks that this kind of acting out occurs at a period when there is an impasse in the analysis. The patient is able to verbalize that he is defending, but he does not work through the defense to bring about change. (Actually the patient still clings to the masochistic position due to the "pleasure" of aggression and revenge feelings.)

The unconscious phantasy is what makes the patient remain in the inhibited position. Gadpaille says that it has been his experience that the repressed phantasies are pregenital in nature: the patient wishes to tear the father apart, or the mother—perhaps both—with his bare hands, or he wishes to devour them; or he believes himself so magically evil that he can bring trouble on people by his wishes to seduce them, to poison them, to castrate them or to kill them. The overwhelming guilt over such phantasies is "intensified by the defective ego's inability to distinguish between the phantasy and reality."

Gadpaille suggests as a way of getting out of this impasse that the analyst confront the patient with the absurdity of the substitute phantasy. He feels that the passive couch position only helps to perpetuate the phantasy, and he feels that as such a point is reached the analyst make known to the patient that he, the analyst, has made no demand on the patient that he lie motionless on the couch. He has in no way indicated that he would be angry if the patient touched him, and so on, depending upon what the substitute phantasy suggests in the way of action. But in doing this the analyst must then be prepared for the action that might follow. The action-inhibition is thus challenged, and the patient is faced with the fact that he himself has imposed these restrictions upon himself. Gadpaille says his only prohibition in such instances is that the patient not indulge in destructive acting out. Gadpaille thinks that in using this technique the analyst acts as the patient's "auxilliary ego."[5]

Rosner (1969) has described an impasse with borderline patients which he believes is associated with the problem of separation, which is an inevitable part of change and "working through." Separation is emotionally felt by such a patient to be life-threatening, since his "identity" is based upon a condition of "pressing against another significant person." The patient cannot conceive of having a separate independent identity, but requires a force to resist in order to experience a feeling of self. The ego is split between the self and the other in a symbiotic, sado-masochistic operation. Without the other (parent or analyst) to serve either as a mirror or as an opposing force, the patient feels he will be demolished. The patient experiences no independent ego force. (This kind of feeling is, I believe, the same as Freud noted in the paranoid in what he called "the end of the world phantasy.") Rosner hypothesizes that "The partial ego only exists if it resists the remainder of the ego" (residing in the other). Consequently, these patients cannot give their all to outside goals; they cannot allow accomplishments to be viewed as evidence of ego expansion because this does not serve to unite the partial ego with the other partial ego. The second resistance against change is fear of emergence of long-repressed sadism. Relinquishing masochism immediately releases anxiety about the emergence of repressed sadistic fantasies, and guilty fear associated with the destruction of the symbiotic partner. Further, masochism cannot be relinquished because pain is the only evidence these patients have of feeling anything. One patient said to Rosner "Pain holds me together. If I give up my pain, I have nothing and there is nothing to take its place." Rosner says that while the mother of this patient communicated her sadism to the patient but acted "as if" she were being a good mother, the patient acted out what the mother tried to deny, i.e., that the patient is the masochistic object. This is the patient's only reality to the parent. Change to the borderline patient is equated with *giving in* to the wishes of the therapist. As another patient said, "I don't want to work things out. That would mean I'm toeing the line, as if I'm a puppet." (Change is equated with abandonment but it is also associated with what the patient feels is a demand on the part of the analyst that the patient "be like me").

The borderline patient has failed to experience "permanency of the self," says Rosner, and he refers to Piaget's book, "Construction of Reality in the Child." The self can be lost, Rosner says, and these particular patients delude themselves that they have separated from their pathological identificaton figures. "They will point to the facts that they have their own families, careers, or that they have placed geographical or life-and-death distances between themselves and their identification figures. . . . Clinging to the introject also serves to defend the patient against having to assume responsibility for independent decision-making and action and possible criticism. . . . Separation leads to anxiety, fears of loneliness and nothingness. . . ."

Rosner recommends the use of the *projective therapeutic* technique as suggested by this author (A. Wolberg, 1960). The goal of the technique is to show the patient that in his projections he sees in others what is also in himself; but this is not done by pointing out the projections. Rather, the analyst accepts the fact that the other is what the patient says that he is, and he makes no attempt initially to confront the patient with the projection. The projective technique serves to externalize the introject and makes it possible to discuss the unconscious motivations, the phantasies and the defenses of the other. Rosner also suggests the use of the paradigmatic technique delineated by Marie Coleman Nelson. In this kind of approach, as has been indicated before, the therapist does not challenge the patient's defenses directly but exaggerates them ad absurdum. As an example, the patient might say: "I am a miserable failure," to which the therapist might respond: "Yes, you can't do anything right!" It must be understood that the therapist uses sarcasm in this kind of retort and makes known thus that he understands that the patient is generalizing when such generalization is not in keeping with reality. Rosner also advocates using the kind of interpretation suggested by Henry Grand in the face of such masochistic maneuvers, that is, to confront the patient with his tendency to be secretive and to withhold thoughts in order to perpetuate the "epinosic gains which accompany his masochism" (Grand, 1952).

One sees in all of these illustrations that the therapist is involved with the patient's sado-masochism and the patient's need to weave the analyst into his sado-masochistic phantasy so that the patient can consider himself the victim, but with the analyst at the same time a target for the patient's sadistic satisfactions.

Moreno's psychodrama has given many therapists the courage to act out with the patient in both verbal and nonverbal ways. Moreno (1967) has reported that one important rule in psychodrama is that the patient change places with the adversary, that is, with the person from the audience who has taken the role of the other person in the psychodrama. "At the crisis of the action, the physician, who is closely following the course of the psychodrama, orders the actors to *reverse roles*: the persecuted plays the role of the persecutor, the weakling the role of the strong man, the son the role of the father, etc. The individual thus gains direct experience of the behavior of his 'opponent' or 'adversary.' As a result, he often gains a genuine insight into his fellow men, which is something far more than a mere process of intellectual compulsion. The psychodrama method also helps the others to understand the often confused personality of the protagonist. When using the so-called double method, an auxiliary ego sits or stands behind the protagonist and imitates his bearing and each of his movements. As soon as the patient, in the course of the action of the psychodrama, falls into an inner conflict, the auxiliary ego speaks the thoughts, feelings and impulses which are not really apprehended by him, thus encouraging him, exposing him, warning him."

Livingston recently wrote a paper (1971) suggesting that the persistence of the masochistic defense may be related to the patient's "refusal to mourn" the "lost object." This has great substance, I believe, in describing the dynamics of borderlines. Livingston recalls that Freud (1914) said that the naming of a resistance, i.e., its identification, does not mean that it will disappear, and that Fenichel reminded us (1945) that, "analysis consists, not merely of an 'abreaction' or of recalling memories, but of a gradual summation of discharge of less distorted derivatives." Insight alone is not enough. While we may not use the concept of "derivatives" in the sense of the instinct theory, we recognize what Fenichel called "derivatives" to be identical with "substitute actions," "substitute phantasies," screen actions, screen memories, displacement, projection and impulses to act out—all defensive operations. It seems a helpful idea in the working through process for the borderline if the analyst understands the negative factor in not wanting to mourn, the oppositional tendency, the fear of closeness, the need to maintain distance and sadistic or revengeful satisfaction he has in his denial and his passive masochistic defense.

We have suggested that in the beginning, treatment, so far as interpretation is concerned, is focused on self-attack, self-denial, fear of assertiveness, and the guilt and the aggression that are involved in these maneuvers. In this way we make inroads on the patient's masochism, and we also begin to outline the identification with the parents, first by pointing to the dynamics of the "others" in the patient's phantasies and dreams. Patients are loathe to admit their identifications with their parents, for they hate themselves for having such identifications. The masochistic mechanism is a way of clinging to the neurosis and of handling the anxiety associated with hatred for the parents. The patient can hide his revenge and sadistic feelings in this way. It is the masochism that helps perpetuate the aggression, that increases the projective mechanisms, and that allows the patient to defend and build up massive resistance, perpetuating his feelings of revenge and projecting them onto others, including the therapist. When we recognize that out of stubbornness and negativism the patient refuses to mourn the fact that his parent was rejecting and that he missed his parent and wanted him, it enables us to understand aspects of the negative transference. There is self-assertion implied in the "negative ego," for the patient "feels like a person" if he can maintain his hostility. To forgive and express affection for parental figures would show weakness and would expose one to further rejection. With continued working through the patient will eventually be able to express these softer sentiments and feelings, and move toward a more un-neurotic life adaptation.

NOTES

[1] Reich's (1931) description of *detachment* was the term "contactlessness," and for the idea of *acting out of neurotic roles* he used the phrase "substitute contact." He pointed to the non-verbal, as well as the verbal characteristics of "substitute contact." It is interesting that at the same time that Reich was writing his "Character Analysis," Melanie

Klein was developing her theories, and about nine years later Fairbairn wrote his first paper on his theory of object relations. While Freud's libido theory was a concept of object relations, it focused on how the instinct seeks objects and how the sexual libido is interwoven in the developmental system. Fairbairn wrote of the adaptation of the infant to the objects around him, and he came to a role theory and the ego rather than an instinct theory: neurotic adaptation was a psychological defense related to the ego.

2 In the profession of psychotherapy, there are no official requirements set for training. Most persons who go to the trouble of learning treatment techniques, particularly psychotherapeutic techniques related to psychoanalytic theory, do so as a self-imposed task. It is not surprising, then, that treatment is often unsuccessful. In the field of psychoanalysis, until recently, it has been felt that little can be done for the more disturbed individuals. With this kind of attitude all sorts of unfortunate practices have emerged. Many studies which purport to devalue the psychoanalytically oriented treatment process have been done, using therapists who have had inadequate training. Thus, the studies are of little worth.

3 According to Mahler, an atrophy of the instinct of self-preservation and the immaturity of the neurophysiological apparatuses at birth result in the human infant's dependency on the mother or the mother substitute for survival: "a species characteristic 'social symbiosis' between the infant and mother is necessary." (Freud called this early stage of development the stage of primary narcissism.) According to Mahler, the infant shows no sign of perceiving anything beyond his own body in the first weeks of extra-uterine life (a period called by Ferenczi "the stage of hallucinatory wish-fulfillment"). The enteroceptive systems function from birth, but the perceptual-conscious system, the sensorium, is not yet cathected. The lack of "peripheral sensory cathexis" only gradually gives way to "sensory perception." The functioning of the "undifferentiated ego apparatuses," that is, the "affecto-motor reactions such as crying," enable the child to communicate with the outside world, particularly the mother. Then the mother becomes an "external executive ego." Mahler (1958) says this is the "pre-symbiotic" or "normal-autistic phase." Under ordinary circumstances this phase gives way to the "symbiotic phase," which begins at the age of three months. During the three-four month phase the baby has temporary perceptions of the outside world in what Melanie Klein has called the "part-object stage"; at this age mothering by any person seems to satisfy the child, so that "mother" is seen only as a "need-satisfying-quasi-extension-of-the-self." This age of dim awareness marks "the phase of symbiosis," in which the infant's own and mother's body-ego boundaries seem fused, confluent and confused. The infant and his mother are "an omnipotent symbiotic dual unity" (Mahler et al, 1959, p. 822). At the end of the first year, ten to twelve months, at the "height of the symbiotic phase," an advance is made towards separation—individuation proper; separation has set in, at least so far as the body is concerned. "This occurs parallel with the maturation and consolidation of such autonomous functions of the ego as locomotion, the beginning of language, and ideation." Mahler stresses what she calls the "circular nature of the early mother-infant somatopsychic relationship," referring to the concepts of Erikson (1950), Spitz (1955), and others. (Spitz postulates that there is an absence of an "inner organizer" in the infant in the first three or four months, so that the "symbiotic partner" must be able to serve as a buffer against inner and outer stimuli, gradually organizing them for the infant and thus orienting it to the inner versus the outer world. This idea seems to support the contention that the mother and child are like a closed system in the early stage of development. Mahler shares these ideas: 1958, 1963, 1963).

The eighteen-month period is an age where ego boundaries seem to crystallize, according to Mahler. The process began at the age of ten months when locomotion was established (the child can experience separation in an active way rather than in the passive mode operative up to this point). "The control of motility, when adequately and comfortably established, provides the pattern for the subsequent development of control of emotions." Mahler refers to Jacobson (1954), saying that in the second year of life the reality testing function comes into play; this depends upon perception, motility and memory, as well as other ego functions, and through these functions the child "achieves a clear distinction between the self and the object world." Mahler says that tics and certain acting out problems indicate that the ego has had a continual experience "of being overwhelmed by inner uncontrolled forces," and this creates a "disorganizing effect which interferes with its further development."

4 Fairbairn's "rejected depreciated little boy," for example, is the masochistic side of the neurotic role that has been fostered by the parents to appease their own neurotic needs, while the "mischievous" person is the sadistic side. These are roles that the child actually did play with the parents, and he continues to play them with others as an aspect of his transference operation. *The roles are based on identification with the parent* (A. Wolberg, 1960). In treatment the patient acts at one time "as if" the analyst were the guilt-ridden rejected child, while at other times, playing the masochistic role he experienced with his parents, he projects the harsh, punitive parent-role onto the analyst—a role that through identification is now the patient's own. The patient plays either role as an aspect of his identification defense to involve the therapist in neurotic interpersonal interplay.

5 There is a belief among many analysts that borderline patients must "act out" before they can "work through." It is certainly true that borderline patients do have the kind of transferential problems that Gadpaille points to in these examples. The passivity and the masochistic position in the transference is obvious.

CHAPTER VII

FAMILY DYNAMICS AND BORDERLINE STATES

Knight (1954), in "Psychoanalytic Psychiatry and Psychology," described the borderline case as one in which normal ego functions of secondary-process thinking, such as integration of ideas and realistic planning, were disturbed. As a consequence, adaptation to the environment, the ability to maintain object relationships, and the creation of defenses against primitive unconscious impulses were severely weakened. Various combinations of factors (i.e., constitutional tendencies, predisposition based on traumatic events, disturbed human relationships and current precipitating stresses) combined to disturb the ego of the borderline patient so that it "labors badly." The ego functions especially impaired are: concept formation, judgment, realistic planning, and defense against eruption into conscious thinking of id impulses and fantasy elaborations. But, said Knight, ego functions related to conventional or superficial adaptation to the environment, which include maintenance of object relationships, do exist in these patients. Memory, calculation, and certain habitual performances seemed to be unimpaired. "The clinical picture may be dominated by hysterical, phobic, obsessive-compulsive or psychosomatic symptoms, to which neurotic disabilities and distress the patient may attribute his inability to carry on the usual ego functions. Occasional blocking, peculiarities of word usage, obliviousness to obvious implications, contamination of ideas, arbitrary inference, inappropriate affect and suspicious behavior are important symptoms." In addition, there is often a lack of concern about the realities of life; difficulties in initiation; lack of constructive achievements; insufficient ability to differentiate between dreams and reality, and a tendency to some degree of disintegration in ordinary routines of everyday life. Defense mechanisms, such as avoidance, evasion and denial, are utilized along with the ordinary defenses.

The point made by Knight, that certain ego functions are impaired while others are not, is of interest to any observer of borderline and schizophrenic patients. It has a relation, it would seem, to Freud's (1940) discovery that a delusion can be corrected in a dream.[1]* Eisenstein paid special attention to this idea of Freud's, which seems to contradict the concept of the ego as being destroyed, or of having lacunae, or defective functions. In the writings on the hysterias, this phenomenon was referred to as "not seeing," "not hearing," and "not knowing." Kernberg, attempting to utilize the structural theory (pages 129ff), in his delineation of the "borderline personality organization" has noted the "selectivity" in acting out patterns. This selectivity has a relation to what Knight has called "impaired judgment" and "blocking," "obliviousness to obvious implications," which in defense terms is connected with *denial* and *undoing*. There is a definite relation to these maneuvers with the masochistic defense. The problem is not that of a "weak ego" nor of a "defect in judgment" nor of "defective ego functions," but of anxiety, inhibitions, masochistic and sadistic patterns, and phobic and counter-phobic behaviors which have perpetuated themselves over the years. The "selective inattention" is related to anxiety, and the consequent hysterical defenses are associated with denial, repression, displacement, isolation and undoing. These patterns are based on conditionings in the family, wherein the choices for action, as Wilhelm Reich has said, forced the individual to take the path of the lesser of two evils. Freud spoke of the individual's ability, even in psychotic episodes, to know what is happening, and we are coming around to the realization that such symptoms as "depersonalization" are special experiences which the person utilizes to immobilize himself so that he will not act upon his perceptions and feelings—a defense used to protect the self and the object from aggression. What we have called "inappropriate behavior" is a cluster of defenses maintained by hysterical or splitting (dissociative) mechanisms, and the acting out of a role or several roles. The whole problem of the *observing ego* vs. the *neurotic ego* (which Freud said was divided into many identifications) must involve the dynamics of dissociation (hysterical maneuvers). There seems little doubt that what is called "inappropriate behavior" or "defective judgment" is sado-masochistic behavior associated with carelessness about the self, typical of some borderline patients. The inappropriate behavior can be seen also to be associated with roles related to identifications which have been fostered by parents to the interest of

* Notes for this chapter start page 161.

maintaining their own neuroses. That these roles are destructive to the child (in some cases being responsible for suicidal or semi-suicidal behavior, as well as homicidal and perverse patterns) has been noted by many observers, including judges, as evidenced in the following excerpt reported in the now defunct New York World-Telegram.

There was much craning of necks in Queens Felony Court in Ridgewood as Magistrate – – – castigated Mrs. – – –, 42, during her arraignment on two charges of impairing the morals of minors. The mother of five children, she is accused of enticing teen-age school children into her own home at – – –, and conducting sex orgies in which her 19 year old son allegedly took part. Devoid of cosmetics except for faint lipstick, and her only jewelry a gold wedding ring, Mrs. – – –, dressed in a grey suit, looked the demure matron as she stood in front of the judge today. She was composed when he started giving her the edge of his tongue, but by the time he finished, her lips were trembling.

"We have one of two things," the judge began, looking at her severely. "Either this poor lady ought to be examined to see if she is sick—there must be something crazy within you, driving you to do these awful things, corrupting the morals of our youths—or else you are amoral, unmoral, and immoral and worse than Sodom and Gommorrah!"

Queens Assistant District Attorney, – – –, interrupted, saying: "Your Honor, in my 12 years in the district attorney's office, this is the lowest, the most sordid case I have ever handled."

Continued the Judge: "You know . . . I'm scared. You have me worried. I hope and pray to God that there aren't many others like you, exposing your own children to such things. I hope they find something wrong with you. I don't see how you can live with yourself after this!" Then the judge ordered her taken to Kings County Hospital for mental observation. Just before taking up her case, the Judge arraigned her son, – – –, Jr., 19, on a charge of rape brought against the youth by a 15 year old girl. She claimed he sexually assaulted her in the – – – home last November 11th, at 4:30 p.m., after Mrs. – – – served her drinks and then left them alone. He ordered the boy held on $500 bail pending a hearing March 4th.

A simplified explanation of Mrs. – – –'s behavior might be that she trained her son to be a "procurer" for her and to act out sadistically with these girls who were actually, in phantasy, her homosexual partners. The latter, in turn, perhaps on a deeper level represented her parents. But we must assume that in the dynamics of this family, the father obviously plays a role. Both the mother and the father, along with the boy, would have to deny, dissociate, "not see," use repression and displacement and many other defenses in order to maintain their sado-masochistic, interlocking defensive patterns. One cannot say either that the parents of the 15 year old girl are innocent of the outcome of their daughter's behavior. Acting out patterns of the parental members of both families could undoubtedly be discovered. The victim is sometimes equally as guilty as the aggressor, in that he or she seeks out the role of victim. The judge referred to above would be filled with disbelief if we were to tell him that in many families perverse patterns are acted out between parents and children; or if we were to say that there is no perverse trait that has not been initiated by parents. It was this discovery that led Freud to deny in part the family pathology that stimulates perverse behavior and to project the "blame" to the Totem Family and the phylogenetic past.

It should be noted that Knight was one of the first to study family relations in respect to the borderline. In the belief that family relations are the stimulus for neurotic behavior, many investigators have now probed into family dynamics. Knight in 1937 surveyed the families of chronic alcoholics, whom he considered to be borderline patients. He reported in a paper that some of his observations coincided with those of observers of the Westchester Division of New York Hospital who did a study in 1935. The mothers of these patients were overindulgent and protective. For example, a typical case was that of a mother who would try to shield the son from the father's discipline and severity, and consistently act as intercessor for him in his attempts to obtain indulgences from the father. If the boy could not get money or privileges directly from his father, he would appeal to his mother and have her act as his advocate. The father was severe, unaffectionate, and undemonstrative to his wife and children. When he did grant favors, he did so sporadically and inconsistently, after being swayed by the wife's pleadings (and we can assume did so with considerable resentment, thus making the child feel guilty for having obtained favors). Occasionally, Knight found the situation was reversed, the father being indulgent and the mother cold and rejecting.

To date, it has not been possible to pinpoint family dynamics in a way that will allow an identification of a specific family-type for a particular syndrome, including borderline cases. Perhaps this will never be possible, for, as we know, in any given family one finds a variety of emotional problems. But it would appear that there is a hierarchy of acceptance-rejection patterns among family members and this is undoubtedly stimulated by the attitudes of the parents. The most severely rejected children are most likely to become the schizophrenics. The borderlines are less rejected than the schizophrenics, but more rejected than the neurotics. In surveying this kind of data we turn to sociologists, social psychologists and to physicians such as Moreno, who has taken into consideration in his theoretical postulates the social dimension or the acceptance-rejection patterns in interpersonal or group life. The "role" is emphasized by Moreno as a measurable variable in interpersonal encounters.

Extensive work on the borderline patient has been reported by Grinker, Werble and Drye (1968). Their research study describes the dynamics of borderline patients in operational terms. They consider the borderline patient an entity different from schizophrenia. Over-all characteristics include anger (the primary emotion); an "anaclitic" affectional relationship (i.e., a "complementary" pattern rather than a "reciprocal" one); absence of indications of consistent self-identity ("as if I were watching myself play a role"); depression; and loneliness.

Grinker and his colleagues group borderline cases symptomatically into four categories, described as follows: (1) inappropriate and non-adaptive behavior, deficient sense of self-identity and of reality, negative behavior and anger toward other human beings, and depression; (2) vascillating involvement with others, overt or acted out expressions of anger, depression, and absence of indications of consistent self-identity; (3) adaptive and appropriate behavior, capacity for "as if" complementary relationships, little affect or spontaneity in response to situations, and defenses of withdrawal and intellectualization; (4) child-like clinging, anaclitic depression, anxiety, and a generally close resemblance to neurotic, narcissistic character disorders.

The Grinker study reports three family types with the following characteristics: first, a highly discordant marriage (chronic or overt conflict or competition), the family not being a mutually protective unit; outright rejection of parenthood or excessive conflict over parenthood; mother-child relationships of a problematic nature, the quality of the mother's affect being predominantly negative, communication within the family confused; second, a family that has not set eventual separation of parent and child as a goal due to neurotic overinvolvement with children; thus submerging the self-identity of the children by the family; third, a family marked by individuals who deny problems, the quality of the mother's and father's affect being ambivalent, and, as a consequence, the children being prevented from developing autonomy.

The nuclear family, from which the borderline patient emerges, has, according to Grinker's research, the following qualities: (1) father's and mother's relationship in marriage is highly discordant; (2) family relationships are marked by chronic overt conflict or competition; (3) outright rejection of parenthood or excessive conflict over parenthood; (4) outright lack of provision of adequate nurturing care for children; (5) the quality of the mother's emotionality in the family is predominantly negative; (6) marital partners unable to achieve a mutuality of purpose in major areas of living, conflicting demands remaining unresolved; (7) the family goals do not embody support for the members; (8) the father's affect and emotionality remain predominately negative; (9) marital partners engage in mutual devaluation and criticism; and (10) father and mother are deficient in achieving reciprocal role relationships.

It is not clear whether the authors think of this family as being specific to borderline conditions, versus families that encourage other types of emotional disorders. My own hunch is that a family constellation which includes neurotic parents may evoke many different kinds of emotional problems in its members. But, in my opinion, specificity depends upon the nature of the choice-rejection patterns in the subgroups within the families. Such subgroups are necessarily confined to the family per se, but can include relatives and friends who live away from the family yet get neurotically involved with one or more members. One family, for example, can produce a child with schizophrenia, while other children in the same family may be neurotic and borderline. Each child is used differently by the parents, and each child has a unique social experience within the same family. The variations in neurotic and psychotic pathology can be great.

The Woll family is a case in point. Louise was the patient. She came to therapy at the age of fifty (1965) and then only at the insistence of her doctor, who told her that she could never be cured of her skin condition (eczema) unless she undertook psychotherapy. No other member of her family had ever sought psychotherapy voluntarily. The family consisted of a father, mother, Clara (the oldest daughter), Henry (the only son), Louise (a middle child), and three younger girls, Bertha, Marie and Alice. The family was upper middle class and wealthy, living in a large city apartment with four maids. The parents owned a small factory assembling automobile parts; they also owned considerable real estate. Information was available regarding the father, mother, Henry, Louise, Bertha and Alice, so that it is possible to reason backward, so to speak, to see how the dynamics of the subgroups give information as to the personality of the individuals in the subgroups.

Subgroup I was composed of father, mother and a female physician who was a cousin of the mother. The father had an affair with the physician cousin which lasted for fifteen years, and the mother, though she knew of this, did nothing about it; in fact, she seems to have encouraged the affair since she was uninterested in sex and was otherwise emotionally withdrawn. The father was an "intellectual," and the mother was considered a "non-intellectual peasant." It appeared that the father had married family money, being a dilettante who did not like work. The mother's family owned the factory, which was inherited by the mother. But the father did work at the factory about two hours each day and then left; he was usually out at least four evenings a week until one or two o'clock in the morning.

Subgroup II included Louise and Henry. Henry guided and counseled Louise. He was seven years older than she. He did not want her to use cosmetics, and when she came home with them, he would scream, wrest them from her and throw them out of the window. He did this, he said, because he did not want her "to become a whore." He advised Louise about what to read: "Only good things, not trash." He personally escorted Louise to the library to supervise her reading. He bought her good books, and had long conversations with her about philosophy, politics, education and sex. He told her how to act, what to wear, what to say. Henry was never close to anyone else. He had no friends outside the family; he was usually alone. When he was in high-school, he was absent from school so frequently that he never graduated. He preferred going to the public library to peruse items of his choice instead of attending school. He signed his parents' names to a series of notes which he sent to the school authorities to explain his absences from school. When the parents finally realized that Henry was not going to graduate from high school, they professed to be mystified.

They claimed that they were totally unaware that Henry was not attending school.

Subgroup III was made up of mother, father and Henry. Henry was berated and castigated by his father on every occasion when they met. The father acted as if he knew everything, Henry nothing. Whenever the father got into a conversation with Henry, he would belittle his opinion and would frequently hit him. Henry was deprived of material things. His only contact with his father was a fighting encounter. The mother was overprotective, babying Henry, asking him to do things for her, taking him along with her. The mother told Henry what to do, where to go, where not to go. Henry obeyed, but he seldom spoke to mother. He never volunteered to enter into conversations with his father.

Subgroup IV contained the maids, Henry and the younger sisters, Bertha, Marie and Alice. The maids would complain that Henry was molesting them sexually, but the mother would never believe this. Henry also made sexual advances toward his younger sisters, but they never dared to tell their mother, knowing she would not believe them. They did discuss this problem with Louise in later life, after Henry was taken to a mental hospital at the age of nineteen with a diagnosis of paranoid schizophrenia (1927). He is still in the hospital at the age of sixty-three. It is interesting to note that the mother, Louise, Bertha, Marie and Alice all had the symptom of sexual frigidity, which persisted in adulthood.

Subgroup V was a combination of mother, Henry and the daughters in the family. After Henry was hospitalized, the mother went to the hospital once a week, every Sunday, to visit him and she still follows this routine. The father never went. The mother forced her daughters to go with her, making them feel guilty if they refused. Henry never spoke to the members of his family when they came to see him; he was almost completely silent for over thirty years. After tranquilizing drugs came into use, Henry was given several courses of drug therapy over a period of three years. He also received shock therapy. Finally, he began to talk. He expressed paranoid feelings, thinking that people were trying to hurt him. In recent years, he was allowed to make home visits. While he was in the hospital, he read about what was going on in New York City—the theatre, the music world, education and other cultural topics. The first time he came home "on leave" from the hospital he insisted he wanted to see "everything" in New York, all the new shows, etc. The mother accompanied him wherever he went, but since she was in her eighties, it was difficult for her to keep up with him. The father continued to remain aloof from his son.

Subgroup VI was the milieu of a particular pattern of interaction between father, Clara and Louise. In this grouping, the father would keep up a battle with Clara. Louise would try to appease the father "so that he would not hurt Clara." The father would then beat Louise. However, in spite of verbal attacks on Clara, he would be "good" to her. She was the only child in the family to whom he gave presents. Clara ran off and married a boy who was not of the same religion. She is the only girl in the family who seems to have had a "somewhat normal adult life. She enjoys sex, has had children, and appears happy."

Subgroup VII consisted of Henry, Clara, and the man she later married. Clara ran away from home at the age of eighteen. She visited London, where she met a prizefighter, the man she finally married. But before the marriage took place, Henry flew to London to ask Clara to come back home. (Henry was sixteen at this time). He brought her back. Three years later she left home again, this time eloping with the prizefighter and marrying him. She went to live in Florida. She visited the family every six or seven years, each time only briefly. Clara's husband represents the "physical," rather than the "verbal" type—a brawny expression of physical action and aggression, rather than the intellectual and educated symbol represented by her father.

Subgroup VIII was composed of Clara, Louise and Clara's peers in the school community. Clara, who was nine years older than Louise, was the one person in the family to whom Louise clung and with whom she had a social life. Clara led Louise into social situations, some of which had disastrous results. Clara herself never got "caught," as did Louise. Louise became pregnant, for example, at thirteen, after having had relations with a boy named Jack, and again at fifteen, when she had relations with five or six boys who had been Clara's friends. Clara left home when Louise was about twelve, just after Henry was hospitalized. Clara taught Louise to steal from department stores and to play truant from school. Often they went to matinees on Broadway. The most humiliating experience in school for Louise occurred when, as a member of a delinquent group, Louise was apprehended by the attendance officer. The principal forced her to make a public statement in school of her misdemeanors. She was expelled, and the family had to find a private school for her. But Louise could not adjust to the school, which was located in North Carolina. She claimed that it was too far from home in New York and that she missed her family. She began to fail in her studies and the family was finally forced to bring her home. She was sent to an art school, having been accepted after exhibiting her paintings in competition with other aspirants. A few months later, Louise was expelled from school after the police revealed that she had been regularly pilfering from a five-and-ten-cent store. She never dared to apply at another school for fear that her misdeeds would be found out through her school record. Her parents made no move to help her in this dilemma, even though Louise had considerable artistic talent and was gifted intellectually.

Subgroup IX was constituted of the mother, Louise, Jack and Jack's aunt, Mrs. Kale, who was a friend of the mother. Jack was nineteen when he impregnated Louise, who was thirteen years old at the time. After having been pregnant for six months, she had an abortion (at age fourteen). (Six years later, the mother wanted Louise to marry this same young man.) The mother was incredulous when she realized that Louise was pregnant and needed to be convinced by the family doctor, to whom Louise appealed, before she would believe it. This doctor would have nothing to do with the abortion; he advised that Louise have the child. The mother would not hear of it and arranged for Louise to have an abortion, even though she was six months pregnant. Louise almost died with an infection (septicemia) when the child was removed from her. The father would have nothing to do with this whole affair. He was not interested in the "goings on," but kept on with his daily routine of being away from home most of the time.

Subgroup X was Paul, Louise, Clara, Phillip (a young man who worked in his father's manufacturing business) and Phillip's friends, George, Harry, Louis, Charlie, Stephen and William. The group formed a "sex ring," and it was in her joining the group that Louise became pregnant the second time. She did not know which boy had impregnated her. It was on the day of the second abortion, at the age of sixteen, that Louise met Paul, the boy who was later to become her husband. He was a friend of Phillip and knew about the abortion. Actually he accompanied one of the boys who met Louise on the street after she left the doctor's office, at which time they were introduced.

The example of the Woll family, as described above, does not exhaust all of the subgroupings which it is possible to outline. The interpersonal relations of the three younger girls in the family have not been stressed. In the subgrouping, the main actors were mother, father, Clara, Louise and Henry. It is obvious that, with respect to scapegoating, Henry was most deeply injured, Louise was the second, and Clara the least injured. Clara resolved part of her problem by breaking away entirely from the family. Louise married at an early age and substituted her husband for her mother. She felt he kept her tied down for twenty-five years working in their drygoods store. After about fifteen years of marriage, Louise carried on an affair with a doctor to whom she went for physical care. Until two years after she began psychotherapy, Louise was tied to the mother, whom she saw three or four times a week and for whom she did a great many household tasks. Louise's major symptom was eczema, which erupted in different parts of her body—under her armpits and breasts and on her thighs, hands and feet. On occasion she would dig her feet until they bled. Her character diagnosis was passive-aggressive personality with paranoid trends. In her early years, Louise had migraine headaches up to the time she started her affair with the doctor. It was as if she substituted the eczema for the headaches. The psychiatrist who took care of Henry told Louise that the mother's diagnosis was paranoid schizophrenia, although she was never hospitalized or treated. He considered the father to be a passive-aggressive personality with grandoise trends. The three younger girls married, but after about eight and ten years of marriage respectively, two of them left their husbands, and the husband of the third girl died. One of the girls remarried. They worked in the public school system—two of them becoming superintendents of schools, the third giving up her principalship to take over the job of manager of a small business. Intellectually oriented, they ignored Louise socially and "looked down" upon her, seeing her only at family gatherings. They considered her "stupid."

If we were to interpret what was happening, we might say that Louise played the role of mother's partner and acted out many of her mother's neurotic but denied wishes. The fact that the mother wished Louise to marry Jack—despite the unfortunate unfeeling way he treated her, and the traumatic situation surrounding the pregnancy at thirteen—was an indication of how active the mother's phantasy was. The father's relationship with Clara seemed to influence her deliquency and her relations with Louise. Louise was the scapegoat in several of the subgroups: in the group with father and Clara, in the dyadic group of herself and Henry, in the sex ring, and in the group with her mother. Clara, like the father, acted out without any dire consequence to herself, but the effects were seen on the other family members.

One should keep in mind four points in relation to neurotic and psychotic role behavior in the family: (1) the connection between the neuroses and/or psychoses of the parents and that of the child is a function of the parent's "use," "exploitation," "scapegoating of," or "aggression against" the child for purposes of maintaining neurotic and/or psychotic dynamic balance through displacement; (2) neuroses and psychoses are based upon *identifications with the parents* which enable the child to comply with the parent's demand that the child perform the neurotic and/or psychotic roles to appease the parent's pressing neurotic or psychotic needs (both the parents and the child use repression, denial, displacement and other defensive measures in the identification process); (3) the defense mechanism of displacement is a function not only of anxiety, but also of both aggression and of identification, the latter always being accompanied by repression, denial and "splitting" or dissociation, and the acting out of roles; displacement is one of the bases for the formation of subgroupings within the family; (4) there is a functional relationship between neurotic and psychotic phantasies[2] (sado-masochistic phantasies), neurotic and psychotic roles, identification, transference reactions and acting out.

If these hypotheses are correct, then Moreno's technique of discovering sociometric choice should enable the social scientist to test the validity of the ideas that certain subgroupings within the family are based on displacement stimulated by the aggression against children from parents. The least rejected should be the child most accepted by the parents (and by the other members of a family as well). The most rejected would be the child most rejected by the parents. Between these two extremes, the other siblings would fall into place on the choice-rejection scale. This scale can correspond to Freud's continuum; those least rejected would belong to the milder categories of neuroses, according to

Freud's developmental scale, while the most rejected would be the near psychotics and the psychotics, or those lowest on Freud's developmental scheme. The most rejected would also have the most anxiety and tension and the greatest prevalence of bodily reactions, somatizations and/or conversions or hypochondria. They would also have the most intensive aggression and the more pervasive depressions.

While I am not suggesting the validity of Freud's developmental scheme, I believe that his idea of placing the neuroses and psychoses on a continuum can be reconciled with Moreno's theory. Intellectual and physical development proceed willy-nilly. It is the emotional factor that makes the difference in the kind of adjustment that is implemented, and it is the communications (by way of interaction) from the parents that create the conditionings, emotional conflicts, and such dynamisms referred to by Freud as the repetition-compulsion, the transference, the defenses and the resistances.

My own observations convince me that the borderline patients possess, as a rule, very disturbed mothers (A. Wolberg, 1952). These mothers fall into four main categories: (a) the severe obsessive-compulsive mother; (2) the narcissistic, competitive mother with strong masculine qualities; (3) the paranoid mother; and (4) the passive schizophrenic-like mother (the child-mother).

The obsessive-compulsive mother may be either compulsively clean or compulsively dirty, and she acts out in the family group her resentment toward men, whom she holds responsible for the fact that women are expected to take a degrading role in life. The mother functions by being perpetually busy, performing various duties for her family, giving no thought to herself as a person. She goes through the role of wife, mother and homemaker, but she openly hates men and repudiates femininity. In her child's feeding and toilet training, she is usually severely punitive.

The narcissistic, sadistic mother is controlling, punitive and competitive with her children. Nagging and constantly critical, she professes avid interest in her children while deserting them for a career. This mother is self-seeking and often has many masculine qualities. She is usually successful at work, but repudiates femininity and will perform no household tasks. This type of mother maintains psychic integration though sado-masochistic (sexual) acting out with her children and others. Her feeling is a kind of monster reaction to the child, and she offers proof of how she has suffered because of the child's ill will.

The paranoid mother is suspicious and constantly on her guard. Mothers with paranoid qualities may influence their children so that they never develop trust or feelings of closeness towards others. Peer relationships may consequently be impaired. The child is always on the periphery of a group, never a part of it. He avoids close relationships. Case histories usually reveal that children of such mothers are unable to become a part of a group on their own, but they may have group experiences under the protection of siblings or sibling substitutes. Such guardians are often not of the child's own age level, so that he is unable to share secrets, compete, or become intimate with a peer as special friend. While we know that the pre-pubertal group life is difficult, it is especially difficult for children with paranoid mothers. Where such a mother is seclusive and detached, remaining at home a great deal, the child will also fail to relate adequately with his age-mates. He is likely to identify with the mother and develop traits similar to hers. The world outside of his own home is a threatening, hostile place. His abysmal inhibitions prevent this child from trusting his own observations and differing from the disturbed parent.

The passive schizophrenic-like mother who is in the house, but "isn't there" at the same time, at least not as a mother, may conceive of herself as one of the children, while the father, or at a later date, an older child, assumes the responsibility of the maternal parent. This mother lives for the most part in a phantasy world, constantly recalling the past, which is glorified and given a fairy story quality. Mothers of this type tend to prevent the child from accepting reality and from establishing an adequate security mechanism. They also shy away from assuming an authoritative role and this blocks the child's superego development.

On the basis of my observation (A. Wolberg, 1968) the fathers of borderline patients can also be categorized: (1) the passive-aggressive father who seems a schizoid type and withdrawn; (2) the hostile, aggressive attacking and controlling father; (3) the paranoid father; and (4) the mildly psychopathic father.

The passive-aggressive father is "good," more or less detached, but is in spite of his "goodness" a destructive member in the family, usually pitting one person against another. He plays a role often in that he is a help to his wife—he serves her. On the surface he does not seem to be very hostile, but he fails in his role in the family as father. He takes no real responsibility, but in small ways he will suddenly assert himself, usually to do something destructive. His sadistic impulses and his oppositional tendencies seem to have the purpose of frustrating others, perhaps in the form of teasing either the mother or a child with whom he is dealing. He works and supports his family, however, and is often a great financial success. This is perplexing, because he seems to allow himself to be completely overshadowed by the mother. He is often described as innocuous, ineffectual, nondescript—a weak person. He shows hostility in what can be described as secretive ways, by withdrawal, generalized passivity, and acting in ways that are inadequate to the occasion. Attached to his wife, who is a strong, controlling person, he accepts her contemptuous attitude towards men, probably because his guilt for his sadism necessitates this masochism. The wife can, nevertheless, be protective of him. This man often allows himself to be used as an errand boy, and he will go to great lengths in permitting others to use him in various ways, including appeasing his wife, who can be very unreasonable. He seems like an obliging sort. He is easily fatigued and often sleeps a great deal, and he employs many avoidance techniques, sometimes working more hours than is necessary. He is careful not to extend himself too much or to become too involved with others. He sometimes acts out sexually with other women and represents himself as a dominated and misunderstood man who has secret wishes to break out of his jail. But he never does, and thus he frustrates the hopes of the "other woman." There is little sexual feeling for his wife; often their living schedules do not completely coincide. If he does not act out sexually, he phantasizes a great deal about idealized love situations with women who "might be."

The second father is often an extremely competent man, controlling, but in an openly competitive way, so that, when he seeks to encompass both the male and the feminine role in the household, he actively "takes over," manages, plans, makes the decisions. He does this in an effort to "show up" the weaknesses and inadequacies of his wife. The woman passively yields her role, and then she feels free to vent her hostility; she feels justified in her anger. Frequently this father faces the mother with her hostility, and he is often openly critical of her. He does a great deal of battling, fighting or bickering with his wife, his children, tradespeople, and carping about the way things are managed in general. This father frequently focuses on money, challenging the way members of his family spend money and belittling their judgment. He implies that they have little regard for money or that they squander it. He feels exploited by everybody. Often he does favors for people, but there is a "busybody" quality about this activity. Secretly he is manipulating people. Such a parent helps to confuse the child as to male and female role. Generally he is sexually adequate with his wife and does not go with other women. She is caught in the trap of this pleasure, and she suffers his domineeringness and his contempt for the sake of the security he provides and the sexual pleasure.

The third type of father is the man who is superior, detached, paranoid-like, and grandiose. He raises himself above the motley crew, the family. He contributes little, often does not support the family financially, but allows the wife to do this, or at least to do most of the work toward providing an income. Demanding worship, he is the counterpart of the so-called narcissistic woman. He is frequently away from home, attending meetings and going to clubs and events. He presents himself as an authority on all subjects: nuclear physics, psychology, history, politics, etc. He is conversational, intellectual, sometimes brilliant. This type of father is intensely competitive with his children, and he often prevents them from developing their own intellectual curiosity or expressing their own ideas and feelings. He has disdain for the world and for the common conventional practices of the human race. He prevents his children from identifying with the group and he encourages isolation.

The fourth father is mildly psychopathic. He lies a little and he cheats a little, and he is usually fast to see how he can take advantage of a situation both financial and personal. He does not have too much respect for anybody, and yet he presents a façade of sociability. He finds a great deal of excitement in pitting one person against the other. He may release competitive conniving feelings through gambling and other forms of acting out. He is the type of father who tends towards addictions of one kind or another—not too severe. He drinks, but you cannot call him an alcoholic. He is a compulsive talker; he eats too much; he smokes too much; he is restless. This father makes unnecessary demands on his children and makes them feel guilty if they doubt his sociability and kindness, and he is inclined to promote in them antisocial behavior by his treatment of them.

In the borderline patient, as in other syndromes, both the oedipal and the preoedipal dynamics are expressed in sado-masochistic patterns. It is the depth or the extent of the pathology which determines the form of the patient's emotional disturbance. In explaining the oedipal problem in women, for example, Freud in 1931 took pains to mention that if a father rejects a daughter or detaches from her, so that she is thrown toward the mother, her relations with men will be disturbed. She may even turn toward women for sexaul encounters. Thus in the rejection of the child, the parent tends to throw the child into more intimate relations with the other parent. There are always sexual implications in this maneuver, which account for the homosexual trends. Moreno has pointed out that each family group is unique; thus, there are infinite varieties in these relationships. In families with neurotic parents, the object relationships are of a pathological nature, embracing interlocking defensive maneuvers. Since the oedipal conflict is a function of family operations and stems from the sado-masochistic relations between parents and children, the dynamics may be schematized as follows:

Type I: The father is more rejecting of the daughter than is the mother. He pushes her toward the mother. The mother engages in, by acting out her own hostility toward men, pitting the daughter against the father. But because the daughter needs the father, she identifies with his hostile patterns. An intensive identification, usually denied, is with the father as a reaction-formation against the anxiety of the deeper rejection. On the surface the daughter has less hate and more kindly feelings toward the mother, with whom she is also identified. Thus there is more ambivalence toward the mother and more guilt toward the father since the hatred is deeper. The injury to the daughter tends to drive her toward female figures in adulthood. A homosexual trend, usually latent, will then be manifested with women in one form or another. Perverse sexual acting out may take place with men.

Type II: The father is more rejecting toward the son than is the mother, and he pushes him toward the mother. The mother expresses her hostility toward men by pitting the son against the father. But because the son needs the father he identifies with his hostile patterns. An intense identification exists with the father as a reaction-formation against the anxiety of the deeper rejection by him. The son has less hate and more kindly feelings toward the mother on the surface. Thus there is more ambivalence toward the mother, with whom he is also identified, but more guilt toward the father since the hatred is deeper. The injury to the son will tend to drive him toward women in adult life. A homosexual trend may be expressed in his acting out the role of a male who has become involved in a seduction and ultimate rejection of women.

Type III: The mother is more rejecting toward the daughter than is the father, and the mother pushes the daughter toward the father. The father expresses his hostility toward women by pitting the daughter against the mother. The daughter becomes identified with both parents, but the more intensive identification is with the mother as a reaction-formation against the anxiety of the deeper rejection by her. The daughter, on the surface, has less hate and more kindly feelings toward the father. Thus there is more ambivalence toward the father and there is more guilt toward the mother since the hatred is deeper. The injury toward the daughter will tend to drive her toward men in adulthood. A homosexual trend may be expressed in her acting out the woman who has become involved in a seduction and who must ultimately reject the man.

Type IV: The mother is more rejecting toward the son than is the father, and the mother pushes the son toward the father. The father expresses his hostility toward women by pitting the son against the mother. The son becomes identified with both parents, but the more intensive identification is with the mother as a reaction-formation against the anxiety of the deeper rejection by her. The son, on the surface, has less hate and more kindly feelings toward the father. Thus, there is more ambivalence toward the father and more guilt toward the mother since the hatred is deeper. The injury to the son will tend to drive him toward male figures and a homosexual trend may be manifested with men in one form or another. Perverse sexual acting out may take place with women.

Type V: The fifth possibility is that both parents are equally rejecting. The child here tends to become "psychopathic" and may very well act out his homosexual trend in overt forms, yet remain bisexual.[3]

Types II and III are the context in which occur the variations found in borderline patients. In the sexual development of the borderline patient, it is obvious, as explicated above, that a confusion of sexual role is present. Male and female are intermixed since the mothers and fathers of these patients usually repudiate to a degree their normal sexual identities, showing latent homosexual trends. In the "use" of the child, the parent expresses compulsive perverse feelings, concealing these within the rearing techniques. Through this means, latent homosexual and other perverse habits are fostered in the child. Compulsive masturbation, with sado-masochistic phantasies depicting the relationship with the parent in symbolized forms is one of the methods the child uses to discharge his excess energy accumulated from excessive stimulation by parents. In extremely inhibited children, the phantasies may exist with masturbatory equivalents, like peeping, skin picking, hair plucking, etc. Because the parents feel guilty about their needs and aggressions, the child is taught to deny that he is engaging in the transactions designed for him. This forces him to repress to a considerable degree thoughts, feelings and knowledge of what is going on, and to act as if he could not understand the reality. However, the "as-if" behavior does not mean that the patient cannot perceive reality. In the defensive maneuver he then substitutes for the existing sado-masochistic relationship with his parents the defensive phantasies picturing sado-masochistic situations that involves not his parents but "others." This is the kind of projection and displacement which must be taken into consideration during therapy.

Aspects of family dynamics have been touched upon by many authors. We have named a few: Freud, Sullivan (1926-7); Levy (1932, 1953); Szurek and Johnson (1952); Fries and Woolf (1953); Wolberg, A. (1952, 1968); Jackson (1957, 1959, 1961); Searles (1958; 1959); Mahler (1958, 1963). Others who have studied certain elements in the behavior of family members are: Lewin (1930); Frank (1944); Tietze (1949); Gerard and Siegel (1950); Lidz and Lidz (1949, 1952); Reichard and Tillman (1950); Beckett et. al. (1956); Lidz and Cornelison (1957); Ekstein and Wallerstein (1954); Freeman and Grayson (1955); Frazee (1953); Freeman et. al. (1959); and Vogel (1960). Many of the family studies stress the role of the mother with the infant in the early stages of life, neglecting the interactive roles between father and mother under the influence of Freud's developmental concepts.

Social techniques for coping with certain kinds of sado-masochistic problems such as "re-parenting" have been suggested by some authors, and recently a self-help organization involving parents who indulge in child abuse has emerged. These steps are not necessarily inconsistent with therapeutic procedures, but they are usually entered into by individuals who find it difficult to maintain therapeutic relationships; the problems reflected are usually more severe than those of the borderline.

NOTES

[1] We now feel that the patient's ego functions are not impaired, but in relation to certain events and situations he responds with the kind of defenses that make it look "as if" his ego functions are impaired. This mechanism is connected with what Sullivan called "selective inattention," or what we are now suggesting may have something to do with phobic and counter-phobic behavior. Often the patient appears to have the "stupidity complex" noted very early by Morel.

[2] Phantasy, as we are using the word, connotes, as we have said, a reaction to stress and conflict created by a reality situation. Phantasies are thoughts organized in a defensive manner, responses to interpersonal involvements which give rise to tension and anxiety.

They originate in the family atmosphere and in interactions where the individual, because of his conflict and frustration over the behavior of family members, particularly the parents (the "double bind" is based on this concept), develops emotional problems. The neurotic or the psychotic phantasy is one of his defenses. In the phantasy there is always a mental organization that represents in some form the family relationships which are sado-masochistic in essence. Miller's frustration-aggression hypothesis can be considered as pertinent in relation to phantasy, for the mental representations depict the frustration and the aggression within the sado-masochistic frame of reference. The greater the phantasy life, the more "used" has the individual been—that is, the greater the hostility, rejection and aggression of the parents, the more controlling and binding the parents, the more complicated the individual's defenses.

³ The manipulations of parents in stimulating the identification process in children can change as other children in the family are born. For example, a mother may "drop" a son if a girl is born; a father may "drop" a girl in whom he has shown intense interest if a son is born; but the relationship will usually eventuate according to one of the five patterns indicated.

CHAPTER VIII

DIFFERENTIAL DIAGNOSIS IN A STUDY OF
TWO PATIENTS: SCHREBER AND DAIRD

Ferenczi once remarked that the mental processes of psychoneuroses and functional psychoses could be distinguished from normal mental activities only by their degree, not by their kind. Today we regard the entire concept of "normal" as diffuse and confusing, but Ferenczi's idea does have a clinical validity. Ernest Jones once pointed out that the difference between the maladjusted and the rational is more quantitative than qualitative. When we consider the defensive operations of borderline patients as contrasted with psychotic individuals we see that the differences are indeed quantitative and can be characterized primarily by the degree of projections and introjections that exist in the one as opposed to the other. We may illustrate this by comparing the mechanisms of Freud's famous paranoidal case, Dr. Schreber, with one of my borderline patients, whom I shall call Dr. Daird, a Professor of Physics in one of the leading universities.

Many of the defensive mechanisms of the borderline patient are of a paranoidal nature. They are often disguised or concealed by the operations of the "reasonable ego," which maintains a relationship with reality. Only under the impact of severe anxiety are the protective arms of the reasonable ego swept aside. Then we may observe the paranoidal system in clear culture. Nevertheless, in bursts of revery or in dreams, paranoidal mechanisms reveal themselves

163

masked by whatever symbolic distortions are deemed essential to evade overwhelming anxiety. If, as is our thesis in this chapter, the difference between psychosis and borderline states is that of intensity, not kind, it would seem appropriate to examine pristine paranoidal operations as revealed in the study of a paranoidal schizophrenic such as Schreber.

In his exposition on Schreber, Freud brought out fundamental dynamics that are applicable to both psychotics and borderlines. Among other important statements, Freud said: "The person to whom the delusion ascribes so much power and influence . . . is either, if he is definitely named, identical with someone who played an equally important part in the patient's emotional life before his illness, or else is easily recognizable as a substitute for him. The intensity of the emotion is projected outwards in the shape of external power, while its quality is changed into the opposite. The person who is now hated and feared as a persecutor was at one time loved and honored. The main purpose of the persection constructed by the patient's delusion is to serve as a justification for the change in his emotional attitude." The implication is that the child once loved the parents but now hates them, and feels justified in view of their behavior, but the whole idea is unacceptable. So it is projected. But the defense in the paranoid mechanism is more complicated than Freud thought, for it reveals what Schreber himself is like, in view of his identifications with his parents. This is the well known defense of projective identification.

Schreber's "homosexual wish," his masturbation and his masturbatory phantasies, as well as his fetishes, were all unacceptable to him, and undoubtedly would be to his father and mother, for they would be confrontations of the way in which Schreber was used by them, and their own similar phantasies would be unacceptable. In defense, they set up denial mechanisms and force the child to deny the secret communications, both verbal and non-verbal that constitute the method by which the parents let the child know the type of neurotic role he must play in their defensive maneuvers. Schreber had to resort to the elaboration of the delusion and to megalomania in order for his ego to tolerate his parent's neurotic demands and his response to them. The megalomania enabled him to accept what Freud called the "wish phantasy," and what we now call his *identification phantasy*, his identification with his neurotic parents as they impressed upon him the neurotic role he must play in their lives. Recognizing neurotic and psychotic phantasies as defenses, one must take a cue from another statement of Freud to the effect that, generally speaking, every human being oscillates all through his life between heterosexual and homosexual feelings, and any frustration or disappointment may drive him over into homosexual acting out (1911). What Freud has touched upon here is something we see in our patients often. Disappointment and frustration or failure creates conflict which is temporarily resolved by homosexual acting out. The fear of success may produce anxiety which is handled by homosexual acting out. Since we are assuming that there is no acting out pattern that is not based on identification, we say there is no neurotic conflict without identification, and in acting out the individual symbolically communicates with the parent (the rejective aggressor) as a means of quieting his anxiety. In the acting out, the individual acts like another person or plays a social role that the other person wishes him to play (A. Wolberg, 1960), and this is symbolic of the original parent-child relationship. Thus, Schreber's need to play a homosexual role was stimulated in the family not only by the parent of the same sex but was fostered by the activities of his parent of the opposite sex. What is obvious in these instances is that when the desire to assert oneself in any important way emerges, either sexually or non-sexually, the anxiety can become so great that it is "bound" by the organization of a phantasy where frustration and sado-masochism enter the picture—the desire for success then being overcome by some form of acting out of the homosexual phantasy. This is the familiar pattern of "giving in to the other." The desire to succeed will be undone by the acting out of the passive-aggressive homosexual phantasy.

Freud said that paranoia resolves into their elements the products of the "condensations" and "identifications" which are effected in the unconscious; thus, the dividing up of his physician, Flechsig, and God, the "splitting" of the souls, are representative of important relationships in which identifications have been made. According to libido theory tenets, regression in paranoia takes the individual back to the stage of development before "objects" were entirely consolidated as "wholes," the beginning of the narcissistic stage. The various identifications or "introjects" represent part objects that have not been assimilated but which have remained as foci of conflict. This concept in one way is reminiscent of the early speculation of Freud and Breuer that a memory could act like a foci of infection or a foreign body around which defenses had to be built. The libido theory, introducing the idea of object relations, places the "introject" in the unassimilable position, but, rather than a memory per se, this represents an identification with the object and therefore a pattern of relationship. Repression and "splitting" (of consciousness?) was an aspect of the defense. We see, however, that the "splitting" phenomenon has a relation to *denial of the identifications and* the need to dissociate the *whole concept of the reality situation and the parent's role.* What Freud has referred to as pieces of the whole, or "part objects," and has related to regression and to a particular developmental phase, appears to be in fact a hysterical defense (a dissociation, and displacement to other objects, as in a dream)—a defense which has been effected to control the anxiety the child has, or later on, the anxiety the adult has, while he is still emotionally tied by identification to the parent in the sado-masochistic mode. He has still not extricated himself emotionally from the identification, nor from the behavior pattern that the identification stimulates. The idea that "pieces" and "parts" are related to hysterical mechanisms of defense (dissociation and displacement to several objects), rather than representing a regression to a former or archaic part-object libidinal state, is a premise that can be applied to the concept of projective identification. To preserve the projective identification, the patient shows great facility in defense. We find this ability to shift rapidly from one defense to another in borderlines, too (Wolberg, A., 1952). The patient "uses, in rapid succession, various control mechanisms such as flight from disturbing situations, escape into bodily satisfactions, and wish-fulfilling phantasies. But the phantasies can be broken into pieces and parts as a means of disguise. Symbolization, displacement, condensations and other mechanisms are used to represent both male and female identifications, or in other words, identifications with father and mother. Characterologic mechanisms are simultaneously employed, especially passivity, dependency, aggression, detachment, masochism and sadism. . . . There are . . . frequent though brief periods of shattering and confusion." Depersonalization phenomena take place as a means of controlling anxiety and can be thought of as hysterical in nature. The "ego shattering" techniques, which, in fact, are associated with the individual's need to "protect the object," can also be thought of in this way. Freud had depersonalization experiences, and it is clear that in his change from the seduction theory to the libido theory he was protecting his own "objects" and denying the perverse traits of his "objects." It is amusing to recall that Freud wrote in indignation of Janet, who accused him of using his theory to conceal his corrupt Viennese sexuality—a doubly entertaining thought when we consider the reputation (at least in literature) of the French. This need to "protect the object" contains some of the dynamics of a phobia in that the object becomes a phobic object. We assume that in the act of projection and displacement there is an hysterical maneuver—rejection of part of the self, or making a "not-me," which appears to have some of the aspects of a phobic avoidance. The mechanism of projection is used concomitantly with the idealization of the objects; yet there is derogation of these same projected objects. In fear of assertion, inhibition is "rationalized" as the object becomes a phobic object. The concept of the ego-ideal and idealization within the concept of superego are "splitting" concepts as well as defensive maneuvers. The superego is associated with a phantasy (sado-masochistic in nature), as is the paranoid projection. In this context it is interesting to recall that Rickman said (1926) that the superego is a *technique for maintaining object relations.* In psychoanalytic theory, the superego is an identification concept which refers solely to relations with parental objects. Thus, the superego, we may say, is actually *a defense,* the defense of identification used to maintain object relations with neurotic or psychotic parents.

Dr. Schreber's upsets, two in number, took place on the occasions of his being promoted to positions he wished ardently to achieve. Schreber attributed his difficulties at these times to overwork, but in perusing Freud's account, it is obvious that his guilt over his success had ushered in the mental organization which was characterized by homosexual phantasies, strong self-recriminations, and delusion. The voices said: "This wants to be a Senatspräsident." It was as if he needed to undo his pleasure attained through accomplishment. In homosexuality, Freud implied, Schreber "gave in to the other."

The first attack was one in which the patient displayed symptoms of hypochondriasis, but Freud could discern no delusions at this time. His intensive hypochondriacal feelings were, nevertheless, harbingers of delusions, or more precisely, somatic aspects which were incorporated later into his delusional system. After a period of treatment by Dr. Flechsig, Schreber's symptoms subsided. During the eight years that elapsed between the first and the second illness. Schreber reported that he was happy with his wife, and that his life was rich, but he claimed that his happiness was marred from time to time by disappointment in his wife's inability to bear children, which made him feel inferior. To complicate the situation, Schreber's wife was so happy that Dr. Flechsig had "returned her husband to her" that she kept his picture on her dressing table. This was interesting in view of the use that Schreber made of Flechsig in the phantasy which accompanied Schreber's second episode, which was precipitated by his having been appointed, in June 1893, to the position of Senatspräsident in the Oberlandesgericht in Dresden. He was to take up his duties in October of the same year. Repeated dreams of Flechsig invaded his sleep. He dreamed also that his old illness had come back. One morning, "between sleeping and waking," he had a phantasy of how pleasureable it was to be a woman submitting to the act of copulation. Upon assuming his duties as Senatspräsident Schreber became acutely ill, his mind being flooded with homosexual thoughts.[1]*

Schreber's anxieties were apparently relieved by the delusion (his sexual phantasies) that he was being mistreated on behalf of a sacred cause, which seems to be an instance of idealization in terms of the "imagoes" or the introjects; he would sit perfectly motionless and rigid for hours thinking masochistically about how he was being tormented—another version of the beating phantasy. These thoughts tortured him to such a degree that he longed for death. He made repeated attempts at drowning himself. He asked to be given cyanide. His condition became so grave that he had to be hospitalized. (Such feelings have been attributed by later writers to the revenge motif—one is willing to die if he can make the "object" feel guilt and remorse.) As his religious delusions began to be elaborated, he lost some of his desire to kill himself. He was in communication with God; he was the "plaything of devils." (Freud wrote in the essay on "Female Sexuality," 1931, that the child can be "an erotic plaything.") Schreber saw miraculous apparitions; he heard holy music; finally, he believed that he was living in another world, after having died. As his religious delusion

* Notes for this chapter appear on page 184.

developed, he was able to act more normally on the ward in the sense that he could deal with some of the responsibilities of everyday life. He no longer sat in a stupor, but he did have a peculiar kind of gait which seemed to be part of his hypochondriasis. He continued to believe that he was being injured by certain people, and he verbalized his hostility in the form of excoriating his persecutors. Being persecuted justified "pouring abuse on them." The most prominent of his persecutors was Flechsig, whom he called a soul-murderer. This is an excellent example of projective identification.

Schreber eventually "became himself" again, while still retaining a few fixed delusions. He was able to converse about many things, keeping abreast of what was going on in the world and discussing contemporary topics expertly. However, he soon expressed the grandiose notion that he was a prophet with a special mission in the world. He had been assigned by God to redeem the world. The most essential feature of his redemptive mission was that it must be preceded by his transformation into a woman. (Today we have seen this phantasy acted out by some homosexuals in their operations to change sex.) He did not wish to be transformed, but God demanded it. The projection of his "homosexual wish" was an aspect of his paranoid defense, but in our present way of looking at matters, in order to feel degraded one must indeed have been degraded by parental figures. Schreber must have been degraded by his parents, but he projected the whole affair on to God and onto himself. It was not his father or mother, or both, who had a secret need to degrade him, and to assign to him a homosexual role, nor was it his father and mother who secretively used him as an object of their own homosexual impulses, but it was a projection of his own impulses which he despised. After having been both rejected and sexually stimulated by his parents, he does indeed have homosexual impulses. His projective defense mechanism is an aspect of the undoing process in the context of denial and projective identification. One must degrade one's self and become second rate if one has desires to be first rate, for to be first rate would be to challenge the whole neurotic structure of the parents and one cannot defy authority that way. It was God's wish, not his father's and mother's and finally his own, that he be converted into a female; his own "wish" was his succumbing to the wish of the high, idealized authority.

God was connected to the dead by "nerves"; thus his "connection" with Schreber. Nerves that were in such a condition of great excitement as Schreber's had a precise property which exerted an attraction upon God, and this accounted for his relationship with God. (This is a statement about the silent sexual "game" between father and son in the family. The child takes the burden of the problem on himself, denying the role of the father, and the father, in his own defense, encourages this displacement.) The communication which took place between Schreber and God was entirely outside human experience (denial of the relationship between Schreber and his parents). The communication, non-verbal, that goes on between homosexuals is well known. They can smell each other out, so to speak; they pick up cues that others cannot. (This is the same kind of communication that goes on in families when parents use their children as transferential sexual objects. The homosexual in his encounters merely repeats in some form patterns to which he was conditioned in childhood in the family.) Schreber was the only person who had ever had this experience with God (denial of the fact that the father or mother and not Schreber himself have homosexual impulses and "use" people in secretive ways to satisfy their perverse traits); therefore, he was the most remarkable man ever to have lived. This obviously refers to Schreber's need to have attention from his father. We can assume that Schreber was a rejected child and emotionally neglected. The overevaluation (idealization) of the father is evident as part of Schreber's defense. We see that the ego is being "split" into "good" and "bad" in this identification. The idealization of the father and of his own identification with the father was an important aspect of his illness. (We have mentioned that, in treatment, the patient can take the role of the parent with the analyst or he can project the role of the parent onto the analyst, playing the role of the bad child himself. The split transference and the identification in the transference is then acted out. This motif is found in child's play and is undoubtedly a means of reliving the anxiety of having been placed in a particular role by the parent. In his 1931 essay, "Female Sexuality," Freud mentions the role of play as a means for the child's acting out active and passive roles. He sees this as a way of working through the oedipal problems. The concept of sado-masochism is not stressed, but it should be, for the only reason anxiety occurs in the oedipal situation is that the parents' performance of their parental roles reveals their sexual and aggressive aims, and the child responds with anxiety to these secret games or aims of the parent. The child is expected to play a particular role in these parental aims.)

During the process of being "transformed" into a woman, Schreber suffered great injuries: he lived for a long time without a stomach, without intestines, almost without lungs, and with a torn esophagus. (Was this displacement upwards, and an internalization and masochistic defense against his feelings of hatred and aggression for women?) But, as these phenomena ceased, he became a woman. Female nerves passed over his body and now, through a process of direct impregnation by God, a new race of men would emerge. Not until then would he be able to die a natural death and, like the rest of mankind, gain a state of bliss. Birds spoke to him in human accents and miraculous things happened everywhere around him. (We do not understand why some individuals must act out this self-destructive phantasy and have themselves actually castrated by operations before they can gain relief from sexual anxiety, while others can find solace in thoughts about such changes. Perhaps the castration is a substitute for the murder that the individual wishes to commit against his parent.)

Freud mentions that Schreber's primary delusion was that of being transformed into a woman, and that "playing the part of Redeemer" was a secondary phantasy. We can see that these are sado-masochistic phantasies and are merely aspects of his main identification phantasy.

The part of the persecutor was originally assigned to Dr. Flechsig, but later was transferred to God. Schreber said, in effect, that his conflict was resolved by the religious delusion: "I shall show later on that emasculation for quite another purpose (other than the gratification of the sexual appetites of a human individual) is within the bounds of possibility, and, indeed, that it may quite probably afford a solution of the conflict."

The voices treated his emasculation as a disgrace. He was mocked and called "Miss Schreber."[2] The voices said: "So this sets up to have been a Senatspräsident, this person who lets himself be f — — — — d; or: "Don't you feel ashamed in front of your wife?" The guilt and the conflict Schreber showed in getting a high position is indicated here. Also, we might suppose that he masochistically takes all the blame for not having children so that he can deny his rage toward his wife. He will phantasize castration himself before he will reveal his deep hostility towards women and his desire not to give a woman children or sexual satisfaction.

God was a strange individual. One had to communicate with him by "root-language" after undergoing a "purification process." God had power, yet power could be exerted upon him. He was almighty, yet he was very earthy too. God called Schreber names: "Scoundrel" he would say. Schreber shouted invectives at God. In a condition of intense excitement, the nerves of living men have a powerful attraction upon the nerves of God, such that he cannot get free again. (In this concept, there is a clear indication of the kind of sexual phantasy being enacted in Schreber's early family and sexual messages which were conveyed from parent to child. Schreber's rage is being expressed in a projective way, and the idea is that he has succumbed, he has been caught in the web of the father's and mother's secret neurotic aims, sexual and non-sexual—but he can make God suffer too.)

Schreber said that God does not understand living man. God was quite incapable of dealing with living man. God had intercourse with corpses. (Here, there is a direct reference to the sexual phantasies of Schreber and his parents. Schreber had been a corpse at one time.) It was because of his inability to understand living man that God persecuted Schreber. (The detachment of the father and the hostility is indicated here.) Schreber could not reach his father, or get to him, except as the father could use him as a sexual object. The father was ungiving, withdrawn and full of hate. But we know that on another level Schreber was describing himself—the denied or rejected part of himself.

Actually, there were two Gods, an upper God and a lower God, each having its separate existence. These Gods were at odds; they fought, yet they were tied together (father and mother and the sado-masochistic relationship).

Freud thought that quarrels between parents and unhappy marital relations stimulated a child's emotional life and led him to experience love, hate and jealousy in varying intensities too early in life, and that this situation determines "the severest predisposition for disturbed sexual developments or neurotic diseases in children."[3] Such problems are indeed the stimulus for the emotional problems in children, the preoedipal and the oedipal problems. (This premise seems to be borne out by the work of Stanton and Schwartz, who found, as noted earlier, that patients were extremely sensitive to disagreements they sensed among staff members and reacted by smearing episodes and other forms of destructive and demeaning behavior.)

To avoid being thought of as a dement by God, Schreber submitted himself to a burdensome system of enforced thinking. (This is obviously a reference to compulsive and obsessive thinking and the masochistic maneuver of taking the blame for the problem, rather than placing the blame on the parents.) If he allowed himself to depart from this system (finally the obsessive thinking took the form of delusion), or to relax and have no particular thoughts, God would jump to the conclusion that Schreber's mental faculties were extinct and that the destruction of his understanding had taken place. (This was un- doubtedly a reference to the controlling tendencies of the father, to his perverse sexuality covered by his puritanism, the father's sublimated homosexual interest in young boys and his piousness. It was also an indication that in being so se- verely controlled by his parents, Schreber had been made to feel intensely guilty when his own ideas were different from those of his parents; he would be doubly guilty if he allowed himself to "divine" the unconscious mechanisms of the parents.)

Schreber had a problem in the evacuation of his bowels. He was preoccupied by thoughts about feces and bowels—the contents of his bowels were smeared over his anus. This act was performed by the upper God (is this the female God, the mother?) and repeated several dozens of times a day. This is associated with an idea that while sexuality may have a biological base, sado-masochism is learned—it does not derive from an innate bisexuality but from relations with father and mother. The activity and passivity so prominent in sado-masochistic behavior are aspects of sadism and masochism (learned responses) rather than innate masculine and feminine trends. Masochism and sadism have roots in displacement behavior. One can notice, for example, that in children aged one or two, if they are chastened, or if they are thwarted, they may well strike out at another person, or bite—the mother, the grandmother, the nurse, the father—whoever may be caring for them at the time, and, when they are restrained or prevented from hitting the adult, they turn on themselves, hitting at their own head or their face, or biting themselves. The displacement has a homeostatic function. *But without the parent's intervention and insistence, this displacement activity could not become a sado-masochistic pattern as we see it in the neuroses and the psychoses.* It was not just that neurotics had sexual thoughts, or memories of sexual events; they had perverse thoughts stimulated by the parents who trained the child in a perverse role as an aspect of the parents' defense. The displacements to others are encouraged by the parents as further aspects of defense—i.e., the displacements are the encouraged or "permitted" aggressions. Patients who are not overt perverts have perverse trends and thoughts. Paranoid phantasies are particularly laden with perverse trends: they are used for masturbatory purposes, and are the stimulant for sexual acting out, as well.

In his essay, "The Defense Neuroses" (1896), Freud made the following connection between *ideas* and *sexual feeling* associated with physiological areas: "The formation of ideas with a sexual content produces, as is well known, excitation processes in the genital organs similar to sexual experience itself. We may suppose that this somatic excitation transposes itself into the psychical sphere. As a rule, this kind of effect is much stronger during actual experiences than during recollection of them. But if the sexual experience occurs at a time of sexual immaturity and the memory of it is aroused during or after maturity, then the exciting effect of the recollection will be much stronger than that of the experience itself because, in the meantime, puberty has increased to an incomparable degree the capacity of the sexual apparatus for response." An inverted relationship of this kind between real experience and memory appears to be the psychological condition of repression. Freud explained in his essay, "Heredity and Etiology" (1896), the way in which early memory can be utilized by the individual during his life to stimulate sexual feelings long after the initial experience has taken place. He mentioned that, when a child is prematurely stimulated sexually by adults, he does not respond the way an adult would; but, later on, the memory of the event will produce the same results as if it were an actual event. We now know that this, indeed, is the way that sado-masochistic phantasies operate: they stimulate the individual sexually so that acting out takes place. The most ordinary cue from the environment can set off such a conditioned response. An example of how the patient can use almost any situation as a "cue" to a paranoid thought and the acting out of a homosexual phantasy will be revealed in the following:

Dr. Quinn, a resident in pediatrics and a Phi Beta Kappa, has a feeling of intellectual and physical inferiority when he is in a seminar or a clinical conference with his peers. He has ideas but does not express them, due to his passivity; when someone else speaks up much more quickly, he sinks back in his chair in a kind of depressed state, but secretly he is in a rage and he wants to destroy the person. He looks at the person who is aggressive and active and "idealizes him"—he thinks of his physique and has a phantasy of himself as a "jerk." He leaves the hospital and acts out homosexually, intending to be the aggressor and indeed he is, so far as picking up the "other" is concerned. During the sexual act he is the aggressor, but in the end he manages to have the other person humiliate him by throwing him out and telling him he is not an adequate lover. He has acted out his aggression symbolically, and then he is punished. One of the problems that is facing Dr. Quinn is the fact that he has found a girl he likes very much and who obviously loves him. He often feels dead emotionally and is jealous when she is able to enjoy herself sexually with him—he becomes angry to see how she can respond so spontaneously. He fends her off because he is afraid of close relationships, afraid of love, afraid of his own tender emotions, and he resents giving pleasure. His need to remain a "little boy," while the circumstances all indicate that he is about to become a well-trained, more than adequate doctor. He is not sure that medicine is what he wants.

It is likely that the great turning point in Freud's career took place in the summer of 1897, when he began his self-analysis. He was discovering the oedipal problem. He had hysterical symptoms of his own (a phobia) and the self-analysis led him into his personal thoughts of perversion. His change of theory and some of his new ideas appear to have been in the interests of his own defense. Letter 70 to Fliess is of note because Freud denies the role of his father in his illness. The paper on "Screen Memories" (1899), considered to be autobiographical, illustrates many of the phantasy defenses and the denial and repressive measures utilized by the neurotic (child and adult) to allay the guilt he feels in "knowing" the reality situation between himself and his parents, in understanding their role in his emotional problem. He "knows," and he denies that he "knows." In his later years, Freud (1936) recalled a visit to Athens which took place in 1904. He described a strange feeling, a confusion, a "de-realization," which he said had "something to do with the child's criticism of his father and the underevaluation which took the place of the overevaluation of earlier childhood"; "overevaluation" and idealization of the parent or the authority figure, as we know, was to play an important role in Freud's concept of identification; it was a forerunner of the concept of the ego-ideal and the superego, a defense which was touched upon in the essay on "Family Romances" (1909) and elaborated in the essay on "Narcissism" (1914). The ego-ideal was an aspect of the dynamism of identification and it was related to the oedipal problem; it was also a dynamic in "splitting," as was repression.

Freud said that, as a child, he felt that his father was "the wisest, most powerful and wealthiest man." The paper entitled "A Disturbance of Memory" illustrated how a child acts toward a father about whom he feels guilty, and it demonstrated the way in which early conditioning can affect mental reactions in later life. The fear of success which we associate with a sado-masochistic trend and guilt was evident in Freud's reaction. But Freud tolerated his success—he did not undo it. This undoing trend is much more severe in the schizophrenic patient such as Schreber. Freud was neurotic. Dr. Daird is borderline, tending toward psychotic, and Schreber was psychotic. There was obviously anxiety felt by Freud in his success, since he had somehow been made to feel guilty concerning his own wishes. In his book, "The Interpretation of Dreams" (1900), he presented the analysis of many of his own dreams, and it was evident that he had much fear, guilt and hostility toward his father which he projected on to others. He wrote of the reaction to his father's death, "to the most important event," the most poignant loss, of a man's life. It is apparent that the "de-realization episode" was a kind of hysterical attack, a "de-personalization" mechanism to make the "self" temporarily immobile. This is one of the mechanisms we have observed in the hysterias, in borderline conditions, and in obsessive-compulsive problems. It was obvious that anxiety could be aroused by anger, and that the "splitting of consciousness" or the repressing, the idealization of "de-realization" and the dissociation and denial could come about as a consequence of the emergence of ideas tinged with anger, rage, and fear.

Freud's relationship with his mother was coupled with sexual and aggressive thoughts. He spoke of females as having inferior status and intelligence, as being sexually loose. His anger and contempt for women seemed more overt but equally highly defended. In his correspondence with Fleiss (Letter 70) Freud reveals some of his inner struggle at the time he was discovering the oedipal problem: he tells of his phantasies—his feelings toward his mother are implied when he mentions his childhood sadism, practiced with a nephew against his niece, and the rage toward his father when he tells of his death wish against his younger brother, who died, although he denies that his father had a determining role in his neurosis. Freud disclosed more: "My emotional life has always insisted that I should have an intimate friend and a hated enemy" (1899).

Adler seems to have played the part of the "hated enemy" after Freud gave up Fleiss, Janet and Breuer, for Freud constantly referred to Adler throughout his life in his writings, calling him a "defector," and a "former analyst." Perhaps, this was because Adler had discovered some of the principles of ego psychology and was explaining ego dynamics in a different way. Ego psychology was, after all, one of the great contributions of Freud. But Adler made great advances in this direction too.

Now, let us consider my patient, Dr. Daird, the physicist, and compare him with Schreber. We shall see that they have traits in common: hypochondrias, the phantasy of being a woman, sado-masochistic masturbatory phantasies, fears of success and anxiety at success which set off both self-effacing and grandiose phantasies. But Dr. Daird does not have the well developed delusional system; he can tolerate success, albeit with intense anxiety, and he can remain in an interpersonal working relationship with a woman even though he considers women inferior. It is clear how his sado-masochistic feelings and maneuvers interfere with the therapeutic relationship and with his relations with others. He is able to sustain himself with his girl friend. Dr. Daird can be called a borderline patient, or perhaps what the American Psychiatric Association classification describes as a case of chronic undifferentiated schizophrenia. A sample session will illustrate dynamics similar to, but not as pronounced as, Schreber's.

He is angry before the session but he cannot say that he is angry nor can he say why he is angry. He uses a phantasy to relieve his anxiety.

PT: I came early and then I was annoyed that you didn't take me early. I was wondering whether the reason that I came early was so that I could be angry—angry at you because you kept me waiting. In a way, it's desirable to wait so that I can feel angry. I had a phantasy: Your secretary called you to tell you that I was here and I wondered whether you could come right out, even though it was early, and not keep me waiting, or whether you would keep me waiting. You did not come out and I was getting mad.

(This is a typical way the patient has of relating to people. The sado-masochistic motif is evident, and the paranoid quality of the phantasy— actually this is an example of projective identification. Often he acts out this phantasy in the sense that he becomes angry at me for what I have done in the phantasy or what I may do to make his phantasy come true—rather than what I actually do. He experiences anger toward me only in response to the phantasy. He has never been able, as some patients do, to say that he wants to be special, although he often acts out the "bright little boy who gives the parent pleasure." The phantasy allows him to feel justified in his anger. The phantasy also reflects the frustration he felt with his parents, and their practice of frustrating him. He now has the same characteristics as his parents. Underneath his anger, there is a feeling of closeness with the analyst which he fears. He cannot express any kind of tender feeling, for he would, at the same time, feel himself engulfed by the object of his good feelings. He himself feels guilty and he projects this to others, having been the object of severe control by his parents. His phantasy is a defense, and, at the same time, a representation of the kind of relationship he actually had with his parents and that he now has when he is in an intimate relationship with others.)

TH: In this phantasy I am doing something that irritates you—I'm keeping you waiting, even though in reality I was on time. I wonder what anxiety you felt that made you have the phantasy just at this time?

PT: It's silly but I thought I should report it. I had the phantasy so I thought I should let you know. (He is being a good patient.)

TH: Yes, I see; it is helpful.

PT: I was having a hard time today on the telephone. Some man, Mr. Yerkes from the administration, called me to tell me that if we were to do anything about the contract, my research contract, that it would have to be done right away. I was having palpitations. I tried to figure it out. I felt that he would see through me. I could not tell him anything because I'm waiting for a message from the woman in Washington who will tell me whether they are going to renew; that is, if they are going to give me another grant this coming year. I cannot tell the University until she tells me. I got all excited and was not sure that I could talk to him. I did, but with tremendous anxiety. I was keeping information from him and I got all upset.

TH: You felt guilty, but you did hold back the information anyway.

PT: Yes.

TH: He must represent some kind of figure to you.

PT: Yes, someone who is pressuring me; someone I can't be entirely honest with.

TH: Can you think of anything else that is making you feel guilty?

PT: I had a dream. I . . . . I was pregnant; and in the dream I had all sorts of phantasies about how I could become pregnant (the homosexual phantasy in disguise). And I felt frightened at the pain I would have in giving birth to the baby. I felt that if something overflows in me—the seminal fluid—that it's like an open-ended tube, and that I can become pregnant because the fluid will seep out and come in contact with—well, I don't know. It's like leaking bladders. Somehow Margaret (his girl friend) and I, on the telephone yesterday, were talking about leaking bladders. I don't know whether it's physically possible to have such a thing. Does a bladder leak? And where would it leak if it did leak? Leaking bladders are anti-Semites. Margaret was saying that it is a figure of speech. Ben Hecht used the phrase to describe anti-Semites. I was thinking of Mr. Yerkes being an anti-Semite. (He was annoyed that he had to deal with Mr. Yerkes before he was ready and he wished Mr. Yerkes dead, only he projects the "wish" on to Mr. Yerkes.) Ben Hecht—anti-Semitic—it's like being self-poisoned; I wonder if Ben Hecht was that deep about it or if he just happened to use the phrase. (He was angry that Mr. Yerkes was putting him on the spot. He felt guilty because he was stalling Mr. Yerkes and putting him off.) Did Hecht really know what he was saying? The full significance of his phrase? While I was still asleep with this dream, I was having the association that perhaps, as a child, I had a fear of pregnancy. This was, perhaps, a basic fear of mine about becoming pregnant. Yes, I used to think of that often. (In the context of this session, the patient reports the dream as a kind of association. When thinking of his relationship with me or with Mr. Yerkes he has these phantasies—I am withholding and so is he, and Mr. Yerkes is making demands—masochism.)

TH: You used to think of yourself as a woman? I remember a few sessions ago that you said that you had a phantasy of being a girl. Something like that; do you remember?

PT: Vaguely. Yes, I'm beginning to remember.

TH: It was something about your father, I think. Do you remember?

PT: Well, I guess, about the enemas—I used to fear them—I probably thought I could get pregnant through the anus. I remember thinking that if I swallowed a seed, a plant would grow in my stomach—that was a fear. Enemas, well, I may have thought that a child could come out through the rear.

TH: Well, then, actually your father had impregnated you through the enema, and you had fear. (Masochism in relation to sadistic father.)

(These thoughts were associated with childhood fears. He has intimated that his father may have been getting some homosexual satisfaction out of the enema practice and that the father was humiliating him at the same time. At present, when he is with his girl friend and she wants sex, he is conflicted about his feelings. He wants sex but he does not want to give sexual satisfaction. Sometimes he needs a homosexual phantasy, or at least a sado-masochistic one to stimulate himself sexually in intercourse with his girl friend.)

PT: (He ignores me.) Then there was another part of the dream, or, perhaps, another dream. I saw this girl, Clara, in the dream. She works with me in the office, and she is pregnant. I kid with her. I say, "Come away with me."

TH: You tease her?

PT: I play this role with her. But, when I'm with her, I really mean it; she does stimulate me.

TH: You do actually like her?

PT: Well, in the dream, I meet her in a rendezvous and after a while she went into the ladies' room. Interesting that there wasn't any men's room. But, outside, there were men's rooms, but they were open like in France—the men urinate in the streets and have bowel movements too—and no one seems to mind; nobody bothers about it—and the women do their dirty work behind doors. That's what I'm thinking about now. There is this theme that has shown up in many of my dreams about being exposed—sometimes it's when I'm having a bowel movement and sometimes when I'm urinating. And I always feel funny being exposed, (exhibitionistic and voyeuristic feelings.) When I had this dream, I felt that perhaps it would reveal a basic conflict.

(There is a basic conflict represented here, his passive-aggressive pattern and his fear of the other person and his need to protect himself and others from his anger and his love. He protects the object and himself. But he is deceitful in his relationships and his passivity is great. His phantasy of the secretary is in the context of an oedipal drama. He wants to take her away from her husband. He wants her to elope. The phantasy reflects a transference feeling and a feeling he had as a child towards his father. He is the one who slept with his mother. He slept in the same room with his mother until he was nineteen. The father slept in separate quarters because he was too "nervous" to be in a room with another person at night. But he was made to feel that he should attach no meaning to this arrangement. And if he had sexual phantasies, he was guilty, not his parents. He was not to think of his penis, of sexual stimulation. Else he would be punished. Freud's typical idea of castration anxiety is implicit here. The idea Freud had, however, was that these feelings would occur despite the parents' behavior, i.e., even if the parents' behavior did not stimulate the feeling. We do not share this idea today. Freud did not deny the accidental cause altogether but tended to feel that all children had experiences of this traumatic kind and that it was only the constitutionally weak ones who succumbed to neurosis.)

Yesterday, I had this set-back and felt this anxiety and the palpitations all over again; and I felt discouraged. I thought that it would be nice, when I went to bed, if I'd have a dream that would reveal the problem to me. That's interesting that I called it the women's dirty work, if they go to the bathroom. As a child, I was afraid of the telephone. I was afraid of that big black thing. I was afraid that I wouldn't be able to understand that black monster! I was just afraid to use it. I've heard theories about the telephone; that it gives your phantasies a chance to work—you can't see the person on the other end of the wire and your phantasies can work. Maybe I'm not interested in having a contract. I don't want to be bothered. I don't want to do the administrative work. I'd like to have the money to go off to Europe, but I don't want to do work on the project. I never took time out to learn about administrative details. I don't see why I have to; there are secretaries who can do these kinds of work. But, I guess I feel guilty. I don't like to work, and I feel guilty.

TH: Is it that you don't like to work? Sometimes you seem to like work.

(He always says that he is lazy and doesn't like to work. He has mentioned the phantasy in the past of wanting to take the project money and go to Europe to have fun, just to steal the money. He has an intense feeling of passivity and inertia; he resents having to act, to make decisions, to be forceful or direct. He resents working in the analysis and becomes angry when things happen which would tend to drive him out of his detachment and his autism. He feels guilty about not wanting to work in the analysis. He resents having to "give" to his girl friend, and to give in the analysis.)

PT: Well I'm lazy. I like to play and dream. (Withdrawal into phantasy and acting the role of the little boy.) Having a baby—there's something homosexual in that. I'm itching my ear, but I don't think it's anxiety.

(In past sessions, when the patient became anxious he rubbed his ear, and he sometimes felt that it was like masturbation—to comfort himself. He remembers that his father pulled his ears as a punishment; and he also remembers, when he was five or six years old, being told by the maid not to play with his penis in the bathtub; he then pulled on his ear instead. This is a kind of symbolic acting out of an identification feeling, an oedipal phantasy. He denies that he is feeling anxiety and that the pulling of his ear has a symbolic, homosexual meaning. He withdraws in the session out of fear of closeness.)

Well, there are these men who flit about like women—and our High School principal—he never married and there were rumors that he was a homosexual. And then there was Tom Murphy in school who used to call me "Mary." (Schreber had the thought that somebody was calling him Miss Schreber, and he incorporated this in his delusional system.)

TH: Did he think that you were effeminate?

PT: I don't know. I don't think so, but he did it anyway.

TH: What would the implication be. He did it just for kicks? What would homosexuality mean to him?

PT: That I'm soft, a sissy, that I'm weak.

(He feels a certain contempt for himself in not wanting to work, but he also feels angry that circumstances force him to work. His passivity bothers him. His work is becoming more and more successful but it is also requiring more of his time and he has less time for dreaming. He will have to step out of his autism and resolve his phantasy world if he continues with his work and with analysis.)

TH: What are your associations about men who flit about like women: What comes to your mind?

PT: As you ask this question, I remember something I used to do for excitement. I'd stand in front of the mirror—this was after puberty—I would put my legs over my penis (he means that he would hide his penis between his legs) and make myself look like a woman—visual excitement—curiosity of a kind. Maybe I allow myself to see a naked woman this way. (This seems to be another version of the homosexual phantasy and similar to some of Schreber's phantasies.) Curiosity, and it's narcissistic, too; and it's also a joke. A joke in the sense that I can make myself look like a woman and then devise some distorted satisfaction from it. Switching myself into another person in order to get the same satisfaction that I would get if I looked at a real woman—that's sort of splitting a personality—if you can't split yourself then it doesn't work. You are the other person. You are yourself and the other person at the same time.

(It has been my construction that the father was using this child to appease his own homosexual impulses and that the game the patient is talking about is the homosexual game between himself and his father. He got not real satisfaction and acceptance as a child from either his father or his mother, for they each used him in their own way. The mother kept him in her bedroom and then was explicit in telling him to turn his head when she dressed and undressed. In past sessions their teasing has been hinted. In this session he shifts from father to mother but in the context of a homosexual phantasy.)

TH: Well, whom do you represent? What other person?

PT: My mother flashes into my mind. (She did not accept maleness.)

TH: You didn't see your mother nude?

PT: No.

TH: You had wanted to?

PT: Oh, yes.

TH: You said "sexual"—no, you said "distorted satisfaction." Did you mean sexual? A sexual feeling? Distorted sexual feeling?

PT: Yes and curiosity. I was never satisfied as to what a woman really looked like.

TH: You never saw your mother, even though you slept in the room with her?

PT: No. Only that once.

(The mother used to sleep with the patient in the same bed until he was about nine years of age. Then he had his own bed, but was still in the same room with his mother until about the age of nineteen when he went into the Navy. The patient has one brother—older than he, a cripple and a paranoid person, who has been sick all of his life as the result of an accident which occurred when the father was driving the car during the brother's early childhood. Brother slept in a separate room. Once his mother rolled over on the patient in her sleep, and he wondered whether she knew what she was doing. He was afraid that he might have sexual feelings. One of his great fears as a child was that if a girl got near him, he might have an erection even in non-sexual situations, and that he would be disgraced.)

I think that the one opportunity I had to look was when I was sleeping, not in her bed, but in the other bed. I'd try to look. I'd look and then I'd look away. I didn't want to be caught looking at my mother. I had a very strong desire to see my cousin Stephanie, though. My boy cousin, Ralph, always used to look at Stephanie; he used to climb up a tree and look at her through the second story window. My boy cousins used to tell me that they saw their sisters undressed. I seemed to be hungry for such an opportunity—to see somebody nude—a woman. Even now, as I talk about this kind of looking, there is an anxiety, a certain anxiety, certain feelings of wanting, of participation—also a frustration, because it doesn't give any satisfaction—yet there is a strong kind of pull to look—it is also linked up with anger.

(In the session, he can only feel angry in a phantasy. This time the phantasy is of how his mother frustrated him. He feels this way in the transference.)

TH: You have the feeling of anger? (My thought is that he feels I am frustrating him by expecting him to work rather than acting out with him as his mother did.)

PT: Yes.

TH: You feel like looking now?

PT: Yes. In looking and peeping there is also the association of a feeling of wanting to get rid of a lot of pent-up emotion. What flashes through my mind is a guilt feeling.

TH: Not anger or sex?

PT: No. I felt guilty when I was with Jack. (He shifts from feelings in the session to an incident with his roommate.) We settled the car business yesterday but we were talking and we got onto the subject of sex. I told Jack that I feel better when I am having a steady and regular sexual relationship with a woman; and he knew that I meant my relationship with Margaret—someone who doesn't excite me too much sexually. I felt guilty because I felt that I was talking about someone—about Margaret to Jack—talking about somebody to another man. Also, I think I was saying it to brag; like saying that I am better than he—the guilt is about exposing a woman though. And then perhaps it's still that old feeling—I still have to prove myself, that I can sleep with a woman. Guilt. It's like on the telephone; I'm constantly afraid that people will find out about me; that I'm not doing my job; and I feel that they will ask me questions, and I will become upset—my breathing will come hard—they will be testing me to see if I know what I'm doing. (This is his fear of assertiveness, his fear of his own masculinity, his fear of impotence, and actually his fear of success. His need to assert himself is coupled with aggression. His only joy in self-assertion is his phantasy of overcoming the other person.) It's disappointing to have a day like yesterday. I don't know how I lived with this in the past. I don't know whether I have less defense now—maybe there are now more opportunities for these things to come up. Am I having the setback in order to frustrate you? Then I can say to you: "Look, I'm not getting any better. What shall I do?"

TH: You have a no-good analyst. A guilty patient, a sneaky patient and a no-good analyst. (His passivity and his aggression are evident. He rushes on to prevent my talking more.)

PT: Yesterday I felt guilty for having phantasies about Jack the other day.

TH: Do you feel guilty when you think of trying to maneuver me into that kind of position—I mean so you can feel angry at me and disappointed?

PT: Well, I guess so.

TH: There seems to be no end to the ways you can manage to feel guilty. If you're not getting better and if you have a setback you are perhaps feeling angry at me.

PT: Well, not really; I had that phantasy when I came in but I'm not really angry at you.

TH: I was thinking that Jack has some of the traits that stimulate those phantasies in you. We spoke of your father's traits as being like Jack's.

(Patient has had difficulty with Jack, his roommate, over a car. During the first part of the school year, the patient had made an arrangement with Jack that if he would take care of parking the car on the street, and moving it from one side of the street to the other, as the parking rules required, then he could use the car for his pleasure whenever he wanted to. Jack is a professor at the same college where the patient works. The patient did not want to be bothered with moving the car and was eager to shift the responsibility to the roommate. The patient had become more and more angry as the year went by, however, because Jack used the car practically every day, and the patient used it hardly at all. Jack used the car weekends and for dates. The patient began to feel he had made a bad bargain; and he became more and more enraged at Jack, sniping at him when they were together in the apartment. The patient felt, too, that Jack was not paying his share for the food and that he was not doing his part of the work around the apartment. Finally, the patient became so upset that he handled the situation by taking the car to his father's house in Pennsylvania and leaving it there. When he got back to the apartment, he told Jack that he could buy the car if he wanted to use it. They haggled for two weeks over the price, and agreed upon $432.50. The patient said that the price of the car was $400, but that the $32.50 represented the sum he just paid a garage for repairs; and, since Jack used the car three-quarters, if not nine-tenths of the time, he should pay the bill. Jack agreed, and the patient went to Pennsylvania for the car. But, while he was waiting for Jack to give him the money, Jack had started using the car again, and the patient then began to have phantasies that Jack would park the car on the street some place that the patient wouldn't know about, and that he would continue to use the car without paying. The patient then had the phantasy that he would be helpless in such a situation, and he would have to call on the police to look for the stolen car so that he could either get the car back in this way or have the police help him collect the money from Jack. The police would come, and they'd begin to track down the car. It was these feelings and phantasies that the patient referred to when he said he felt guilty about his feelings toward Jack. The patient has the same feelings about analysis. He wants it, but he does not want to go through what one must to undergo the analysis. He resents having to give up his phantasies. He resorts to them frequently in his relations with people.)

TH: Actually you don't want the car?

PT: Well, I want it but I don't want to keep going out to change from one side of the street to the other. Jack is willing to do that.

TH: Will you miss the car?

PT: My associations just now make me think that I have some self-exciting mechanism—to excite myself sexually. But there is something about anger. Would you say that men behave like women in order to excite themselves sexually—is that why homosexuals act like women?

TH: Perhaps that is why—I guess they do that for the purpose of exciting themselves. But you say there's something about anger.

PT: You mean that it's a kind of masturbating activity.

TH: Uh-huh.

PT: But they go around constantly!

TH: Yes, they sometimes seem to be in a chronic masturbatory state—perpetually masturbating, or doing something that is the equivalent, during their waking hours—or most of their waking hours.

PT: I can't quite catch it, but there is something very quick that goes on in my mind, that makes my heart pound—it's a kind of compulsive thing—I feel the need to obey—a kind of compulsion to obedience (the need to give in to the other). This seems to be reactivated in certain situations—like yesterday in the telephone conversation—and it happens sometimes with Jack. Also, at department meetings—the feeling that somebody is going to catch me and I will be reduced to a hysterical, helpless mass. It reactivates that feeling that I'm about to be caught. I can't go on forever escaping. Am I going to get it? Oh! Those words! I wonder why I used them. My father used to say that: "Now you're going to get it!" No, I'm not sure—he said—I guess he said: "Now I'm going to give it to you!" That was when he was going to hit me with the strap. It seems to me that that is the kind of phantasy that can scare me; that could frighten me. (These are the beating phantasies similar to the ones Freud wrote about in his essay, "A Child is Being Beaten." Often, the homosexual will have a beating phantasy as a prelude to acting out. Freud noted that such phantasies are acted out by hysterical patients—they bring on attacks.)

TH: Do you feel that if you're angry at me you'll get it?

PT: Why do you always bring yourself into it?

TH: I was thinking that in your phantasy the person on the other end of the telephone is your father; the man in the phantasy is like your father? If you come early here and then I keep you waiting by being late, you will be angry and I will be like your father; I'll punish you for being angry or hostile. You put me in the phantasy that you confessed about when you came in today. You'd like me to take you early so we could spend more time.

PT: Yes, I guess so.

TH: It's like something is going to happen so that you'll have to be beaten.

PT: I guess so. The person asks me a question and I get frightened and I stiffen up and go into that spell.

TH: What spell?

PT: Oh, you know—that panic, sweating, breathing hard!

TH: Did you argue with your father a lot?

PT: No, I don't think so.

TH: Did he make you feel guilty?

PT: Yes, a lot.

TH: About what?

PT: Everything.

TH: Did you have sexual feelings about your father?

PT: No, no.

TH: For your mother?

PT: No, no, she's not sexual looking. Although I may have had those feelings anyway. Certainly curiosity. I always wondered if she knew she was rolling over on me.

TH: What did you think?

PT: I never could decide.

TH: Did your father criticize you?

PT: I can't remember; it doesn't seem so. He was critical, though. He'd listen to my violin playing and criticize me. But I always assumed that he didn't know what he was talking about—that he didn't know anything really about the violin. It's hard to remember my father being like that. This feeling that someone tried to catch me, or is trying to catch me, to find me out. Well, he must have been. He was, to some extent. I can't remember. I can intellectually think that he was critical but I can't *feel* it at all.

Well, what have we accomplished here? It doesn't seem that anything has come out here today. Yesterday, when I had that setback and began to feel that way while talking on the telephone, I was very discouraged. It's very discouraging. I was hoping that I'd dream and the whole thing would be cleared up. Now, I feel very dissatisfied. Nothing is clear. I can't even seem to think what I have been talking about.

TH: Everything seems meaningless?

PT: Well, I can't "cotton on" to anything.

TH: We have been talking about your father and your mother and homosexuality, and we have been saying that homosexuality in some ways is a form of chronic masturbation, and that there is a phantasy where the individual represents himself and somebody else at the same time. You call this the split personality. Perhaps you represented your mother when you looked at yourself in the mirror, and perhaps you reacted toward yourself as you would have reacted toward your mother if you had allowed yourself to react. You said it was some kind of a joke. I am reminded here of Freud's idea that the joke is a way of ridiculing the other person as he himself has been ridiculed—that it means he has a desire to demean but he turns it on himself. Did I do anything or say anything to you that you felt was demeaning?

PT: No. But I guess the whole idea of analysis is demeaning. It's for weak people. People who need help. Can't make it on their own.

TH: You think I feel you're weak, no strength, no guts.

PT: You don't. I guess—well, sometimes I think so. I know you don't.

TH: You're anxiety on the telephone, you're holding back—does anything else come to your mind?

PT: Well, being put on the spot by being asked all sorts of questions, and the feeling that I won't be able to speak—fright, heart palpitations.

TH: Those are the collapsing symptoms. You feel that part of your phantasy is that you will have to obey, compulsively, and that you will be criticized or humiliated, and will be found out. When you came in here you "confessed" that you were having some kind of feeling about me—you told me the incident but not about the *feelings*—maybe you were repressing the feelings, concealing them from me—maybe from yourself. In all these phantasies, there seem to be arguments, anger; fighting; there's something about these phantasies, compulsive obedience. (These are sado-masochistic phantasies.) Do you feel angry that we have not gone further?

PT: No, just impatient; and I would like to get to the core of things. I have been feeling and acting so much better and I would not want to think that I am just fooling myself.

TH: Do you think that is possible?

PT: Anything is possible!

TH: How do you think you would feel if it were true that you really have accomplished something in this analysis and that the gains are real?

PT: That's a pretty silly question!

TH: Well, how would you feel if I agreed with you that we have accomplished nothing in four years?

PT: I'd say you were a liar. But I'd like to say it—I'd like to blame you.

It was during the next session that the patient mentioned, in an off-hand way, that a famous university had suggested he work as an exchange professor for a year, on the basis of several papers he had written which presented an advanced aspect of a certain theory. In inquiring about this, and how he felt about the invitation, it was revealed that he was at times happy, at other times fearful, then grandiose, and then he would have phantasies of being used scornfully by the other professors when he presented his material. He had a phantasy of his secret pleasure in presenting his paper and his desire to "put others down" with his knowledge. He also felt: "If they knew what I'm really like, they'd never have given the invitation." He was conflicted about the analysis, for if he took advantage of the opportunity, he would have to leave analysis and come back a year later. He felt guilty about wanting to leave and accept the invitation but the urge to go was great. Then he had fears that if he were on his own, he'd mess everything up—he'd have a return of his symptoms. The session reported here was the one before he was able to talk about his good fortune and the accolades he had received for his papers. (In the course of his treatment he had two such opportunities, both of which he finally accepted, and after each he returned to analysis, eventually finishing.) As soon as he realized, during the next session, that this immediate conflict was in regard to his feelings about me and his opportunities, his symptoms cleared.

NOTES

[1] Many analysts have interpreted such thoughts as being related to sado-masochism. The sexual act is considered a passive surrendering, of being hurt, perhaps having the connotation of the beating phantasy that Freud wrote about in the essay, "A Child Is Being Beaten." The idea of sexual encounter and being a woman carries with it a masochistic trait in this way of thinking. Schreber was also extremely troubled by hypochondriacal ideas: he thought he had softening of the brain, and that he would soon be dead. Shortly thereafter he expressed the idea that he was already dead and decomposing and that his body was being handled in all kinds of repulsive ways. (This idea can be correlated with the childhood experience of the parents using the eyes to express eroticism by "looking" at the various parts of the child's body. Levy's paper, "Body Interest in Children and Hypochondriasis," is relevant in this context. This kind of explanation is much more likely to approach the truth of the origin of hypochondriacal traits than Freud's idea that the problem is due to regression to the "part object" stage of development.)

Many borderline patients act out sexually in ways that are reminiscent of some of Schreber's phantasies. For example, the patient, Mrs. Gloss, was stimulated by "filthy talk." Almost any man who would approach her and begin to talk in a derogatory way would stimulate her erotic phantasies. The men who attracted her most always presented her with sado-masochistic possibilities, such as: "I know you are dissatisfied with your husband. I will ram it into your anus. I will ram it into your vagina. I will give you something to scream about."

[2] The role of masturbation is clear; and the phantasies have an obvious masturbatory connotation. Freud wrote of the connection of the oedipal phantasy (the identification phantasy) with sexual stimulation as handled by masturbatory techniques. Wanting to be a girl, or having to become a woman, was obviously a compulsive need based on Schreber's feeling that his parents did not accept his sexuality. If we agree with Starcke (and there seems to be no reason not to), who was firmly convinced that all unconscious phantasies are ultimately repetitions of early situations, then we shall understand that Schreber's father was seductive in one way or another and extremely detached and denying in other ways, and that Schreber must have been teased and demeaned. His mother cooperated in this type of relationship.

After I had written this manuscript I came across an article in the Roche Report of January 1, 1972 to the effect that Morton Schatzman, M.D. of Arbours Housing Association, Ltd., London, wrote in Family Process 10:177, June, 1971 that research reveals Schreber's father, a well known orthopedist, who wrote 18 books and booklets on child-rearing, was sadistic. In these writings, according to Schatzman, Dr. Schreber, Sr. "told parents to persecute their children" and practiced this in his own methods. "Schreber did not imagine he was persecuted; he was persecuted." Dr. Schatzman seems to feel that this disproves Freud's theory of the origin of homosexual feelings, and that paranoia is an attempt at defense against homosexuality. This disclosure does help to bring into focus my thesis that parents must take an active role in an aggressive way with their children for neurosis or psychosis to emerge in the child as a defense. The cruelty of the parent is one of the things that binds the child in a homosexual way—the mother must play her part too. Other aspects are secretive seduction, rejection and taunting or teasing.

[3] Page 181, "The Structure and Meaning of Psychoanalysis."

CHAPTER IX

RATIONALE OF THE PROJECTIVE
THERAPEUTIC TECHNIQUE

The projective therapeutic techniques which are so important in the treatment of the borderline patient and which are illustrated in detail in this chapter have a history in psychoanalytic literature. Although the techniques have never been appropriately delineated, described and conceptualized, nevertheless they have roots in some of the experimental deviations from the classic techniques which were attempted by such analysts as Ferenczi (1924, 1929) and Clark (1919, 1926, 1933, 1933a, 1933b).

Ferenczi inaugurated a variety of therapeutic forms, some of which could be conceived of as projective techniques. Ferenczi's efforts at innovation were geared primarily toward helping the character disorders. We find this of interest in view of the fact that the borderline patient has a passive-aggressive character pattern. Ferenczi called his technique "active therapy." It was a combination of suggestion, encouragement of self-direction, and psychoanalytic interpretation. *His aim, he said, was "to lay bare latent tendencies to repetition," i.e., the patterned manifestations of transference behavior.* He was apparently referring to *character patterns*, which we now recognize as an inextricable part of the patient's *defenses* of sado-masochism, projective identification and acting out. Ferenczi said that another of his goals was *to connect the repetitions with memories.* We may expand this idea by saying that the "repetitions" are

185

associated not only with transference behavior, but also with the patient's neurotic phantasies which are affiliated with his identifications.

Many of Ferenczi's techniques resemble what we now call "behavior therapy," for they were in the form of a desensitization process in order to reduce anxiety. However, the goal toward which he directed his efforts, unlike the current behavior therapies, was a revival of memories. He did try, as the behaviorists do today, *to reinforce successful unneurotic behavior*, and he was not against giving reassurance and praise at appropriate times if this could be used by the patient as a reinforcement of behavior that he felt was constructive, or ego-building. He believed in the "corrective experience" as a means of modifying the ego.

Behavior therapists speak today of *behavior rehearsal, training for assertiveness, aversive therapy, thought-stopping, emotive imagery*, and other techniques which they use to block "self-defeating" patterns. In some sense, these techniques resemble Ferenczi's *forced phantasy methods*, and in other ways they apparently borrow from Moreno's psychodrama and from role theory. *Forced phantasy methods can and should be used in the treatment of borderline patients.* They are adapted to the purpose of exploring patterns, and outlining particular neurotic roles, with the aim of helping the patient gain control over acting out. *The forced phantasy will have the same structure and organization as the phantasy the patient would have been able to recall or remember, if he did not repress so severely.* By using the forced phantasy *the therapist works to discover the defenses, to outline the interpersonal roles and to lay bare the identifications (introjections).* Those things and people in the phantasies are explored without insisting that the patient is "just as," which is the phrase used by Freud in "The Interpretation of Dreams" to indicate identification.[1]* *Just-as* is a concept similar to the *as-if* phenomenon. *One must explain to the patient in some fashion that a phantasy becomes activated in moments of extreme anxiety.* One does not at first confront the patient with the idea that the qualities of the "other" (in the phantasy) are qualities and characteristics of the patient as well. When the patient is ready to deal with this problem he will himself recognize the *just-as* phenomenon; then the problem may be explored in relation to the patient himself.

Projective techniques are based on Freud's formulation that *the characters in dreams and phantasies are identification figures and they represent patterns of behavior that the patient is currently acting out or that he fears he will act out.* Since borderline patients do not willingly reveal their phantasies, and often forget their dreams, we must "listen with the third ear" for the latent content in the session. *This is another way of saying that when the patient speaks of others in the session, he is defending against his identification with these others, but he is nevertheless describing his own characteristics.* The productions in the session, when the patient is employing projective defenses,

* Notes for this chapter start page 232.

resemble dream-thoughts. *By listening, we find the projective meaning of the verbalizations and can use them in our understanding of the patient's dilemma.* One may readily speculate, for example, or ask the patient to speculate, as to the defenses of any identification figure, and one may encourage verbalizations regarding the motives, problems and activities of all identification figures. This shields the patient's ego from anxiety. The delusions with which we often have to deal in the borderline, being simply a particular form of phantasy, can be used in the same way.

Ferenczi *recognized the relation of phantasy to transference behavior and "acting out," i.e., to character problems,* and he discovered early that patients with character disorders are prone to "forget" their dreams and usually refuse to reveal their phantasies; it was for this reason that he resorted to the "forced phantasy" technique as a way of discovering the dynamics of the patient's problem in the face of denial mechanisms, and other frustrating defenses, such as consciously holding back material. This latter is a passive-aggressive, masochistic maneuver (Grand, 1952), and also a means of frustrating the therapist; it is a means of controlling guilt feeling for wanting to be different from the parent. Ferenczi would ask for phantasies even if the patient said that he could not remember them. He might ask the patient to make up a phantasy.

Clark (1919) suggested a different kind of projective technique. He deliberately "promoted regression," which the orthodox analysts of the time stressed so strongly, by asking the patient to imagine himself as an infant.[2] This technique has been used in various forms by several modern therapists. What Clark really wanted was to recapture the patient's mode of behavior as a child and through the patient's phantasies learn the essence of the child's experience and his identifications with parental objects.

More important than his regressive technique was Clark's recommendation that *one use a method of gradual education of the patient in his use of projective mechanisms, while actively interpreting the hostile transference reactions.* Spotnitz (1969), Searles (1961) and Coleman and Nelson (1957) also advocate interpreting the hostile transference in the early stages of treatment. In my experience, such interpretations made too early appease the masochism of the patient rather than work through the transference. In chapter VI we have noted that Kernberg mentions the latent negative transference and suggests that it not be ignored; he handles this phenomenon by direct confrontation. My feeling is that direct transference interpretation is not wise in the early phases of treatment; but the transference as it affects other interpersonal relationships can be considered as soon as feasible, i.e., as soon as the patient indicates a willingness to accept that his behavior with others contains repetitional elements. The I-Thou transference behavior cannot be worked through until the third phase of treatment. In the early phases of encounter the patient uses the identification figures that Freud mentioned in the "Interpretation of Dreams" as a means of defending against the expression of too much aggression in the one-to-one situation. This defense has been called the "splitting of the ego," "regression in the service of the ego," or the breaking up of the identifications into their early objects. Interpretations regarding these objects in the initial phases of treatment are best handled by projective therapeutic techniques. One points to certain hostile reactions of the patient without trying to work them through or to relate them to the transference. Success is greater if one stresses the self-defeating patterns first. These are invariably associated with masochism, the paranoid feelings, and the depression. The emphasis is on self-attack, self-denial, fear and guilt concerning assertiveness. Then it follows that one will come upon the aggression that is involved in the fears of self-assertion. There is less resistance on the part of the patient to consider self-defeating patterns than to deal with aggressions, which ultimately means dealing with sadistic feelings. What should be done is to focus on the guilt feelings surrounding self-assertion, which lead to self-denying patterns. It is because of the self-denigrating mechanisms that it has often been said that the borderline seems to have no ego, no sense of self. Actually this is the masochism at work—masochism that helps perpetuate the aggression and strengthens the projective defenses.

In utilizing the projective technique in relation to the identification figure, one would initially, then, emphasize the self-attack, the self-denial, the fears of assertiveness *and particularly the guilt* the person has in thinking of himself as an autonomous figure; one can move then to the aggression in its projected form.

Clark also suggested the use of a projective technique in the handling of hallucinations. He treated the people in the hallucination as the "other" by acting *as-if* these people represented other persons rather than being a projection of the patient, and he explored with the patient the behavior of these other persons. This technique worked well with one of my patients, Mrs. Jonathan, a Ph.D. candidate who had been having severe anxiety attacks which brought her into treatment. She reported in connection with these attacks "bad dreams," and particularly a resurgence of fears of ghosts and hallucinations from which she had suffered periodically most of her life (she was age thirty-two at the time of entering treatment). As a child she had called "the ghost figure," Harold. At that time, the figure was benevolent; she could talk with him. But later he seemed malevolent. She said in one session:

PT: I was visited by my monster again last night. The thing is, I was in a horrible panic, shaking, sweating and I could hear footsteps. Of course, I knew that there was nobody walking around in the apartment, but at times like this, I'm not sure—I believe there is someone; a figure, and I see the figure. It used to be a nice figure, when I was a child—I've had this monster since I was a child. But lately it's become malevolent. As a child I used to have conversations with it—talk things over—but now I'm terrified, I just quake.

TH: What does this thing look like? It's a person evidently? Or is it an animal?

PT: Oh, no a person—yes a person.

TH: A menacing person?

PT: Well—a big hulk—a massive hulk.

TH: Male or female?

PT: It used to be a tall blond man with blue eyes. Now it's a big massive figure.

TH: A man?

PT: Yes—like a Viking—or a Scandinavian man—now more terrifying.

TH: Scandinavian?

PT: Yes, strong.

TH: Frightening?

PT: Yes—er—it's strange! My father is tall and blond and German—that's like Scandinavian. (There is an obvious identification with the father, and from this point on we concentrated on the actual object symbolized by the ghost, her father.)

TH: Yes it is. That reminds me of the first dream you told me. A man, a sailor or somebody who liked sailing, he was the captain of a boat and you were on the boat. And your father and brother, I believe, were on the boat with you, and the Nazis were coming to get you all. You were going to stay on the boat, on principle, but your father and brother were going to escape before the Nazi's got there. And then you had the phantasy (or dream) of the bird that got loose from your apartment. The bird flew down to the next floor and got caught in the iron grilling. You wanted to reach in to save it, but if you reached in you might disturb the grille and the bird's neck would get caught in the grille. You were afraid to try to get the bird for fear you would hurt it. And then you told me about the feeling you have while swimming—that some monster would come up and catch your foot.

PT: Well, it's not the same. That monster will grab me, it seems. I don't go that far with this menacing monster.

TH: What are you afraid of—will he hurt you?

PT: I don't go that far with the phantasy. But the figure seems very real. I can tell myself that it is not real, but when I'm shivering at night I know it is real. And I feel helpless. My husband is right beside me in the bed, but he sleeps like a rock. Nothing bothers him when he's asleep. We've had books fall out of the case, making a great racket in the middle of the night, and he sleeps through it all. Once the apartment house was on fire and he slept through the alarm. I got up and everything was handled so I didn't wake him. In a way, that's good, for he doesn't react to things when he's awake the way I do. I can get very excited. He stays calm. He reads a book, he goes into another room, he refuses to argue.

TH: He withdraws from the situation.

PT: Well, yes, I do too. I never get too close to anyone. My husband is the first person I ever got close to and we had a terrible time the first year of our marriage, but we finally came through it. Possibly, if he were different, I couldn't tolerate it—I still don't like to get close to people. I have few friends.

TH: You are probably right. Your husband's detachment makes you more comfortable—and he gives you space and distance, which you need.

(The symbolism of the bird caught in the grille and her fear that if she attempts to rescue the bird she will hurt it is significant of several problems. One is her fear that her detachment will be invaded. Another problem is her aggression that is presently associated with her activities—she is motivated by aggression in her work, yet she feels guilty and defends against it. In this sense, she is more identified with her father than with her mother. She expects, however, to be famous in her field, once she becomes a colleague of her present professors, and she is both fearful and grandiose when she thinks of it. She has realistically been given high praise, but finds it difficult to accept these kudos.)

PT: Oh, yes, definitely—but he is helpful—he does some of the housework, too. I'm a woman's lib. I don't mean that I'm in the movement, but I've thought of it. I don't like the attitude of men and the world towards women.

TH: What kind of attitude is that?

PT: Denigrating, scornful, hostile. My mother's position is a good example. She is an intelligent woman, but she acts flighty and stupid. She's clever, but she always takes a secondary position. My father is the boss—about everything.

TH: But you say he's away a lot.

PT: Yes, but he's still the boss. Of course, my father is an extremely capable and adequate man, and my mother is hostile to him. He takes an awful lot from her. She gets hysterical and screams and yells and calls him all sorts of names. He never says a word.

TH: He withdraws.

PT: Well, I guess you'd call it that. He never answers her back. But sometimes I feel as though they play a game. She can't make him react, no matter what she does. My husband thought that, when he visited at my parent's home. He felt that my father tries to draw you into an argument and then belittles you and makes you angry, and then he withdraws. My mother always rises to the bait. My father doesn't like my husband. (*The husband has developed a passive-aggressive character, while the father has an active-aggressive personality structure.*) He won't engage. And my father doesn't like the easy way my husband lives. My husband doesn't let things bother him and he doesn't strive for the commercial order of this culture, this American culture. This gets to my father.[3]

My husband would be happy on a desert island, and perhaps I would too. I'm struggling for my Ph.D. and my husband is too, but he's thinking of giving it up because the oral exams frighten him. He has a block. I'm the opposite. I don't mind the orals but I can't stand the thought of the written exams.

TH: Jack Spratt and his wife (laughs).

PT: Yes (laughs).

TH: You said you husband would like to be on a desert isle.

PT: Yes. His grandparents have a place in California on an island near the coast; and he can go there—and he may do that—we may—and write some books and forget about Ph.D.'s. They are a drug on the market anyway, and there's not much point in getting one—that's what my husband says.

TH: Your father would call that a "cop-out."

(She actually feels that way, too, and this is the basis of her present conflict. She will go with her husband, even though she realizes subconsciously and even consciously that it is a destructive thing for both of them. In the dream she stays on the boat *on principle*, even though the Nazis are coming. We have not touched upon the destructive feelings she has in her identification with her father, and incidentally with her husband, although we have alluded to the projected problems in the symbolism of the bird and the grille and in the dream—she has indicated however, that her father will not allow himself to be destroyed—he and the brother would save themselves—but they could not work out their emotional problems. They will use their aggression to win. She is more masochistic.)

PT: Yes. He always says he wished my husband had some ambition. My husband is very intelligent, but he doesn't believe that one should kill oneself in the commercial hub-bub. (Her husband is also masochistic.)

TH: I see.

PT: I say he should do what he wants to do. There are too many people doing things every day—killing themselves doing what they hate. They have no freedom. Why get caught up in that?

TH: How would you feel being on a desert isle—would you be lonely for the city?

PT: Probably—I do love the city—but I'd go if he wanted to. I'd write.

TH: Wouldn't you feel badly giving up the Ph.D.?

PT: Perhaps, but I would.

TH: Well, you're going to finish your courses this semester anyway. You're all finished except for the thesis—and the writtens. (This is a reinforcement of her constructive intentions.)

PT: Yes. Oh, I'll finish sometime!

TH: Oh yes, you will. (Another reinforcement, and an acceptance, a projection of the constructive side of her ego onto the therapist.)

PT: I've asked to take a typewriter into the examination room. There's another girl who has a similar problem. I need the typewriter because my hands shake so that I can't write. We are allowed to go into a separate room (away from those who can accept the regular examination conditions) and write the exams out on the typewriter.

TH: Well, it's great that you are allowed to do that—it helps you get around the block. Later you can perhaps figure out what makes you act that way. (She manipulates to keep her defenses and so never has to work out the problem.)

PT: I almost feel as if it isn't me; but it is. ("As if I were playing a role"—this is a denial or a "split," a feeling of being dissociated. She's acting out a role which is destructive to her but she does it anyway. She cannot face her rage towards her husband, nor towards her parents, but it gets in her way when she wants something for herself. Her guilt is great. In one sense, she plays the masochistic role as her mother does. She feels this as "not herself."[4]

TH: I wonder what could be done for your husband so that he wouldn't fear the orals. I wonder what his hang-up is? (Probing for motivation.)

PT: I suppose it's got something to do with his father—his father is so efficient, so great, such a . . . figure! (She identifies with the husband.)

TH: I wonder how your husband will feel if you take the writtens, having already finished with the orals? Will he be jealous? (Indicating that something is going on between them, too—a game. This is the employment of a projective technique using the interpersonal situation as the place for defining a pattern.)

PT: Oh, he's never jealous—no, he takes everything calmly. (Denial and a pointing to the purpose of the husband's withdrawal mechanism, i.e., to protect himself from the over-riding competitive activities of his own parent.) But I've wondered about this. (An indication that subliminally she realizes there is a "game" being played between them.) He changed his major and then I changed mine—I don't know why. I told myself it was because what I was doing seemed so shallow, it didn't go deep enough. My husband was in literature and then he just changed. Now he thinks he'll take a year off and write. There's something that goes on between us—I can't put my finger on it. In a way it seems competitive. But I guess I'm the competitive one. (Masochistic blaming of self and denial of husband's role in the sado-masochistic game.) He doesn't compete. But he does in a way. He always comes through examinations at the top, even when he hates the subject. Even if he waits until the last minute to study. But then he doesn't value it. (This is reminiscent of Freud's comment, 1913, on the obsessive-compulsive mechanism to the effect that the desire for knowledge can have a sadistic basis.)

TH: He wants to win out and then acts like it's of no consequence to him to have done so? (He denies his aggression but he acts it out in winning, then he becomes bored.)

PT: Yes. He even says he does not want to teach college. Even if he got the Ph.D. he'd do something else altogether. He'll teach high school—he doesn't want to teach college—or he'll leave the teaching field and do something with his hands. (She would participate in this, even though she disapproves of such behavior. She is "protecting the object" as an aspect of her defense against aggression.)

As we go along in the session, the husband's behavior is discussed, the patient eventually explains her identification with the "other" (i.e., the husband) and his conflict, but we do not confront her with this. Instead we use the important principle suggested by Freud concerning interpretation. We find in the phantasy the area of least resistance (Freud, 1911, page 92; 1923, page 110). In learning how to do psychoanalytically oriented psychotherapy the therapist must practice this principle assiduously *and learn how to find the area of least resistance.* The analyst can, by selecting the areas of least resistance, help the patient eventually connect her own *identification phantasy* with the defenses, which are operative in that aspect of the conflict that the patient can tolerate to handle directly. *In other sessions one can then show the patient that she uses the phantasy and the acting out as a means of controlling her own anxiety, i.e., as a defense.* This process will take many months, perhaps a year. This woman will not challenge her husband's behavior in any way at present, because she has a great belief (defensive) in "individual freedom" and "self-determination," even if one dies in the process. Therefore, she is planning to *act out with him* and leave civilization. She feels guilty about this, but she denies her own normal feelings and defends against her identification with her own father, who is hostile to her husband. She identifies with her husband as a defense against her identification with her parents. In order to deny her own hostility towards her husband for his defensive "weak" behavior and his inability to stay in the situation, she will go with him. She resents the fact that in many ways she actually is "identified" with her father, as well as with her mother. (In my opinion, the therapist should merely outline the situation and make no attempt to influence the patient to urge her husband to stay. If they insist upon going, the therapist should encourage a resumption of treatment when they return from their sojourn. They will learn that isolation is not satisfying, as she has learned that detachment and withdrawal do not make for good interpersonal relationships.)

L. Wolberg (1945, 1948) used the projective technique of forced phantasy analysis under hypnosis to find connections which were inaccessible in the free association method and where it was impossible for the patient to discuss the transference implications associated with the resistance. He utilized association techniques under hypnosis, using words and their symbols, to ferret out connections between odd dissociated mental "bits" expressed in extraneous thoughts, and the underlying repressed aspects of the sado-masochistic phantasy to which these thoughts were connected. He emphasizes that *the best way to establish a working relationship with the patient is to discover the patient's motivations and then let the patient realize these are understood.* One will find that the most practical way to accomplish such an aim is to interpret some area of the problem (the least resisted area), thus, that aspect of the problem that the patient is willing to consider, and then establish that something can be done about relieving the problem (positive reinforcement). Wolberg makes use of phantasy to explore the area of least resistance so as to avoid direct confrontation of the patient's defenses (1945).[5]

Where is this area of least resistance with the person who tends toward delusion and paranoid ideation? Clark gave us a clue in his principle of discussing the behavior of the "other person" in the phantasy, in dreams or in interpersonal encounters. As the behavior of the other is analyzed or talked about, the patient eventually explains his identifications with the other person. This is the same principle that one uses in the interpretation of dreams when asking for associations to the dream, or to parts of the dream. As soon as the patient's identification with the projective object becomes clear, then the analyst can, by selecting the point of least resistance, help the patient connect the identification phantasy with areas of the patient's anxiety, and it will become more obvious then to the patient that he uses the phantasy and the acting out as a means of controlling his anxiety, i.e., as a defense. My students have called the projective technique the "off-target technique." But actually, even though the analyst seems to be aiming "off-target," he does hit the bull's eye. *He is utilizing the dynamics of dreams and phantasies and, particularly, the dynamics of identification to make his discoveries and his interpretations of the actions of "the other."* The off-target technique is used chiefly to identify, explain and explore defenses, connecting these with anxiety. Even when the patient is talking about his parents or his early friends, one must keep in mind the principles of projective identification,[6] the idea of exploring defenses and connecting these with anxiety.

The analysis of resistance is one of the major techniques in psychoanalytic work, and it occupies an important part of the work with borderline patients. What generally happens is what Freud so beautifully described in saying that "wherever in our analytic delving we come upon one of the hiding places of the withdrawn libido, there ensues a battle; and when we follow a pathogenic complex from its representative in consciousness (whether this be a conspicuous symptom or something apparently quite harmless), back to its root in the unconscious, we soon come to a place where the resistance makes itself felt so strongly that it affects the next association, which has to appear as a compromise between the demands of this resistance and those of the work of exploration. Experience shows that this is where transference enters the scene. Over and over again, when one draws near to a pathogenic complex, that part of it which is first thrust forward into consciousness will be some aspect of it which can be transferred; having been so, it will then be defended . . ." Projective techniques can be used to handle such transference manifestations with the borderline patient in the beginning phase of treatment. Freud said that where the libido is withdrawn, there is phantasy. In looking over his material on resistance, we find that Freud said that anything which interferes with the course of analysis is resistance and that resistance represents "the wish of the unconscious ego." But there were five main kinds of resistance, according to Freud; (1) ego unwillingness to give up repressive countercharge; (2) ego reluctance to renounce symptom gain or relief; (3) transference resistance (an attempt to evade recollection through reenactment or repetition of infantile experience)—we now call this "acting out"; (4) the id-repetition compulsion (this is also acting out); and, (5) the need for punishment arising out of the demands of the superego. (This produces acting out.) One can see that these are all aspects of a sado-masochistic pattern and that they are all interrelated, and connected with identification in its projective forms. Freud thought that the id-repetition compulsion showed itself in the perpetuation of a neurotic pattern. He said that when analysis seemed to be complete and the ego resistances appeared broken down, but the behavior nevertheless persisted, then we are dealing with the id-repetition compulsion, i.e., an aspect of the instinct. The process of "working through" was connected with the repetition compulsion, or what we now think of as the patient's practicing of new patterns while consciously coping with resistance, i.e., with fears, aggression, anxiety, guilt and defenses which are still operative as the patient attempts to give up his old patterns of adaptation. In (S-O-R) terms, we would say that extinction of the neurotic pattern has not taken place, although the individual has worked out some of the meanings and significance of the neurotic pattern. The behavior probably persists because the proper amount of practice in new behavior has not been instituted and the meaning of the neurotic behavior is not totally clear. As the individual stops the behavior at various points, suffering the anxiety and becoming aware of the phantasies that accompany the anxiety, the analysis of the phantasy helps in understanding the meaning, and the inhibition of the pattern and its gradual extinction become possible. The neurotic response becomes weaker as therapy proceeds, the response being used by the patient less and less. From a functional point of view, we may think of the neurotic pattern as a manifestation of learning rather than due to an instinctual repetition of id impulses, i.e., impulses associated with a periodic manifestation of the instinct. Thus we could say that all resistance is related to the ego.

The "alloplastic" or projective mechanisms, evident in the borderline patient, can be discerned even in the initial interview; actually, the patient's psychodynamics and psychopathology can be delineated in some form in the first contact. Moreover, it may be possible to determine leads for the practice of the projective techniques that will be employed later on. The following initial interview illustrates some of these points.

PT: Yes, uh, well, actually I'm from Ireland. I've been here for six months now and just before I came I was with a psychiatrist in London.
TH: I see, for how long?
PT: I was with her for about six to eight weeks.
TH: Uh-huh.
PT: And she felt I should come back and continue the treatment when I got here—and so I came and found a job and decided that I would stay and I went back to England—now I'm back again for good, for a while, and I decided to come here.
TH: What kind of work do you do?
PT: Film editing.
TH: Film editing, uh-huh. And you are working in New York City?
PT: Yes.
TH: Why did you leave Ireland?
PT: Well, because, uh, one reason, you know it's very difficult to get film editing work there.
TH: Oh, no, I didn't know.
PT: And I don't know, I thought for some reason I should get out of my environment.
TH: Uh-huh. Well, why did you want to see the psychiatrist in England?
PT: I had a breakdown and uh—
TH: Were you in the hospital?
PT: No, no, I just—
TH: What happened? I mean, what do you mean by a breakdown?
PT: Well, I had an experience with a teacher in London. I was studying acting.
TH: Oh, I see.
PT: And the teacher was using a mixture of Stanislavsky and Freud to teach his students. He didn't really know what he was doing, I don't think.

TH: Uh, huh.

PT: And uh—Stanislavsky's principle is that one creates out of one's subconscious.

TH: Yes.

PT: It's an ally of Freudian principle—so this was what he was trying to do, you know.

TH: Uh-huh, uh-huh.

PT: . . . and one way or another he managed to bawl me out, but it wasn't quite what he'd expected, my performance, I mean.

TH: I see; do you know what it was that upset you or what he did to upset you?

PT: No, I'm not sure.

TH: I mean specifically.

PT: Specifically—you mean, at the time what did he say?

TH: Yes, I mean, what was the incident that was upsetting to you?

PT: He was a very dogmatic person, and his idea in teaching was that he knew what he was doing, what he was saying, and that you didn't, and that you came to learn from him and you took everything. I did that for two years. Over a period of time I gradually began to question certain things—I thought I understood his basic ideas—and then this thing sort of mounted.

TH: It was gradual and you got more and more annoyed by him.

PT: And then he—uh—(pause).

TH: Did you have any particular symptoms? I mean, were you tense, have any headaches, or sweating; did you have any symptoms of that kind?

PT: When?

TH: When you felt you were having a breakdown?

PT: Oh, no, when I had the breakdown, I mean—(pause).

TH: Well, what did you do, I mean, why did you feel you had a breakdown?

PT: I started screaming, and then I collapsed. I sort of completely passed out. (This is suspicious of a psychotic-like episode and alerts me to the possibility that he may be borderline.)

TH: You were unconscious?

PT: Yes, and I woke up afterwards on a couch in his (the teacher's) office.

TH: Oh, I see.

PT: And, you know, the immediate things that preceeded this, I don't remember. You know, the whole thing—suddenly everything was all right and then suddenly the whole thing—

TH: Oh, it was all of a sudden. I see. Was that frightening to you?

PT: Well, afterwards I felt relieved. I felt better. I always felt—you know, that he was right about everything.

TH: Uh-huh. You mean even when you sensed he might be wrong?

PT: Yes. That was my image of him and I never felt I knew him to speak to him and I was afraid if I said anything that disagreed with him that I would be penalized for it.

TH: Well, was he a vindictive person or was that just a theory of yours?

PT: I don't know. The person I went to see (the psychiatrist) saw him as well, and he (the teacher) was very concerned with my case. The doctor told me afterwards that (the teacher) was in a lot of trouble himself and that he had some kind of phantasy or other that he was trying to dominate and he was very idealistic. He wanted to control everything and he was idealistic at the same time.

TH: He had this kind of a problem and you idealized him, sensing that he had a problem but denying it at the same time (a positive projection).

PT: Yes, yes.

TH: Do you have a family in Ireland?

PT: Yes.

TH: How old are you, by the way?

PT: Twenty-three.

TH: Ah, I see. Where did you go to school? What kind of school?

PT: I went to an Irish public school which is boarding school.

TH: Are your father and mother living? Do you have a mother and father?

PT: No, just a mother. My father left when I was four. He separated from my mother. They later divorced and he remarried.

TH: I see, I see. Have you seen him at all?

PT: No.

TH: You don't have any relationship with him?

PT: No.

TH: Do you have brothers and sisters?

PT: Yes, I have a sister; she's younger than I.

TH: Two of you then.

PT: Yes.

TH: Younger than you.

PT: Yes, two years younger.

TH: What goes on in your family? What kind of family life did you have?

PT: Well, I don't know. You mean, uh, from the point of view of quarrels?

TH: Oh, how you felt towards your mother and how you felt towards your sister. What kind of people are they?

PT: That's difficult. They seem to be two different things. You know, I mean, I could praise my mother's character, or—the way I feel, I'm not sure whether I—it's more easy to think—she's very nervous, she worries a lot. (The thought occurs to me that he is identified with her—she is an obsessive worrier, and thus cannot long sustain any feeling of pleasure.)

TH: Worries, uh-huh.

PT: She, after my father left, to my knowledge, she completely devoted herself to the children and she had no outside distractions or interests. She never remarried and she was never going to remarry—

TH: Do you remember your father at all?

PT: No.

TH: Don't remember him?

PT: Well—

TH: Let's see, how old were you when he left?

PT: I was 4½ or 5.

TH: Uh-huh. But you don't have any memories of him?

PT: Not really, no. I have a kind of picture of what I think he looked like which doesn't seem to tally with a photograph.

TH: Well, isn't that interesting—I mean, what are the differences in your picture of what he is and what he looks like and—

PT: Well, he seems to be younger, healthier, stronger, more dynamic than he actually is, I suppose—(he feels this way about himself, too).

TH: You mean in your picture of him he was younger and stronger?

PT: Yes, he seems to be.

TH: I see. Uh—what does your mother say about him?

PT: Very little. In fact—

TH: Does she talk about him?

PT: No, until I was 20 or 21, I always thought that I could never ask her about him.

TH: Uh-huh, you didn't dare to speak about him.

PT: And she never offered any information. And then when I went to see the doctor in London, I realized that these things would be useful to find out. I did start to ask her those questions—

TH: Uh-huh.

PT: . . . and the general thing was that she would say, you know, "You're exactly the same as he was." But, I mean—

TH: Meaning what?

PT: Exactly, meaning what? Meaning absolutely nothing.

TH: Was she being critical of you when she said that? Was she angry at him?

PT: I don't know.

TH: I mean was that supposed to be a criticism of you? Or was it a compliment? (His mother identifies him with the hated man. I am trying to get his ideas about this identification.)

PT: Well, not one or the other and both at the same time. I mean, I suppose she was attracted to him in some way or other. The fact that he left her—for what reason I'm not clear. I know nothing about why.

TH: She thought that you were attractive and your father was attractive.

PT: Well, no.

TH: Do you look alike, you and your father?

PT: I don't think so. I think I look more like my mother, actually.

TH: But you don't remember missing him or anything of that kind?

PT: No.

TH: Did you imagine that you had a father or did you have fantasies about a father?

PT: No, well, uh, at the beginning when I was very young. From all I can remember, the idea was that he was some sort of traveling salesman who was always away. I was never told . . . that he left.

TH: Oh, oh, I see. You felt that he was a traveling salesman.

PT: So I never missed—I don't think—consciously, never missed not having had a father. But the doctor told me that as a result of this, this is why I was so easily influenced by someone who was older and a man who had something to say that I could respect, like this man, you know, at the age of 21 or 22. You know he had me completely—Uh, this seemed logical. (He was also influenced by his mother who was worrisome, controlling and, he seems to imply, obsessively martyred, taking care of the children. It is likely that he did not dare to criticize his mother. It would seem that he has defenses with women that he does not have with men.)

TH: Uh-huh, but you became very disillusioned, was that it? You got very angry at him and became disillusioned with this man.

PT: The teacher?

TH: Yes, the teacher.

PT: Yes, well, I tend to completely accept or completely reject. Once there is one flaw, that means the whole thing is no good. This is a terrible thing, and it is this thing I want to find out about—why? *The ability to evaluate, criticize and appraise things as they really are and not as I am sort of compelled to do it. This is one of the problems I want to—*

TH: If you see a flaw in somebody you begin to resent them. You want them to be perfect?

PT: That may be it. Yes. I'd like to work that out.

TH: I think that is perfectly possible and most desirable. What kind of girl is your sister?

PT: Uh—(long pause). Well, she's younger than I was.

TH: Uh-huh. Well, were you close with her at all? Did you have different friends?

PT: Yes, we had different friends. But we were always together—always on top of each other—

TH: Your sister and you?

PT: In the sense that we were always in this little group—the three of us, you know, the family, living conditions, and then I went to school at eleven, but before that we had always lived together.

TH: Did you go to day-school? Did you come home at night?

PT: No, I went away.

TH: About how old were you when you went away?

PT: I was 10½.

TH: Uh-huh. And you stayed until when?

PT: Until I was 17 (pause).

TH: Uh-huh. How did you feel at school?

PT: I hated every minute of it.

TH: Every minute?

PT: Practically.

TH: That's a long time. You weren't happy at all there? There was nothing you enjoyed?

PT: No.

TH: Oh, my.

PT: It was, you know, it was one of these very insular places, something like Eton, You know, Eton?

TH: Uh-huh.

PT: Where they have a hierarchy of older boys and masters and you're absolutely powerless. And within those walls they are capable of doing anything and they do anything, practically. It's a very unhealthy way of bringing children up, as one can see by the state of the English and Irish upper classes, the government and what not, you know. They're all—

TH: They're not in very good condition? (Laughs)

PT: They're not in very good condition. I mean they might look all right on the surface—they're behind—the whole thing is—this is how I feel about it, you know.

TH: The whole thing is crumbling?

PT: Yes, you know, they're struggling to keep this tradition and this way, and it's gone, you know, so they fight to preserve this way—

TH: Very difficult for them to change, you mean? (This is a use of the projective technique. He is really thinking about himself when he talks about the English and the Irish, but it is not possible for him to realize this at this early stage.)

PT: Yes, I always from the moment I went there, resented the place and I resented the people. The thing was that it was a foundation school for children, for boys who didn't have fathers.

TH: I see.

PT: All the boys there were the same more or less—either they had lost one parent or two parents. And it was free, and mother was forced to send me there for financial reasons and so I did stay. I mean, the education was of good standing, intellectual standing, but God knows what the other has done—(pause).

TH: Well, what are your worst fears about what it has done to you?

PT: Well, I'm not sure. That's one of the reasons I wanted to come here. I want someday to find out. (He blames the school rather than his father and mother for his emotional troubles—obviously a projection.)

TH: Was that the first time you had gone to a psychiatrist? When you went just recently?

PT: Yes, yes.

TH: And you think this whole incident really precipitated it.

PT: Yes.

TH: In other words, you wouldn't have gone probably . . .

PT: Oh, no.

TH: . . . if it hadn't been for that a—

PT: I always believed that I could handle everything myself and when this happened it was—I've never been physically ill. I've never had an operation or been in a hospital or anything, and this was the first time in my life that I really felt completely helpless, and I thought it's time to stop being—and go to somebody who really knows something—(pause).

TH: Well, that's right. You were right. Do you remember any of your dreams?

PT: Well, oh, I don't remember them really.

TH: You have a tendency to forget them?

PT: To completely forget them. Especially if I must remember them. Then I forget them. I can remember having remembered certain things about them over a period of time, but— (His oppositional tendencies—his need to deny his dependency feelings.)

TH: And then they sort of disappear.

PT: Yes.

TH: Oh, if you are asked, do you resent it? Do you put up a resistance, you mean?

PT: Well, it just seems to go out of my mind.

TH: It just disappears.

PT: Yes, it disappears.

TH: Well, I don't want to force things out of your mind, but if you can think of any—I mean, I would just like to get an idea. What do you think your dreams are about, I mean, in general. If you don't remember anything in particular. (The forced phantasy technique.)

PT: Well, uh, there's usually some sort of conflict, in the sense that I have to do something I can't do or—I know this is very general—

TH: Yes, yes, I just wondered what the general trend or tenor of them—you try to do something, you are forced to do something, you can't do?

PT: Umm, not forced, usually it's something I have to do, I want to do and—

TH: And you can't do it.

PT: No.

TH: You're not able to perform, you mean, in your dream?

PT: Then, various dreams about either killing people or fearing them, being afraid of people. And, uh, then even if I sort of manage to overcome it, I feel as though I have made the biggest mistake now and everything is going to collapse. (His dreams seem to indicate a devalued self-image, great feelings of ineffectuality, desire to attack and fears of being attacked. He is marshalling defenses to cope with these conflicts.)

TH: Uh-huh.

PT: I don't really know—it's something—

TH: Do you feel that way consciously?

PT: No.

TH: You don't feel so inadequate consciously?

PT: Not—

TH: Or as though—well, in the dreams are you fumbling or are you ruining things, or are you just immobilized or what is the idea?

PT: Immobilized, I suppose.

TH: You're immobilized. Uh-huh.

PT: That's the nearest, yes. And then consciously, you know, in everything I do I know I'm working at sort of 50 per cent of the capabilities. For some reason, everything is being held—there is always a level that I can't get out of or get any further with. I can do anything up to a point and then no more. And not because I feel that I am incapable of understanding or going on—just some completely unconscious reason it's blocked.

TH: Blocked, you're sort of stopped.

PT: Yes. I feel I can't get out of it. Like if I'm reading something and, uh, my object at the beginning when I started was to find something out or learn something, you know, the concentration will begin to disappear and, uh, I have to go back and read the pages over again, and then I'll start out with the idea that now this time I must really read it and three pages later I've lost it again. And it's this kind of pattern throughout everything.

TH: I see, uh-huh.

PT: My energy—(pause).

TH: Uh-huh, uh-huh. Do you know whether things come into your mind and crowd out what you are trying to do?

PT: No. (pause) I'm not conscious of anything coming in.

TH: You don't know. You're not conscious of a daydream coming in and interfering with what you are trying to do?

PT: Maybe a little, but not—no, it's just—like a pressure. You know, I find myself off. Not in anything, just off of what I'm doing.

TH: Blank?

PT: Yes. (He apparently withdraws into phantasy.)

TH: Does it bother you at work? Or just when you're—

PT: No, it bothers me at work. It bothers me all the time, my whole waking day in some form or another, and to some degree.

TH: Well, uh, do you feel fatigued—from that?

PT: Yes.

TH: You feel physically fatigued.

PT: Physically.

TH: Uh-huh. What about your—do you know people here in New York? Do you have friends?

PT: Yes, I have lots of friends, people I've met.

TH: Relatives?

PT: No, no just friends.

TH: Uh–do you have girl friends?

PT: Yes, I have a girl friend.

TH: Here in New York?

PT: Yes.

TH: What kind of a relationship do you have with her?

PT: Well, uh–(pause) a very intense, kind of self-destructive thing. In other words, I'm not able to relax and she's not able to relax, and I tend to explain everything. Anything that comes up, I have to find an explanation for it. She has the same tendency, so between us we really drive ourselves into the ground. (They "drive each other crazy".)

TH: Well, when you say "explain," do you mean you are trying to explain your motives all the time? Why you do things?

PT: Yes.

TH: And why she does things? That could be very tiring.

PT: Right.

TH: But you feel sort of compulsive—that you have to do it.

PT: Yes, I can't leave it alone. (We are again reminded here of Searle's essay on "Driving the Other Person Crazy.")

TH: Uh-huh. Well, what happens? If you spend some time together, what would you be likely to focus on? And what would she focus on? I mean, what do you say or do to each other?

PT: Well, uh—you mean now or a month ago or two months ago—

TH: Anytime, say, now.

PT: Well, now, uh—we've reached a stage where we keep calm for most of the week because otherwise it's just completely exhausting and distractive.

TH: What does she do?

PT: She's a model and she does some secretarial work, and she goes to acting class. That's where I met her.

TH: Oh, I see, and you're going to acting classes, too.

PT: Yes.

TH: Uh, do you have any idea what kind of a person you had in mind for somebody to do therapy with you? What's your idea of the kind of person who could be of help to you here?

PT: I don't know, I really don't.

TH: Don't have any preconceived ideas?

PT: No preconceived ideas.

TH: Or nothing that you want from the person?

PT: Oh, well, in the sense that only broadly I don't think I want to know in terms of directives, you know, like coming each week to be—in, fact like a dispensory, in a sense, a prescription-giving—you know. But it's rather where one goes back and finds out the cause of what is creating the problem now rather than casting around from week to week, trying to deal with the things now. But to get to the root of them—this is what I want—to find out what is in the unconscious.

TH: Do you know something about psychoanalysis?

PT: Oh, yes, only superficially.

TH: You know people who are in treatment?

PT: Yes.

TH: You say only superficially?

PT: Well, I mean my knowledge is only superficial. I wouldn't think that I could discuss it with anybody who had really studied it. I have a broad general knowledge, which is a problem because it's just general, and it's broad, and I tend to apply it in specific things.

TH: Well, that's normal. You know something about it and tend to have ideas about it.

PT: Yes.

TH: Well, how did you get along with—was it a woman you saw?

PT: Yes.

TH: How did you get along with her?

PT: Oh, very well and I always felt very happy to have been to see her each week, and I left relaxed and better for having—

TH: What were you working on with her? Anything in particular?

PT: No.

TH: Or just—

PT: No, just a sort of week to week thing, because she knew that I already had decided to come here. It was just more or less to tide me through this period.

TH: Is your girl friend in treatment, at all?

PT: Yes.

TH: How long has she been?

PT: I think she has been in treatment about a year or so.

TH: Do you know why she went into treatment? Do you know what was bothering her?

PT: Not specifically. She didn't know. She sort of began to find out various problems within the family, her background, her relationship to her parents, and this sort of thing. And, uh, she has difficulties in this area.

TH: Uh, what about your sex life? Uh, do you have problems or do you have a good sex life?

PT: No, I wouldn't say it was good. It isn't—certainly I have a problem.

TH: What about your girl friend, does she have any problem sexually?

PT: Yes.

TH: What would you say your problems are?

PT: That's very difficult. See, this is the thing. I'm thinking how I can best explain it to you in your terms rather—and this is one of the problems.

TH: Rather than saying what you want to say.

PT: And it gets to the point where I can't say what I want to say because I've forgotten—because I'm thinking about how to say it.

TH: You want to please me—

PT: Yes, sort of—(He wants to appease me and answer, but he resents having to tell me these things.)

TH: You want to use my language instead of your own. You belittle yourself that way, don't you?

PT: Yes.

TH: You don't—(pause). Well, you can allow yourself to talk about what you want to say. Try, relax and just try.

PT: I'll try. Well, it's a problem of a—I don't know. I sort of become mean and vicious; not vicious, that's too hard, too definite a term. But somehow I get—I don't really like her—afterwards. For a certain period afterwards.

TH: After sex—(Sexuality seems to be a fertile source of conflict for him.)

PT: Sex relations, yes. And then, you know, it'll go, it'll pass, and so this whole thing of my state of mind has become mixed up with it, you know. So now when I go into it, I go into it with these ideas—am I going to start feeling like this again? And then I get exhausted and I think, well, I'm better off not having any, just keeping her away from me and leaving the whole thing alone. Now I'm really not capable of handling myself in the situation.

TH: Do you ever get to the point where you have sex? I mean, where you have relations?

PT: Yes, it's a very uh—(pause)

TH: Are you able to have any satisfaction at all?

PT: Well, partially, a sort of brief physical satisfaction. But the whole thing—(pause)

TH: Ejaculation?

PT: Yes, but it's, well, I suppose it is satisfactory at the moment, but it's not a kind of complete thing where one relaxes mentally and physically; the whole thing isn't what it should be, or what I think it should be.

TH: What abour your girl friend? Is she able to have orgasms? Does she get satisfaction from sex?

PT: Well, she says she does, but I don't know, you know, from the way she behaves; I'm not sure at all.

TH: You think that she's not; she's lying and she's faking.

PT: Not lying and faking, you know; she says all the right words. But I'm not convinced from knowing what I know about her, and knowing how I feel myself, and knowing that we have similar states of mind. The whole business becomes very disillusioning. (He cannot feel accepted.) You know, this is the thing—then what I'll do is what I've done before. I realize now, looking back, because I'll go from one to the next and—you see, the beginning is fine, for the first few weeks—everything is exciting, everything's new and I'm very elated, but the moment it comes to—when you really start to get to know the person, the interest disappears, the sexual interest. (He cannot maintain pleasure—he cuts it off; does he resent giving pleasure?) The only thing that's kept us together is the fact that we have this kind of mutual analysis thing going—which is sort of neurotic, I think. (Their relationship is sado-masochistic.) You know, I really want to get away from it because I don't know enough, *I think it's dangerous*, and I don't think I'm capable of handling it. I've just come to the end. I'd just like to put myself in somebody's hands who knows what they're doing and who will take a little of the strain off. (He wants to make himself dependent on some reliable authority, the effect of which would have to be studied, since instead of quieting his anxiety it might excite it more by enhancing his sado-masochistic phantasies.)

TH: Do you feel that the analysis that you do to each other is destructive?

PT: Yes. I feel it would be much better if—you know—if we could just go for a walk and enjoy the walk and relax and perhaps do two or three ordinary simple things. This would be much healthier—than all this—picayune—

TH: When you say your mother was a worrier, was she a worrier like that? Was she a picky worrier?

PT: Yes.

TH: She was?

PT: Intensely.

TH: And did she keep at something a lot?

PT: Yes, all of the time.

TH: Is that similar to what you do? (This is a cue that we may be able to use his mother as a projective vehicle to get at his own feelings.)

PT: Well, I think I do it—you know, I say to myself I never will be like that, but I don't know whether I actually do it. I suppose in a sense I do on a different level, an intellectual level, I pick up things in a mental way. But a—you know, she would pick up material things, everything in the house was cleaned, just constantly. You couldn't walk into a room without the feeling that you disarranged something. Her life was one constant kind of clearing up.

TH: I see, uh-huh.

PT: She couldn't relax herself. Whenever she was sitting down, she was waiting to get up again. And she gets, as a result, migraine headaches, and things of that kind that would knock her out for two days. She can't eat and she can't—

TH: Uh-huh, physical symptoms.

PT: Yes.

TH: But you don't have physical symptoms, do you?

PT: Well, I have, I've been getting headaches since I've been here (in this country) more frequently. I never used to get headaches, but I get headaches which come and go. Never very strong in the sense of a physical—you know you bang your head, but the kind that creeps up and stays there and then I get tense. Yes, sometimes I just can't pick things out. I get fumbly and then my work capacity—I work with a film editing machine that stops and starts all the time, and on a good day sometimes I can work it very freely and easily and handle the machine, and then the thing gets on top of me and it takes the whole day to do what I could do in an hour, usually.

TH: Oh, yes, that's fatiguing, terribly fatiguing. Uh, I'm going to ask you to do something—would you? This is not to be artistic. But would you draw a picture of a person for me? Any person you decide to draw.

PT: I've got to think about it; I mustn't think—

TH: You'll be lost if you think about it?

PT: Well, no, I'll start thinking about what I'm drawing in terms of—a whole person?

TH: Whatever you want. Relax. (Silence except for the sound of pencil an paper). That's a man, right?

PT: Right. (He finishes the drawing.)

TH: Would you draw a woman? (Long silence while patient draws.) Thank you. Are you a good actor? (The drawings have form and he differentiates the two sexes. The faces looked like masks, and the woman was markedly larger than the man. He labored over the drawings in an obsessive way. The man's arms were fixed to his sides; the woman's were free.)

PT: Uh, not yet.

TH: No? Are you coming along, though, Are you—satisfied?

PT: Well, I'm learning things.

TH: Uh, do you know whether you felt annoyed when I asked you to draw?

PT: I felt hesitant—No, I don't think I could say—

TH: You don't think you felt annoyed?

PT: Well, I may have, but not consciously.

TH: Because when you said, "Now, I have to draw; now I'll have to start thinking and I won't be able to draw because I'll have to start thinking," you see, it occurred to me that maybe it's like a command again that—it's like back in school when the headmaster told you to do something and you got annoyed because you are following someone's command. It's like when you said when you talked to me you would have to think about how I would want to hear it.

PT: Right.

TH: The same kind of mechanism. So I was just wondering if you were conscious of feeling annoyed.

PT: No.

TH: If you were, you would have repressed it?

PT: Yes.

TH: What days are you going to come, or you don't know yet.

PT: I don't know. I'm free from—I mean, I can take time off from work any time during the day.

TH: Oh, I see, that's good. Perhaps you can come in Thursday at 4 o'clock?

PT: Yes. Thank you, I appreciate it. Do you think I can work this out?

TH: I think you should be able to—It'll take time, but I think if you stick to it . . .

PT: Yes, yes.

TH: It will take time but you can work this problem out if you really want to.

PT: O.K. Thank you very much.

TH: I'll see you on Thursday.

PT: Yes. Thank you.

Zilboorg (1952) spoke of a session in which he used what can be interpreted as a projective technique in exploring the dynamics of a patient's problem by illustrating, through the dream of a woman with whom the patient was living in a common-law relationship, the patient's dynamics evident in the latent content of his companion's dream. The "positive" transference, said Zilboorg, was evident in the patient's wearing a bow tie, which he never had done before, similar to the ties worn by the analyst. We see here the acting out of an identification with the analyst, in an appeasement or an idealization. One use of the projective technique is to explore the connection (in the context of the dream or phantasies—this includes delusion) between the dream of the "other person" and the transference reaction to the analyst, and to discover what the relationship means between the individual and a real other person in the here-and-now. In the case cited by Zilboorg, the latter was the patient's paramour, and the identification as delineated in the dream would reveal the character of the interpersonal relationship of the patient and his paramour, particularly that aspect of the relationship where the patient attempts to deny his role. Zilboorg did not talk about his interpretations to this man, or how he utilized the material he had uncovered through the use of the projective technique. He spent a good part of this particular paper trying to tear down analysts who use unorthodox therapies, particularly brief methods, intimating that they do not produce "cure" or "insight," which he defined as reorientation and reintegration of the ego, gained through understanding and resolving of the transference reactions. Transference, he said, reiterating Freud, cannot be related exclusively to infantile sexuality or to infantile experiences, but must also be connected with the here-and-now, i.e., the way in which transference operations are currently expressed.

A projective therapeutic technique allows the relation with the here-and-now to be handled through the use of the "other person," emphasizing the defensive aspect of the transference behavior of the "other" and letting the patient avoid the personal confrontation with the analyst until he is able to tolerate the anxiety he feels in the interpersonal relationship, without resorting to massive defense. *The aim of treatment is to help the patient let up on the creation of defenses rather than to force him by premature confrontation to increase his defenses.* The here-and-now intimate relationship with the analyst is almost intolerable for the patient at first. He is afraid of close relationships and wards off his fears and other untoward feelings through detachment, isolation, dissociation, not hearing, not seeing, not understanding and by withdrawal and phantasy. A direct I-you transference interpretation stirs up too much anxiety in the beginning phase of treatment and should be done only obliquely (page 206).

One can do with the projective technique many things that one would do with other techniques, such as: (1) exploring what happened in a situation (who was doing what, how, and when); (2) discussing the dynamics of an interpersonal encounter; (3) thinking through the motives and the intrapsychic dynamics of a person (boss, mother, father, sister, brother, friend, enemy, celebrity, etc.); (4) wondering how the other person accomplishes a certain task; (5) talking about the dreams of another person, and other mechanisms, such as their slips of speech and certain kinds of behavior; (6) delineating the phantasy which accompanies a piece of acting out behavior on the part of a parent; (7) analyzing phantasies, as one would a dream; and using the productions in a given session as one would a dream (*listening with the third ear*). In using interpretation, the rule to follow is to deal with the area of least resistance (for example, the history of the other person's problem, how the latter affects the patient, etc.); gradually the therapist can talk about the patient himself.

It is almost impossible to list the varieties of defenses and resistances used by the borderline patient in the initial stages of treatment, for they are myriad and often subtle as well as glaring and overt. The subtle defenses are the most difficult to discover, for they are secretive in a sense. For example, the recalling of traumatic material and family history is usually used by the borderline patient in the service of his masochistic defense in the first phase of treatment. Thus, it almost always refers to the patient's identification with the individual under discussion. Whenever the patient uses the word "I" in connection with a pattern, in this early phase, and relates it to the original family, the therapist can assume that the anxiety is less; but he must be tentative in exploring the pattern even then, for when the patient discusses the possibility of identification and admits to a likeness, the passive-aggressive pattern is particularly operative, and at the slightest provocation the patient will try to sweep the therapist into a sado-masochistic engagement. It is one thing for the patient to say "I" and it is another thing for the therapist to confront the patient with what he has said that his problems are.

An illustration of the mechanism of *use of family history for projective defense* is evident in the following extract from a session. The patient, Lisa, is speaking of her mother, who has been hospitalized on many occasions and who has been diagnosed paranoid schizophrenia.

PT: I talked with my mother today. She seemed all right, but my father was belittling her as usual. He wanted me to take a trip to Philadelphia to go shopping with her. But I didn't bite this time. (Formerly, the father would never let the mother shop by herself but would send the patient with her and the patient would play a mothering role with her mother, but a kind of punitive and controlling mothering role, preventing her from buying what she wanted, talking her out of certain kinds of purchases and questioning the advisability of one against another article. At the same time, the patient would tell her mother how to act: "Stand there, do that, do this, etc.").

TH: You decided your mother can shop by herself?

PT: Yes. She never has bought things in a foolish way, but my father acts as though she's a nitwit. And he got me to act that way towards her too.

TH: You did act that way?

PT: (The patient begins to cry.) Yes, but I didn't want to. It was my father's idea. And now I feel like my mother, I'm identified with her. I think I'm helpless. But I always manage; I come through. My father treated me the same. Always my brother got praise. Me, nothing. I can't do it either. (She is writing her dissertation for a Ph.D.) I was writing last night and I asked James (her husband) to read my work. He tore it to pieces. He's so sure of himself. Why do I try? These men are all so brilliant—my father, my brother, even my sister-in-law. And, I'm nothing (*masochism*). I was so mad at James. He's so sure of himself. When did he become the great writer?! I'm so mad. I told him that I couldn't stand another attack. He's cruel, like you. As Marion says (a member of the group which I conduct in which they are both patients), you are cruel, you laugh. Why don't you ever give me a good word, why always the attitude, "stand on your own feet, don't lean on me." Why can't you give some reassurance once in a while. (She tries to make the therapist feel guilty, like she does her husband, denying her own sadism.)

TH: What makes you feel you need all that reassurance?

PT: Well, I do—so I want a mother—and you're no mother. How did your own children ever survive? You have no feelings about me, one way or the other. I was thinking the other day that there is nothing about me that you like.

TH: Nothing.

PT: Nothing.

TH: That must be a bad kind of feeling. You couldn't think of a thing I might like about you?

PT: Nothing. (This is a projection of her own hate and sadism—identifying with both her father and her mother.)

TH: That's amazing. (She identifies me with the mother and father who want a masochistic daughter.)

In the next session, we went through a similar kind of encounter, but finally the patient admitted that I might think well of her fortitude, her ability to come through under distressing conditions, all of which meant, on a latent level, that I would like her masochism, i.e., her ability to survive under difficult conditions. (Her husband has decided to work for his Ph.D. and to leave his job. On top of this, she is his second wife and he has alimony to pay, and she can look forward to lean times for the next three years.)

PT: You may admire my qualities of surviving in dire circumstances.

TH: I have thought of these characteristics in you.

PT: Now you're trying to find something good to say. That doesn't make me feel good.

TH: I still have contempt for you then?

PT: Yes.

TH: You have said that your own mother was the only person who was ever good to you, who even liked you.

PT: Yes.

TH: Can that be true, the only one?

PT: Yes.

TH: Your mother was gentle and kind, and submissive.

PT: Yes, and loving. I'm like that. People like me because I'm always helping, always doing for others, always the kind one (denial of her sadism).

TH: That's funny. I've never seen you as the helper. I've thought that you have other traits.

PT: Oh, yes, I'm always the helper.

TH: A regular Girl Scout (I laugh).

PT: See, you are sadistic.

TH: You feel you "mother" others as you were made to do to your own mother?

PT: Yes, yes, yes.

The basic aim of the projective therapeutic technique is to be able to handle conflict material of a sado-masochistic nature, which has been incorporated into the defense of projective identification, to talk about the material in the session, and to analyze certain aspects of the delusion (the projective identification phantasy) without making a direct reference to the patient's behavior except in those areas where the patient can tolerate confrontation, i.e., the area of least resistance. The patient, in this short example, is willing to say that she mothers others, but *we shall have to have several more sessions before we can point to the controlling nature of the "mothering," the demeaning characteristics and the other sadistic aspects of the defense.* The patient denies the sadistic side of the controlling or mothering mechanisms and says that she is really "good." She would never have acted that way with her mother if her father had not made her do so. She denies that she acts this way today with her husband, although in previous sessions she has alluded to this.

An important step in projective therapeutic technique is *to outline the manner in which interlocking defenses operate* between the parents in the interpersonal encounter. The patient's description of her defenses, and the actual utilization of her defenses with the therapist and with others, are expressed at the beginning of treatment in projective and acting out terms. The patient speaks of her defenses, and she talks about her aspirations mostly by referring to others about whom she may feel envy or guilt. She describes her inhibitions and her sado-masochistic behavior (some call this the dependent or the symbiotic behavior) by talking about others, i.e., about family members—her father, her mother, her brothers, her sisters. At times, the patient acts towards me as her parents did toward her. For example, she may be self-critical in a harsh and sadistic way (Freud described this as the operation of a primitive punitive superego), and berate herself, just as her father or her mother might have done. She acts out her father's role towards herself (this is, of course, a masochistic maneuver), or she belittles herself or her husband by saying that he cannot understand a situation, or that he cannot see the implications of a situation, or that he is unthinking. She then says she will surely fail at what she attempts to do. And, indeed, these are not mere words. She may very well act out the failure as she did in childhood. She represses the fact that her parents helped her defeat herself; that there were things the parents did not wish to see, or to understand. She shifts roles and acts towards the therapist as the parents did towards her.

In attempting to perpetuate a masochistic role, this patient may react to an interpretation by saying: "That's just what my father would have said!" This kind of statement can be discomforting to a therapist who is establishing his difference from the parents. The patient knows that the therapist does not want to be thought of as "like the parents," and yet, in this mechanism, the patient is reflecting, by accusing the therapist, an aspect of herself, her identification with her hostile, punitive parents against whom she is defending. Counteracting her own guilt, she tries to make the analyst feel guilty. When the analyst responds to this guilt-provoking maneuver, he must do so in a way that does not rebuke the parents or humiliate the patient in any way, for to criticize the parents or the "other person" would be to criticize that aspect of the patient's personality that the patient's projective maneuver helps to deny. In denial, the patient defends against the constructive side of the ego, as well as against the incorporated or introjected (parental) destructive and punitive side of the ego. The behavior is both sadistic and masochistic on the part of the patient and is intended to defend by throwing the therapist out of the therapeutic role, casting him in the role of a parent (or both parents) whom the patient attempts to make feel guilty. Thus the patient implies that it is not he who acts in a provocative way, but only the other person—the mother, the father, the boss, the analyst, etc. The transference is evident here, but one will recognize that, in the beginning of treatment, it would be difficult to make a direct transference interpretation, for the transference is expressed in a projective operation, such as "acting out." *The phantasy behind the acting out must be delineated first, and then the relation of the acting out to the phantasy will be clearer. Projective interpretation is the first step in outlining an interlocking defensive pattern between two people.* One would, therefore, have to respond to the patient's statement that the analyst is acting or talking like the father by interpreting the defensive maneuver of the father. One might say: "Your feeling was that when your father spoke to you in a harsh way, he was trying to hurt you, or to make you feel guilty. It seems to me that at the same time that he was doing this, he would be trying to *protect himself* by accusing you. He would be denying his part in the hostile reaction when really he had a part in it. Perhaps deep down he felt guilty, but would never admit it." In this way, one would be outlining the dynamics of the patient's behavior, for when she speaks of her father she is really using the defense of projective identification and denying that she is speaking about herself—the "just as" pattern. The interlocking interpersonal defense is clear.

The phantasy is one of the most meaningful aspects of the defense, and the analysis of the phantasy, as of a dream, leads to the reconstruction of the past—so that it can be brought into appropriate relationship with neurotic patterns operative in the present, i.e., into the transference situations. *How can we connect the phantasy with the patient's acting out pattern when the phantasy takes the form of delusion?* At best, this is a long tedious task. Let us say that the patient has introduced into the session an incident in the immediate past with a friend, which makes the patient feel guilty, and in the process of exploring the dynamics of the friend and his relations with people and with the patient, the patient's associations have lead to incidents in the remote past. If the mother is the focus of the association to the past, then a discussion of the mother's dynamics and the similarity of those to the dynamics of the friend must be done in a way that will relate to the *patient's present mode of functioning, without stating this fact.* Thus, the therapist might say: "Oh, your mother would say something to you that would make you feel guilty?" (The therapist knows that he is speaking of the patient's dynamics as well as the mother's, for the patient has just acted in a way to make the analyst feel guilty.) "Did you have a particular memory in mind?" the therapist asks.[7] In one instance of this kind, a patient then recalled a time when he let his mother do all of his homework for him; she apparently resented this, but did it anyway. One must be aware that the mother's resentment is irrational, in the sense that she has taught the patient to depend on her doing his work for him, due to her own controlling tendencies. *She burdens herself with her child's so-called dependency and then finds an outlet for her aggression in resentment of being in this position with her son.* The paranoid or projective quality of the relationship is evident. (This particular dynamic is most prominent in schizophrenic children and in behavior disorders. The child becomes a thorn in the parents' side, but what we may forget is that the parents have trained the child in this role. Neurotic children are often thought of as "monsters" by their parents, and they are presented as such by the parents to others when the parents discuss the children.) What is happening in this particular session with my borderline patient is that he is resisting therapy and feels guilty: he tries to make the therapist do all the therapeutic work; his defense of passivity, which he developed in his relations with father and mother, is operative. His inhibitions are related to his passivity and his anger at his therapist is what Freud called the invasion of the patient's narcissism (his autism or phantasy life), which the patient resents and defends against. He feels the therapist will be angry, as his mother was, when she did all the work. And, on a deeper level, the patient wishes to throw the therapist out of her therapeutic role, into the mother-role as a defense against treatment. The patient recalls one occasion when he came home to tell how critical the teacher was of the homework the mother had done. (The child was pitting the mother against the teacher, the mother participating in the maneuver.) The mother became infuriated and said to the patient: "That is the thanks I get; do you think that I don't feel hurt? Why do you torture me so?" As we now know this angry mother created the patient's dependency by doing the homework, at the same time denying her role in the maneuver. She then made the child feel guilty for his counter-aggression. This whole association came about when, in the particular session, the therapist had challenged the patient's defenses by agreeing with one of the patient's friends (as the patient reported) who had commented that the patient was "nervous and inattentive in the interpersonal relationships." The patient, the therapist agreed, sometimes acted that way with people, and she said that she, too, had noticed this in the patient. (*The therapist does not pursue this idea beyond noting the similarity of the patient's actions in and out of the session, and saying that there must be a good reason for this behavior. Then, the therapist asks if the friend has any of these characteristics.*) The therapist does not, for example, explain the transference feeling that is operating between herself and the patient, or explain the patient's attempt to throw the therapist out of her role, or explain what is going on between himself and his friend, or analyze what happened with the mother. These interpretations will come later. She merely agrees with the friend, speculates about the friend's dynamics, and adds that there must be an explanation for all this behavior. One wonders whether the friend, too, has the same characteristics as the patient. *The goal of the technique is to be able eventually to show the patient that he is defending: the act of withdrawing is a defense.* One must show first that this happens and then go over the kind of situation where it happens; then one must relate the defense to anxiety.

The first insight is to demonstrate and admit that the defense occurs. This particular patient, as part of his defense, has been pitting the therapist against another therapist (his friend's), saying that the other therapist was more direct, more "orthodox" and thus more "scientific." The patient had himself been in treatment with two other therapists—one who had had no therapeutic training, but who was a "legitimate doctor" and had a tremendously successful psycho-therapeutic practice, economically speaking, and another therapist who followed the non-directive (Rogerian) technique. The patient insisted that neither of these therapists had helped him, but since they were "successful in their practices," obviously one did not have to have psychoanalytic training to practice psycho-analysis. This was a way of trying to make the therapist feel inferior, but it was also a way of "defending" against "probing," while at the same time taunting the therapist with what he considered the orthodox technique of "intensive" probing. The patient was aware that the therapist was connected with a training program and placed a great deal of emphasis on adequate preparation for a therapeutic role. He had brought up the matter of the "other therapists" when his present therapist agreed with the friend as to the patient's withdrawal tendencies. (He showed his anger in this way when his defense was pointed out.) In agreeing with the friend, the therapist estimated this as the patient's least defended area: it was a problem where the patient could speak directly in terms of "I" ("my friend says I do this"), albeit in the hope of persisting in his denial and his wish to perpetuate this particular kind of defense. Agreement with the friend was a form of interpretation, or perhaps, more precisely, a form of accenting or underlining a phrase which had a particular meaning with respect to one of the patient's defenses. This "interpretation" or "accenting" aroused the patient's anxiety and he began to attack the therapist and treatment. He denied the other therapists had helped him, although it was obvious that in some ways they had been useful to him. Eventually the patient and the analyst will have to analyze the sado-masochistic phantasy attached to the defenses the friend had described in the patient—the defenses of what Melanie Klein called the "schizoid position"—"tuning the other person out" by withdrawing into phantasy and thus temporarily leaving the relationship. At the end of the session, the patient admitted that he does often withdraw and "tune out" the other person in the relationship. The connection was then made with his pattern of passivity and his anger at the implication that he too must take an active role in his own treatment. This was, as explained before, because he had been trained in passivity by his mother.

Another example of explaining that a piece of behavior is a defense can be related to an instance when the individual acts out a homosexual phantasy in some form or other. If we think of the homosexuality as an oedipal problem related to conditionings in childhood, we ask: "Why now?" "Why is this oedipal feeling occurring at this time? What interpersonal problem and *what anxiety is being defended against in the acting out*? Furthermore, what kind of unconscious communication is involved in the present neurotic interaction?" To be consistent with the theory of sado-masochism, we know that self-denigration, as well as denigration of the "other," is being enacted in the homosexual encounter, so that the oedipal feeling is a reenactment of relations with father and mother. It is the acting out of a transference feeling to quiet anxiety. When my patient, Frank, acts out in a homosexual incident, I must think to myself: "Why this symptom: Why now?" I must ask what went on during the day and what were the anxieties stimulated during the day (the same principle as in the interpretation of dreams). I must also remember what I have already learned about him. His associations reveal that he does not want to go to work at all; he prefers to stay at home and listen to records, i.e., to withdraw. The patient's father, even after the patient had graduated from engineering school and held a position of some prominence, managed his money, telling him that he was incapable of handling finances. After he began to challenge his father, encouraged by therapy to take care of his own money, his father wrote him a most hostile and denigrating letter in which the mother joined by a scribbled postscript, telling him among other things that he would probably lose all his savings within one year if he persisted in what he was doing. In view of this background, the patient has transference reactions in every interpersonal encounter. For example, if he has an exchange with a peer at work he feels the peer is looking down upon him. (As a child he was inept, he could not play ball with the other boys; his father was always telling him he was awkward, and he acted awkward.) His father, however, would never show him how to do anything; he would always take things out of his hands and do it for him instead. The father never praised him for anything, even when he graduated from a famous university *cum laude* and had become an accomplished engineer.

One would think that after having successfully challenged the father and mother concerning the money, and after he had taken over the management of his money, his assertiveness would generalize and that the neurotic pattern would yield in other areas; but this was not the case. It had to be worked through on other issues as well, for the obsessional mechanism had not been broken. It persisted for two more years, until other aspects of the problem had been worked through, such as: "Could he live with a woman; could he accept the fact that he was a successful engineer?" His obsessional doubting was connected with all matters that concerned himself—his aspirations, his thoughts about recognizing his abilities and his wishes for a good life. In 1952 I wrote that the basic problem in such cases is associated with sado-masochistic cycles, which the patient often goes through. This might be called a phobic and counter-phobic cycle, the latter part associated with depression and guilt. The guilt is over self-assertion and recognition of self, as well as a reaction to aggressive and revenge feelings. Guilt must be overcome before working through can take place.

Arieti has suggested a technique in the treatment of schizophrenics, to be used at times when a hallucinatory defense is in operation, which helps the patient to understand that the hallucination is not constant but is organized at periods when the patient has an especial "listening attitude." I take this to mean that the patient has a "listening attitude" at points of *special anxiety* and that the hallucination is a defensive response (a projective sado-masochistic defense) to the anxiety. One can apply this technique to the sometimes momentary hallucinatory or delusional experiences of the borderline patient. Eventually, the therapist explains to the patient that hallucinations may appear at periods when anxiety is most intense and that their function is to help relieve anxiety. The patient and the analyst can then explore the situations in which the intense anxiety appears just as one would do if the symptom were a headache or a phobia. Often, the anxiety is aroused by feelings of aggression or desires to be self-assertive or both. The hallucinatory experience although a withdrawal mechanism is also associated with a paranoid-like type of defense. The phantasy is projected into the environment in a delusional sense. After the patient understands the hallucinatory experience is a defense, then the hallucination can be used like a dream.

A projective technique should begin early in treatment to support the patient's "normal" ego strivings and to counteract his masochism, since he has overwhelming guilt over his self-assertive needs. Some authors look at this as a way of the therapist's representing reality, the therapist acting as the patient's ego. *It is important that the therapist reinforce the patient's productions concerning his recognition of reality, as well as his normal assertive strivings by repeating the phrases that the patient has used to describe these strivings, the therapist feeding back to the patient the latter's ideas as ideas which the therapist confirms.* This helps to undermine the masochism, but the therapist must, in these instances, make sure that he mentions the *culpability* that neurotic people have when they wish for success and the good life. The relations with parents have been such that they have been made to feel extraordinary guilt for wanting to be self-assertive. Such strivings are too much of a challenge to the patient's need to debase himself. This is the opposite of the paranoid person who becomes successful on the basis of his aggression—a persistent counter-phobic mechanism that carries him through to overcome others. The borderline patient vacillates between being phobic and counter-phobic in his tendencies, and the obsessive-compulsive mechanisms reinforce these patterns. The projective technique is a way of managing transference within these kinds of projective defenses so that the possibility of an elaborate transference psychosis does not take place. Rather, the transference is handled in small parts and pieces until, finally at the end of treatment, the patient can tolerate the direct *I-you* transference, looking back at the pieces and parts and putting them together in an integrated form without fear and guilt. Toward the end phase of treatment, the patient can face direct transference feelings. During the middle phase of treatment, transference attitudes are handled largely by intermediate reactions to the others with whom the patient is in an interlocking defensive relationship.

My treatment of George Adler, the pediatrician, provides an excellent example of how one may use the projective technique in the management of transference:

PT: I felt good, but when I came here I got depressed. I just don't know whether you know what you are doing. After four years I have the same doubts and feelings I had initially.

TH: The same?

PT: Yes, the same!

TH: Are you sure?

PT: You sound like my mother. "Do you think you really want that? Are you sure that is the best idea?!"

TH: Well, I wasn't aware that I'm like your mother. The way you've described her.

PT: You're not; but you're making me feel the way she did. (This seems to be an effort to make the therapist feel guilty because she challenged his statement about his feeling the same as he did four years ago, a challenge to his hostility and his denial of his success.)

TH: I had thought you said you felt better? (Therapist stresses reality.)

PT: I did, but today all was lost. I just wondered all of a sudden what on earth I think I'm doing. I just didn't seem real (a depersonalization feeling).

TH: What happened today?

PT: I was at work—I didn't want to go to work at all—I never want to go to work.

TH: You told me the other day you were interested at work—you hoped you could maintain that feeling (again stressing reality as a challenge of his denial of this change).

PT: It was very temporary.

TH: Yes, but exciting, you said. I hope you feel that way everyday soon.

PT: I can't imagine such a thing.

TH: You really mean that? Your phantasy doesn't take you in that direction? You can't imagine enjoying your work and your life?

PT: That's right—as a matter of fact it's just the opposite: when I feel good I always say it won't last.

TH: Yes—that's strange: you feel good and then you cut it off. (This has to do with attitudes of his father and mother towards him. Their obsessive-compulsive pattern, their obsessive doubting. Their questioning of him. "Is this what you really want?", etc., cutting off his pleasure and challenging his decisions.)

PT: Right. Why is that? That's what I want you do to—help me with that. I'll never get rid of that feeling. I don't see that you are doing anything to help me. (Therapist ignores the hostility and gets on with the exploration of the problem as the patient has asked her to do.)

TH: You said you didn't want to go to work this morning.

PT: As usual. I forced myself out of bed and then I listened to records and I didn't want to leave. But I got myself to go. Then when I got to work, the class was there and I was annoyed that I had to talk to them. For a brief moment I enjoyed talking and I was animated, telling them some thing I was really interested in, but they were waiting for Dr. Green. (The patient works in a university setting, one aspect of his work being teaching; Dr. Green is the head of the department.) He's their God. I can never compete with him.

TH: Why do you have to; he's been at the game twenty years longer than you. Why do you have to compete with him?

PT: Well, I want the students to respect me.

TH: You feel they don't respect you?

PT: They—how could they? Dr. Green walks in and we are discussing something, and he puts his two cents worth in, and always adds something to what I've said. He can never just agree with me. He's always got to do me one better. (This, he feels, is like his parents: Are you sure? Wouldn't this way be better? The father and mother could never let him be right about anything—their competitiveness could not allow it.)

TH: Perhaps he's competitive. He can't let you have it with the class.

PT: He can't give me a good word. (The masochistic orientation.)

TH: That reminds me of someone. (I mean the patient's father and I hope the patient will pick up this cue.)

PT: Yes, my father. I say to myself when Dr. Green comes into the room: "That bastard can't give me an inch; he always has to put me down." He always says, "Yes, but" to everything I say, and then makes some brilliant remark.

TH: Your relations with your father contaminate the relationship with Dr. Green. (A projective transference interpretation.)

PT: He is like my father—in that way.

TH: Yes, but do you have to act toward him as if he were your father? He's a colleague.

PT: Why not, if he is like him—my father?

TH: Because he's not your father and you're not his son. You are a junior colleague.

PT: He's like my father.

TH: He's not your father; you are not his son. Even when he puts you down, he's not your father.

PT: Well what is he?

TH: A senior colleague. What do you feel when he says, "Yes, but . . . "

PT: Depressed, defeated—I want to run out.

TH: Why aren't you angry at him?

PT: I am, but what good is it?

TH: Well, do you feel angry?

PT: No, not really—only depressed.

TH: You feel like giving up?

PT: Oh I feel like yelling my head off.

TH: Yelling—then you do feel angry!

PT: Yes, no—not angry, but like yelling; like saying, "Why can't you appreciate me; why can't you give me the time of day—why do you put me down?" (The masochistic attitude.)

TH: You don't feel like saying: "Why do you put me down, you son-of-a-bitch?" (The therapist takes the role of the patient—the sadistic side of the patient's sado-masochism—the therapist acting as a projective instrument.)

PT: No, because then I say to myself that's not reasonable. Why should I be angry? I've been taught to be reasonable.

TH: But you are angry, and anyone might feel angry under those circumstances.

PT: But it's not sensible.

TH: If you're angry, you're angry.

PT: All right, I'm angry—so where do we go from here?

TH: Well, for one thing, if he's trying to put you down, you don't have to react as if he's your father and you are six years old. You become six years old and you complain in your phantasy to big daddy. Big daddy, why do you use me this way? You are not six years old. He's not your father.

PT: I tell myself that, but it doesn't help.

TH: You act that way anyway?

PT: Yes.

TH: It's a phantasy, you see, you use a phantasy: *He is putting me down and I'm six years old. I'm helpless, I'm pleading with him.*

PT: Yes, what do you mean a phantasy?

TH: That's what I mean—a phantasy. He's big daddy and you are six. Neither thing is true. But you act *as-if* it were true. It's a phantasy, and in your phantasy you plead with him.

PT: Yes, I see that.

TH: What does the phantasy do for you in the situation? We've got to figure that out.

PT: I don't know—you tell me. (His passivity is manifest.)

TH: Well, think—think about the phantasy: is there more to it?

PT: Perhaps.

TH: Well—what's the rest?

PT: I guess it's different at different times.

TH: Well, tell me about the different phantasies.

PT: Well, sometimes I think: "Drop dead you bastard." The other day I had a phantasy I'd like to choke him. I had a phantasy I would tell him off, but then I got scared because I was sure he'd punish me. He'd get me out of the department. He'd refuse to promote me. He'd deprive me of money, a raise.

TH: He'd be a vindictive, hostile, punitive, bastard if you yelled at him or challenged him. (He has now expressed his sadistic side.)

PT: I guess so.

TH: You don't handle him because you fear his retaliation. (His parents did punish him if he challenged them. They responded with hostile, punitive attitudes and made him feel guilty.)

PT: Yes.

TH: Is there any way you could handle it without choking him?

PT: Yes. It's funny—right now I hear music—and I can't think—I don't seem to hear what you're talking about. (The patient is using a repressive mechanism to avoid anxiety and is withdrawing into phantasy in anger.)

TH: You're blotting the whole thing out of your mind.

PT: Yes—it's frustrating. I can't remember what we were saying.

TH: You're withdrawing into the music. Well, you've mentioned this often before.

PT: I was getting a homosexual phantasy, too. I feel like going out and picking someone up and forcing them to suck me off. I've done it before.

TH: Are you angry at me?

PT: Sort of, not really—I won't do it but I feel like it.

TH: What does the music remind you of?

PT: My father comes to mind.

TH: Your father?

PT: I used to sit with him and listen to records. (At this point, the patient turned on the therapist and said angrily: "You know that! How many times have I told you this—you don't remember anything—that's something I can't stand, saying these things over and over again. What do you do with it? Just sit and repeat it over and over again!" Patient is manifesting here a partial transference reaction. It will be noted that a rapidly shifting defensive system, so typical of borderline cases, is being shown here.)

TH: Yes, that's so. We keep talking about that music. When you want to get something out of your mind and not have to think about it.

PT: I don't do it deliberately—the music comes to my mind and I can't think. I do forget what we're talking about.

TH: You can't remember at all?

PT: No.

TH: If you relax and think about it can you remember?

PT: No.

TH: Well, try relaxing; just relax, relax.

PT: Well—I guess we were talking about work.

TH: Yes.

PT: Dr. Green.

TH: Yes—just relax and the thoughts will come back to you.

PT: The phantasy.

TH: Yes.

PT: That's fantastic. I really did forget the whole thing and I heard the music and I wanted to act out with a homosexual. But I did remember having a nice time over the weekend with Ruth (his current girl friend). I really did enjoy it, but after a while I started observing. She didn't look too good to me. She was withdrawing too much. She had a pimple on her face. I can't stand that.

TH: You put a stop to your enjoyment. (Characteristically, the patient cannot sustain feelings of pleasure due to his masochism.)

PT: Yes.

TH: It reminds me of what you said about your father and mother. You start to enjoy something and then you say: "Are you sure this is what you want? Don't you think that—or, you can't have this—who are you to want something like this? (The obsessive compulsive mechanism of cutting off pleasure comes from the internalization of the hostile parent—the introject—or to put it another way, from identification with the parent.)

PT: Yes—yes—when am I ever going to stop this?

TH: Well, last year you talked about the pattern—you were going through this then, too, but this year you're talking about it in a different way. You're talking about stopping the pattern.

PT: That is very true; and sometimes I can stop the reaction.

The following extracts from three sessions with another borderline case, Kurt Blau, are further examples of handling transference in a projective form, thus dealing with the defensive aspect. The attempt here is to show the patient that in his interpersonal relations he acts as if the other person were his parent; but, this does not help work through the problem. The patient must begin to see that his transference maneuvers are defensive and that they are connected with sado-masochistic phantasies: the "as-if" maneuvers are defensive and connected with phantasy, which defends against and depicts the role the patient played in his family and which he perpetuates today by acting at one time like his parent with others, and at other times like a little boy. He, like George Adler, can play either role—the little boy or the hostile parent.

FIRST SESSION

PT: I took the test. (A battery of Rorschach, TAT and others for candidacy as a psychoanalytic student.) I think I'm depressed—there weren't so many responses. No quantity. I'm depressed—going to Manhattan. I guess I'm going to join the middle class; intellectual party. I'm going with the intellectual snobs. She called me doctor. (He refers to the psychologist who gave him the tests. He has finished his Ph.D. thesis, but has not received the degree yet. One member of his committee refused to accept his thesis on the grounds that it was poorly written. So he has to rewrite it. He says he cannot write it and he may hire a writer. They accept the thesis, but this one man refuses the write-up.)
TH: Why is it embarrasing?
PT: Because I don't have the Ph.D. yet.
TH: Any other reason?
PT: I don't feel I deserve it, I really don't (masochistic defense).
TH: What were your feelings about Mrs. Green this time? (Mrs. Green is the psychologist who gave him the tests.)
PT: I didn't like her. I don't know if I was angry at her—er—
TH: Angry? Angry; didn't like her. (This is probably a transference feeling)
PT: There's really nothing to be angry at. Like I said to her, I guess I'll see you in two more years—like I knew. I think they'll show I have difficulty in growth, and that I think of myself as very small. (He is thinking of himself as a little boy.) Let me see (silence), I don't know why—it's irrational. Again, could I compete with Charlotte Green (projected transference feelings). Not only that. People were complaining about me again—a lot—our group; they seemed to be doing fairly well. While I was talking I was fearful. (He means while he was giving a lecture to his colleagues at work. He is much more advanced professionally than his colleagues who are treating personnel in the child guidance clinic, because he is one of the few who has special training.)
TH: What people?
PT: At the agency. Many people questioned me after the lecture.
TH: About what?
PT: About what I was doing. People turned around. "What kind of a trouble-maker are you," some said.
TH: What do you mean, trouble-maker?

PT: This is what they would say. If I made a suggestion, or criticized any procedure, or if I talk about the work I do, they'd say, "What are you doing?"

TH: If you want to improve things at work?

PT: Well, I'm making trouble. Yes, that's what they mean. I'm too anxious; I do too much; I shake up the place with my ideas. (His way of approaching changes or of suggesting improvements is to express aggression against "the system.")

TH: That's what you mean when you say you feel guilty?

PT: Yes. Then I say to myself I really hate to feel adequate because there's something queer about it. (Masochism is being shown.)

TH: Well, if you are doing a good job, you don't have to feel like they do about it, do you?

(In this kind of exchange there is a transference involved, in that he feels competitive with the analyst and he feels guilty about that. He also fears his competitive feelings towards the analyst, because his parents had attitudes like his colleagues: if anything happened to shake their adjustment or their ideas and attitudes, they did not like it. As a child he was punished for his attitudes and ideas, even though they were often rational ideas as opposed to his parent's irrational ones. The technique to be used is to speak of his colleagues rather than his parents, to focus on the irrationalities of his colleagues, rather than his parents. He feels guilty, too, because his ambitions are couched in terms of aggression. He wants to replace the analyst, demolish her position, take over, etc.)

PT: That's true.

TH: You're feelings are more normal?

PT: What do you mean?

TH: Adequate—you get along—you do well. But you're feeling guilty about being adequate, or more than adequate? Aren't you? (Interpreting his defense.)

PT: I was handling this children's group, and they were throwing things around. A teacher walked in. I am trying to explain what they are doing. She said about one boy: "He'll put some boy's eyes out." I had to spoil what I was doing, because she walked in.

TH: You told him to stop because she was there?

PT: Also the time the principal walked in. He said, "You are working with this group? These kids are just eating!" I feel demands are brought to bear on me and they make me change, or they want me to change and do what they would do. (He has a paranoid and masochistic reaction to these school personnel when he is at work because, in their resistances to change, they attack him.)

TH: You didn't feel angry at the teacher?

(The teacher and the principal are like the parents: they have irrational attitudes. To put the matter in another way, they are defensive. It creates anxiety in them to see things done in a manner they don't understand, or in a way so as to upset their cherished ideas about handling children, although these are the very children with whom they have failed. The feelings towards the principal and the teacher are transference feelings. The teacher and the principal are similar in their attitudes to those of the parents. The patient feels towards them as if they were adults and he a child, and he should not upset them in any way. They criticize and interfere in something they know nothing about. He feels that people who are butting in are not really right in doing so. They should

be learning, in view of their own failures, rather than criticizing. He also feels
like killing them.)

PT: Well, yes, I would like to say: "You let me take care of this. He's not
going to put any boy's eyes out!" I would like to put her eyes out. (His extreme
anger is transferential.)

TH: You were really very angry?

PT: I could kill.

TH: Well, next time maybe you can say what you wanted to say: "You let
me take care of this. He's not going to put anyone's eyes out." Why did you say
you hate to feel that you are adequate?

PT: Well, I gave an orientation lecture at the Agency about group therapy
for lower income kids. It teaches them so much more—provides something for
them. No one is talking about that. I did the same at my previous job. I'm afraid
the same thing is going to happen at the Agency; I'm afraid people will cut me
down?

TH: How?

PT: Argue with me; disagree with me.

TH: How does that cut you down?

PT: They act as if I'm the one who is in error. I feel ashamed; I feel no
good; that cuts me down. (A masochistic little boy phantasy, and paranoid
feelings.)

TH: That bothers you—if you're making a good statement, talking out of
your own experience? Why should you feel you're the one who is wrong? Isn't
that some kind of a phantasy? (Supporting his positive qualities.)

PT: (Long pause) I guess it's because on such a deep level I feel so unsure
of myself. Maybe I want to shake them up! (His guilt about his competitive and
sadistic feelings.)

TH: Unsure? (Therapist lets the sadism go and focuses on the anxiety)

PT: Um huh.

TH: Unsure? (To get more associations.)

PT: (He shifts to his parents and to an actual episode he recently had with
them where he acted out the little boy role.) I can't make the right decisions for
my parents. I have thought of moving to the Village or to Manhattan, but that is
going to be upsetting to my parents. They won't like that idea at all—they'll
think it's foolish, we'll be going into a slum. I can just hear it. They'll say,
"You're harming your children; you're going into a slum."

TH: They'll think you're harming your children and going into a slum?

PT: Yeah.

TH: Why a slum?

PT: We won't be moving into a slum. (He turns on the therapist) What
makes you think we'll be moving into a slum? (Negative trasnference.)

TH: I didn't think you would; I didn't say you would.

PT: No, but you act like you agree with them. We won't be living in a
slum; we won't, but they'll think so. (*He implies that therapist agrees with the
parents*—a manifestation of transference feelings.) They'll say you are hurting
the kids; it's crazy—I know the whole story. (Silence) I don't know why I'm so
quiet—I've noticed that I'm a lot quieter lately. In school, too. This is why I
think I'm depressed—because I think I'm quieter. I don't think I'm sapped—but
quiet.

TH: Maybe that's more normal—your feeling before may have been on the hopped up side. (His overactivity hides his depression, but he is beginning to realize he has been depressed, now that he is thinking about being less overactive.)

PT: I got my five months evaluation: "He can only keep this up by maintaining a rigorous schedule." It's knocking me out—I'm just. . . . How do you terminate a patient? How do you treat a patient like this? How do you say to this woman—besides her not being able to pay—I know there is a real money problem, and there is a feeling on her part. Sometimes she shows and sometimes she doesn't show. Ten to eleven dollars would be little enough. I took her for five dollars. That is almost like taking her for nothing. (Rebelling against his masochism.)

TH: You feel you should do something about her—change the situation. I think you're right. We'll have to talk about her next time.

In the next session, the patient identifies with the teacher he mentioned in the previous session and with a child he is seeing in the school. He transfers onto the therapist feelings he had about his mother, but, more than that, he uses the defense of projective identification when he speaks of his vocational ambitions. He speculates that if he attempts to go into the field of psychology and becomes an analyst I will be angry with him. The safe role, he then assumes, is the masochistic one, but he now wants to break out of the masochistic way of life. He brings the problem more clearly into the current transference situation.

SECOND SESSION

PT: I had a dream. I was running away from you; I was running up the stairs. Then I realized it was the exact same flight I used to run up when my mother would catch me and beat the hell out of me. I'd do something she didn't like and she'd run after me and I'd run up these stairs, and she'd catch me at the top and beat the hell out of me. Then I'd go to the last step on the very top and just sit there. I'd sit there and sulk; I'd stay by myself for an hour or more. I felt injured, hurt, beaten, and I was in a rage, but I never said anything to her. In another dream, I was thinking of my sister and telling her to go to hell. My sister was the favorite."

TH: Why do you think I'm in the dream?

PT: Running away from therapy? Negative transference. Anger.

TH: Did you want to say something to me? Instead of having the feeling I mean. What could you have said? Did I say anything that hurt you last time?

PT: You're wrong. I could have said "You're wrong."

TH: When?

PT: When you said that about the school bulletin, but I didn't. I could have simply said, "You're wrong."

TH: But you didn't dare because I'd . . . .

PT: Sometimes I feel shorted by you.

TH: What's shorted?

PT: Cheated!

TH: Cheated?

PT: Yes. I couldn't say you're wrong or else I'd be shorted some more. Is that anxiety? Am I anxious when I'm with you? Am I trying to be you? Do I want your attention?

TH: What do you mean?

PT: Is it infantile if I want your attention?

TH: Infantile . . . ?

PT: I want you to be here always.

TH: You expect me to be here? Always? Well . . . .

(There is inherent in this statement of the patient, "I want you to be here always," the kind of resistance Reich spoke of as a problem associated with the narcissistic neurosis, i.e., the secret hope that the analyst will finally fulfil the patient's preoedipal longings, or love demands. George Adler, the pediatrician, became aware of this longing in the form of a phantasy, and so did Lisa, the girl who spoke of shopping with her mother. Reich said that one must uncover unresolved guilt feelings which have a relation to sadistic impulses towards a childhood object. In this remnant of a "non-genital infantile fixation" to the analyst as the representative of the mother, he hopes she will be protective; otherwise she will become the sadistic, bad mother, especially if he shows any anger towards her. We may add that as therapist, she may confront him with his sadistic feelings, and his need to express this longing is a defense against getting at his sadism).

PT: Only one time you weren't here; but my mother was never there when I was home. When I needed her, I guess I wanted her to be home. People have always said: "You're wrong, you're wrong, you don't know," or "you don't really want that!" Teachers talking to me—setting me up as a good boy. That's the worst thing anyone can do—set you up to be a good boy. My mother set me up to be that way too. And you? You expect me to be good. A good student, get ahead!

TH: What did you want to be?

(I am taking this away from transference to use a projective technique, employing the relationship with the mother in the past instead of exploring the present with me, because I believe it would be more valuable to get at the hostility toward his mother and phantasies he may have had of getting back at her. The order of my working is first on the defense, to make the phantasy apparent, then on the relation of the defense and phantasy, to the anxiety, and finally I move to the I-Thou transference.)

PT: I wanted to be free. I didn't want to be in the store. I was climbing the fence and my mother wouldn't let me climb the fence. I felt so embarrassed, ashamed. She'd prevent me from climbing. I'd have to be in the store and be the errand boy. "Get that box of nails or screws." I was supposed to keep smiling. I didn't want to carry the garbage can out. "Do you want to go to your Aunt Martha's?" It wasn't a question; it was a demand. I couldn't say "no," and I couldn't show any anxiety. I couldn't show anything, but I just had to smile.

TH: I had another patient once who called himself "the smiler": if anyone said anything to him, he'd just have to smile, whether he liked it or not (this was Dr. Daird).

PT: I'm insensitive to anxiety in my children too. (Here he speaks of himself directly. He had referred to these traits in a projected way, speaking of his aunt, and, in the previous session, implying transference feelings in an attitude of the therapist.) I couldn't do anything except sit on the stoop with my mother, or go play with the girl next door. If I slid down the bannisters, I'd have to feel guilty. I'd have to think: I hope nobody sees me. I once traded a pencil box for a mask—my mother almost killed me. I wanted the Lone Ranger mask. I was never able to get a 2¢ Lone Ranger mask, but I could have a pencil box. I didn't want a pencil box. (The mother had infantilized him, or, to put it another way, she castrated him and immobilized him with girls by protecting him "because of his asthma.")

TH: Why couldn't you get a Lone Ranger mask?

PT: I had to borrow my cousin's toy gun. They never bought me any toys.

TH: Your mother never bought you any?

PT: No, I couldn't play ball. I couldn't run. I couldn't be active at eight or nine. I could play hopscotch with the girls. As a younger kid I had to be in the store—nowhere else. They watched me in the store—and there I was the errand boy—get that! Get this! I had asthma, and my mother said I was sick.

TH: What am I doing to you that reminds you of all that? (Back to the transference)

PT: Wanting me to study, wanting me to get my doctorate—move ahead to success. I decided I should become an educational psychologist; I just didn't want to be identified as a social worker.

TH: You feel I wanted all that?

PT: Yes, that's what I feel. (*The patient is projecting his ambitions and wishes onto me since he is still afraid to accept them as his own.* The transference feeling is that I would be against his progress, I would be jealous, I would think: "How do you aspire to such things?")

TH: What are your animosities to social workers?

PT: Lousy group of people—that's not so—low status. I don't know why status means so much.

TH: Why wouldn't it mean something?

PT: Like the head social worker said to me: "You should be a psychologist, not a social worker." What is she telling me? That she can't stand what I'm doing. They keep saying I rock the boat. On the one hand, I want social work to mean something to me, and on the other hand I'm dissatisfied with it. (Silence) Last week I just didn't feel like having sex. I don't know whether I was disinterested or tired or angry or what! We never have sex on week days. Only on weekends, because I work nights. I work Monday, Tuesday, Wednesday, Thursday, and Saturday morning. I've started a private practice on Saturday morning.

TH: You work how often?

PT: Monday, Tuesday, Wednesday, Thursday and Saturday morning.

TH: That leaves Friday.

PT: This is killing me—this work. I'm working with a very anxious kid. I must have realized he was anxious, but on the other hand I was very insensitive to it. He was jumping all over the place.

TH: You didn't realize that the hyperactivity meant anxiety? And maybe depression?

PT: Yes. I didn't perceive him as being so hyperactive—I just—. Somehow I have too much of a tolerance and denial. I deny a lot. (He had said in the previous session that his father denies.)

TH: Your tolerance makes you deny certain kinds of behavior?

PT: Like hyperactive—like hallucinating—but I get very angry at such behavior too. This kid will leave the room for ten minutes. Today we were working with models. He broke three models. I was so angry. He didn't have to leave the room that time. The principal called and complained about another kid. This kind of behavior gets me very angry. But on the other hand, I'm tolerant of some things. I'm tolerant of pathology but only of some kinds. (Silence) I have this group of Sisters I work with, nurses, nuns. There's one lay teacher in the group. It's turning out to be a therapy group, and I haven't fought it. I'm becoming a therapist intead of a social worker. (He is in the process of getting his Ph.D. in Psychology.) This lay woman is in a straight jacket. She wants to break out. She's in this superego jacket. What's the world coming to? She's largely depressed—being alone, even though she's with so many people all the time. She said, "How come you never call me Mary? You only call me Mrs. Asti." I said, "Let me tell you—maybe this is wrong—but you feel alone—depressed. The feeling is somehow being reflected in this question. And all the time I was thinking how attractive she is and how I'd like to "make" her, and then I was thinking that is probably why I don't call her Mary. I thought that very clearly last week. Here she was, dressed very restrained, but very seductive, ready to be "made," but not. Maybe my mother was that way too.

TH: Is she? (The patient can use this statement to refer to the present and the analytic situation if he so chooses to respond.)

PT: When she was young, she always dressed restrainedly. She's old now. How was she before? Inhibited, very embarrassed at times. She'd blush continuously.

TH: She'd blush?

PT: She'd have hysterical tantrums—crying spells—but then she'd hold it in. But in my mind this is somehow associated with my wanting to be alive—and . . . . But I feel this is kind of "schitzy"—a schizoid feels that way. And I think this woman feels that way too. (Sexuality is equated with hostility, or sadism.)

TH: She wants to be alive yet she feels dead; that's "schitzy"? You sense that in her? In the teacher?

PT: Not the loneliness and despondency. She wanted to reach out, but couldn't. And in a way she gives a sophisticated appearance.

TH: She did want to reach out? But couldn't because she was depressed.

PT: I think so. How do you just go about getting it out. How do you help someone to feel free, to feel, to kind of enjoy life? She's a masochist. She must be an excellent music teacher. She's working in a private school for very poor money—$3,000 a year—and she won't ask—she just won't ask. You have to kind of prime her. ("Breaking out" means expressing sadism too; the sadistic feeling makes the person feel alive.)

TH: Do you think she feels too guilty to enjoy life? Guilt is usually one of the reasons people remain in a masochistic position. Guilt is a strange thing. Why do people have to feel so guilty over pleasure?

(He is apparently feeling guilty about wanting to be a therapist: it is an insult to the therapeutic school and the therapist—something he should not wish for. Since I believe he is unable to accept his own guilt, I use a projective technique, employing how he says his mother, the therapist and the teacher feel. He does not recognize the transference feeling.)

PT: Well, I guess it depends on what gives them pleasure. (Guilt over the sadistic desires.)

TH: Well, if she wanted to earn more money, that doesn't seem to be a crime. She'd not be hurting anyone, would she?

PT: No. And what about me? I want to earn more.

TH: Well! Why not?

PT: Yes, why not!

TH: Why are so many people afraid of all kinds of pleasure?

PT: I'm the patient—you tell me!

TH: Do you think this woman feels depressed and sorry for herself?

PT: I don't know about sorry for herself.

TH: Does she realize she's depressed?

PT: Yes—I don't know—perhaps. She doesn't say it that way. Just that she's lonely.

TH: Uh-huh. Does she sense her feelings of guilt?

PT: I didn't think of it—so I didn't try to find out.

TH: Perhaps you can find out.

PT: I'll try. (Actually the patient will begin inquiring into his own guilt and depressive maneuvers.)

The third session brings out more of the patient's defensive mechanisms, particularly those of denial and projection. It illustrates how one may delineate those mechanisms through the use of projective techniques.

THIRD SESSION

PT: I just had the feeling again today that I don't want to die. (One of the symptoms that brought the patient into treatment originally was the fear of death.) The feeling only seems to happen when I'm in the shower washing and drying myself. I almost drowned once when my aunt stepped on me at the beach. She was walking in the water and stepped on me. She was a big fat hulk and didn't seem to know or care that she had stepped on me. A woman has no care for others, does not recognize the rights and existence and the welfare of others. (The assumption is that he projects these feelings onto the therapist in a transference maneuver—the therapist is like the aunt, unfeeling. But in actual fact he is like the aunt, so that the projection onto the therapist is in the interest of denial of his own behavior. This is an example of projective identification.) I used to like to stay in the bathrrom when my father was taking a shower. I used to sit on the toilet reading a joke book while he was showering and I'd sneak looks at him. (Guilt about wanting a relationship with father. He had to have the relationship in secretive ways and under certain conditions.) I remember once he threw me out of the bathroom when he was washing my mother's back. He said: "Get out!"

TH: Why did he do that? (The patient may be asking why he and his father had to have such exclusive secret relations. This may possibly refer to the patient's presumed transference feelings, which are secret because they are expressed in such a round-about way.)

PT: He felt he didn't want me to see my mother nude, but he could! I felt left out. (The father's actions made the child try to find a rationale for the father's behavior, which becomes a defense on the part of the child.)

TH: Did that make you feel angry?

PT: Dejected; left out; lonely. I remember that at times when I was a child, especially when I was left alone, I refused to go with them. The whole family was away on a picnic. I'd go into my mother's room and sit on the bed with a B.B. gun. I was afraid to be alone; I waited for ten hours like that, once, for somebody to come in, for some relative to break in. I imagined I would shout if they broke in. Sometimes I used to take the B.B. gun down to the basement. I'd shout and masturbate, lying on some dirty old cloth. I'd get out my rage. Nobody was home to hear me. I'd conjure up phantasies of girl's breasts that I would hold, suck and feel, and I'd look at girlie magazines. (He didn't want to be with the family because he felt rejected, but when he refused to go with them and they were willing to leave him alone, he was fearful and angry. He sits on his mother's bed with a B.B. gun. We must assume he wants to shoot his parents, but denies this, exploding with rage instead of being left alone.)

TH: Who was going to break in?

PT: I remember my aunt brought me a soldier set. I'd set them up and shoot them down, for hours and hours and hours. (He does not respond to the therapist's question—just remembers how he handled his rage.)

TH: When were you shouting in the basement—what age were you?

PT: 13-14-15-16.

TH: And in the bathroom with your father in the shower?

PT: Five or six. I never would defecate in school. For some reason, I'd never "go" in school. I couldn't. One time I defecated in my pants. My mother gave me hell. They always said I had to be controlled—I had to put up some kind of front. I felt I shouldn't "go" in school. (*He jumps from the past to the present.*) I told them that we were going to move to Manhattan. (The patient's family lives in Queens. We must remember that this patient is married and has children, but he has always lived in the same neighborhood where his parents reside. Recently he has thought of moving out, establishing a new life for himself, separating from his family and leading a separate existence. In this session, he makes transitions from present to past, sometimes in the same sentence, as he did at the beginning of the session, and as he is doing in this statement.) I told them (*them* refers to his parents) we are going to move. They didn't say anything, but after I left I found out from my sister that my mother "split a gut."

(*In planning a move like this, he may not only be considering moving out from under the aegis of his family, but I would suspect that he may be contemplating the possibility of eventually leaving analysis. He would possibly like to leave now, and not have to resolve his problems, but he wants to become a psychologist and give up his present work as a school social worker. He originally had aspirations to become a physician, but he never got any help from his family in a financial or even a supportive emotional way. As a student in psychology, he has had to finance his own way.*)

TH: Your mother doesn't want you to move? (This is an indirect way of referring to the transference feelings, but using the mother as the object rather than the therapist.)

PT: My mother doesn't want me to do anything or think anything different from what she thinks. (Women, he intimates, are selfish, unfeeling, demanding and only want to use you.)

TH: Do you feel guilty? I mean, if you do feel differently?

PT: I realized I had a tremendous headache. I felt frightened at finding a place. I thought of the expense. I felt depressed. I thought I should go and take my family and live on a farm and become a mechanic, (He does not respond directly to the question, but he describes his feelings when he thinks of separation.) I think my family should help me, not hinder me. They should even help me with the expense of the move. They help my sister, but never me. I identify very strongly with my father. I'm mad at his brother. During the war they refused to help my father. I'm very bitter at that, angry and upset. They were wealthy; they were making money out of the war. My father was the patriot; he gave up his store and went to the Brooklyn Navy Yard to work. They never helped us. I was very upset by that. I was seven or eight at the time. I never could understand why I had to be out every night. We visited my grandmother every night. Sometimes we ate there for weeks on end. And when we went on picnics, we ate the burned frankfurters and my uncles had the good ones. I still can't understand why we had to live that way. We weren't rich, but we weren't that poor either. We always had to be under the shadow of our rich relatives. We had to do their bidding. That psychologist (a direct reference to the psychologist who took his Rorschach the same week as this session), she's writing down things again: "He's too sick in this area,' or "He's too sick in that!" (In trying to qualify for a special course in psychology he needs to have a certain kind of Rorschach report, showing that he is free from particular attitudes towards authority and that he is using therapy profitably to work out his problem. Actually his Rorschach indicated that he was not ready at this point; but he decided to go to the psychologist for testing for a second try.) She's preventing me from getting my work goals by those damned reports. (He is not far enough along in analysis either and he is probably angry at the analyst for his failure.) I feel sexually maladjusted. But I don't want her to have such control. I want to be free. I don't want to take her shit. And I don't want to be your boy—I want to be free. (A direct transference response.) I don't want to take second place. Why do I always have to work hard and never get any help? My parents could help me but they won't; they could help economically. All the time I was a "good boy" and I got nothing for it but a broken arm.

(His paranoid feelings come to the fore as a defense. He resents having to work out his problem, particularly his sexual disinterest in his wife. He does not want to go into that; he feels too anxious. He would like to avoid having to resolve his problems. He is angry at the therapist for not having helped him more, for not having resolved his problems for him.)

TH: Your father—he felt he had to be near his mother. You went to his mother's house?

(Projective technique: this is a way of talking of separation without a direct confrontation with the patient. This is done because of the patient's paranoid-like reaction in transference. The least defended area is with the father and mother in the interpersonal encounter, and therefore this is the easiest to handle.)

PT: Yes, I don't know why he felt that way. He visited her every day, and usually he took us.

TH: Out of duty, or because he loved her?

PT: They don't know the meaning of love! Are you joking? Only hate—rage, rage, rage.

TH: Was he feeling guilty?

(This again illustrates the projective technique, using the father to say what we would say directly to the patient if we could do so without increasing his defense. The use of the father was indicated in his verbalization concerning his identification with the father. He feels guilty about wanting to separate from the therapist and he feels inordinately tied down. He feels he gets no special attention or help. It is a fact that his parents favored his sister over him and gave her more material things, especially money.)

PT: He doesn't feel anything. He would say you were crazy if you said that to him. (He is talking about his father's denial mechanisms, detachment and withdrawal. He identifies with these mechanisms.)

TH: Well, I'm not likely to say it. I don't think he'll ask my opinion. (This is a way of saying: I will make no demands on you. I am not trying to break into your detachment. He would think I was crazy if I asked him if he felt guilt towards his mother?)

PT: I'm sure of it. Well they didn't feel guilty about me—at least they didn't show it. He won't ask your opinion either, I mean my father. Neither would my mother. I'm thinking of my fourth grade teacher. She gave me the order to do the blackboards and I was allergic to chalk. I made in my pants. I didn't dare to tell her—I just wheezed, and did the boards, and made in my pants. It's funny, I'm not allergic any more. As a child I was allergic to everything. As a child I always had to help, but I got no help. I had to help my cousins. They had less than we did. They belonged to the poor side of my mother's family. My cousins' father was an alcoholic and a giant. I was afraid of him. I always used to think that one day I'd probably kill him in self defense. I'd have to save my own life. He'd come after you when he was drunk. (Is he displacing feelings—from his own parents to the uncle—a defense against wanting to kill his parents?)

TH: You had to give and give and you got nothing—only a broken arm. (The therapist ignores for the time being the implications of the patient's identification with the drunken uncle who was so full of projected rage and who was so dangerous. She chooses to deal with the least defended area of the patient's problem—his masochism.)

PT: Why was I second? My father always took care of my cousins first.

TH: You were never first with him?

PT: Never.

TH: Neither your father nor your mother would let you be first?

PT: No.

TH: Do you feel you were rejected?

PT: No. Yes, I was. Very subtly. No, what am I saying! It was gross rejection! Like you read about! In school there was this teacher—she liked me and I used to get prizes, but were they interested at home? Never! Always I could have done better. I got this prize in chemistry and they didn't even go to my graduation. So I didn't go either.

TH: That was too bad. They deprived themselves of the pleasure of hearing about your success.

PT: They didn't care.

TH: Well, that's hard to believe—if they had a son who was able to get a chemistry prize in a big city school, they must have cared. (Challenging the patient.)

PT: Well they didn't; at least they didn't act it.

TH: Was the teacher pleased? (A reference to the positive side of the transference and the difference in the attitude of the therapist and the parents.)

PT: Yes, I was a favorite of hers.

TH: How did that make you feel?

PT: Good, but I guess I wanted recognition from my family.

TH: Yes; that's understandable. I was thinking—you said: "I identify with my father"; you also said last week that he was always second to his brothers. Yet he was always visiting his mother. Did they visit her every day too?

(Projective technique: referring to the father's dependency—a defense against hostility?—and oversolicitude to the father's dependency—a defense against aggression?—as a way of opening the door to the patient's dependency, and aggression.)

PT: No, but they did go once a week. This principal in the school where I work now, he reminds me of my parents. He never is satisfied, always critical. I think to myself: "I'm not going to bother with you; go cut somebody else!" Yet I keep talking to him because I think it's important for him to understand my work. But he's resistive—he refuses to listen. He's "uptight"—he's defensive. I keep talking to him because I think he could do so much for those boys with little effort, really. But he gets nervous.

TH: Why do you care how he feels?

(This is part of the projective technique in that the therapist is trying to indicate that in adulthood it is not so important to consider every implication of another's feelings as one was trained to do as a child. The "other" must learn to cope with his own feelings and to be confronted. The implication is that eventually the patient will have to deal with his own feelings openly rather than secretively. The therapist is using the patient's relationship with the school principal to emphasize this.)

PT: Well, I think he could be helpful, but he criticizes. He doesn't understand what I'm trying to do with those boys. They do respond.

TH: You got frustrated with him, but you also protect him.

(By not challenging the patient's defenses directly, the therapist is acting with the patient the same way the latter believes he is acting with the principal. The therapist realizes that outlining the defenses and delineating how they operate is all the patient is able to do at this point.)

PT: We carry on this antagonism, and the teachers, some of them slash away at me and the kids. I don't want to die! They're killing me each time they attack. (The patient is responding in a paranoid-like masochistic way, but justifies it by pointing to the aggression of the teachers. He uses the relationship to appease his masochism.)

TH: You can't help the principal by direct explanation of what you are doing with the children? (The implication is that eventually this must happen.)

PT: No, he couldn't take it. He'd be too resistive; he'd wreck my program.

TH: He'd be too anxious; He can't take change?

PT: He's rigid.

TH: Well, we can all be that way at times. I guess we can all be rigid when we're challenged. (This is universalizing the fact that when the defenses are challenged, the individual suffers anxiety.)

PT: You? Even you? (He laughs)

TH: Even me.

PT: Well, now that you mention it, why were you so defensive the other day?

TH: When was that?

PT: Monday, when you said that I was misunderstanding what was written in the school bulletin. (Patient had given me the bulletin and I actually did misunderstand a sentence.)

TH: I guess I made a mistake.

PT: But you were adamant at first.

TH: That's true; but apparently I misunderstood.

PT: Well, you're not supposed to misunderstand! (An expression of disappointment at my failure to be omnipotent.)

TH: Perhaps not; it would be better if I didn't misunderstand. Should I feel guilty that I made a mistake?

PT: Well, you had the wrong week and the wrong situation (referring to the misunderstood sentence—we were talking about two different things).

TH: Yes, I began to realize that.

PT: You didn't at first.

TH: No, I didn't.

PT: Well, it's all right now. You finally understood.

TH: I guess it bothered you to see me act that way.

PT: Well, why not?

TH: Well why? I can make a mistake!

PT: Well, don't make too many of them; my life is in your hands. That's no joke. (The patient is actually saying: "I am helpless in your hands. You are strong and I am weak." This may mask a desire to remain dependent on authority.)

TH: Well, let's say your life is in both our hands. We're in it together. But you have had enough of irrational authorities; that's what you'd like to say to me.

PT: Yes, yes, yes indeed! I'd like to say that and a great deal more.

TH: Like what?

PT: Like you're a dizzy dame.

TH: Is that all?

PT: No, I'd like to swear and curse, or I'd like to throw you down and maybe rape you—or something. Not that I'm attracted to you as a sex object! But I always have this feeling, I'd like to grab your leg or hit you on the thigh.

TH: Would that be good or bad?

PT: Well?

TH: The sexual feeling—is that good or bad; hostile or loving?

PT: If I feel it, it couldn't be good.

TH: Why not?

PT: Well, because I'm really mad at you for that and I feel trapped by you. I'd like to give up, but I know there's more.

TH: You feel I'm chaining you here?

PT: Yes, but I know that's irrational.

TH: You're not so sure you can depend on me if I make such mistakes.

PT: Well, yes, but I know I've had other experiences with you.

TH: Well, I guess we'll both have to trust each other. (This is a response to let the patient know that I understood what he was telling me; he could be dangerous and he feels me at times as being dangerous, but we will both have to trust each other if we are to work through this problem.)

PT: Well, I guess I'm in it to the bitter end.

TH: We both are.

The patient could not tell me directly what was bothering him, although we got to one of the problems that aroused his transference reactions and his defenses in the incident where I had made a mistake in reading the school bulletin. But there were other problems (his wanting to become an analyst, his need for me as a nurturing, protecting, non-challenging mother, etc.) in relation to me which were equally plaguing him, which came out in the next session. In the past three sessions we have been dealing with his fear of his aggression, and his oedipal guilt. The sessions illustrate how persistent working with the projective technique will in the end liberate raw transference feelings. The transference reaction to me indicates that he has his oedipal and preoedipal feelings fused. As his disappointment in preoedipal love or wanting and nurturing expectations comes to the fore, his rage against the object will be more apparent. The use of the projective technique helps to control the intensity of the rage reaction towards the analyst by deflecting part of it towards other objects. In these sessions the patient has used the father, the mother, the school principal, the director of social work, the uncle and the aunt, for example. *The therapist encourages the direction of rage towards these figures to water down the intensity of the rage in transference, since to feel the full force of the rage in transference at this time would be more than the patient can handle.*

NOTES

1 In the "Interpretation of Dreams" Freud wrote (1900) of the "just as" mechanism as reflected in dream formation; this was a characteristic of identification. He said that in analyzing a dream the therapist takes into consideration the fact that a mechanism in dream structure exists that depends on *similarity, consonance,* and *approximation.* "We find that parallels of instances of "just as" inherent in the material of dream thoughts, constitute the first foundations for the construction of a dream. . . ." (Thus, a dream is a projection, Freud said, of his hysterical patients. I feel one can apply this concept to the dreams of all patients.) "Identification is a highly important factor in the mechanism of hysterical symptoms. It enables patients to express in their symptoms not only their own experiences but those of a large number of other people; it enables them, as it were, to suffer on behalf of a whole crowd of people and to act all the parts in a play single-handed." He went on: "I shall be told that this is not more than the familiar hysterical imitation, the capacity of hysterics to imitate any symptoms in other people that may have struck their attention—sympathy, as it were, intensified to the point of reproduction. This, however, does no more than show us the path along which the psychological processes in hysterical imitation proceeds. The path is somewhat different from the mental act which proceeds along it. The latter is a little more complicated than the common picture of hysterical imitations; it consists in the unconscious drawing of an inference." Freud said of hysterical phantasies, that, just as in dreams, it is enough, for the purposes of identification, for the subject to have thoughts about acting out without the acting out having actually taken place. Usually such thoughts are in the form of fears.

2 Sechehaye, for example (1951, 1955, 1956, 1957), and Azima and Willkower (1956) gave symbolic objects, bottles, clay, apples, etc., to make up to the person what he had missed in his relations with depriving, hostile parents. They called this "gratification of basic needs" in schizophrenia. In my opinion, there is little to be gained from these "regressive techniques" in the treatment of borderline patients.

3 This is a teasing relationship. Such sado-masochistic maneuvers have been related in psychoanalytic literature to the instincts and to the oedipal problem. Freidman, for example

(1966), in his article, "Toward a Unitary Theory on the Passing of the Oedipal Conflict," stressed the concept of *teasing*. He refers to several papers in the psychoanalytic literature (Lewin, 1930; Sperling, 1951, 1951a) in which the sado-masochistic and the defensive aspect of teasing have been stressed. The defensive part includes the idea that nothing in life is serious, this is actually a masochistic stance, and that everything is a big joke. Sperling says this means that the patient denies the seriousness of the oedipal strivings and the teasing helps to libidinalize and master painful experiences of frustration. The borderline patient manifests this trait of making light of serious feelings and of his frustrations, and early in treatment this must be pointed out. Often the patient tells jokes on himself and is really humorous. The therapist can laugh at the jokes. I find that eventually I have to say to the patient, "It's funny but why are we laughing—we're making fun of you and your feelings." This is the first step in breaking into the defense. Many therapists fall into the teasing pattern with their patients. Once one of my patients became angry when I would not respond in that way, saying she liked someone who played ping pong with words. The smart repartee is in this category, and often when the therapist will not engage in this way the patient feels the situation is vapid, non-stimulating, and that the therapist is stupid, uninteresting.

Freud wrote that the oedipal problem is extinguished because it is doomed to failure, but in relations with parents this is not quite true, for in order for the child to develop a perverse trait the parent must have used the child in some way as a perverse object, and teasing is one way, and there are many other disguised ways. Freidman says that the neurotic does not accept the fact that he cannot have the parent. This is certainly true of the borderline patient. But my feeling is that this is a defense against the recognition of the rejecting attitude of the parent and the parents' use of him at the same time. The parent uses the child when the child is an object in the parent's defensive position. The child simply refuses to accept the fact that the parent is rejecting and sadistic. The knowledge is too threatening. The sexuality accompanying this problem arises from actual sexualized experiences associated with the teasing.

[4] This identification has been given a variety of names. Sullivan calls it the "not-me" or the false self; Laing calls it the false-self system; the "orthodox" analyst calls this the harsh introject; Reich called it a "substitute action." Grinker refers to this mechanism as a trait in borderline "as if I were playing a role." Actually the parent and the patient do play roles.

[5] There are other ingenious ways that have been reported by many authors to uncover the phantasies of the patient, although some authors do not always recognize the dynamic significance of what is happening. They tend to feel that the mere eliciting of material of this kind is sufficient, that the expression of the emotional effects that accompany the phantasies is the essence of therapeutic goals.

[6] Klein, who elaborated on the concept of projective identification considered the introject an example of one of the viscissitudes (defenses against) the *instinct* rather than an *ego-security operation*. The introject, having a connection with the parents and thus with the superego, was an incorporated struggle with the instincts. Freud said it was a struggle against the instinct seeking expression. The struggle is actually against learned behavior.

[7] The therapist wishes to relate the present to the past, but the discussion concerns defenses, since this is the aim in the first phase of treatment, where a delineation of the interpersonal dynamics as they relate to defensive maneuvers are the concern, or the focus, of treatment.

CHAPTER X

THE WORKING THROUGH PROCESS

Success or failure in the psychoanalytic treatment of the borderline is largely dependent upon the adequacy of the working through process. This is difficult and time consuming because of the volatility of emotions and the complicated network of defenses. As a consequence, some therapists, their patience worn thin, abandon the goal of personality reorganization in favor of supportive expediencies. Yet reconstructive objectives may be achieved if the therapist is mindful of the dynamics underlying the interpersonal maneuvers to which he will be exposed.

One of the most common tactics employed by borderline patients is his tendency to fend off a close relationship. On the surface he may seem congenial and cooperative, but this façade easily vanishes the moment one attempts to work through certain transference maneuvers, particularly those associated with aggression. Sooner or later the patient will subtly employ projective defensive patterns, even when he is motivated for treatment. He will fend off a therapeutic alliance by acting out identification roles of a sado-masochistic nature. Many varieties of maneuvers are apparent, but some are so disguised that they are not easily detected. For example, the patient may seem eager to cooperate and will comply punctiliously with what he believes is demanded of him. But behind these gestures is a need to submit himself; what looks like cooperation is an appeasement gesture. Some patients who are more self-destructive in their acting out of neurotic roles than others tend more toward hysterical patterns, while others are more obsessive or more delusional. It is difficult for the borderline patient to give up his preoccupation with his own needs and to think of others with consideration.

Because the patient repeats sado-masochistic patterns over and over again, even after these have been discussed, the therapist may find this a frustrating experience. He may become annoyed and disgusted with the patient. In addition, the patient may be provocative and grandiose, and act demeaning toward the therapist, taunting him and behaving in a competitive, rejecting, controlling or punitive way. Negative transferential patterns are reflective of the interlocking defenses originating in the parent-child relationship.

The interpersonal therapeutic encounter will thus understandably be difficult to tolerate, inasmuch as it is accompanied by denial mechanisms and a refusal on the part of the patient to accept responsibility for his own actions, particularly his hostile behavior. The problem of maintaining a working relationship is made more harassing by the patient's detachment, his withdrawal into phantasy and his poignant need to manipulate the situation to his advantage. Behind the patient's obnoxious operations is the hope that he will be accepted as he is, even though he is convinced that he will not be loved or even tolerated. His search is for an idealized parental relationship, which he is convinced will never come to pass but for which he constantly hopes. And his behavior is such that a close relationship is not possible unless he changes and analyzes his aggressive tendency.

The therapist should not deceive himself into believing that he can evade the parental role designed for him by the patient. In spite of meticulous behavior, and a thoroughly studious therapeutic stance, the patient will continue to misinterpret and accuse the therapist unfairly. From time to time, his fortitude exhausted, the therapist may, despite himself, explode and show natural exasperation, and even neurotic counter-transference. Should this occur, the therapist can do nothing but admit that he is angry. This admission, made without indignation, or with a show of humor, may eventually achieve a desired goal. However, the therapist must be ready to receive more hostility from the patient, since the latter's defenses are literally life-saving. He may at such a point turn on the therapist, accusing him of not having been sufficiently analyzed himself, and taunting the analyst, wondering how he can work through to a successful end with an unanalyzed person. This is a difficult position, and often one can only hope that the patient will rally and let reason take over, rather than developing a more paranoid defense. The revengeful side of the patient's character or his punitive superego has an opportunity for expression in this kind of situation, and the patient may break off treatment out of fear of retaliation. There are several instances of this type of transference—counter-transference problem, where challenge makes the patient flee. Usually, these are instances where the aggression has been rampant, yet expressed in a way that the patient is able to defend and deny. The patient may be "putting one over on the analyst," either consciously or unconsciously—all of which is defensive. The analyst in his turn may be unconsciously inviting such behavior. The patient acts as if he does not know what is happening, and when this behavior is challenged, the patient resorts to paranoid maneuvers. The following examples indicate this type of problem:

Miss Girard, a fifty-five year old unmarried woman, had been in treatment for five years on a twice-a-week basis. She had spent her life as a singer, but was usually unemployed. She refused to "go on relief" but would play on the sympathy of friends, so that she managed finally to receive a small income from a wealthy acquaintance. She usually went to the best specialists, who took care of her for little or no fee. She entered treatment on the basis of a low fee. Every so often she would make a token payment for her treatment, when she was working as a helper in a store. She refused to go to clinics and had a haughty attitude if anyone suggested such a thing. This longstanding pattern was finally challenged when the therapist brought up the possibility of the patient applying for treatment through Medicaid. She became angry but let it go. In the following sessions, however, when the therapist brought up the possibility again, and wondered what her feelings were about the matter, the patient became enraged and accused the therapist of being cruel and attacking. She said she would "feel like a failure" if she had to accept Medicaid. The therapist countered by wondering what that meant—"Why not talk about it?" she asked. The patient responded with an attack and attempted to make the therapist feel guilty, implying that the therapist was a dirty dog who was showing her true colors after so many years. The therapist asked Miss Girard to think about why she would deprive the therapist of money. The patient said that apparently the therapist had resented the relationship all along and was now showing her sadism, her revenge feelings. (This is precisely what is being exposed in the patient, it is her principal problem.) The therapist was in a dilemma. She had seen the patient for several years at a low fee and had helped her considerably. She realized that the patient could earn a living as a singing teacher but would not do so. She wondered whether her counter-transference problem was evident in the beginning when she agreed to take the patient at the low fee. On the other hand, the patient had overcome a rather deep depression and had worked through some of her problems. At this point the therapist did not feel that she wanted to go further, unless the patient did something about her life. She was getting along in a marginal way and could certainly survive the way she was. But the patient had settled down into a groove of coming to treatment and not making any more progress. She had been attending group sessions for the past four years. What to do? The therapist decided to challenge. The patient verbalized that she had been coming to the group as one would to a "nice family." This was lovely, and she needed a nice family. The therapist repeated that she was only suggesting a way the patient might pay and she wondered why the patient wanted to deprive the therapist of money that could easily and legitimately be obtained. The patient became unduly angry and said she would leave, for now she realized the true nature of the therapist. Should the therapist have refused to accept the patient at the initial interview, or should she

sacrificially (or therapeutically?) act as a good supporting parent and help the
patient that way? Should the therapist have told the patient that it was not
necessary for her to consider the money at all, and that she should come to the
group free as she would to a good family. Perhaps the patient might not work
through her own problem but she might help others. Can a patient use the group
as a good family and then, after a period of time, work through her problem?

Abby Newbold was referred to me by another therapist who was leaving
town. A young woman about twenty years of age, she was one of two
sisters—the sister having a successful career (college, work, a good marriage) and
Abby being exactly the opposite. She felt she was always rejected and as long as
she could remember she was disturbed. She had had treatment all her life. As a
child, she had screaming fits. In school, she was a behavior problem; in college
she was a drop-out. Finally, she settled down to work as a receptionist, but being
a rather brilliant girl she began to reorganize the office without having been
asked to do so. Soon she was interfering in aspects of the business that were
none of her concern. She managed to have some kind of relationship (through
scheming) with people at the top, and before they realized it they were involved
with her. She had few friends and led a rather lonely life. She made attempts to
become intimate with "authorities" at work, entering into a child-parent
relationship of a somewhat stormy nature. She was taken into the confidence of
people and she insinuated herself into their lives until they would have to reject
her. She was like a pestiferous gnat.

In treatment, she would scream the minute she entered the room, and
throw a tantrum of some kind. If the therapist told her not to scream she would
become insulting. After two sessions the therapist announced that she would not
see her if she carried on like that. The next session she indulged in another
tirade; the therapist asked her to go, but she refused. The therapist warned her
that she would be removed bodily if she did not go. (Patients sometimes test the
limits with their therapists. Where unreasonable limits have been reached, the
therapist will have to take a stand. "So far, and no further." The therapeutic
situation will usually survive this test if a proper relationship with the therapist
exists.) With that, the therapist left the room and went towards the entrance of
the building, the patient following. Finally, when we were on the street, the
patient said she wanted to continue the sessions and would never make a
disturbance like that again. The therapist agreed to continue. Sessions were held
without disturbance from then on, although the patient showed great resistance,
sometimes being silent for minutes at a time, or being emotional and resistive.
Treatment continued for about four years. All this time the patient had been
working and her father had been paying for sessions. She changed her job and
advanced herself. Then she decided to go back to college. She started and it
became difficult for her to attend sessions regularly. She began to involve the
teachers and the administration in much the same way that she had provoked
authorities in her last job, from which she had been fired finally. But the
teachers were "psychiatrically oriented" and put up with a great deal. Finally,
she got into a furious altercation with one of the teachers. When she told the
story in the session, I refused to "take her side" when she asked me to. At that
point, the patient began to scream as in her initial sessions and she made such a
blood-curdling sound that three therapists on the same floor left their patients
and ran into the room, the door having already been opened due to my asking
the patient to leave. Shortly thereafter it became apparent from messages and

telephone conversations with the patient over a period of six months that she had made enormous progress. She got excellent marks in college and graduated. She started to work and now she plans to go to graduate school. No mention was made in the telephone exchanges of the last episode between the therapist and the patient. Her letters were signed affectionately. She reported only progress. No more actual sessions were ever held.

The last example is that involving a young woman with one child. Originally, she was married to a doctor, whom she divorced, taking her child with her, a boy three years of age at the time of divorce. The patient was a professional person, in the mental health field herself. She had entered treatment when she realized her own detachment and inability to form a relationship with men. She had been in treatment for about three years, when she began to question her relationship with her son. Was it good for him to be with her? He was getting symptoms. He was beginning to have a far away look in his eyes, he was having trouble in school, although he was a child with a high I.Q. Her sexual acting out was such that the child never knew what man he was going to see in the apartment in the morning. Yet he seemed to make an adjustment and he appeared happy, but he did not make friends. She pressed the therapist for an opinion. Should she give up the child and let her husband have him, since he had remarried and had a stable home with other children? There was little "culture" in the father's home, but he might be better off with his father. The therapist stopped analyzing and began to give advice. In the end she said, "Yes, I think it would be better for both of you if he went to his father. He is beginning to react to this life you lead, and you resent having to care for him. You feel the burden of his care. You feel held down. And these men you see—most of them are creeps—are no kind of influence for your son." Calling a spade a spade as I did, was, she admitted later, the best thing that happened to her. The child went to his father. It was necessary because of her job for the patient to establish herself in another city. She did go into treatment, however, with another therapist. She wrote of her continuing progress.

There is no doubt but that there were negative transference problems that had never been worked through in all of these cases. The transference was more towards the psychotic side than is usual; yet these patients were, with the exception of the singer, working regularly and making an adjustment, even having a certain kind of social existence.

These are more difficult patients, but they do seem on some level to be asking for treatment. There are no hard and fast rules to follow, yet it does seem to me that points arise in these cases where a challenge must be met, even if the patient leaves treatment and working through does not take place. Hopefully they go on to someone else with whom they may succeed in the working through process.

In the treatment of all cases, eventually *the defenses in their operational dimension,* i.e., in the overt behavior, must be connected with the patient's *identification phantasy* on the intrapsychic level. The association is then made with anxiety and *the situations in the here-and-now which create anxiety.* These situations must be explained over and over again, and attention must be drawn to the phantasies which are aroused in the situation, for these are related to transference phenomena.

The identification phantasy is the major defense around which all other defenses are organized. As has been repeatedly emphasized, this is the intrapsychic representation of the patient's having become enmeshed as a person in the defensive operations of his parents. As the child became a transferential object for the parent, i.e., an object of projection, displacement and defense, the stage was set for an identification with the parents and the reenacting of the identification role with others after the individual has left the parental home. The transference behavior is a function of the identification phantasy. The patient's dreams reflect that aspect of the patient's problem with which he is dealing at any given time. In the longer dreams the whole problem is depicted; in the short dreams, merely some part of the conflict. In dreams we follow the identification figures and through them the patient's progress. The "objects" or the "identification figures" change as the patient changes.

Several authors, including Fenichel, have referred to the first phase of treatment with the borderline as a pre-analytic phase. Actually, this is the phase where projective analytic techniques are most in use, due to the negative transference. This is a most difficult phase and can sometimes last as long as four or five years. But during this period the patient has acknowledged much of what he must work out if he is to be relieved of his problem. Towards the end, this first phase of treatment overlaps with the second phase, which, according to L. Wolberg (1967), is the period when the therapeutic task is to identify important patterns, deal with transference and resistance and make connections with early experiences with parental figures and other "early objects." Some of the goals of transference behavior may also be identified towards the end of the second phase. My feeling is that *working through* for the borderline patient, a process which probably starts in minute form in the first phase but which becomes the main thrust in the second and third phase of treatment (this is the phase where insight is converted into action), *must be preceded by conscious and clear acknowledgement on the part of the patient that he realizes he can trust the therapist in order to work out his problem. Such an acknowledgement must be made in a succinct and direct way, without qualities of appeasement, but rather with the stated knowledge that with suitable cooperative work between patient and therapist, the therapeutic process may go through to a successful finish.*

The variations in the working styles with borderline patients are great, as are the varieties of adjustment patterns the patients have made. Kernberg has touched upon some of these styles. For example, some patients may be able to work on their problems in a concentrated way for four years, while others may require a short hospitalization period. Others may need drug therapy, either for depression or for anxiety, while many patients get along without medicinal treatment and seem able to work through to a finish in seven years. Some patients manifest a "transference psychosis," while others plod along in a slow, passive-aggressive way for ten or eleven years. Some patients break from treatment when they approach a transference psychosis or when they are in the midst of it; they then usually seek out another treatment person, often of the opposite sex to the one with whom they have done the bulk of the treatment, as a flight away from the "bad" analyst to the "good" one. Feelings of revenge and a compulsive need to demean the analyst create problems which sometimes cannot be resolved, since these serve as a defense against good or loving feelings which are fused, in the beginning, with transferential homosexual feelings, which the patient tries to fend off. As the patient seeks out another analyst, he focuses his hatred on the first one, thereby saving the second situation from the devastation of the sadism. In such a contingency the patient's fears of closeness have not been sufficiently worked through to the point of trust. He flees out of fear of his phantasy of being taken over and controlled, and his neurotic need to "give in to the other" or to be unduly hostile and punitive with the other. His "fears" are projections of his own feelings of distrust and his desires to take over and control, which he attributes to the analyst. It is for this reason that many borderline patients make several starts in treatment with different analysts, each time staying three or four years, then breaking off, but finally working through after the third or fourth try.

Working through is impeded primarily because of the enormous repressed aggression. Aggression is always destructive to the individual himself and to the others with whom the patient is in relationship. One of the reasons that treatment of the borderline takes so long is that he defends against analyzing his aggression. He often learns to express his aggression without guilt, but this is not "working through."

My patient, Harriet Hamburger for example, has been in treatment off and on with different therapists for twenty years. Only in six of these years was she in what would be considered intensive treatment. She has progressed in many ways; she has gotten out of a bad marriage and into a good one. After having spent years as a poorly paid secretary, she attended school and became a highly paid executive—having worked for and received a Masters Degree in business management. Her position as an executive and her good marriage, both of which she finally had the strength to accept, have, however, placed her in a position where she has had to come face to face with her aggression. As an executive it is difficult for her to accept colleagues who are efficient without feeling jealous and upset by their competitiveness, and angry at their maneuvering behind her back. She recognizes that when she thinks of these characteristics in others, she has paranoid ideas and feelings. She came back to therapy because she now wants to work through these problems. She sees her relationship with her husband in the same light that she regards her relationship with her colleagues. She becomes inordinately angry at him; she feels like calling him an idiot. He has a tendency to be passive; he is against going into personal analysis. Actually, he makes an excellent living, but he does have the traces of passive-aggressive personality with a tendency to withdraw. He nevertheless has the strength to challenge her when she gets "on his back" in an obsessive ("bugging") way. She respects his "calling her" on this when she behaves this way. She now wants to get rid of her anger and rage at him, and to eliminate her untoward feelings about the people at work for whom she is administratively, and in a supervisory sense, responsible.

Several times over the years she stopped treatment—once at my suggestion, when I felt that she would be better off struggling on her own, rather than using me in a dependent way, and twice at her own insistence. During one period she went to treatment with a male analyst for two years, and then discontinued with him. One of the reasons we were blocked in making progress was that she was inordinately detached and out of contact with her feelings, particularly anger. It was, for example, impossible for her to criticize me in any way. What is encouraging now is that she verbalizes feeling angry toward me. She has become angry, she says, when she thinks of the years we have been working together, and then she wants to know: "What have you been doing all these years? Why haven't you helped me more? Why am I not having a better sex life? Why do I have to be such a miserable bitch at work?" The negative side of the transference has not emerged all these years in such an open way. She is serious now and says: "I want to get rid of this hostility, this rage. I want my husband to be happy with me and I want you to do some work so that we can finish off this business." For the first time in her life she is actually breaking through her detachment. She has not yet, however, said that she trusts me and that she is convinced we can work the problem through. As soon as she can say this, and mean it, we will then be in a position to finish. But Harriet is not the mouse she has imagined herself to be all these years. In reality, she did periodically lash out at people, but she has never considered this as aggression and hostility. This ambivalence was obvious in group therapy, where she was competitive, brilliant, grandiose and hostile. She enjoyed attacking and controlling. She was usually referred to as a "ball buster." She denied the meaning of her behavior. Only now is she beginning to realize that she experiences pleasure in her hostile attacks. She also is beginning to feel that she is truly afraid of men, and is unduly hostile to others.

Elizabeth Osgood is also about to finish her analysis. She has been in treatment for six years. The ending phase, which may last for another two years, was ushered in by a dream, which I shall explain later in some detail. She lived with a man for about four years in an economically advantageous liaison. She used this arrangement to buy clothes, to feel domestic and feminine, to rest after having struggled to attain some standing in her field (she is one of the better young scenic designers in the theatre), and to learn what some of her work problems were after she was fired by an outstanding artist. (This man is a homosexual who always appeared in her dreams as a substitute for her father.) Her marital partner, an acting out borderline person who has never had treatment, had great respect for her and wanted, on some level, to "make it" with her. He could not tolerate a close relationship, however, and broke away to have sexual episodes with other women. She attempted to tolerate these adventures, feeling that the man, after all, liked her and was willing to support her. She also felt that she would perhaps try to use the relationship to work out her sexual problem of being non-orgiastic. This did not work out, but she was nevertheless able to tolerate sexuality much more than she ever had before. She herself had many "affairs" and frequently talked of her various "lovers"; but these "affairs" were short-lived and there was very little love in them, since the participants had problems similar to her own—that is, the inability to tolerate close relationships, inordinate hostility, detachment, teasing attitudes, and latent homosexual trends.

As a child she had been unattractive, although now she is exceedingly beautiful. Her mother was considered a "flighty, nit-witty" woman, who lived on pills most of her life, although she was capable of straightening herself out, at times, and acting in an integrated fashion. She had the "why me" attitude of the mother of the "Wolf Man." The patient's father is a scientist, who escapes to his laboratory; whenever she wanted, as a child, to have a relationship with him, she had to listen to his accounts of what he was doing and admire him, rather than engage in a give-and-take father-daughter encounter, which she would have preferred. Her father was intensely competitive, had always to be right. Withdrawn and detached, he traveled through life by "reasoning everything out" and avoiding feelings. She has two brothers, both brilliant. She recently was shocked when one of her brothers announced to her that he had become a homosexual. Her other brother has become a mystic.

Money has had a peculiar place in her life, for it was used by the patient's family, particularly her mother, as a means of controlling her. Even though money was plentiful, the patient as an adolescent was given only twelve dollars a month, and among other things she had to buy her clothes with the allowance. As a consequence, she learned to make her clothes, and usually looked somewhat odd in her creations. She was awkward as a child and she wore big eye glasses. She never had a date in high school; she could not mingle with the girls in the "jet set" because she had neither the social presence nor the money. She was uncomfortable with the children with whom she could mingle, since they were not of her intellectual caliber. She had no boy friends because she looked so ugly that no boy would date her. She had the habit, as a child, of attaching herself to an older person and idealizing that person. She clung to the person, followed her around, talking compulsively and acting "like a leach" until she would be rebuffed by the person, who would finally have to tell her to "stop pestering." Finally, she joined a "hippy crowd" group—a crowd that did not mind her peculiar clothes and could appreciate her mind. She began to love the theatre, enjoyed acting and dancing.

Her parents sent her to a good college, one with a "liberal" and "advanced" program. Here she was able to express herself. She was artistic, with the ability to draw. With men she would develop feelings of wanting to attach herself and monopolize their time, feeling rejected if she could not "dominate their scene." Sexually she would begin to enjoy herself, and then in the middle of intercourse would "turn off," finally dissolving into tears, never having a climax. This would be disconcerting to her partner. On the occasions when this did not occur she would "just lie there" and let the man have his orgasm. (This cutting off of the sexual pleasure is reminiscent of Reich's description of the neurotic character, particularly the masochistic aspects.) Initially, the only way Elizabeth could have sexual feeling would be to imagine being hurt in some way. She often felt like asking men to hit her in the buttocks. Even as a child when engaging in masturbatory behavior (behavior which was "substitutive" rather than handling her genitals, i.e., she would rub her thighs together), she would have a phantasy of being beaten. When one man did hit her buttocks, she was highly stimulated.

Because she could not develop a good relationship with a man, she decided to come into therapy. After working through the first phase of treatment we were finally able to get at the phantasy she had during sex. It was not only a "beating phantasy," but when she allowed herself to think about it on one occasion she reported seeing the face of her father, suddenly, laughing and saying in a scornful way: "You can't make it!" She had worked through with me to a considerable degree her identification with her mother who, "on the surface," seemed like a feminine woman, but who suffered as a consequence of her husband's detachment and continued neglect. In one of her sessions, she began to realize that her mother had always been "pleading for closeness, and for love and attention." At home in the family group, the mother had acted as the conciliator. At the table, for example, she would try to break the silence (the family became a group of detached people) by asking questions about what each member had been doing during the day; or, she would ask for an explanation of some phenomenon she had heard about on the radio. Finally the patient admitted that the mother would never meet an issue "head on." For example, when Elizabeth wanted to ride horseback so that she would "get on" with the jet set, her mother would not say "No; we can't afford it"; nor "No, I would be thinking all the time that you could get killed." While she said all of these things about horseback riding in general, she acted as if she wanted Elizabeth to ride, but made a condition which precluded the possibility. She said: "If you will earn enough money you may go horseback riding." Elizabeth being eight years of age could naturally not do this. Elizabeth expressed contempt for her mother's sneakiness and her weakness. She openly identified with her father, who was strong, but from childhood on she acted out her identification with her mother by seeking closeness, "bugging people" and talking compulsively; she also acted "nervous," as her mother did, gesticulating as she talked with jerky bodily movements, using peculiar gestures with her hands. She always asked for advice and often behaved as if she had to be programmed like an IBM machine before she could act. She complained that she could not make the appropriate connections between other people's behavior and how she should respond; she was often rejected because of her compulsive talking and her clingingness. She never knew when it was appropriate to leave if she was visiting friends. For example, there would come a point when they would obviously want her to leave, and finally, when she would realize this, she would become angry. She would talk of this and then say that they should tell her to leave if they felt that way—how was she to know? In that sense her behavior was often inappropriate.

Elizabeth often said that her problem with men was that she could never find one who could "stand up to her." She was very bright and could always get the upper hand intellectually. This wasn't so good for a woman. She was in favor of "Women's Lib" and felt for a long time that I frowned on sexuality and saw "femininity" in a "middle class way." She felt that I wanted her to become a middle-class woman, married to an uninteresting man, and for a time she conjectured she might have to give up the therapeutic relationship and seek out another therapist who was more modern and more in tune with the "current scene." She was not able at this point, she believed, to "get through" to me. Finally, in working over certain transference feelings where her rational reasoning took precedence over her almost delusional defense she began to feel she might be able to communicate and that she and I might find a common ground. On the other hand, she said she would be willing to give up work and all the glamour of the theatre to have a home and babies and a man who loved her. Preferably she would like to leave the city and live on a farm in Connecticut. As she began to work through her transference and her projection onto me, of her defensive attitudes towards men and women, she became aware that she would have to cope with her withdrawal tendencies, her pestering of people, her need to be on top intellectually (and in bed), her competitiveness and finally her rage in interpersonal business encounters. She finally found a man who she said was not afraid of her, who could tolerate her intellect, but was "impossible socially." He took her frigidity as a challenge and was working with her towards eliminating it.

Then she had a period of doubting whether she or I knew what we were doing. However, she decided she would have to "take a chance" because she had seen others who had benefited by working with me. At this point she had the following dream, which illustrates how there is a fusion in dream structure of the past, the present reality situation and the transference, a preamble to the working through process.

PT: I have no idea where this was, but in my dream I was putting books away—from somewhere I was getting a big jeweled book to have—I'd have room for it because I was taking books from the bookcase and sending them back to Connecticut (her parent's home). I was sending back all my children's books, "Heidi" and "Little Lord Fauntleroy," those favorite books of mine, and "Pollyanna."

TH: What was it that you loved about those books? (Projective technique.)

PT: Oh, that the child finally won over these cruel adults: Heidi won over the glum uncle; Pollyanna, the favor of the mean old aunt; and Lord Fauntleroy finally succeeded in getting the favor of the Earl. As I was putting this beautiful book into the bookcase the sun was pouring into the room. It reminded me of some of the design research in Cambridge—how the old houses are modernized—beautiful design—the kind of house I'd like to have—in the country an old remodelled New England House—nature, serenity, joy, family. We used to have a bookcase like that at home—the sun came in—that's where I store everything I don't want—at home in the barn (she means her parents' house), furniture, books, everything. (Is it that her motivation is to seduce, win over, cajole the analyst, rather than work through her problem?) Then the bookcase seems to have changed into a room which was a museum. My father was there. I was talking to him—the bookcase was metamorphosed, so to speak, into a museum. And they had changed the nature of the museum so that it was a total picture, a unity of an old scene—sort of like Sturbridge Village, a total picture of some older period. I said to my father: "Look what they have done to make this look so much nicer. See, they've even taken portraits of old masters and made photostats and they're almost life-like." I'm trying to get him to understand. He makes no comment. It's a little out of his realm but I'm trying to make this simple. It reminds me that I asked dad if I could get lasers free. He sent them right away. (She can only communicate with her father in terms of science—she wanted these lasers for the lighting designer in the theatre). He sent them in two days but mom forgot to mail the letter that had all the instructions. She forgot to mail the letter for two weeks. Thank heavens that I can respond to her now without getting too furious. I didn't want to read the letter, really, because I felt it would be something so kindergarten-like—I offer him these tid-bits—to communicate—and then he responds as if I'm an idiot.

(She is speaking of her relationship with her father and mother and how frustrated she was as a child trying to communicate with them. She has had these feelings towards the analyst, as well, and at this point I begin to wonder whether she is not telling me that she feels the only way she can develop a relationship with me is to "win me over" rather than analyze her problems. She has had the feeling that if she were to have a relationship with me she would have to put herself into a certain mould—be exactly what I want her to be.)

PT: The next thing I knew in the dream, the scene shifted to a week-end resort. A party of ladies—you know—real ladies. Ronny (her current man) was going to sneak me in. It seemed they didn't want me—or I don't know. I didn't seem to fit in—these ladies. I don't know, why I had to sneak in, I don't even know if I wanted to be there. (The patient in real life often does not feel like a female, and she seems to be saying that she is not sure that she wants to be a female if being a female means meeting middle class standards.)

The room was like a drawing room and only ladies were there. I was outside on a balcony, or a railing, a kind of porch railing, looking in at them all dressed up. I was climbing on a balustrade then, sort of in the room, but away on a balcony. I was straddling the railing tom-boy style, sort of—a tom-boy gesture on my part. Ronny had gone away, seemingly to find out how I could get into the circle of ladies, but he never came back and finally people were leaving. They seemed to be signing a book. I seemed to see a name, something like La Cocchio. I was reminded of an electrician I once worked with in the theatre.

Suddenly a huge wave came up and washed right over me. The wave didn't frighten me—I didn't panic. Somehow I thought it was amusing about the party-goers. The party seemed to be breaking up. *When Ronny didn't come back I was terribly rejected and hurt.* I thought he couldn't get me into the party and he had literally run away. The whole effort didn't seem worth it. I felt that he was afraid to face me. He couldn't say, "We didn't get in." I was very hurt in the dream. (She apparently is seeking to become female through her relationship with Ronny. He will make her a woman and she will not have to analyze her problem. But the relationship with him will be tinged by her scornful attitude towards him and she will transfer this to the analyst.) He'll have to face the fact that he couldn't get me in. (She will try to prevent him from making her into a woman by deriding him and demeaning him and then she will attack him for it. Her passivity is evident here.)

That "wave image." That has been in many of my dreams. It has to do with my letting myself be carried away. (She now approaches for the first time her own feelings and her problem as she sees it currently.) One of the last times when I did have a panic feeling, like the waves used to be in my dreams, I thought of sex. In this dream, I was lying on the beach and the wave was rocking over me. Usually the wave is like a huge tower, swelling and cascading. It sucks me back into it, and draws me in and I feel panic and fight for air. In this dream it was a big wave, but I did not panic. (She has had to fight off feeling in sex relations and her frigidity may serve this function; she still uses the beating phantasy in sex, but this is diminishing.)

TH: Are you saying that if you're not so afraid of the wave in the dream it means you are not so afraid of sex? You don't fear being taken over or sucked in by it?

PT: I wasn't swept away with the wave. I have the image that if the thing came crashing down I'd ride with the wave. I wouldn't have to fight for air. In this dream I was rejected, but I felt I could go back to the city by myself. I felt I could. In other instances, I've had that awful feeling I might dream I was driving a car but it would be in a reckless manner—too fast—out of control—what my mind does when it's desperate. And even in regular situations, I have the answer before the question is finished. Somebody could say: "How do you figure that out so fast?" I'd know the answer, but then I'd have to go back and figure out how I did it. I can look at a column of figures and give the answer. The quick answers, I'm usually right. (She often says this of her father.) I found several women, one who seemed to have a child. I was constructing a way to get back to the city—I'll show them, I'll solve the problem.

TH: We're back to the dream. You mean you were angry. "I'll show them!"

PT: Frantic, depressed, angry, but not really. I didn't really feel that way after awhile. Well, anyway, the last image in the dream was that we were riding into the city and I was with a lot of women and girls. I'm sitting in the middle of the front seat. I'm messing with the controls of the car, and because I'm messing with the controls I feel the car may careen. And then the dream ended. (She goes to women when the man rejects her—or when she rejects him.)

TH: What did you think of the dream?

PT: Well, retiring the books, I'm done with that part of the phantasy—the other book, I'm substituting the bigger book. Then my father—I'm showing him around my life. I'm showing him the dead part, the past. I'm not showing him that beautiful place where the sun is. I don't have access to that part yet. (This may very well refer to her pleasure in sadism—her secret.) The design research. I saw this when I visited Harvard. I was very impressed but now its more like just a store, *less of a shrine*. When I think of it now I see it is a place to buy nice things.

TH: Less of a shrine? (The idealized father is now giving way to a more realistic image.)

PT: Yes—more like a daffodil shining in the sun. I was thinking—about Ronny—was it more of a put-down on my part? I don't think he's going to achieve it. Like I'm saying: "You're not good enough to get me into that thing—it's very easy to do and you're going to fail." Then my feeling about the man would account for his running away. My feeling about his abilities and capacities. Am I angry, frantic or in good shape? I'm having that trouble at meetings again. They get off the point and I feel angry. When my anger is triggered off, this distracts me. Somehow, I'm thinking of Isaac. (Isaac was the man she lived with for four years.) My response was appropriate; he'd go away and be with someone else, and then come back and want sex. No wonder I couldn't make it with him. Why should I have sex under those circumstances? I think frigidity was an appropriate response; why should I play sex games? I beg your pardon! What nerve! It's a wonder it didn't get worse. (She used him as a defense). But lately I've had a feeling of helplessness in dealing with people. Ronny says: "You don't make me feel like a lover." I want someone to love me. How could I feel loved by Isaac?

TH: You were staying with Isaac to have a place to live? You saw what the situation was?

PT: Yes, but I liked him and he liked me. He was always busy, no time for me. He'd say next week we'll have time together—next week. I believed in that for almost two years. Then I realized he couldn't deal with me when we were alone.

TH: Like in the dream—the man couldn't deal with you.

PT: Yes. When we were in Venezuela together, I can barely remember what happened between us. We had a fair amount of sex, *but we didn't seem to have any relationship*. Isaac at one time drew ten sketches—terribly large and ugly cunts—*demanding*.

TH: That seems to have demonstrated his problem.

PT: Yes, he had a dream while we were there—a group of homosexuals, talented, didn't respect anything—true talent scares the commercial theatre. In this dream there was an image similar to mine—excitement in working in things—in the commercial theatre you can't express yourself. Any sacrifice is worth it. Isaac is successful, of course, in the commercial theatre, but he has to work with these characters. He manages, though. That's where I get hung up—dealing with them. The other day, though, I had to laugh. We were with the director, a whole group of us—actors, scenic designers, lighting designers, electricians. A whole group talking about the final trappings before the opening. And the director, who is a genius but mad, and who gives everybody such a hard time—we were all ready to kill him—he suddenly turned around in a very relaxed manner and said: "I used to go home after a day like this and beat myself up, telling myself what a hostile, terrible, impossible person I had been to everybody. But since my analysis I don't do it so much anymore. I just say to myself: 'Well, that's their problem.' " After a stunned silence of about a minute everybody began to roar with laughter.

TH: He's the same bastard, but now he doesn't feel so guilty about it.

PT: Yes—isn't that a riot?

TH: He's gotten something out of his analysis. (I am using the projective technique—She has been talking about her anger towards men, but she is still very defensive about it.)

PT: Yes (she laughs in an amused way).

TH: What is it that this man actually does that drives people up the wall?

PT: He must have his way and the last word, even when he doesn't know what he's talking about. Example: For five days he argued with me and the lighting designer about colors—his colors and mine. We told him and he refused to accept our ideas. *I'm* the artist and he knows more than I do about color! Or more than the lighting designer. We set up a design to suit him and that took four days. After it was all over, he ranted and raved. What did we mean? Why did we do something that had such an effect! Of course, it was all his idea, against our advice. Then towards the end of the day he said he had figured out what could be done and he outlined the plan we had given him five days previously. Now it was his—his scheme, his ideas, his show. I was ready to throw the thing in his face, but the lighting designer simply handled him beautifully. He said it would take four days to redo it and the opening was in two days. He'd have to put day and night crews in. He went on to suggest—this-and-this might cut down on the time. But I blew—and he looked at me coldly and said: "In a working relationship of this kind, your behavior interferes with the kind of teamwork that is required of all of us in the theatre!" I fled because I would have split him or myself wide open. I felt like going into a crazy hysterical fit and tearing him to pieces. That reminds me of the phantasy I used to have of scratching out my eyes, or fearing that something would come to destroy my face. (The child inside of her has a "hysterical fit" in dealing with an irrational authority.)

TH: What was your association to your father's being in the dream?

PT: Yes—well (she hesitates).

TH: What comes to your mind?

PT: Well, I can't talk to him—I can't get through. I was not going to show him the beautiful book because he'd never understand. And you can't confront him. He'd go to pieces. (What she seems to be projecting here is transference feelings. I know she feels this way about me.)

TH: You can't confront him?

PT: Not at all.

TH: He wouldn't be able to take it?

PT: No—he'd go to pieces.

TH: You're certain?

PT: I'm sure.

TH: I remember about five weeks ago you felt the same about me—you did not know whether I'd ever understand and you felt you couldn't get through to me.

PT: Yes—but that's passed.

TH: I must have felt to you like your father.

PT: Yes—I guess so, but he always has to be right and he can never discuss anything—*and he has no feelings—he can't stand feelings—any feelings.* . . . (She is also talking about herself—feelings are very frightening to her.)

TH: Your father sounds to me a little like this director who lost so much of his guilt in analysis. He doesn't have to walk around feeling guilty anymore, like a criminal (projective technique). At least he must be able to sleep at night and feel more comfortable. I don't know whether that part applies to your father.

PT: Well, my father is not as crazy, and he is fair in a way. He's not openly hostile. He's hostile by default, or in withdrawing, or in his detachment. He's not attacking—well, except in having his own way. (This is not quite true; both she and her father have very sharp hostile tongues.) His opinion is the last word, however, and he has this contemptuous attitude towards others. But the problem is often he's absolutely right. He figures things out in his mind. My mother is the suffering, hysterical one, the crazy one—the irrational one. Of course, he withdraws and then she is frantic. But back to me—I'm having trouble talking too much, and at the union meetings I'm afraid these older men are going to give it to me one of these days. I'm always arguing and differing with them. I try to do it diplomatically and they seem to accept me—but—well, you know (she smiles) I'm always right. (She acknowledges her problem to some extent but still refuses to accept that in the controlling tendencies there is a sadistic pleasure.)

TH: You never make a mistake?

PT: Well, hardly ever! (She laughs.)

We see in the interview the "fight against the introject" or the "identification." Yet, we understand that she is getting ready to cope with that aspect of herself that is most like her father, and the irrational part of her that is like the mother. We see, too, that she would like some normal peer relationships.

A short time later, in a group therapy session, Elizabeth began to talk about her mother.

Elizabeth: My mother is in town and I'm going crazy. I am so angry, I don't know what to do with myself. She is staying at the Holiday Inn with two friends and every day she calls me. I got Sally to go with me the last trip because I can't stand those ladies. She was great. She said, how do you do, Mrs. Osgood, you look great, you've lost weight. She has no feeling about it. She's not *connected.*

Therapist: You're connected with your mother?

Elizabeth: Yes. We were walking along the street, my mother and I, and she was bumping into me every minute until I was right up against the walls of the buildings. I was so enraged. And then she hangs onto me with that anxious expression, but I can't move either because she's telling me: "Don't cross the street yet, walk here; look out! I'm afraid." Believe me, I'm in a trap. She's so dependent; but she has to control my every movement. I have to move completely within her orbit.

Elaine: Why don't you just hold her hand and guide her along and don't make such a fuss?

Elizabeth: Because I don't want to touch her (she almost screams) and I don't want her to touch me! And I don't want to feel so angry. I am beside myself with anger. I feel like yelling and screaming—I could burst—I feel like my face will blow up.

GROUP THERAPY AND THE BORDERLINE

A therapeutic group, jointly combined with individual sessions, can be of inestimable value in the working through process. From the time that Marsh (1931) used groups in his work with physically ill patients until today, the group has been an important vehicle in psychological treatment. Ideally the patient is seen once or twice weekly in individual therapy (although when the patient gets into a crisis this can be increased), and once weekly in a group. Because the borderline patient has had little experience with peers in his development, a group is especially important for him. It helps him break up his character defenses, and to move from what Wolf and Schwartz (1962) call the hierarchic to the peer position.

Group members often proceed from preoccupation with authority to rebellion and then to interdependence (Benne, 1960), the latter affecting the resolution of dependency (in borderline patients this is expressed in the form of sado-masochism) and the emergence of independence. What usually happens with the borderline patient in the group is that one person may be considered a "friend" while certain others will be felt to be adversaries. "Friendly" figures can change as the idealization pattern gives way to hostility. This pattern, which is a reflection of the "split ego," i.e., "the good and bad objects" (the projective identification figures), is acted out in life too, but for a long period of time this defense should not be disturbed, even though the figures that come and go, at first as friends and then as disappointing personages, constitute the patient's main interpersonal contacts.[1]*

In the group, as in the one-to-one situation, the patient's recognition of defenses (including transference reactions) and the realization that they are operating repetitively and compulsively do not guarantee that modifications of behavior will occur. Change, to a large extent, depends upon motivation, and as L. Wolberg (1967) says: "Among the motivating influences . . . are a sense of frustration induced by an inability to fulfill normal needs, and the growing awareness that neurotic strivings are associated with suffering in excess of compensatory gratifications." Working through is enhanced as the individual accepts his autonomy more and more and feels no guilt about this. The punitive

*Notes for this chapter start page 256.

side of the introject is reduced. The detection of contradictions and conflicts in the person's life helps him develop motivation for change, and it is one of the tasks of the therapist to point up these contradictions in both the group and the individual sessions. We must remember that the defenses and the transferential behavior help to control anxiety and the patient is loathe to give up these supports. L. Wolberg continues to describe the course of working through which is particularly applicable to borderline cases. "The curve of improvement is jerky. The initial chink in the patient's neurotic armour is made by penetrations of insight. . . . An insight takes hold and the patient improves. This improvement is momentary, and the patient goes backward with an intensified resistance. He reintrenches himself with all his previous defenses as he delves deeper into his problem. . . . The patient returns repetitively to his old modes of living while making tentative thrusts in a new and more adaptive direction . . . change is never in a consistently forward direction."

We now know that this movement is helped definitively as the analysis uncovers guilt and the sado-masochistic tendencies. This means the releasing to the self from the restraint and tyranny of superego defense, i.e., the introjects (identifications), and the freeing of the individual from paralyzing fears, guilts, and conflicts. "The emergence of self-respect, assertiveness and self-confidence is accompanied by the release from the tryannical superego (the castigating side of the self) which is rooted in the unconscious and in the repressions." Change occurs only as the patient begins to gain satisfaction from his new responses. Pleasure finally outweighs pain as success is acknowledged. In the group, the patient receives the reinforcement of acceptance for his attempts at eliminating his neurosis. The group takes as its goal helping each individual to undo his neurotic defenses and to lay bare the neurosis. The reporting by each individual of his personal way of overcoming neurotic behavior patterns is of great significance; each individual strives to meet the group norm, which is to eliminate fears and overcome inhibitions.

The individual who uses many people upon whom to project is more defended than one who needs fewer projective objects. In the group, the actively hostile person will be more difficult to treat than the passively hostile one, for active aggression arouses more active counter-aggression in other group members. It is this kind of person who, when he gets into a group, tends to become a monopolizer, and this mobilizes the group to want to expel him or isolate him. The group therapist must consequently utilize every measure to prevent the monopolizer from goading the group on toward incessant coping with his aggression, for this paralyzes the group's progress in problem-solving.[2]

Probably the most difficult part of working through with borderline patients is coping with the specific patterns of perverse behavior that have definite links with actual ritualized, repetitive parental practices. For example, James Fuchs, whom I wrote about in my paper, "Patterns of Interaction in Families of Borderline

Patients" (1968), was arrested as a peeping tom. His mother used to go into the bathroom with him, watching him, as he defecated or urinated (she followed him every time he went in for any reason: a shower, morning ablutions, defecation or urination). It seems to me that one must call her a "peeping tom," who forced her son to identify with her as a defense against the degradation and humiliation he felt in having his mother hovering over him. We do not know what her sexual phantasies are but we can make some assumptions by understanding some of the patient's phantasies. One was of the analyst letting him look at her bare breasts and of helping him out in learning about sex, as in the "Tea and Sympathy" theme. If we turn the characters around we may say that the patient's phantasy probably reflects some of the mother's phantasies as well—phantasies that the patient gleans from the mother's conversations with him as she watches in the bathroom. James' mother had the habit of reviewing with him his relations with girls when he came home from dates. Thus, on the preoedipal level, James thinks of breasts, while on the oedipal level he has homosexual phantasies and phantasies of phallic women who nevertheless have feminine and passive traits. James' father, on the other hand, was always defying the law, driving through red lights, cheating on his income tax, shoplifting, lying to people, and involving his son in some of these practices. James identified with many of these traits of his father. The father of Dr. Daird, rather than the mother, took him on vacation, and they always went to a nudist camp. At home the boy slept with his mother, and on vacation he slept with his father. When he grew up, Daird had a feeling that he might want to molest a child, although he never did; he had homosexual phantasies and for several years lived under the spell of an older professor, but there was no overt homosexuality between them. His fear with women was that he might have an erection at an inappropriate moment. In each of these cases, one of the problems was the patient's pleasure in sadism or in sadistic thoughts. Patients are loathe to give up this pleasure, for it is associated with the person's desire for revenge and it helps keep loving feelings out of awareness as a defense against the fear of being engulfed rather than loved.

The identification process, at least in borderline patients, has definite links with the perverse repetitive parental patterns, as well as with the hostility that the parent shows to the patient. Thus the identifications have the goal of helping the child maintain relationships with his neurotic parents or their substitutes (Rickman's idea of the superego). Identifications with severely neurotic or psychotic parents necessitate complicated systems of defense. The identifications work like the dream in that a psychologically significant but not recent element, a train of thought, or a recollection may be replaced for the purpose of dream-formation by a recent but psychologically indifferent element, provided the two following conditions are fulfilled: (1) the dream-content (the identification phantasy) preserves a connection with things recently experienced; (2) the dream-stimulus is a psychologically significant event (Freud, 1900, p. 248). "I am persuaded to advance the proposition that a dream works under a kind of compulsion, which forces it to combine into a unified whole all the sources of dream-stimulation which are offered to it." The defense as it is represented in the mind is, more or less, a complete statement of the problem. The problem is reflected in both preoedipal and oedipal terms. In the group, as in the dream, the patient identifies with one person or another as his defenses shift and change, and he selects or rejects members as his defensive needs shift. His defensive relations with group members are a reflection of his intrapsychic defenses. The patient's relations with people outside the group change, too, as he begins to work through his problem, as in individual therapy the therapist must alert himself to ways of expediting actual behavioral changes in the patient's relationships with others. In psychoanalytic treatment we note these changes by discovering the shifts in object relations, and with borderlines we look for a reduction in sado-masochistic relations. Hunter (1954) wrote a paper on the changes in object relations that he noted in the course of his analysis of a fetishist. In order to help facilitate change, the therapist must point up the conflicts that are being resolved as these changes take place.

When it comes to working through perverse traits, the sadism comes out as the patient shifts in his focus from one group member to another. In one of my groups, a physician showed his sadism in one session by taunting an alcoholic member and calling him weak because he was using Antabuse as a means of controlling his habit. At the same time, he attacked a young girl for her withdrawal tendencies, saying that she was a tease and a sexual harlot at heart. Then he turned on one of the men and called him a cheat and a faker who got his just deserts when his wife recently left him. Teasing provides a kind of sublimation for perverse patterns and helps the patient endure his oedipal conflict. In all probability there is no oedipal conflict that is not based on sado-masochistic experience with parents, which includes teasing. Agreeing with Freud that the oedipus complex becomes extinguished by its lack of success, and the result of its impossibility, Friedman (1956) notes that it is precisely this conclusion that many neurotic patients refuse to accept, and he credits this obstinacy to denial and *reality factors that tend to keep the oedipal wish alive.* With respect to this second point, he emphasized teasing as an aspect of the behavior of the parental figure. This problem is certainly true in the case of the borderline patient. Perverse patterns are a form of teasing—an implied seduction and then frustration. James Fuchs used to get into the subway and rub his arm against women's breasts, particularly the nipples. He said that it was amazing how many women stood for the rubbing and acted as he did, "as-if-the-whole-procedure-were-not-taking-place." There is excitement in this act, but what excites is both the danger of exposure and the sadism that is symbolically acted out. The parents have behaved as if the whole neurotic pattern were not taking place. This kind of mechanism has been accredited to lack of judgment, a defective ego, masochism, a poor superego, and identification with a masochistic parent. I am suggesting that it is a hysterical mechanism with denial and dissociative processes, affiliated with masochism, but also that underneath it is the pleasure associated with sadism. The sadism can be turned towards the self and toward others as well. In the group the sadism is more obvious and the pleasure in the sadism becomes more evident.

The peculiar rigidity of behavior in borderline patients, its seeming immutatability, may be due to the fact, emphasized by Maier (1961), that "behavior acquired under excessive frustration may become 'abnormally fixated.' " We must recognize that fixation of neurotic behavior depends upon the activity of the parent and that it is conditioned behavior. The borderline syndrome is a life-saving technique, a sado-masochistic way of life: the patient is the product of a situation in which he was constantly thrown into anxiety by the behavior of the parents. Thereafter he anticipates anxiety constantly. *When he feels no anxiety momentarily in treatment, he immediately feels guilty. For this reason, he tries to conceal his progress or manifestations of success, which tend to bolster his self-image but which, at the beginning, increase his anxiety.*

In this book I have stressed that identification in the borderline serves as a neurotic defense and not as a natural or normal accompaniment of maturation, an aid in learning. Quite the contrary, it is a detriment to learning. The identifications must be undone in treatment, and this means that the patient must work through his feelings about having been rejected as a child, and having been used as a projective defense of the parent. But more than that, he must eliminate the behavior patterns that are like those of his parents, he must work toward giving up the sadistic pleasure associated with revenge and denigration. The fears of competition and rivalry must be worked through, and the impulse to "give in to the other," as a defense against the fear of annihilation, must be overcome. Fears and guilt concerning success must be eliminated. On the sexual level, the patient lives in sexual resignation and engages in perverse activities. These perverse traits must be identified and worked through.

Finally, it must be emphasized again that in doing reconstructive therapy with the borderline patient, the transference neurosis, or the transference psychosis, must be worked through, and this can be done only by understanding the intricate pattern of resistances, realizing that detachment and isolation, withdrawal and self-protection from others, is a prime object in defense. It is desirable but not always possible to avoid a *transference psychosis,* and projective techniques help in this goal. The appropriate spacing of sessions over a period of years aids in watering down the transference, so that eventually it will be worked through. Lipschutz (1957) has written a paper on the proposition that the group helps the patient divest himself of the too intense hostile transference towards the analyst. We know that such a transference easily leads to a paranoid projection which prevents working through.

One must realize that the borderline patient's tactics are to relieve anxiety by maintaining relationships with several people who serve different purposes at different times. Interpersonal contacts are held at superficial levels and are broken after anxiety has been temporarily relieved by acting out in the interpersonal sphere. In those contacts that remain steady, interpersonal defenses break the constancy of the relationship by periods of withdrawal, by hysterical defenses of not seeing, not hearing, not knowing and by resorting to phantasy while staying in the situation. These dynamics must become clear to the patient before the oedipal and preoedipal problems can be resolved. The defensive maneuvers will continue until the "observing ego" can distinguish those patterns that must be changed and the anxieties that must be worked through so that termination can be considered. The many "objects" in the patient's life, mostly used in a superficial way, help dissipate the transference, and his brief contacts with people and his distancing behavior are ways that the patient uses to avoid the intensity of deep relationships that may lead to a transference psychosis. At least 75 per cent of the borderline patient's relationships at the beginning of treatment are transferential in nature. We know that in treatment, if we attempt to gain closeness with the patient before he has reduced his transferential mechanisms, his anxiety easily leads to a paranoid projection which enhances a transference psychosis and interferes with working through. It is for this reason that we use projective therapeutic techniques.

We may well heed the wise words of Freud, who, in 1914, wrote that the working through of the resistances "may in practise amount to an arduous task for the patient and a trial of patience for the analyst. Nevertheless, it is the part of the work that effects the greatest changes in the patient. . . . The transference," he said, "forms a kind of intermediary realm between illness and real life through which the journey from the one to the other must be made. . . . If the patient does but show compliance enough to respect the necessary conditions of the analysis, we can regularly succeed in giving all the symptoms of the neurosis a new transference coloring, and in replacing his whole ordinary neurosis by a 'transference-neurosis' of which he can be cured by the therapeutic work." But what makes treatment most difficult of all is what Freud (1911) so aptly emphasized when he indicated that in each individual case we must "leave the high ground of generalization and descend to the detailed consideration of actual circumstances—which are undoubtedly very much more complicated."

NOTES

[1] The concept of traumatic interpersonal relations in early life accounts for the facts of defense and the idealization that exists in neurosis or psychosis. The patient withdraws in some measure from real life; he is alienated from that aspect of reality which is unbearable. The most extreme type of this kind of alienation is the psychosis, which, as Freud said, not only denies reality but remakes it in the defense. *Idealization,* of course, is an example of altering reality which is typical of neurosis and psychosis as well. It is considered a function

of the ego and the superego in psychoanalytic theory. The splitting techniques which have been attributed to a weak ego, or to an inability on the part of the ego to integrate impressions and experience with objects, appear to be defenses (some of which could be called hysterical) that help to distribute the aggression so that object relations can be maintained. We may redefine the superego as a *defensive technique* which contains the idealization mechanisms and the identifications with the parents. In my opinion these are always related. In defending against aggression, a projection onto several objects makes the aggression towards each become manageable. Rickman (1927), we have mentioned before, called the superego a *technique* for maintaining object relations, and I have suggested that the superego consists of mechanisms which properly could be called defensive, and are related to the identification phantasies.

In sleep there is a withdrawal and relief from external stimuli which also happens in phantasy. But mental activity goes on, albeit in a reduced form. Dreams, for example, reflect the cognitive function and often reveal basic defenses in their pristine state, as well as aspirations, problem-solving propensities, identification figures, etc. Phantasy may well reflect these same mental characteristics; certainly phantasy expresses the identifications and the idealizations as well as the myriad other defenses. The patient's group activity mirrors what we see in the dream. The need for disposal of hostility is great, but until some of the aggression is worked through, the defenses that contain hostility have to be maintained during group therapy and outside the group with others. I have often thought that this was the significance of Freud's remark that in the dream the patient suffers on behalf of a group of persons, in that he is identified with each person in some way; each person represents some aspect of the dreamer, and each person, we may add, or his representative, serves in the defense.

2 The psychoanalyst tends to think of the therapeutic group as a family, the members becoming transference figures for each patient. Freud had a dual concept of the group as he had of the individual. On the biological side he said that the group was a continuation of the multi-cellular organization of all higher organisms (i.e., the continuity between the individual and the group were two orders of the organism). On the other hand, he gave the group a phylogenetic origin, the dynamics of which he said were based on the Totem Family. All social organization, according to this theory, has a family dimension: the leader is like the parent and the members are like the siblings in the family. The dynamics are similar to those of the Totem Family. Needless to say, sociologists do not agree with Freud. In another place (A. Wolberg, 1972) I have written that there are three dimensions in the group that must be the focus of attention for the group therapist, and these ideas come primarily from the work of Moreno and one of his early co-workers, Jennings. The latter suggested that in thinking of groups we take three dimensions of interaction into account: (1) the projective; (2) the problem-solving, and (3) the choice-rejection patterns, or the socio-metric choices (Moreno). Moreno introduced three important techniques, all of which are useful to group therapists: sociometry; psycho-drama and group therapy. In his "First Book on Group Psychotherapy" (1931, p. 11) Moreno wrote that "the most important discovery was that every group has a specific structure of its own with a varying degree of cohesiveness and depth, and that no two groups are alike. The structure of groups can be explored and determined; they are phenomena which can be studied scientifically in their own right. This discovery led to the development of sociometry and small group analysis." The group, of course, is not a family.

The projective dimension in groups is the one most familiar to psychoanalysts, for it is a reflection of the transference needs of the patient as demonstrated in identification and in projective identification. This is perhaps why psychoanalysts, beginning with Freud, always refer to the group as a family. *It is in the interests of defense that most members choose or reject other members in the group.* But these choices are not permanent, for as the defenses change or are reduced, the choice-rejections change. The problem-solving dimension can be understood in psychoanalytic terms as the work of the rational or observing ego or as the "working through process," i.e., the *learning* that takes place in the therapeutic process.

Learning patterns in psychotherapy depend upon the rational ego and these are ushered in by clear statements on conscious levels of the complexity of the emotional problem, and of the individual elements of the problems that are under consideration. This must not be confused with intellectualization as a defense. I do not mean to disregard what has been called incidental learning or subliminal learning, but I only emphasize that in psychotherapy there must be some clear statements as to what the therapist and the patient are trying to do together, in order for the working through process to take place. Such statements are necessary, as, for example, this insightful expression on the part of a patient: "I see that I am very attacking with my husband. While he has some passive traits that make me angry, I do not want to attack him for them. If he is to change, he cannot do so by my attacking him. I shall have to stop this attacking anyway, because it occurs often and interferes with my relations with co-workers, and in my need to act as a supervisor. This pattern is becoming very frustrating to me." Without a reason to be working through and without motivation there is no goal and nothing is accomplished.

REFERENCES

Abel, T. M.: Neuro-circulatory reaction and the recall of unfinished and completed tasks. J. Psychol. 6:377-383, 1938.

Abraham, K.: A short study of the development of the libido. (1924) In: On Character and Libido Development: Six Essays. New York: Basic Books, pp. 67-150, 1966.

_____ : Selected Papers. London: Hogarth Press, 1927.

Ackerman, N.: The Psychodynamics of Family Life. New York: Basic Books, 1958.

_____ : Family Therapy. New York: Basic Books, 1960.

Adler, A.: The Neurotic Constitution. New York: Moffat, Yard and Co., 1917.

_____ : Individual Psychology. London: Kegan, Paul, Trench, Truber & Co., p. 8, 1925.

Adler, D. L. & Kounin, J.: Some factors operating at the moment of resumption of interrupted tasks. J. Psychol., 7:255-267, 1939.

Aichhorn, A.: Wayward Youth. (1925) New York: Viking Press, 1945.

Alexander, F.: The neurotic character. Internat. J. Psycho-Analysis., 11:292-311, 1930.

Allport, G.: The historical background of modern social psychology. In: Handbook of Social Psychology. (Lindzey, G., Ed.) Vol. I. Cambridge: Addison-Wesley, pp. 16-17, 1954.

Alper, T. G.: Task orientation vs. ego-orientation in learning and retention. Amer. J. Psychol., 59:236-248, 1945.

_____ : Memory for completed and incompleted tasks as a function of personality: Correlation between experimental and personality data. J. Personality, 17:104-137, 1948.

_____ : The interrupted task method in studies of selection recall: A revaluation of some recent experiments. Psychol. Rev., 59:71-88, 1952.

American Psychiatric Ass'n.: Diagnostic and Statistical Manual, 2nd Ed., Prepared by the Committee on Nomenclature and Statistics. Wash., D.C.: Amer. Psychiat. Ass'n., p. 42, 1968.

Antrobus, J., Dement, W. & Fisher, C.: Patterns of dreaming and dream recall: An EEG study. J. Abnorm. Soc. Psyhcol., 64:341-344, 1964.

Arieti, S.: Interpretation of Schizophrenia. New York: Brunner, 1955.

_____ : Schizophrenia, Encyclopaedia Britannica. Chicago: Encyclopaedia Britannica, Inc., Vol. 20, pp. 69-71, 1964.

259

Arlow, J. A. & Brenner, C.: Psychoanalytic Concepts and the Structural Theory. New York: International Universities Press, pp. 144-178, 1964.

Atkinson, J. W.: The achievement motive and recall of interrupted and completed tasks. J. Exp. Psychol., 46:381-390, 1953.

Azima, H. & Wittkower, E. D.: Gratifications of basic needs in schizophrenia. Psychiatry, 19:121-129, 1956.

Bales, R. F. & Strodtbeck, F. L.: Phases in group problem solving. J. Abnorm. Soc. Psychol., 46:485-495, 1951.

_____ , _____ , Mills, T. M. &Roseborough, M. E.: Channels of communication in small groups. Amer. Sociol. Rev., 16:461-468, 1951.

Bateson, G., Jackson, D. D., Haley, J. & Weakland, J.: Toward a theory of schizophrenia. Behavioral Science, 1:251-264, 1956.

Beckett, P. G. S. et al.: The significance of exogenous traumata in the genesis of schizophrenia. Psychiatry, 19:137-142, 1956.

Bellak, L.: Dementia Praecox. The Past Decade's Work and Present Status. A Review and Evaluation. New York: Grune & Stratton, 1948.

_____ : The treatment of schizophrenia and psychoanalytic theory. J. Nerv. Ment. Dis., 131-39-46, 1960.

_____ : The Schizophrenic Syndrome. Research in Ego Functional Patterns. New York, Grune & Stratton, pp. 14-20, 1969.

_____ : The concept of acting out; theoretical consideration. In: Acting Out (Abt and Weissman, Eds.) New York, Grune & Stratton, pp. 3-19, 1965.

Bentham, J.: An Introduction to the Principles of Morals and Legislation. (1st Ed., 1789). Oxford: Clarendon Press, 1879.

Berelson, B. & Steiner,   : Human Behavior, New York, Chicago: Harcourt Brace & World, 1964.

Beres, D.: Ego deviation and the concept of schizophrenia. In: The Psychoanalytic Study of the Child. New York: International Universities Press, 2:164-235, 1956.

Bernheim, H.: De la suggestion et de ses application à la thérapeutique. (1886) Boston: Putnam. Suggestive Therapeutica: a treatise on the nature and uses of hypnotism, 1895.

Bertalanffy, S. von: The theory of open systems in physics and biology. Science, 111:23-29, 1950.

Bianchi, L.: La Meccanica del Cervello e la Funzione Dei Lobi Frontali. Forino Bocca, 1920.

Bleuler, E.: Affectivity, Suggestibility, Paranoia. (1906) Utica, New York: State Hospitals Press, 1912.

_____ : Lecture on ambivalence, given in Berne in 1910. Abstracted in Zentralblatt fur psychoanalyze, Bd. 1, S. 266.

_____ : Dementia Praecox, or the Group of Schizophrenias. (1911) New York: International Universities Press, 1950.

_____ : Autistic thinking. Amer. J. Insanity, 69:873, 1913.

_____ : Mendelismus bei Psychosen, Speciell bei der Schizophrenie. Schweiz Arch. Neurol. u. Psychiat., 1:1, 1917.

_____ : Schizophrenie und psychologische Auffassungen. Zugleich ein Beispiel, wie wir in psychologischen Dingen ananeinder vorberieden. Allgemeine Ztschr. f. Psychiatrie, 76:135-162, 1920.

_____ : Research and changes in concepts in the study of schizophrenia. 1941-1950. Bull. Isaac Ray Med. Library, 3:1, 1955.

Boyer, L. Bryce: A hypothesis regarding the time of appearance of the dream screen. Internat. J. Psycho-Analysis, 41:114-122, 1960.

Boyer, L. & Giovacchini, P.: Psychoanalytic Treatment of Characterological and Schizophrenic Disorders. New York: Science House, Inc., 1967.

Buber, M.: I and Thou (2nd Ed.). New York: Scribner, 1958.

Burnham, D.: Schizophrenia and the Need-Fear Dilemma. New York: Internat. Univ. Press, 1969.

Bychowski, G.: The preschizophrenic ego. Psychoanal. Quart., 16:225-233, 1947.

_____ : Remarks on some defense mechanisms and reaction patterns of the schizophrenic ego. Bull. Amer. Psychoanalytic Assn., 7:141-143, 1951.

_____ : Psychotherapy of Psychosis. New York: Grune & Stratton, 1952.

_____ : The problem of latent psychosis. J. Amer. Psychoanal. Assn., 1:484-503, 1953.

_____ : On the handling of some schizophrenic mechanisms and reaction patterns. Internat. J. Psycho-Analysis., 35:147-153, 1954.

_____ : From latent to manifest schizophrenia. Congress Report of the Second International Congress for Psychiatry. (Zurich) 3:128-134, 1957.

_____ : Struggle against the introjects. Internat. J. Psychoanal., 39:182-187, 1958.

_____ : Schizophrenic partners. In: (Eisenstein, V., Ed.) Neurotic Interaction in Marriage. New York: Basic Books, pp. 135-147, 1963.

_____ : Obsessive compulsive facade in schizophrenia. Paper presented before the 24th International Psychoanalytic Congress, Amsterdam, 1965.

_____ : The archaic object and alienation. Internat. J. Psychoanal., 48:384-393, 1967.

Cantril, H.: Perception and interpersonal relations. Amer. J. Psychiat., 114:117-126, 1941.

_____ : Interpersonal Experience. New York: MacMillan & Co., 1957.

Carmichael, L: Manuel of Child Psychology (2nd ed.). New York: John Wiley and Sons, Inc.: pp. 124-125, 1954.

Charcot, J. M.: Encyclopaedia Britannica: Vol. 6, Charcot, pp. 244-5, 1953.

Clark, L. Pierce: Some practical remarks upon the use of modified psychoanalysis in the treatment of borderline neurosis and psychoses. Psychoanal. Rev., 6:306-308, 1919.

_____ : The phantasy method of analyzing narcissistic neuroses. Med. J. Rec., 123:154-158, 1926.

_____ : Narcissism as a factor in neuroses and psychoses. Med. J. Rec. 137:59-64, 1933.

_____ : The queston of prognosis in narcissistic neuroses and psychoses. Internat. J. Psychoanal., 14:71-86, 1933.

_____ : Treatment of narcissistic neuroses and psychoses. Psychoanal. Rev., 20:304-326, 1933.

Clark, Ramsey: Crime in America. New York: Simon and Schuster, 1970.

Coleman, M. L.: Externalization of the toxic introject: A treatment technique for borderline cases. Psychoanal. Rev., 43:235-42, 1956.

_____ & Nelson, B.: Paradigmatic psychotherapy in borderline treatment. Psychoanalysis, 5: 3:28-44, 1957.

Delboef: Le Magnetisme Animal. Paris: Bailliere, 128 pages, 1889.

Desmonde, W. H.: Mead and Freud: American social psychology and psychoanalysis. In: Psychoanalysis and the Future. New York: National Psychological Association for Psychoanalysis, pp. 31-50, 1957.

Deutsch, Helene: Neuroses and Character Types. New York: International Universities Press, p. 21, 1965.

Dollard, J. & Miller, N. E,: Personality and Psychotherapy. New York: McGraw-Hill, 1950.

Eisenstein, V. W.: Differential psychotherapy of borderline states. In: Specialized

Techniques in Psychotherapy. (Bychowski, G. & Despert, L. J., Eds.) New York: Basic Books, pp. 303-321, 1952.

Eissler, Kurt R.: Limitations to the psychotherapy of schizophrenia. Psychiatry, 6:381-391, 1943.

_____ : Remarks on the psychoanalysis of schizophrenia. Internat. J. Psychoanal., 32:139-156, 1951.

_____ : The effect of the structure of the ego on psychoanalytic technique. J. Amer. Psychoanal. Assn., 1:104-143, 1943.

_____ : Notes upon the emotionality of a schizophrenic patient, and its relation to the problems of technique. Psychoanalytic Study of the Child, 8:199-251, 1953.

_____ : Remarks on some variations in psychoanalytic technique. Internat. J. Psychoanal., 39:222-229, 1958.

Ekstein, R. & Wallerstein, R.: Observations on the psychology of borderline and psychotic children. In: The Psychoanalytic Study of the Child, Vol. 9. New York: International Universities Press, pp. 344-369, 1954.

Erikson, E. H.: Ego development and historical development. In: The Psychoanalytic Study of the Child, Vol. 2. New York: International Universities Press, pp. 359-396, 1946.

_____ : Childhood and Society. New York: Norton, 1950.

_____ : Growth and crises of the healthy personality. In: Personality, Society and Culture in Nature (Kluckholm, C., Murray, H. A. & Schneider, D. M., Eds.) New York: Knopf, 1953.

_____ : Identity and the Life Cycle. New York: International Universities Press, 1959.

Fairbairn, W. R. D.: A revised psychopathology of the psychoses and psychoneuroses. Internat. J. Psycho-Anal., 22:250-279, 1941.

_____ : Endopsychic structure considered in terms of object relationship. Internat. J. Psychoanal., 25:70-93, 1944.

_____ : Endopsychic structure considered in terms of object relationship. Psychoanal. Quart., 5:54, 1946.

_____ : Object relationships and dynamic structure. Internat. J. Psychoanal., 17:30, 1946.

_____ : An Object-relations Theory of the Personality. New York: Basic Books, pp. 93, 61 & 169, 1952.

Federn, P.: The analysis of psychotics. Internat. J. Psychoanal., 15:209-214, 1934.

_____ : Ego Psychology and the Psychoses. New York: Basic Books, 1952.

Fenichel, O.: On the psychology of boredom. Collected Papers of Otto Fenichel. (1934) 1:292-302. New York: Norton, 1953.

_____ : On the theory of the therapeutic results of psychoanalysis. Internat. J. Psychoanal., 18:133-138, 1937.

_____ : The counter-phobic attitude. The Collected Papers of Otto Fenichel (1939) 2:163-173. New York: Norton, 1954.

_____ : Problems of Psychoanalytic Technique. Albany, New York: The Psychoanalytic Quarterly, Inc., 1941.

_____ : The Psychoanalytic Theory of Neurosis. New York: Norton, 1945.

Ferenczi, S.: (1909) Introjection and transference. In: Sex in Psychoanalysis. New York: Basic Books, pp. 35-93, 1950.

_____ : (1911) On Obscene Words. Sex in Psychoanalysis. New York: Basic Books, pp. 132-153, 1950.

_____ : (1911) Stimulation of the anal erotic zone as a precipitating factor in paranoia, contribution to the subject of homosexuality and paranoia. In: Final Contributions to the Problems and Methods of Psychoanalysis. New York: Basic Books, pp. 295-298, 1955.

_____ : (1911) On the part played by homosexuality in the pathogenesis of paranoia.

In: Sex in Psychoanalysis. New York: Basic Books, pp. 154-186, 1950.

_____: (1912) Transitory symptom-construction during the analysis. In: Sex in . Psychoanalysis. New York: Basic Books, pp. 193-212, 1950.

_____: (1922) Paranoia. In: Final Contributions to the Problems and Methods of Psychoanalysis. New York: Basic Books, pp. 212-215, 1955.

_____: (1924) On forced phantasies. In: Further Contributions to the Theory and Technique of Psycho-Analysis. London: Hogarth Press, pp. 68-77, 1950.

_____: (1925) Contra-indications to the 'active' psycho-analytical technique. In: Further Contributions to the Theory and Technique of Psycho-Analysis. London: Hogarth Press, pp. 217-230, 1950.

_____: (1925) Psychoanalysis of sexual habits. In: Further Contributions to the Theory and Technique of Psychoanalysis. London: Hogarth Press, pp. 259-297, 1950.

_____: (1929) The principle of relaxation and neocatharsis. In: Final Contributions to the Problems and Methods of Psychoanalysis. New York: Basic Books, pp. 108-125, 1955.

Fisher, C,: Dreams and perception. J. Amer. Psychoanal. Assn., 2:389-445, 1954.

_____: Freud Lecture Given March 1969, reported in Frontiers of Clinical Psychiatry. Vol. 6, No. 16, p. 1, November 15, 1969.

_____, Byrne, J., Edwards, A. & Kahn, E.: A psychological study of nightmares. J. Amer. Psychoanal. Assn., 18:747-782, 1970.

Fleischl, Maria & Waxenberg, Sheldon: The therapeutic social club: A step toward social rehabilitation. Internat. Ment. Health Res. Newsletter, (Ed. Reiss, B.) Vol. 6, No. 1, Spring, 1964.

_____: Specific problems encountered in social rehabilitation: Theoretical formulations, Amer. J. Psychother., 18:660-669, 1964.

Fliess, R.: The Psychoanalytic Reader. London: Hogarth Press. p. 254, 1950.

Foulkes, S. H.: Introduction to Group-Analytic Psychotherapy. London: Heinemann, p. 29, 1948.

Frank, J.: Indications and Contra-indications for the application of the standard technique. J. Amer. Psychoanal. Assn., 4:266-284, 1956.

Frank, L. K.: The adolescent and the family. In: Adolescence (43rd Yearbook, Nat. Soc. for the Study of Educ., Jones, H. E., Ed.) Part I, pp. 240-254. Chicago: University of Chicago Press, 1944.

Frazee, H. E.: Children who later became schizophrenic. Smith College Studies in Social Work, 23:125-149, p. 148, 1953.

Freeman, H. E., Simmons, O. G. & Bergen, B. J.: Possessiveness as a characteristic of mothers of schizophrenics. J. Abnorm. & Soc. Psychol., 58:271-273, 1959.

Freeman, R. V. & Grayson, H. M.: Maternal attitudes in schizophrenia. J. Abnorm. & Soc. Psychol., 50:45-52, 1955.

Freud, A.: (1930) The Ego and the Mechanisms of Defense. New York: International Universities Press, 1946.

_____: Normality and Pathology in Childhood: Assessments of Development. New York: International Universities Press, 1965.

_____ & Dann, S.: An experiment in group upbringing. In: The Psychoanalytic Study of the Child. Vol. 6. New York: International Universities Press, p. 127, 1951.

(References to *Freud, S.,* except where otherwise indicated, are found in The Standard Edition of the Complete Psychological Works of Sigmund Freud. London: Hogarth Press, 1966.)

Freud, S.: (1887-1902) The Origins of Psychoanalysis. Letters, Drafts, and Notes to Wilhelm Fliess. New York: Basic Books, 1954, p. 425; also: (1895) letter #27, p. 122; (1895) letter #32, p. 129; (1896) letter #39, p. 140; (1896) letter #52, p. 173; (1897) letter #55, p. 184; (1897) letter #57, p. 188; (1897) letter #59, p. 193; (1897) letter #61, p. 196;

(1897) letter #70, p. 218, 219; (1897) letter #75, p. 229; (1897) draft L, Notes (1), p. 199; (1897) draft M, Notes (2), p. 202.

_____ : (1888, 1889) Hypnotism and suggestion (preface to the translation of Bernheim's Suggestion), 1:75-85.

_____ : (1893) On the psychical mechanism of hysterical phenomena, 3:26-39.

_____ : (1893) Charcot, 3:9-23.

_____ : (1894) On the grounds for detaching a particular syndrome from neurasthenia under the description anxiety neurosis, 3:87-117.

_____ : (1894) The neuro-psychoses of defense: An attempt at a psychological theory of acquired hysteria and obsessions and of certain hallucinatory psychoses, 3:45-61.

_____ : (1896) Further remarks on the neuro-psychoses of defense, 3:159-185.

_____ : (1898) The psychical mechanisms of forgetfulness, 3:288-297.

_____ : (1898) A case of successful treatment by hypnotism, 1:116-128.

_____ : (1899) Screen memories, 3:301-322.

_____ : (1900) The Interpretation of Dreams, vols. 4 and 5.

_____ : (1901) Psychopathology of Everyday Life, vol. 6.

_____ : (1905) Three essays on the theory of sexuality, 7:125-245.

_____ : (1905) Fragment of an analysis of a case of hysteria, 7:3-122.

_____ : (1907) Delusion and dreams, 9:3-95.

_____ : (1908) Hysterical phantasies and their relations to bisexuality, 9:157-166.

_____ : (1909) Family romances, 9:236-241.

_____ : (1910) Contribution to the psychology of love. A special type of choice of object made by men, 11:164-175.

_____ : (1910) Psychogenic visual disturbance according to psychoanalytical conceptions, 11:211-218.

_____ : (1911) Formulations regarding the two principles in mental functioning, 12:215-226.

_____ : (1911) Psychoanalytic notes on an autobiographical account of a case of paranoia (dementia paranoides), 12:3-82.

_____ : (1912) The employment of dream interpretation in psychoanalysis, 12:91-96.

_____ : (1912) On the universal tendency to debasement in the sphere of love, 11:179-190.

_____ : (1912-13) Totem and taboo, 13:1-161. Animisms, magic and the omnipotence of thoughts, 13:75-99.

_____ : (1912) Contributions to the psychology of love: The most prevalent form of degradation in erotic life

_____ : (1912) The dynamics of transference, 12:98-108.

_____ : (1913) The predisposition to obsessional neuroses 12:313-326.

_____ : (1914) On narcissism, 14:69-102.

_____ : (1914) On the history of the psychoanalytic movement, 14:3-66.

_____ : (1914) Further recommendations on the technique of psychoanalysis: Remembering, repeating, and working through, 12:147-156.

_____ : (1915) Observations on transference-love, 12:159-171.

_____ : (1915) Instincts and their vicissitudes, 14:111-140.

_____ : (1915) Repression, 14:143-158.

_____ : (1915) The unconscious, 14:161-215.

_____ : (1915) Some character types met with in psychoanalytic work, 14:311-333.

_____ : (1916) A metapsychological supplement to the theory of dreams, 14:219-235.

_____ : (1917) On transformations of instinct as exemplified in anal erotism, 17:127-133.

_____ : (1917) Mourning and melancholia, 14:239-258.

_____ : (1918) From the history of an infantile neurosis, 17:3-122.

_____ : (1918) The taboo of virginity, 11:193-208.

_____ : (1919) A child is being beaten, 17:177-204.

_____ : (1919) The uncanny, 17:219-256.

_____ : (1920) The psychogenesis of a case of homosexuality in a woman, 18:147-172.

_____ : (1920) Civilization and its discontent, 21:59-145.

_____ : (1921) Group psychology and the analysis of the ego, 18:67-143.

_____ : (1922) Some neurotic mechanisms in jealousy, paranoia and homosexuality, 18:223-232.

_____ : (1923) Remarks upon the theory and practise of dream interpretation, 19:108, 121.

_____ : (1923) The ego and the id, 19:3-66.

_____ : (1924) Loss of reality in neurosis and psychosis, 19:182-187.

_____ : (1924) The economic problem in masochism, 19:157-170.

_____ : (1924) Neurosis and psychosis, 19:148-153.

_____ : (1925) Some additional notes upon dream interpretation as a whole (c) the occult significance of dreams, 19:125-138.

_____ : (1925) Psychoanalysis and delinquency, 19:272-275.

_____ : (1926) Inhibitions, symptoms and anxiety, 20:77-175.

_____ : (1927) Fetishism, 21:149-159.

_____ : (1931) Female sexuality, 21:223-243.

_____ : (1933) New introductory lectures in psychoanalysis, 22:3-182.

_____ : (1936) A disturbance of memory on the Acropolis, 22:238-248.

_____ : (1937) Constructions in analysis, 23:256-269.

_____ : (1937) Analysis terminable and interminable, 23:211-253.

_____ : (1938) The splitting of the ego in the defensive process, 23:273-278.

_____ : (1938) An outline of psychoanalysis, 23:141-207.

Friedman, D. B,: Toward a unitary theory of the passing of the oedipal conflict. Psychoanal. Rev., 53:38-48, Spring 1966.

Fries, M.: Interrelationship of physical, mental and emotional life of a child from birth to four years of age. A.M.A. Amer. J. Dis. Child, 49:1546, 1953.

_____ : Studies on Integrated Development: The Interaction between Child and Environment. Commentary for Film 2: A psychoneurosis with compulsive trends in the making. New York University Film Library, 1953.

Fromm-Reichman, F.: Transference problems in schizophrenia. Psychoanal. Quart., 8:412, 1939.

_____ : Problems of therapeutic management in a psychoanalytic hospital. Psychoanal. Quart., 16:325-356, 1947.

_____ : Notes on the development of schizophrenia. Psychiatry, 11:263-273, 1948.

_____ : Notes on the personal and professional requirements of a psychotherapist. Psychiatry, 12:361-378, 1949.

_____ : Principles of Intensive Psychotherapy. Chicago: University of Chicago Press, 1950.

_____ : Some aspects of psychoanalytic psychotherapy with schizophrenics. In: Psychotherapy with Schizophrenics: A Symposium. (Brody, E. B. & Redlich, F. C., Eds.) New York: International Universities Press, 1952.

_____ : Psychoanalytic and general dynamic concepts of theory and of therapy: differences and similarities. J. Amer. Psychoanal. Assn., 2:711-721, 1954.

_____ : Clinical significance of intuitive process of the psychoanalyst. J. Amer. Psychoanal. Assn., 3:82-88, 1955.

Frosch, J.: Management of specific ego defects in the treatment of borderline patients. (Amer. Psychiat. Conf. Section I: Contribution of Psychoanalytic Thinking to the Psychotherapy of Borderline Patients. Joint Panel with Amer. Psychoanal. Assn.) May 11, 1970.

Gadpaille, W. J.: Homosexual activity and homosexuality in adolescence. In: Science and Psychoanalysis (J. Masserman, Ed.) Vol. XV. New York: Grune & Stratton, pp. 69-70, 1969.

_____ : Research into the physiology of maleness and femaleness. A.M.A. Arch. Gen. Psychiat. 26:193-206, 1972.

Gair, H.: A Report on the Battered Child. Speech given before the Women's Bar Association on January 27, 1970 at New York Bar Association, New York City.

Gardner, M. (Ed): The Wolfman. Basic Books: New York, 1971.

Garma, A.: (1931) La realidad exterior y los instintos en la esquizofrenia. Rev. de Psicoanalisis, 2:56-82, 1945.

Geleerd, E. R.: Some observations on temper tantrums in childhood. Amer. J. Orthopsychiat., 15:238, 1945.

_____ : The Borderline States in Childhood and Adolescence. Paper Delivered at New York Psychoanalytic Institute, 1958.

Gerard, D. L. & Siegel, J.: The family background of schizophrenia. Psychiat. Quart., 24:47-73, 1950.

Giffin, J., Johnson, A. M. & Litin, E. M.: Specific factors determining anti-social acting out. Amer. Jour. Orthopsychiat., 24:664, 1954.

Glover, E.: The Technique of Psychoanalysis. (1928, 1940) New York: International Universities Press, 1955.

_____ : Ego distortion. Internat. J. Psychoanal., 39:260-264.

Goldstein, K.: The organismic approach. In: American Handbook of Psychiatry. (Arieti, S., Ed.) New York: Basic Books, pp. 133-147, 1959.

Grand, H. G.: Conscious secretiveness as a masochistic defense. Amer. J. Psychother., Vol. 6, No. 2, April, 1952.

Greenson, R. R.: The struggle against identification. J. Amer. Psychoanal. Assn., 2:200-217, 1954.

_____ : On screen defenses, screen hunger, and screen identity. J. Amer. Psychoanal. Assn., 6:242-262, 1958.

_____ : The Technique and Practice of Psychoanalysis. New York: International Universities Press, 1967.

_____ et al: Variations in classical psychoanalytic technique. Internat. J. Psychoanal., 39:200-242, 1958.

Griffith, G. S. & Mahler, H. R.: DNA ticketing theory of memory. Nature 223 (No. 5206):580-582, 1969.

Grinker, R., Werble, B. & Drye, R. C.: The Borderline Syndrome: A behavioral study of ego functions. New York: Basic Books, 1968.

Guntrip, H.: Personality Structure and Human Interaction. London: Hogarth Press, 1961.

Harlow, H. F.: Motivational forces underlying learning. In: Learning Theory, Personality Theory, and Clinical Research—the Kentucky Symposium. New York: John Wiley & Sons, pp. 35-52, 1954.

_____ : Primary affectional patterns in primates. Amer. J. Orthopsychiat., 30:670-84, 1960.

_____ : The development of affectional patterns in infant monkeys. In: Determinants of Infant Behavior (Foss, B. M., Ed.) New York: John Wiley & Sons, pp. 75-97, 1961.

_____ : The development of learning in the Rhesus monkey. Sci. Progr. 12:239-69, 1962.

_____ : The effect of rearing conditions on behavior. Bull. Menninger Clin., 26:213-24, 1962.

Hartmann, Heinz: Ein Bettrag zur Lehre von den reaktiven Psychosen (1925). Monatsschr. f. Psychiat. u. Neurol., 57:89-108, 1925.

_____ : An experimental contribution to the psychology of obsessive-compulsive neurosis: On remembering completed and uncompleted tasks (1933). In: Essays of Ego Psychology. New York: International Universities Press, pp. 404-418, 1964.

_____ : Internationale Zeitschrift für Psychoanalyse, XXIV, 1939. Partly translated in D. Rapaport: Organization and Pathology of Thought. New York: Columbia University Press, 1951.

_____ : Technical implications of ego psychology. Psychoanalyt. Quart. 20'31-43, 1951.

_____ : The Genetic Approach in Psychoanalysis (1945). Psychological Issues Monograph 14,4:7-26, 1964.

_____ : Notes on the theory of aggression (1949). Psychological Issues Monograph 14,4:56-85, 1964.

_____ : Comments on the psychoanalytic theory of the ego. In: The Psychoanalytic Study of the Child, Vol. 5, pp. 74-96. New York: International Universities Press, 1950.

_____ : The development of the ego concept in Freud's work. Internat. J. Psychoanal., 37:425, 1956.

_____ & Kris, E. & Lowenstein, R. M.: Comments on the formation of psychic structure. In: The Psychoanalytic Study of the Child, Vol. 2, p. 11. New York: International Universities Press, 1946.

Healy, W., Bronner, A. F. & Bowers, A. M.: The Structure and Meaning of Psychoanalysis. New York: Alfred A. Knopf, 1930.

Heath, R. G., Martens, S., Leach, B. E., Cohen, M., and Feigley, C. A.: Behavioral changes in nonpsychotic volunteers following the administration of taraxein, the substance obtained from serum of schizophrenic patients. Amer. J. Psychiat. 114:917-920, 1958.

_____ , Leach, B. E., Byers, L. W., Martens, S. & Feigley, D. H.: Pharmacological and biological psychotherapy. Amer. J. Psychiat. 114:683, 1958.

Heimann, P.: A contribution to the reevaluation of the oedipus complex. The early stages. In: New Directions in Psychoanalysis (Klein, et al., Ed.) London: Tavistock; New York: Basic Books, 1955.

_____ : A combination of defense mechanisms in paranoid states. Ibid.

Hobbes, T.: Leviathan. Reprint of 1st (1651 ed.). Cambridge, England: University Press, 1904.

Hoch, P. & Polatin, P.: Pseudo-neurotic forms of schizophrenia. Psychiat. Quart., 23:248-276, 1949.

Hoedemacher, E.: Psychoanalytic technique and ego modifications. Internat. J. Psychoanal., 41:34-46.

_____ : The therapeutic process in the treatment of schizophrenia. J. Amer. Psychoanal. Assn., 3:89-109, 1955.

Holt, R. R.: A critical examination of Freud's concept of bound vs. free cathexis. J. Amer. Psychoanal. Assn., 10:475-525, 1962.

_____ : Two influences on Freud's scientific thought: A fragment of intellectual biography. In: R. W. White (Ed.): The Study of Lives, Essays on Personality in Honor of Henry A. Murray. New York: Atherton, 1963.

_____ : A review of some of Freud's biological assumptions and their influence on his theories. In: N. Greenfield and W. Lewis (Eds.): Psychoanalysis and Current Biological Thought. Madison, Wis.: University of Wisconsin Press, 1965.

———— : Ego autonomy re-evaluated. Internat. J. Psychoanal., 46:151-167, 1965.

———— : Beyond vitalism and mechanism. Freud's concept of psychic energy. In: The Ego (Masserman, J., Ed.), Science and Psychoanalysis, Vol. XI. New York: Grune & Stratton, pp. 1041, 1967.

Holzman, P. S.: A note on Breuer's hypnoidal theory of neurosis. Bull. Menninger Clinic, 23:145, 1959.

Horney, K.: Neurosis and Human Growth. London: Routledge, Kegan, Paul, 1951.

———— : The compulsive drive toward revenge. Amer. J. Psychoanal. 8:3-12, 1948.

Hunter, D.: Object relation changes in the analysis of a fetishist. Internat. J. Psychoanal., 35:302-312, 1954.

Jackson, D. D.: The question of family homeostasis. Psychiat. Quart. Suppl., Part I, 31:79-90, 1957.

———— : Family interaction, family homeostasis and some implications for conjoint family psychotherapy. In: Science and psychoanalysis, Vol. II. (Masserman, J., Ed.). New York: Grune & Stratton, pp. 112-141, 1959.

———— : The monad, the dyad and the family therapy of schizophrenics. In: Psychotherapy of the Psychoses (Burton, A., Ed.). New York: Basic Books, pp. 318-328, 1961.

Jacobson, E.: The self and the object world: Vicissitudes of their infantile cathexes and their influence on ideational and affective development. In: The Psychoanalytic Study of the Child. New York: International Universities Press, 9:75-127, 1954.

———— : Contributions to the metapsychology of psychotic identifications. J. Amer. Psychoanal. Assn., 2:239-262, 1954.

———— : On psychotic identifications. Internat. J. Psycho-Anal., 35:102-108, 1954.

———— : Depersonalization. J. Amer. Psychoanal. Assn., 7:591-610, 1959.

Janet, M. P.: L'Automatisme Psychologique. Paris: Alcan, (1st Ed.) 1889, (9th Ed.) 1913.

Johnson, A. M.: Juvenile delinquency. In: American Handbook of Psychiatry (Arieti, Ed.), Chap. 42. Vol. I, pp. 840-856. New York: Basic Books, 1959.

Jones, E.: Papers on Psychoanalysis. Chapter II, Rationalization in everyday life. New York: William Woodward Co., pp. 12-15, 1918.

Jung, C. G.: On the psychogenesis of schizophrenia. J. Ment. Sci., 85:999, 1939.

———— : The Psychology of Dementia Praecox (1913). New York: Nerv. & Ment. Dis. Publishing Co., (1936.

———— : Psychology of the Unconscious. (translated by Hinkle, B. M.). New York: Moffat, Yard & Co., 1921.

Kanner, L.: Problems of nosology and psychodynamics of early infantile autism. Amer. J. Orthopsychiat., 9:416-426, 1949.

Kasanin, J. S.: Language and Thought in Schizophrenia. Berkeley & Los Angeles: University of California Press, 1944.

———— : Developmental roots of schizophrenia. Psychiatry, 6:770-776, 1945.

———— & Hanfmann, E.: Conceptual Thinking in Schizophrenia. New York: Nervous and Mental Diseases Monograph Series, 1942.

———— , Knight, E. & Sage, P.: The parent-child relationship in schizophrenia. J. Nerv. & Ment. Dis., 79:249-263, 1934.

Kahlbaum, L.: Gruppierung der psychischen Krankheiten. Danzig: Kafermann, 1853.

———— : Die Katatonie oder das Spannungirresein. Berlin: August Hirschwald, 1874.

Kalogerakis, M. G.: Homicide in adolescents: fantasy and deed. In: Dynamics of Violence, American Medical Assoc. pamphlet, 1971.

Kelly, H. H. & Volkart, E. H.: The resistances to change of group anchored attitudes. Amer. Sociol. Rev., 27:453-465, 1952.

Kelman, H.: Chronic analysts and chronic patients: The Therapist's Person as Instrument. Paper given at the 17th Annual Conference of the Academy of Psychoanalysis in Dallas, Texas, April, 1972.

Kernberg, O.: Structural derivatives of object relationships. Internat. J. Psycho-Anal., 47-236-253, 1966.

_____ : Borderline personality organization. J. Amer. Psychoanal. Assn., 15:641-685, 1967.

_____ : The treatment of patients with borderline personality organization. Internat. J. Psycho-Anal., 49-600-619, 1968.

_____ : Factors in the psychoanalytic treatment of narcissistic personalities. J. Amer. Psychoanal. Assn., 18:51-85, 1970.

_____ : A psychoanalytic classification of character pathology, J. Amer. Psychoanal. Assn., 18:800-821, 1970.

Klein, G. S. et al: Cognition without awareness: Subliminal influence upon conscious thought. J. Abnorm. & Soc. Psychol., 57:255-266, 1958.

Klein, I. J.: Childhood schizophrenic states simulating retardation and auditory impairment. Nerv. Child, 10:135, 1952.

Klein, M.: Der Familienroman in statu nascendi. Internat. Ztschr. f. Arztliche Psychoanalyse, 6:151-155, 1920.

_____ : The importance of symbol-formation in the development of the ego. Internat. J. Pscyhoanal., 11:24-39, 1930.

_____ : The psychotherapy of the psychoses. Brit. J. Med. Psychol., 10:242-244, 1930.

_____ : The Psycho-Analysis of Children (1932). London: Hogarth Press, 1950.

_____ : A contribution to the psychogenesis of manic-depressive states. Internat. J. Psychoanal., 16:145-174, 1935.

_____ : Notes on some schizoid mechanisms. Internat. J. Psychoanal., 27:99-110, 1946.

_____ : Contributions of Psychoanalysis. London: Hogarth Press, 1921-45, 1948.

_____ : Developments in Psychoanalysis. London: Hogarth Press, p. 300, 1952.

_____ : On identification. In: New Directions in Psycho-Analysis (Eds. Melanie Klein, Paula Heinmann, and Roger E. Money-Kyrle). London: Tavistock Publications, Chapter 14, 1955.

Knapp, P. H., Levin, S., McCarter, R. H., Werner, H. & Zetzel, E. R.: Suitability for psychoanalysis: A review of 100 supervised analytic cases. Psychoanal. Quart., 29:459-477, 1960.

Knight, R. P.: An Evaluation of Psychotherapeutic Techniques, Psychoanalytic, Psychiatry and Psychology (Knight, R. P. & Friedman, C. R. Eds.) (1952). New York: International Universities Press, pp. 65-76, 1954.

Knight, Robert P.: Management and psychotherapy of the borderline patient. Bull. Menninger Clinic, 17:139-150, 1953.

Kraepelin, E.: Dementia Praecox and Paraphrenia (1896) (trans. from 8th Ger. Ed.). Edinburgh: Livingston, 1925.

Laforgue, R.: Schizophrenie, Schizomanie und Schizonoia. Ztschr. f. die gesamte Neurologie u. Psychiatrie, 105:448-458, 1926.

_____ : Scotomazation in schizophrenia. Internat. J. Psychoanal., 8:473, 1927.

_____ : Absperrungsmechanismen in der Neurose und Bezichung zur Schizophrenie. Internat. Ztschr. f. Psychoanalyse, 15:246-258, 1929.

_____ : Contribution a l'étude de la schizophrenie. Evolution psychiatrique, 3:81-96, 1935.

_____ : The Universal Tendency to Debasement in the Sphere of Love, Standard Edition, Vol. IX (1912). London: Hogarth Press, 1962.

_____ : Certain Neurotic Mechanisms in Jealousy, Paranoia and Homosexuality. Standard Edition, Vol. 18, pp. 223-232. London: Hogarth Press, 1962.

_____ & Henri Claude: Sur la schizophrenie et la constitution bipolaire due charactère schizoide. Evolution Psychiatrique, 1:27-36, 1925.

_____ & Angelo L. M. Hesnard: Les processus d'autopunition en psychologie des nevroses et des psychoses en psychologie criminelle et en pathologie generale, 1930-1931. Revue Francaise de Psychoanalyse, 4:2-84, 1931.

Laing, R. D.: Knots. New York: Pantheon Books, Random House, 1970.

_____ : The Divided Self. Pantheon Books, p. 100-112, 1970.

Lashley, K. S. & Colby, K. M.: An exchange of views on psychic energy and psychoanalysis. Behavioral Science, 2:231-240, 1957.

Levinson, E. A.: A treatment facility for college dropouts. Ment. Hyg. Bull., Vol. 49, No. 3, July 1965.

Levy, D. M.: Body interest in children and hypochondriasis. Amer. J. Psychiat., 12:295-315, 1932.

_____ : The Early Development of Independent and Oppositional Behavior. Midcentury Psychiatry. Springfield, Ill.: Thomas, pp. 123-131, 1953.

Lewin, B. D.: When adults tease. Child Study, 7:106, 1930.

Lidz, R. W. & Lidz, T.: The family environment of schizophrenic patients. Amer. J. Psychiat., 106:332, 1949.

_____ & _____ : Considerations arising from the intense symbiotic needs of schizophrenic patients. In: Psychotherapy with Schizophrenics (Eds. Brody, E. B. & Redlich, F. C.). New York: International Universities Press, 1952.

Lidz, T., Cornelison, A. R., Fleck, S. & Terry, D.: The intrafamilial environment of the schizophrenic patient: I. The father. Psychiatry, 20:329-342, 1957.

Lippman, W.: Public Opinion. New York: Harcourt, Brace, 1922.

Lipschutz, D. M.: Combined group and individual psychotherapy. Amer. J. Psychother., 2:336, 1957.

Litin, E. M. & Griffin, M. E.: Parental influence in unusual sexual behavior in children. Psychoanal. Quart., 25:37-55, 1956.

Livingston, M. S.: Working through in analytic group psychotherapy in relation to masochism as a refusal to mourn. Internat. J. Group Psychother., 21:339-344, 1971.

Lowenstein, R. M.: Concluding remarks. Internat. J. Psychoanal., 39:240-242, 1958.

Mack Brunswick, R.: A Supplement to Freud's "History of an infantile neurosis." Internat. J. Psychoanal. 9:439, 1928.

Magoun, H. W.: The ascending reticular system and wakefulness. In: Brain Mechanisms and Consciousness. Springfield, Ill.: Thomas, pp. 1-20, 1954.

_____ : Subcortical mechanisms for reinforcement. In: Moscow Colloquium on Electroencephalography of Higher Nervous Activity (Jasper, H. H. & Smirvov, G. D., Eds.). EEG Clin. Neurophysiol. Suppl. 13, 1960.

Machiavelli, N.: The Prince (trans.) New York: Hendricks House, 1946.

Mahler, M.: Autism and symbiosis: Two extreme disturbances of identity. Internat. J. Psychoanal., 39:77, 1958.

_____ : Thoughts about development and individuation. Psychoanalytic Study of the Child. 18:307-324, 1963.

_____ : Certain aspects of the separation-individuation phase. Psychoanal. Quart., 32:1-14, 1963.

_____ & Furer, M.: Observations on research regarding the 'symbiotic syndrome.' Psychoanal. Quart., 29:317-327, 1960.

_____ , _____ & Settlage, C. F.: Severe emotional disturbances in childhood: Psychosis. In: American Handbook of Psychiatry, (Arieti, S., Ed.) New York: Basic Books, Chapter 41, Vol., I, 1959.

_____ , _____ , _____ & LePerrier, K.: Mother-child interaction during separation-individuation. Psychoanal. Quart., 34:483-498, 1965.

_____ , Ross, J. R. Jr. & DeFries, Z.: Clinical studies in benign and malignant cases of childhood psychosis (schizophrenic-like). Amer. J. Orthopsychiat., 19:295, 1949.

Maier, N. R. F.: Frustration, The Study of Behavior without a Goal. Ann Arbor: University of Michigan Press, 1961.

Marsh, L. C.: Group treatment of the psychoses by the psychological equivalent of the revival. Ment. Hyg., 15:328-349, 1931.

McConnell, J. A.: Memory transfer through cannibalism in planarians. J. Neuropsychiat. 3 (suppl. 1) S, 42-48, Aug., 1962.

Mead, G. H.: A behavioristic account of the significant symbol. J. Philos. Vol. 19, 1922.

_____ : Mind, Self and Society. Chicago: University of Chicago Press, 1934.

Meerloo, Joost A. M.: Hidden suicide. In: Suicidal Behaviors (Resnik, Ed.), Boston: Little, Brown and Co., Chap. 6, pp. 82-89, 1968.

_____ : Persecution trauma and the reconditioning of emotional life: A brief survey. Amer. J. Psychiat., 125:1187-1191, 1969.

_____ & Laury, G. V.: Mental cruelty and child abuse. Psychiat. Quart., 41:203-254, Suppl. Part 2, pp. 1-52. Utica, N.Y.: State Hospital Press, 1967.

Menninger Foundation Conf.: Sandoz Pharmaceutical Co. of Hanover, N.J., Vol. 6, No. 1, April, p. 305, 1969.

Menninger, R. W. and Modlin, H. C.: Individual violence, prevention in the violence threatening patient. In: Dynamics of Violence, American Medical Assoc. pamphlet, 1971.

Merton, R. R.: Social Theory and Social Structure. Glencoe, Ill.: Free Press, 1947.

Meyer, A.: The dynamic interpretation of dementia praecox. Amer. J. Psychol., 21:385, 1910.

_____ : The nature and conception of dementia praecox. J. Abnorm. Psychol., 5:274-285, 1911.

_____ : The Role of Habit Disorganizations in Studies in Psychiatry. Nervous and Mental Disease Monograph, No. 9, 1:95, 1912.

_____ : Constructive formulations of schizophrenia. Amer. J. Psychiat., 1:355-364, 1922.

Miller, N. E.: The frustration-aggression hypothesis. Psychol. Rev., 48:337-342, 1941.

_____ : Theory and experiment relating psychoanalytic displacement to stimulus-response generalization. J. Abnorm. & Soc. Psychol., 43:155-178, 1948.

Mittleman, B.: Psychodynamics of motility: Studies of adults, children and infants. Bull. Amer. Psychiat. Assn., 8:238-240, 1952.

_____ : Motility in Infants, Children and Adults: Patterning and Psychodynamics in the Psychoanalytic Study of the Child, Vol. IX, p. 142. New York: International Universities Press, 1954.

Money-Kyrle, R. E.: Normal counter-transference and some of its deviations. Internat. J. Psychoanal., 37:360, 1956.

_____ : British schools of psychoanalysis. I: Melanie Klein & Kleinian psychoanalytic theory. In: American Handbook of Psychiatry (Arieti, S., Ed.), Vol. III. New York: Basic Books, pp. 225-229, 1966.

Morel, B. A.: Traite des Maladies Mentale. Paris: Victor Masson, 1860.

Moreno, J. L.: Who Shall Survive? A New Approach to the Problem of Human Interrelations. Washington, D.C.: Nerv. & Ment. Dis. Publ., Co., 1934.

———— : Foundations of sociometry, an introduction. Sociometry, 4:15-35, 1941.

———— : Who Shall Survive? Foundations of Sociometry, Group Psychotherapy and Sociodrama. Beacon, N.Y.: Beacon House, 1953.

———— : Reflections of my method of group psychotherapy and psychodrama. In: Active Psychotherapy (Greenwald, Ed.). New York: Atherton, 1967.

Mowrer, O. H.: Learning theory and the neurotic paradox. Amer. J. Orthopsychiat., 18:571, 1948.

———— : Learning Theory and Personality Dynamics. New York: Ronald Press, 1950.

———— : Anxiety theory as a basis for distinguishing between counseling and psychotherapy. In: Concepts and Progress of Counseling (Berdie, R. F., Ed.) Minneapolis, Minn.: University of Minnesota Press, 1953.

Nelson, Marie C.: Effect of paradigmatic techniques on the psychic economy of borderline patients. In: Active Psychotherapy (Greenwald, Ed.), New York: Atherton Press, 1967.

Papez, J. W.: A proposed mechanism of emotion. Arch. Neurol. & Psychiat., 38:725, 1937.

———— : Neuroanatomy. In: American Handbook of Psychiatry (Arieti, S., Ed.), Vol. II. New York: Basic Books, pp. 1585-1619, 1959.

Pavlov, I. V.: Lectures on Conditioned Reflexes, Vol. I. New York: International Publishing Co., 1928.

Penfield, W.: Memory mechanisms. Arch. Neurol. & Psychiat., 67:178-198, 1952.

———— & Roberts, L.: Speech and Brain Mechanisms. Princeton, N.J.: Princeton University Press, 1959.

Piaget, J.: The Child's Conception of Physical Causality. New York: Humanities Press, 1951.

———— : The Origins of Intelligence in Children. New York: International Universities Press, 1952.

———— : The genetic approach to the psychology of thought. J. Educ. Psychol., 52:275-281, 1961.

———— & Inhelder, B.: The Growth of Logical Thinking From Childhood to Adolescence. New York: Basic Books, 1958.

———— & ———— : The Early Growth of Logic in the Child. New York: Harper & Row, 1964.

Piotrowski, A. & Lewis, N. D. C.: An experimental Rorschach diagnostic aid for some forms of schizophrenia. Amer. J. Psychiat., 107:362, 1950.

Plato: Dialogues of Plato, The Republic and Phaedo. In: The Great Books, Encyclopedia Britannica, 1952.

Poetzl, O.: Experimentally provoked dream images in their relation to indirect vision. Ztschr. f. Neurol. u. Psychiat., 37:278-349, 1917.

Pratt, J. H.: The influence of emotions in the causation and cure of psychoneuroses. Internat. Clinics, 4:1, 1934.

Rado, S.: The Psychodynamics of Behavior, Vol. II. New York: Grune & Stratton, 1962.

Rangell, L.: Similarities and differences between psychoanalysis and dynamic psychotherapy. J. Amer. Psychoanal. Assn., 3:734-744, 1954.

Rapaport, D.: The Development and the Concepts of Psychoanalytic Ego Psychology: Twelve Seminars given at the Western New England Institute for Psychoanalysis (Miller, S., Ed.). Mimeographed ms, 1955.

———— : A theoretical analysis of the superego concept. In: The Collected Papers of David Rapaport (Gill, M., Ed.). New York: Basic Books, 1967.

Reich, W.: The characterological mastery of the oedipus complex. Internat. J. Psychoanal., 12:452-467, 1931.

_____ : Character Analysis (1933). New York: Orgone Institute Press, 1945.

_____ : On character analysis. In: The Psychoanalytic Reader (R. Fleiss, Ed.). New York: International Universities Press, 1:129-147, 1948.

_____ : Character Analysis (3rd ed.). New York: Orgone Institute Press, 1949.

Reichard, S. & Tillman, C.: Patterns of parent-child relationships in schizophrenia. Psychiatry, 13:247-257, p. 257, 1950.

Rich, M.: Aggression as a variable in the school failure of children in the 8th, 9th, and 10th grades. Doctoral thesis, School of Education, New York University, 1972.

Rickman, J.: A survey: The development of the psycho-analytical theory of the psychoses, 1894-1926. Brit. J. MEd. Psychol., 6:270-294, 1926.

_____ : A survey: The development of the psycho-analytical theory of the psychoses, 1894-1926. Brit. J. Med. Psychol., 7:94-124, 321-374, 1927.

Riviere, Joan: On the genesis of psychical conflict in earliest infancy. Internat. J. Psychoanal., 17:395-422, 1936.

Rosenfeld, H.: Transference-phenomena and transference-analysis in an acute catatonic schizophrenic patient. Internat. J. Psychoanal., 33:457-464, 1952.

_____ : Considerations regarding the psycho-analytic approach to acute and chronic schizophrenia. Internat. J. Psychoanal., 35:135-140, 1954.

Rosner, S.: Problems of working-through with borderline patients. Psychotherapy: Theory, Research and Practice. Vol. 6, No. 1, Winter, 1969.

Rothstein, D. A.: The assassin and the assassinated as "non-patient" subjects of psychiatric investigation. In: Dynamics of Violence, American Medical Assoc. pamphlet, 1971.

Sabath, G.: Parental negative suggestion as a stimulus for anti-social behavior. Corrective Psychiatry & J. Soc. Therapy, 11:323-326, 1965.

Sanua, V. D.: Sociocultural factors in families of schizophrenics. Psychiatry, 24:246-265, 1961.

Sarbin, T. R.: Contributions to role-taking theory. I. Hypnotic behavior, Psychol. Rev., 47:255-270, 1950.

Schmideberg, M.: Some unconscious mechanisms in pathologic sexuality and their relation to normal sexual activities. Internat. J. Psychoanal., 19:225, 1933.

_____ : The borderline patient. In: American Handbook of Psychiatry (Arieti S., Ed.). New York: Basic Books, Vol. I, Chapter 21, p. 400, 1959.

Schwartz, M. S. & Stanton, A. H.: A social psychological study of incontinence. Psychiatry, 13:399-416, 1950.

Searles, H. F.: Positive feelings in the relationship between the schizophrenic and his mother. Internat. J. Psychoanal., 39:569-586, 1958.

_____ : The effort to drive the other person crazy—An element in the aetiology and psychotherapy of schizophrenia. Brit. J. Med. Psychol., 32:1-18, 1959.

_____ : Integration and differentiation in schizophrenia. Brit. J. Med. Psychol., 32:261-81, 1959.

_____ : Phases of patient-therapist interaction in the psychotherapy of chronic schizophrenia. Brit. J. Med. Psychol., 34:169, 1961.

_____ : The differentiation between concrete and metaphorical thinking in the recovering schizophrenic patient. In: Collected Papers on Schizophrenia and Related States. New York: International Universities Press, pp. 560-583, 1965.

_____ : Transference psychosis in the psychotherapy of chronic schizophrenia. Internat. J. Psychoanal., 44:249-291, 1963.

_____ : The contributions of family treatment to the psychotherapy of schizophrenia. In: Collected Papers on Schizophrenia and Related States. New York, International Universities Press, pp. 717-752, 1965.

———— : Integration and differentiation in schizophrenia: An overall view, In: Collected Papers on Schizophrenia and Related Subjects (1959). New York, International Universities Press, pp. 317-348, 1965.

Sears, R. E. Maccoby, E. E. & Levin, H.: Patterns of Child Rearing. Evanston, Ill.: Row, Peterson, 1957.

Sechehaye, M. A.: The transference in symbolic realization. Internat. J. Psychoanal., 37:270-277, 1956.

Segal, H.: Some aspects of the analysis of a schizophrenic. Internat. J. Psychoanal., 31:268-278, 1950.

———— : A note on schizoid mechanisms underlying phobia formation. Internat. J. Psychoanal., 35:238-241, 1954.

———— : Depression in the schizophrenic. Internat. J. Psychoanal., 37:339-343, 1956.

Selye, H.: Stress, The Physiology and Pathology of Exposure to Stress. Montreal: Acta, 1950.

———— : The Stress of Life. New York: McGraw-Hill, 1956.

Shainberg, D.: The Dilemma and the Challenge of Being Schizophrenic. Paper given at the 17th Annaul Conference of the Academy of Psychoanalysis, Dallas, Texas, April, 1972.

Sharpe, E.: Dream Analysis. London: Hogarth, 1937.

Sheffield, F. D. & Tenner, H. W.: Relative resistance to extinction of escape training and avoidance training. J. Exp. Psychol., 40:287-298, 1950.

Sherrington, C. S.: The Brain and Its Mechanism. London: Cambridge, 1936.

Shevrin, H. & Luborsky, L.: The measurement of preconscious perception in dreams and images: an investigation of the Poetzl phenomenon. J. Abnorm. & Soc. Psychol., 56:285-294, 1958.

Simmel, G.: The Sociology of George Simmel (Trans. & Ed. by K. H. Wolff). Glencoe, Ill: Free Press, 1950.

Sperling, S. J.: On the psychodynamics of teasing. Bull. Amer. Psychoanal. Assn., 7:356, 357, 1951.

Sperling, S. J.: On teasing. Psychoanal. Quart., 20:343-344, 1951.

Spitz, R.: The Smiling Response. Genetic Psychology Monograph. 34:57, 1946.

———— : The psychogenic diseases in infancy: An attempt at their etiologic classification. In: The Psychoanalytic Study of the Child. New York: International Universities Press, 6:255-278, 1951.

———— : The primal cavity: A contribution to the genesis of perception and its role for psychoanalytic theory. In: The Psychoanalytic Study of the Child, Vol. X. New York: International Universities Press, p. 215, 1955.

Spotnitz, H.: Modern Psychoanalysis of the Schizophrenic Patient: Theory of the Technique. New York: Grune & Stratton, 1969.

Stanton, A. H. & Schwartz, M. S.: The Mental Hospital. New York: Basic Books, 1954.

Stärcke, August: Psychoschyis. Amsterdam: Staatsdrukkerij, 1904.

———— : The reversal of the libido-sign in delusions of persecution. Internat. J. Psychoanal., 1:231-234, 1920.

———— : Psychoanalyse und Psychiatrie. Leipzig, Vienna: Int. P.V., 1921.

Stoller, R. J.: A further contribution to the study of gender identity. Internat. J. Psychoanal., 49:(Parts 2-3) 364-369, 1968.

———— : Earliest Parental Influence on the Development of Masculinity in Males. Presented at the American College of Psychiatrists, February 1, 1969.

Sullivan, H. S.: Affective experience in early schizophrenia (1925). Amer. Jour. Psychiat., 6:467-484, 1926-1927.

_____ : The modified psychoanalytic treatment of schizophrenia. Amer. J. Psychiat., 11:519-40, 1931.

_____ : Therapeutic investigation of schizophrenia. Psychiatry, 10:121, 1947.

_____ : The Interpersonal Theory of Psychiatry. New York: Norton, 1955.

_____ : The International Theory of Psychiatry (Eds. Perry & Gawl). New York: Norton, 1953.

_____ : Conceptions of Modern Psychiatry. New York: Norton, 1955.

_____ : Schizophrenia as a Human Process. New York: Norton, pp. 84-88, 1962.

Szurek, S. A. & Johnson, A. M.: The genesis of anti-social acting out in children and adults. Psychoanal. Quart., 21:323-343.

_____ & _____ : Etiology of anti-social behavior in delinquents and psychopaths. J.A.M.A., 154:814-817, 1954.

Thompson, C.: Sullivan and psychoanalysis. In: Contributions of Harry Stack Sullivan (P. Mullahy, Ed.). New York: Hermitage House, pp. 101-115, 1952.

_____ : Concepts of self in interpersonal theory. Amer. J. Psychother. 12:5-17, 1958.

_____ : The interpersonal approach to the clinical problems of masochism. In: Science and Psychoanalysis, Vol. 2 (Masserman, J. H., Ed.) New York: Grune & Stratton, pp. 31-37, 1959.

_____ : Developmental psychology. Am. Rev. Psychol., 10:1-42, 1959.

_____ : Ferenczi's relaxation method. In: Interpersonal Psychoanalysis. New York: Basic Books, pp. 67-71, 1964.

Tietze, S.: A study of mothers of schizophrenic patients. Psychiatry, 12:55-65, 1949.

Tinbergen, N.: The Study of Instinct. Oxford: Clarendon Press, 1951.

_____ : Derived activities, their causation, biological significance, origin and emancipation during evolution. Rev. Biol., 27:1-31, 1952.

_____ & Vandersel, J. J. A.: Displacement reactions in the three-spined stickleback. Behavior 1:56-63, 1947.

Transactional Analysis Bull.: Vol. 8, No. 31, Special Number: Reparenting in Schizophrenia. Jacqui Schiff, Guest Editor, July 1969.

Ungar, G.: Molecular mechanisms in learning. Perspective in Biology and Medicine, 11:217-32, 1968.

_____ : Chemical transfer of learning fear. Nature (London), 217:1259-1261, 1968.

Vaihinger, H.: The Philosophy of As If. London: Paul, Trench, Trubner, 1924.

Vogel, E. F.: The marital relationship of parents of emotionally disturbed children. Polarization and isolation: Psychiatry, 23:1-12, 1960.

Vogt, C. & Vogt, O.: Importance of neuro-anatomy in the field of neuropathology. Neurology, 1:205, 1951.

Von Bertalanffy, L.: An outline of general systems theory. Brit. J. Phil. Sci., 1:134, 1950.

_____ : The theory of open systems in physics and biology. Science, 111:23, 1950.

Von Domarus, E.: The specific laws of logic in schizophrenia. In: Language and Thought in Schizophrenia (Kasanin, J. S. Ed.). Berkeley: University of California Press, pp. 104-113, 1944.

Waldhorn, H. F.: Assessment of analyzability: Technical and theoretical observations. Psychoanal. Quart., 29:478-506, 1960.

Wahl, C. W.: Some antecedent factors in the family histories of 392 schizophrenics. Amer. J. Psychiat., 110:668-676, 1954.

_____ : Some antecedent factors in the family histories of 568 male schizophrenics of the United States Navy. Amer. J. Psychiat., 113:201-210, 1956.

Weakland, H. Jr.: The 'double bind' hypothesis of schizophrenia and three-party interaction. In: The Etiology of Schizophrenia (Jackson, D., Ed.). New York: Basic Books, 1960.

Wexler, M.: Hypotheses Concerning Ego Deficiency in Schizophrenia. In: (Scher, S. C. & Davis, H., Eds.) The Out-Patient Treatment of Schizophrenia. New York: Grune & Stratton, pp. 33-43, 1960.

Winnicott, D. W.: Metapsychological and clinical aspects of regression within the psycho-analytic set-up (1955). Collected Papers. New York: Basic Books, pp. 278-294, 1958.

Wolberg, A.: The borderline patient. Amer. J. Psychother., 6:694-710, 1952.

_____ : The psychoanalytic treatment of the borderline patient in the individual and group setting. In: Topical Problems of Psychotherapy, Vol. II, pp. 174-197. (Hulse, Ed.). New York: Basel & Karger, 1960.

_____ : Patterns of interaction in families of borderline patients. In: New Directions in Mental Health (Reiss, B., Ed.). New York, Grune & Stratton, p. 108, 1968.

_____ : Intensifying the group process in psychoanalytic group psychotherapy. Psychiatric Annals. Vol. II, No. 3, pp. 70-73, March 1972.

Wolberg, L. R.: Hypnoanalysis (1945). New York: Grune & Stratton, 2nd Ed., 1964.

_____ : The Technique of Psychotherapy, New York: Grune & Stratton, 2nd Ed., 2 Vols., 1967.

_____ : Medical Hypnosis (2 Vols.) (1948) New York, Grune & Stratton, 8th printing, 1958.

_____ :Psychotherapy and the Behavioral Sciences. New York: Grune & Stratton, 1966.

Wolf, A., & Schwartz, E. K.: Psychoanalysis in Groups. New York: Grune & Stratton, 1962.

Wolfson, Martha: The struggle for autonomy in Hank, a borderline patient. Case Presentation for Certification of Postgraduate Center for Mental Health, New York, 1972.

Woltman, A. G.: Personal Communication to Eisenstein, V. on cases Examined between June 1949 & March 1950. In: Specialized Techniques in Psychotherapy. New York: Basic Books, p. 321, 1952.

Zilboorg, G.: The deeper layers of schizophrenic psychosis. Amer. J. Psychiat., 88:493-511, 1931.

_____ : The emotional problem and the therapeutic role of insight. Psychoanal. Quart., 21:1-24, 1952.

_____ : The conceptual vicissitudes of the idea of schizophrenia. In: Schizophrenia in Psychoanalytic Office Practice (Rifkin, A. H., Ed.) New York: Grune & Stratton, pp. 30-39, 1957.

INDEX

Acting out
    identification in, 11-13, 48
    assumption of roles in, 20
    as variable in psychoanalytic theory, 21
    and the imagoes, 22
    and ideas in the brain, 25
    relation to phantasy, 25, 44
    and family dynamics, 32-36
    a sexual role, 41
    effects on relationship, 43
    and sado-masochistic motif, 44
    relation to transference and resistance, 44
    as a realization of phantasy in action, 44
    and the "fate neurosis," 45
    and sadism, 46
    and negative transference, 46
    called by Reich artifical contact relationship, 126-127
    screen action, 139
    a homosexual episode as reaction to frustration and anxiety in competition, 164-165

Adaptation
    neurotic and psychotic, 3, 73
    alternate choices of, 3

Aggression
    and shifting defenses, 4
    "as if" and repression, 11
    of parent in promoting neurosis, 11
    and transference, 12
    "permitted" and "unpermitted," 13
    and masochism of parent, 13, 20
    in family members and borderline patient, 32-38
    as reaction to experience in family, 40
    as reaction to rejection, 100

Anxiety, and parental projective use of child, 25

Appeasement, related to shifting defenses, 4

"As if" behavior
    and suggestion and identification, 11
    Sarbin's theory, 13
    relation to fiction and phantasy, 14
    private logic and rationalization defenses, 15
    a projective defense, 53-54

Autosuggestion, differentiated by Freud from suggestion, 17

Borderline patient
    large number seen in clinics, 1
    and mixed conditions, 1, 58